workbook

FOR LECTORS AND GOSPEL READERS

James L. Weaver

LTP

LITURGY
TRAINING
PUBLICATIONS

New American Bible readings are taken from *Lectionary for Mass for Use in the Dioceses of the United States of America, second typical edition* © 1998, 1997, 1970 by the Confraternity of Christian Doctrine, Washington, D.C., and are reproduced herein by license of the copyright owner. All rights reserved. No part of *Lectionary for Mass* may be reproduced in any form without permission in writing from the Confraternity of Christian Doctrine, Washington, D.C.

WORKBOOK FOR LECTORS AND GOSPEL READERS 2007, UNITED STATES EDITION © 2006 Archdiocese of Chicago. All rights reserved.

Liturgy Training Publications, 1800 North Hermitage Avenue, Chicago IL 60622; 1-800-933-1800, fax 1-800-933-7094, orders@ltp.org, www.LTP.org

Editor: Kris Fankhouser
Typesetter: Jim Mellody-Pizzato
Original book design: Jill Smith
Revised design: Anna Manhart and Jim Mellody-Pizzato
Cover art: Barbara Simcoe
Interior art: Anna Manhart

Printed in the United States of America.

ISBN-10: 1-56854-571-1
ISBN-13: 978-1-56854-571-4
WL07

Nihil Obstat
Reverend Louis J. Cameli, STD
Censor Deputatus
February 8, 2006

Imprimatur
Most Reverend George J. Rassas
Vicar General
Archdiocese of Chicago
February 13, 2006

The *Nihil Obstat* and *Imprimatur* are official declarations that a book is free of doctrinal and moral error. No implication is contained therein that those who have granted the *Nihil Obstat* and *Imprimatur* agree with the content, opinions, or statements expressed. Nor do they assume any legal responsibility associated with publication.

CONTENTS

The Author

James L. Weaver was received into the Roman Catholic Church at the age of 26. He received the sacraments of Baptism, Eucharist, and Confirmation during the Easter Vigil Mass at St. Thomas More Chapel of New Haven, Connecticut, in 1995. Jay holds degrees from Yale and the University of Chicago in History, Divinity, and New Testament and Early Christian Literature. He is currently at work on a doctorate in the Department of New Testament and Early Christian Literature at the University of Chicago.

Dedication

This book is dedicated with love, gratitude, and respect to my grandfather, Dr. Oliver Cornelius Weaver, and to the memories of my grandparents, Laura Moore Weaver, James Henry Middleton, and Eleanor Marie Middleton. It is also dedicated to Sister Betsy Pawlicki, OP, and Sister Laurie Brink, OP, of the Dominican Sisters of Sinsinawa; to Father Greg Boyle, SJ, and Homeboy Industries; and to Nicole Erin Urbach.

INTRODUCTION

The Purpose of *Workbook*

The intention of the *Workbook for Lectors and Gospel Readers* is to offer assistance to all who proclaim scripture in Roman Catholic worship. In the spirit of the instruction of the Dogmatic Constitution on Divine Revelation *(Dei verbum)* issued by the Second Vatican Council on November 18, 1965, this edition of *Workbook* has been made available so that "ministers of the divine Word may be able to distribute fruitfully the nourishment of the Scriptures of the People of God" (*Dei verbum*, #6.23). *The General Instruction of the Roman Missal* also stresses the importance of the ministry of proclaiming God's word, saying that lectors "should be truly suited to perform this function and should receive careful preparation so that the faithful by listening to the readings from the sacred texts may develop in their hearts a warm and living love for Sacred Scripture" (#101).

Laypeople, as well as the ordained, who are charged with catechesis, direction of liturgy and music, religious education, preaching, and other pastoral ministries may find *Workbook* a useful tool in their attempts to understand the readings of the Lectionary in the literary, historical, cultural, and theological contexts of the authors who produced them, as well as the diverse traditions of their interpretation in the Roman Catholic Church.

The Church, according to the edition of the *Catechism of the Catholic Church* published by the United States Conference of Catholic Bishops and quoting the text of *Dei verbum*, concludes that "access to Sacred Scripture ought to be open wide to the Christian faithful" and encourages the "frequent reading of the Divine Scriptures" by all Christians (Catechism, #131, 133). If the study of scripture is therefore a duty, one should hasten to add that the performance of this duty can be a profound joy. It is the hope of this author that this edition of *Workbook* will help kindle this joy.

The Roman Catholic Bible: Unity amid Difference

The Roman Catholic Bible contains writings composed over more than a thousand years of human history. The early Hebrew poetry of Exodus 15, for example, was composed well before Alexander's conquests spread the Greek language throughout the Mediterranean, before a little village on the Italian peninsula called Rome even existed. By contrast, the Greek of 2 Peter, perhaps the latest of our texts, was first written down when Rome was no longer a village, but a metropolis, and not merely a metropolis, but an empire ruling the entirety of the author's known world. The Bible contains the vast difference one expects among authors writing in different places, social and cultural settings, languages, and historical circumstances. But the variety within the Bible is even greater than this. It includes in its pages histories, letters, love poetry, war poetry, novellas, oracles, apocalypses, and Gospels. Its contents run from Psalm 118, a liturgical text of the Jerusalem Temple in celebration of the monarchy of Judah, to Paul's letter to a well-heeled friend called Philemon in search of mercy for a runaway slave. They span the philosophical speculations of Ecclesiastes and the book of Wisdom to the

In the beginning was the Word, and the Word was with God, and the Word was God.

prophetic oracles of Jeremiah, from the practical theological wisdom of Paul's letter to the Philippians to the vision of heaven and of the end-time future disclosed to John of Patmos in Revelation.

To this fact of the Bible's variety, one may add the fact that the Roman Catholic Bible, in part or in whole, is authoritative for a variety of peoples, denominations, and religions. This is true not only for other Christian denominations, but also for the religions of Judaism and Islam. People of uncertain or no religious commitment also make beneficial use of it. Scripture, therefore, is shared treasure. As was recognized by the late Pope John Paul II in his encyclical letter *Ut unum sint* ("That They Might Be One"), contained within this fact is the seed of greater fellowship among the human family. It is doubtless a help to the effective proclamation of scripture, and not only in ecumenical contexts, to bear firmly in thought and prayer all those with whom Roman Catholics share their sacred writings.

A third fact stands beside these two. In addition to the varied contents of the Bible and the authority it has for other denominations and religions, the teaching authority of the Roman Catholic Church, the Magisterium, interprets the Bible in the theological context of its traditional use within the Roman Catholic Church. It declares the Bible's Old and New Testaments to be a single unity revealing and testifying to Jesus Christ. The Catechism, borrowing the words of Hugh of St. Victor, describes this unity quite plainly: "All Sacred Scripture is but one book, and that one book is Christ, because all divine Scripture speaks of Christ, and all divine Scripture is fulfilled in Christ" (Catechism, #134).

For ministers of the word to "be attentive to what the human authors truly wanted to affirm and to what God wanted to reveal to us by their words" means difficulty in some cases, particularly where the Old Testament is concerned (Catechism, #109). If "all divine Scripture speaks of Christ," then ministers must grapple with how to be faithful to the human authors of scripture living well before the advent of Christ and the development of the institutional Roman Catholic Church.

The Gospel of Luke

For the Catholic Church, the issue of canon was essentially settled by the widespread acceptance in the West of the Latin version of scripture translated by Saint Jerome, which became known as the Vulgate. The Catechism acknowledges four canonical Gospels, those according to Matthew, Mark, Luke, and John. The formation of this quartet of scriptural voices from among the chorus of the great literary output of the early Church was likely due to their perceived apostolic authorship and/or character, as well as their relative antiquity. The cycle of the Roman Catholic Lectionary in the United States is three years in length, with the three so-called synoptic Gospels comprising the bulk of the readings during each three-year cycle: Matthew in Year A, Mark in Year B, and Luke in Year C. The Gospel of John occurs on particular feast days, solemnities, and in some of the seasonal readings.

The Gospel of Luke is the principal Gospel of Year C. Like Matthew, Mark, and John, the principal subjects of Luke are the ministry and Passion of Jesus. Luke, however, has particular themes and areas of concern that distinguish his Gospel from the other three. Two bear mention here, for they arise repeatedly in the commentaries. First, Luke's interpretation of Jesus' death stresses his innocence; by Christ's Resurrection God vindicates a righteous man wrongly accused. Second, Luke especially emphasizes Jesus' incorporation of the poor, as well as other social outcasts, misfits, and people on the edge of society, into the kingdom of God. Those familiar with the authentic and traditional teaching of the Catholic Church on issues of poverty, social justice, and the fair apportionment of wealth and resources will find many scriptural bases for these teachings in Luke's Gospel. The Catechism's discussion of the seventh commandment is particularly instructive in this respect (Catechism, #2401–2463).

An additional feature distinguishing Luke's Gospel from the other three is that it is the first of a two-part work. It is clear from a variety of similarities that the author of Luke and the Acts of the Apostles are the same person. And although this Gospel and Acts were probably not penned by the Luke mentioned in Colossians 4:14, Philemon 24, and 2 Timothy 4:11, but were probably the work of a second- or third-generation Christian, it is still conventional to refer to their author by this name. This convention has been observed in the commentaries.

Many secondary sources have helped the production of this edition of *Workbook*. They are often cited in the commentaries. Chief among them have been Father Joseph Fitzmyer's two-volume commentary on the Gospel of Luke in the Anchor Bible series and Luke Timothy Johnson's commentary on Luke in the Sacra Pagina series.

Commentaries: Contexts of Interpretation

The commentaries are intended to assist the informed proclamation of scripture by ministers of the word. There is no way to provide everything that a lector or Gospel reader may wish or require for a given reading, particularly in the light of the unique needs and interests of his or her worshipping assembly. What an average commentary offers, in most cases, is the fruit of prior attention paid to the linguistic, literary, historical, cultural, and theological contexts of the reading in question. A basis for much of this approach may be found, once again, in *Dei verbum*, which instructed that interpreters of scripture "must look for that meaning which the sacred writer, in a determined situation and given the circumstances of his time and culture, intended to express and did in fact express, through the medium of a contemporary literary form" (*Dei verbum*, III.12).

The following are descriptions of some of the circumstances of time and culture pertaining to the texts of scripture. Many others could be added to these. These are offered because it has been repeatedly demonstrated to this author that many Roman Catholic laypeople are interested in them. It is also the personal experience of this author that knowing something about the world in which the texts of scripture were produced increases the enjoyment of proclaiming them in worship.

Linguistic

The linguistic context is almost always established either by Hebrew or Greek. The reason for this is that these are the languages in which the texts were composed and from which the translators and editors of the NAB have rendered them into English. Attention to the particular vocabulary and style used by biblical

> God so loved the world that he gave his only Son, so that everyone who believes in him might not perish but might have eternal life.

authors helps to understand their meaning with additional accuracy and precision. In many cases, the commentaries will contain specific information born of attention to the linguistic context of scripture.

Literary

The literary context assumed for most readings is the full book or relevant portion of text from which the reading has been excerpted. Sometimes, most often in the case of Old Testament readings, the literary context of the reading is provided by the interpretation of the text by Jewish and Christian writers working during the formative years of the Church in the ancient period.

It is true also that the Lectionary itself provides a literary context for the interpretation of scripture. The readings for a given day have been excerpted and joined together in the Lectionary because they have been determined to complement one another in the service of a particular theme or message for that day.

This is especially clear on feast days, where the biblical basis for the feast is usually the theme uniting the readings. The commentaries in this issue of *Workbook* usually, though not always, leave alone the issue of how the readings for a given day relate or "speak" to one another.

Historical

The historical contexts of scripture are many. A word about dates is in order. No universal method of dating was in place in the ancient world. A typical way to date something was according to the year, in the Roman period, of the emperor's reign. Thus, when Luke 3:1 says that God's word came to John the son of Zechariah (John the Baptist) in the fifteenth year of the reign of Tiberius Caesar, and we know that Tiberius began his reign in 14 AD, then we can say that John began to preach in 28–29 AD. In Israel in an earlier period, the regnal years of the kings of Israel and Judah served the same function (see, for example, 2 Kings 22 and Isaiah 6:1). Sometimes other significant events were used in addition to the kings' reigns. The introduction to the book of the prophet Amos reports that Amos received his oracles "in the days of Uzziah, king of Judah, and in the days of Jeroboam, son of Joash, king of Israel, two years before the earthquake" (Amos 1:1). To someone who knew about this earthquake, it was apparently enough to say *the* earthquake without confusion.

The date for Jesus' birth that caught on in the Church was based on the calculations of a monk named Dionysius Exiguus who lived in Rome during the sixth century AD. His calculations unfortunately contained a few errors. This is why biblical scholars talk about Jesus having been born before or after the year 1 AD. When they do so, they are making their own calculations, which (they hope) are superior to those of Dionysius.

Some of the seminal historical events in the scripture of Israel, and therefore in salvation history, are the era of the patriarchs and the Exodus in the second millennium BC; the period of the judges between the Israelite invasion and settlement of Canaan and the monarchy of Israel, which probably began in the eleventh century BC; the period of the divided monarchy of the realms of Israel and Judah, spanning the late tenth century BC to the Assyrian conquest and end of the northern kingdom of Israel in 721 BC; the independent kingdom of Judah's increasing submission to the empire of Babylon in the late seventh century BC and the Babylonian destruction of Jerusalem and the Temple in 587/6 BC; the exile of a substantial portion of Judah's citizenry, particularly its elite, to Babylon, beginning in 606 BC; the Persian victory over Babylon in 538 BC and a decree of Cyrus of Persia two years later permitting the return of exiles to Judah; and the completion of the new Temple in 516 BC.

Between his coronation in 336 BC and his death in 323 BC, Alexander the Great of Macedonia conquered Egypt and much of the Middle East. Greek shortly became the principal common language of the Mediterranean. Successor Macedonian regimes based in Syria (the Seleucid dynasty) and in Egypt (the Ptolemaic dynasty) vied for control of Israel. In 168 BC, a brutal attack on Jerusalem by Antiochus IV (175 BC–164 BC) presaged a Jewish uprising leading to the establishment of an independent Jewish kingdom (the Hasmonean dynasty). In 63 BC, Israel and Jerusalem were invaded by the Roman general Pompey and came under Roman authority. In the ensuing two centuries, Roman rule was exercised either directly through governors, such as the procurator Pontius Pilate (26 AD–36 AD), or indirectly through client kings, such as Herod the Great (37 BC–4 BC) and his family.

The period of the New Testament begins with the birth of Jesus near the death of Herod the Great and during the reign of Augustus Caesar (27 BC–14 AD). Both Matthew and Luke, the two Gospels containing accounts of Jesus' infancy, place Jesus' birth at

This is my commandment: love one another as I love you.

Magnify the LORD with me; let us exalt his name together.

the end of the reign of Herod (Matthew 2:1; Luke 1:5). Matthew puts Jesus' birth near Herod's death (4 BC). The detail of Matthew 2:16 (Herod ordering the murder of all children two years old and under in Bethlehem and nearby regions) suggests that he believed Jesus to have been born between 6 and 4 BC. Luke's dates pose a bit more of a problem, for neither was Quirinius the governor of Syria during those years nor was a census taken in Judea at that time (Luke 2:1–2). A census must have been taken, however, in 6 AD when Judea came under direct Roman rule. What seems to have happened is that Luke has combined at least two traditions about the date of Jesus' birth, one placing it 10 to 12 years later than the other. Most biblical scholars think that the agreement between Matthew and Luke concerning the birth of Jesus during the close of Herod's reign warrants a date between 6 and 4 BC.

There is no way to tell from the Gospels what was the precise duration of Jesus' ministry. If John the Baptist began his ministry in 28 or 29 AD, then Jesus began his own some time after that. During the reign of Tiberius Caesar (14 AD–37 AD) and the procuratorship of Pontius Pilate (26 AD–36 AD), Jesus was crucified during Passover celebrations in Jerusalem. Jesus died, therefore, some time before 36 AD. His ministry spanned, at most, a few years.

The Church began its growth very soon thereafter. One of its ablest missionaries was the apostle Paul. Thirteen of 27 New Testament texts claim him as author, while the Acts of the Apostles, though not by him, is overwhelmingly about him. His life as a follower of Jesus Christ probably spanned the years 33–64 AD. (If these dates are correct, and Paul was indeed a persecutor of the Church for a time as Acts reports and Paul himself claims, then Jesus must have

been crucified between 30 and 32 AD.) The earliest Christian document we have (Paul's first letter to the Church of Thessalonica) was composed in the late 40s AD. His last letter to the Christians of Rome was composed in about 60 AD. The chronology of Paul's life is difficult to establish with precision and it is not a simple set of calculations. Its broad outline, however, Paul himself provides in his letter to the Church of Galatia (Galatians 1:12—2:14).

In 70 AD, the Roman general Titus, attempting to put down a Jewish rebellion, pillaged and destroyed the Temple in Jerusalem. The force of this event on the subsequent developments of Judaism and Christianity was considerable, although in the case of Christianity their precise effects are hard to state with precision.

To these historical data one could add many more, such as dates, both firm and not, for the composition of all of the documents of the New Testament, the missionary journeys of Paul and his team, and so on. When relevant and possible, these will be dealt with in the commentaries. The data given above have been provided because it is helpful to have at least a skeletal outline of them for reference purposes when using the commentaries. Where relevant and when possible, non-Christian Roman, Greek, and Jewish writers have also been cited in the commentaries.

Cultural

The cultural contexts of scripture are many as well. It is a problem that the word "culture" does not have an easy or obvious definition. Language, history, ethnicity, location (urban or rural), economy, class, status, form of government, art, and literature all play a role in defining the culture of a given people or individual. To the degree possible, the commentaries have been written to provide interpretations in relation to some of these cultural variables whenever they are meaningful for understanding the composition and/or interpretation of scripture.

Theological

The theological context in which the commentaries have been composed is quite broad. Put simply, the commentaries have been written with the conviction that scripture is divinely inspired and is a product of collaboration between God and human beings. Important Christian interpreters of antiquity, such as Clement of Rome, Justin Martyr, Irenaeus of Lyon, and Origen of Alexandria to name only a few, have been repeatedly consulted in order to show how some early Christians read and interpreted the Bible in antiquity. The first-century Jewish writers Philo of Alexandria and Flavius Josephus have also been consulted. The theological insights of rabbinic Judaism and Islam, while clearly relevant, lie well outside this writer's competence and thus do not appear much at all. Additionally, the Catechism has also been extensively consulted. After the Bible, it is probably the most frequently cited source in the commentaries. The insights of modern Roman Catholic theologians have also occasionally been cited.

The theological context of the commentaries' author is that of a layperson, a convert to Catholicism, who has spent the bulk of his ten years in the Church working at graduate studies and worshipping in his neighborhood parish.

Blessed are the poor in spirit, for theirs is the kingdom of heaven.

Lastly, and most importantly, the commentaries are meant to be helpful and constructive for those who seek not only to improve their own closeness to God, but that of their brothers and sisters in Christ.

Scripture and Prayer

The nourishment that scripture's proclamation provides both lector and community is enhanced if the lector makes a regular practice of prayer and meditation on the pages of scripture.

Scripture is not divine; rather, it reveals the divine. As a matter of tradition, Roman Catholics have not worshipped the pages of scripture, but rather the one to whom they point. The Catechism cites Luke 24:45 in this connection, where Luke reports that the risen Jesus joined his disciples in a village outside of Jerusalem and there "opened their minds to understand the Scriptures" (Catechism, #108).

Pronunciation Guides, Margin Notes, and General Suggestions

Proclaiming a reading of scripture requires practice and preparation. If it is at all possible, a lector or Gospel reader should go over the reading several times, silently and out loud, before getting up to proclaim it in worship. Strive to know your text well enough to be confident when you deliver it.

The pronunciation guides are meant to help with the clear proclamation of scripture. Some biblical words and names, such as "David" or "Jerusalem," are so common as to require no guide. Other words and names, while commonly known, may still not be known by all. They have been listed in the guides according to their standard pronunciation and accenting. Words and names that are relatively unknown and have no standard English pronunciation have been accented as they are found in either Hebrew or Greek as the case may be.

The margin notes are suggestions that will likely help with the effective proclamation of scripture. Perhaps the most consistent directions are "slow down," "stress," "emphasize," and "pause." (The reason for "slow down" perhaps has more to do with the author's personal experience as a lector than anything else.) It is difficult for some people to avoid rushing through a reading, particularly in a public setting and one feels the weight of many pairs of eyes and ears. In such a situation, it is a relief to recall a simple truth: the message, not the messenger, is what people have come to hear. It is the lector's task to read in such a way that God's people, gathered together for worship, may best take the words of scripture to heart, mind, and spirit.

It is almost always the case that electing to read more slowly than one is originally inclined is a good choice. A number of the Lectionary's selections are pieces excerpted from fairly complicated theological arguments. To speed through anything from Hebrews or Galatians, for example, is almost always to leave many people behind in a cloud of "therefores," "hences," and "howevers." Aim for a slow, patient, and clear delivery—loud enough for people to hear, but without shouting. In the event that one has a habit of reading too quickly, make it a practice to take a moment of brief silence for oneself before beginning. Use it to ask for any help God might care to give.

The modulation of one's reading speed and the volume of one's voice is an effective means of emphasizing particular words in relation to those going before and coming after. To deliver readings in the cadence and rhythm appropriate for typical public speech is helpful to the ear in general. The words "stress" and "emphasize" in the margin notes usually

The LORD's word is true; all his works are trustworthy.

refer to particular words or lines. The direction to pause in the middle of a reading also has to do with emphasis. The margin notes, for example, often direct lectors to pause after the words "brothers and sisters" and to make eye contact with the assembly. The pause is here intended to emphasize the content of what has just been proclaimed and to encourage the assembly to understand themselves as a family united by God.

In the margin notes, it has often been pointed out when there are multiple speaking parts. Please do not take this as encouragement to perform an overly dramatic reading. Rather, simply proclaim the multiple speaking parts in such a way that the difference

among the chorus of voices is clear. Take Luke 15:11–32, the return of the prodigal son, for example. The mood of the first son, the one who claims his inheritance and promptly squanders it, changes in the course of the reading. He goes from demanding money from his father to eating with barnyard animals. His father, it is safe to say, is happy beyond description when his son, whom he feared dead, comes walking home. The second son, the one who stayed behind and slaved away for his father, is understandably angry. It is quite possible to communicate all of this without unseemly and overwrought delivery. Ask yourself how you like to hear scripture proclaimed. Do you like it when someone makes a spectacle of him or herself, or do you prefer it when you can concentrate on what's being read, without being overly distracted by the person reading it?

Eye contact in normal speech is very important to effective communication. This is no less the case in the proclamation of scripture. Know your text well enough that you only need to look down at it from time to time. Sometimes, of course, one gets the call to fill in for someone else and there really is not time to learn the reading well enough that such eye contact can be maintained. In this case, make sure that you read slowly enough that you at least have a shot at looking up once or twice.

One should also dress in an appropriate manner. Naturally, this will vary from place to place. Ostentation and sloppiness are the two poles to avoid. Once again, it is the message, not the messenger, that is the focus. Modest, unpretentious, and clean dress almost always fits the bill.

Proclaiming a reading you have practiced, prepared, and learned something about can be immensely enjoyable and gratifying. Public reading is among the most ancient forms of Christian ministry. Consider, for a moment, that when someone calling himself Paul, an apostle, wrote letters to various Christian communities, it fell to lectors to stand up and read them aloud.

If there is a simple way to encapsulate the advice for the proclamation of scripture, perhaps this will do: prepare, relax, read, and rejoice.

1ST SUNDAY OF ADVENT

Lectionary #3

READING I — Jeremiah 33:14–16

A reading from the Book of the Prophet Jeremiah

The days are **coming**, says the LORD,
  when I will **fulfill** the promise
  I made to the house of **Israel** and **Judah**.
In those days, in that time,
  I will raise up for David a j**ust shoot**;
  he shall do what is **right** and **just** in the land.
In those days **Judah** shall be **safe**
  and **Jerusalem** shall dwell **secure**;
  this is what they shall call her:
"**The Lord our justice.**"

The Church has traditionally understood this prophecy to refer to the advent of Christ. Stress the word "is" to emphasize the present reality of its fulfillment.

Stress the words "those" and "that" in the second stanza and the word "those" in the third.

READING I — The author of *Brideshead Revisited* and *A Handful of Dust,* two monuments of modern fiction, is best remembered in the English-speaking part of the Roman Catholic family for an eccentric life and some combative remarks in defense of his Christian belief. We can name a great many people, from Winston Churchill to Yogi Berra, whose reputations eclipse their work. Among Old Testament prophets, Jeremiah is sometimes in the same situation. Because his book tells of an unusual life lived in dangerous times, and also because such a delightfully engaging prophetic voice calls out in the telling, Jeremiah's personality can easily overshadow what he had to say.

One of the persistent themes of the book of Jeremiah is a theological principle of Judah's national well-being: the people's fortunes, for good or ill, depend on its fidelity to God. In Jeremiah 33, the prophet proclaims that the Chaldeans, or Babylon, will do unimaginable violence in Judah and Jerusalem. The reason Jeremiah gives is Judah's failure to hold up its end of its covenantal obligations. But even if Judah is not faithful, God remains faithful. Despite everything, even destruction and exile, Jeremiah prophesies that God will one day raise up a "just shoot" of David's line to rule Israel. In 33:17, Jeremiah prophesies that this line will never fail.

In Roman Catholic teaching, the "just shoot" that Jeremiah prophesied has usually been understood to refer to Jesus, whose Davidic ancestry receives particular attention in the infancy narratives of Matthew and Luke (see Romans 1:3), and whose royalty is examined at greater length in the commentaries for November 25, 2007.

Emphasize the words "Brothers and Sisters," pausing to look at your own assembled brothers and sisters— the worshipping assembly.

The first half of this reading, up to "Amen," is essentially a prayer. The second half is instructional. Pause between them and deliver the second half in a more commanding tone than the first.

READING II   1 Thessalonians 3:12—4:2

A reading from the first Letter of Saint Paul to the Thessalonians

Brothers and sisters:
May the Lord make you **increase** and **abound** in **love**
    for one another **and** for all,
    just as **we** have for **you**,
    so as to **strengthen** your hearts,
    to be blameless in holiness before our God and Father
    at the coming of our Lord Jesus with all his holy ones. Amen.

Finally, brothers and sisters,
    we earnestly **ask** and **exhort** you in the Lord Jesus that,
    as you received from us
    how you should **conduct** yourselves to please God
    —and as you are conducting yourselves—
    you do so **even more**.
For you know what instructions we gave you
    through the Lord Jesus.

READING II | In 1 Thessalonians 5:14–22, Paul offers a set of instructions. He states them with such brevity that they could easily fit on a note card or post-it note and be slipped into one's wallet. Even so, it's a very tall order. In 5:17, he writes, "Pray without ceasing." Even if we assume, as is likely, that Paul exaggerated his expression somewhat in order to make it very clear that the Thessalonians ought to pray a lot, the point stands that the Thessalonians, and we who read the letter as also addressed to ourselves, are to be men and women of constant prayer.

Today's reading also contains the prayer of Paul and his missionary team on behalf of the Thessalonians. This is clear enough in our English-language translation, but even clearer in Paul's Greek where we encounter a customary verbal mood used for prayers and wishes. Following the prayer of 3:12–13, Paul instructs the Thessalonians "as you received from us how you should conduct yourselves to please God—and as you are conducting yourselves—you do so even more." Is Paul telling the Thessalonians how to behave? Yes, but he is telling them how to behave based on what they know of

his own behavior. His instruction to "pray without ceasing" in 5:17 comes near the close of a letter in which Paul not only urges people to behave as they once saw him behave in person, but also as they now see him behave in the written word.

GOSPEL | As the skies darken ever earlier and biting winds whirl yellowed leaves in flocks, Advent arrives, a lush season for our senses. Candles, three purple and one rose, rise from wreaths of green like wax silos crammed with a harvest of the Spirit. Crèches appear in churches,

Proclaim this reading slowly.

GOSPEL   Luke 21:25–28, 34–36

A reading from the holy Gospel according to Luke

Jesus said to his disciples:
"There will be **signs** in the sun, the moon and the stars,
    and on earth **nations** will be in dismay,
    perplexed by the **roaring** of the sea and the waves.
People will die of **fright**
    in **anticipation** of what is coming upon the **world**,
    for the powers of the heavens will be shaken.
And then they will see the **Son of Man**
    coming in a cloud with **power** and great **glory**.
But when these signs begin to happen,
    stand erect and **raise** your heads
    because your **redemption** is at hand.

"**Beware** that your hearts do not become **drowsy**
    from **carousing** and **drunkenness**
    and the **anxieties** of daily life,
    and that day catch you by surprise like a **trap**.
For that day will assault **everyone**
    who lives on the face of the earth.
Be vigilant at **all** times
    and **pray** that you have the strength
    to escape the tribulations that are **imminent**
    and to **stand** before the **Son of Man**."

Give special emphasis to the words "And then they will see the Son of Man coming."

Emphasize the word "everyone."

cubicle desks, and kitchen tables display tiny figures leaning and gazing rapt toward an infant wrapped warm against the night and lying amid straw. His mother, draped in blue, leans in closest of all. Advent calendars mark our time, the door to each day concealing images, trinkets, and chocolates. The Advent calendar, its common cardboard laden with hidden sweets, symbolizes how good it is to be Roman Catholic—to have grace without measure revealed by the simple passage of time, to be able to pluck it from the world's ordinary stuff, and to savor it moment to moment.

This vivid, shocking, even terrifying reading comes from a part of Luke's Gospel called the "little apocalypse," a term also used of the parallel portions of Matthew and Mark (Luke 21:7–36; also see Matthew 24:3–44; Mark 13:3–37). To his disciples, who have been marveling at the Temple, Jesus declares that "the days will come when there will not be left a stone upon another stone." "Teacher," they ask, "when will this happen?" The little apocalypse is Jesus' answer. He predicts natural disasters and calamities of human cause, forecasts the persecution and death of his followers,

and prophesies that amid signs and portents in the heavens "the Son of Man coming in a cloud with power and great glory." In addition to the first advent of Christ, his birth, there will be a second, when he returns to earth.

IMMACULATE CONCEPTION

Lectionary #689

READING I   Genesis 3:9–15, 20

Keep in mind the multiple speaking parts. God is initially inquisitive, then angry. Adam and Eve are frightened and perhaps bewildered.

A reading from the Book of Genesis

After the man, Adam, had eaten of the tree,
    the LORD God called to the man and asked him,
        "Where **are** you?"
He answered, "I heard you in the garden;
    but I was **afraid**, because I was **naked**,
    so I hid myself."
Then he asked, "**Who** told you that you were naked?
You have eaten, then,
    from the tree of which I had **forbidden** you to eat!"
The man replied, "The woman whom you put here with me—
    she gave **me** fruit from the tree, and so I ate it."
The LORD God then asked the woman,
    "**Why** did you do such a thing?"
The woman answered, "The **serpent** tricked **me** into it,
    so I ate it."

Then the LORD God said to the serpent:
    "**Because you** have done this, **you** shall be banned
        from **all** the animals
        and from **all** the wild creatures;
    on your **belly** shall you **crawl**,
        and **dirt** shall you **eat**
        all the days of your life.

Slow down and emphasize God's curse of the serpent.

READING I   The Hebrew names of people and places in the Old Testament often have a particular significance that is lost in translation. In Exodus 17:1–7, after much complaint from the Israelites about their need for water, Moses, with God's help, causes water to flow from a rock by striking it with his staff. "The place was called Massah and Meribah because the Israelites quarreled there and tested the Lord" (Exodus 17:7; compare Numbers 20:2–13). Why name the place Massah and Meribah? The word Massah means "despair"

or "test," and Meribah means "strife" or "contention." The name of the place, according to Exodus, has to do with something important that happened there. In this reading Eve's name has a similar significance, for in Hebrew her name is related to a family of words having to do with "life" and "living things." The man, Adam, calls his wife Eve "because she became the mother of all the living."

The serpent's promise to Eve in Genesis 3:3–5 is twofold. First, she and Adam will not die if they eat of the fruit of the tree of the knowledge of good and evil (see Genesis

2:17). Second, when they do eat of it, their "eyes will be opened" and they "will be like gods who know what is good and what is bad."

Some Christian traditions and strains of Judaism have often associated the devil with the serpent of today's reading. Early evidence for this association, and a doctrine of the fall (see Wisdom 10:1), comes from the book of Wisdom in the course of an argument for the immortality of the soul: "For God formed man to be imperishable; the image of his own nature he made him. But by the envy

I will put **enmity** between you and the woman,
   and between your offspring and hers;
he will **strike** at your **head**,
   while you **strike** at his **heel**."

The man called his wife Eve,
   because she became the **mother** of all the living.

READING II   Ephesians 1:3–6, 11–12

A reading from the Letter of Saint Paul to the Ephesians

Brothers and sisters:
Blessed be the God and Father of our **Lord** Jesus Christ,
   who has blessed us in Christ
   with **every** spiritual blessing in the heavens,
   as he chose us in him, **before** the **foundation** of the world,
   to be **holy** and without **blemish** before him.
In **love** he destined us for adoption to himself
      through Jesus Christ,
   in accord with the **favor** of his **will**,
   for the **praise** of the **glory** of his **grace**
   that he granted us in the beloved.
In him we were also **chosen**,
   destined in accord with the purpose of the One
   who accomplishes all things according to the **intention**
      of his will,
   so that we might exist for the **praise** of his **glory**,
   we who first hoped in **Christ**.

Emphasize the words "brothers and sisters," pausing to look at the assembly as you do so.

These three stanzas are also three fairly complicated sentences. Proclaim them slowly, pausing briefly when you hit a comma. The logic of the clauses is easy to lose.

Give special emphasis to the names of the persons of the Trinity.

of the devil, death entered the world, and they who are in his possession experience it" (Wisdom 2:23–24; compare Romans 5:12).

READING II   For his first followers, the shock of Jesus' Crucifixion must have been profound. It is scarcely conceivable that they expected the man for whom they had left behind home and family, who had only days before been hailed as a king upon entering Jerusalem (see Commentary I, November 25, 2007), to die on a cross charged as a criminal subversive. Whatever the plan had been, this death had *not* been part of it. But what had the disciples thought was the plan? The conversation between the disguised risen Jesus and two of his disciples on the road to the village of Emmaus reveals that they had hoped Jesus "would be the one to redeem Israel" (Luke 24:21). Even after the risen Jesus discloses his identity, the question persists during the 40 days prior to his Ascension: "When they had gathered together they asked him, "Lord, are you at this time going to restore the kingdom to Israel?" (See Acts 1:6.) The plan, it seems, remained unclear. Not until the Church, under the guidance of the Holy Spirit, is born and begins to grow do Jesus' followers learn that he was and is more and different than a royal messiah come to satisfy Israel's national aspirations.

Today's reading from Ephesians takes up the issue of plans. "Before the foundation of the world," it seems, God chose the membership of the Church to be in Christ (Ephesians 1:4). This is a conviction about providence, which the early Greek fathers of the Church commonly called *pronoia,* or

Keep in mind the two speaking parts. You should deliver the words of the angel Gabriel in a clear, strong, forthright tone appropriate for a divine envoy of God.

Pause before each stanza containing Mary's response. Proclaim her words slowly and clearly.

GOSPEL Luke 1:26–38

A reading from the holy Gospel according to Luke

The angel **Gabriel** was sent from **God**
  to a town of **Galilee** called **Nazareth**,
  to a **virgin** betrothed to a man named **Joseph**,
  of the house of **David**,
  and the virgin's name was **Mary**.
And coming to her, he said,
  "**Hail**, full of **grace**! The **Lord** is with **you**."
But she was greatly troubled at what was said
  and **pondered** what sort of greeting this might be.
Then the angel said to her,
  "Do **not** be **afraid**, Mary,
  for **you** have found **favor** with God.
Behold, you will conceive in your womb and bear a son,
  and you shall name him **Jesus**.
He will be **great** and will be called **Son** of the **Most High**,
  and the **Lord God** will give him the **throne** of David his **father**,
  and he will rule over the house of **Jacob** forever,
  and of his Kingdom there will **be no** end."
But Mary said to the angel,
  "**How** can this be,
  since I have **no** relations with a man?"

"foresight." The confused disbelief after Jesus' Crucifixion has, in a few decades, given way to an understanding that everything has gone, goes, and will continue to go exactly according to God's plan.

GOSPEL The Immaculate Conception is a doctrine misunderstood by many in and out of the Roman Catholic Church. The common misconception is that it refers to Mary's conception of Jesus by

the Holy Spirit (Luke 1:35; also see Matthew 1:18). In fact, the doctrine refers to the conception of Mary herself. The *Catechism of the Catholic Church,* quoting Pope Pius IX, explains that Mary was, by virtue of the grace of God and the merits of Jesus, "preserved immune from all stain of original sin" (Catechism, #491). Like the doctrine of Mary Theotokos (see Gospel Commentary, August 14, 2007), the reason for the doctrine of the Immaculate Conception has more to do with Christology than with Mary.

But the place of Mary in the minds and hearts of Roman Catholics cannot be explained simply by an appeal to christological doctrine. The results of a 2001 survey by Dean Hoge of *The Catholic University,* and presented by Father Andrew Greeley in The Catholic Revolution, finds devotion to Mary the Mother of God to be highly rated as essential to faith by Roman Catholics between the ages of 20 and 39. In the survey, devotion to Mary comes fourth behind the

And the angel said to her in reply,
"The Holy Spirit will come upon you,
and the **power** of the Most High will **overshadow** you.
Therefore the child to be born
will be called **holy**, the Son of God.
And **behold**, **Elizabeth**, your relative,
has also conceived a son in her old age,
and this is the sixth month for her who was called **barren**;
for **nothing** will be impossible for God."
Mary said, "**Behold**, I am the handmaid of the Lord.
May it be done to me according to your **word**."
Then the angel **departed** from her.

presence of God in the sacraments, charity for the poor, and the presence of Christ in the Eucharist.

Mary is indeed the Mother of God and duly revered for it. As the Dogmatic Constitution on the Church *(Lumen gentium)* states, "By reason of the gift and role of divine maternity, by which she is united with her Son, the Redeemer, and with His singular graces and functions, the Blessed Virgin is also intimately united with the Church. As St. Ambrose taught, the Mother of God is a type of the Church in the order of faith, charity and perfect union with Christ. . . . For in the mystery of the Church, which is itself rightly called mother and virgin, the Blessed Virgin stands out in eminent and singular fashion as exemplar both of virgin and mother. . . . By her belief and obedience, not knowing man but overshadowed by the Holy Spirit, as the new Eve she brought forth on earth the very Son of the Father, showing an undefiled faith, not in the word of the ancient serpent, but in that of God's messenger." Indeed, Mary's place in the Church is uniquely her own.

2ND SUNDAY OF ADVENT

Lectionary #6

READING I   Baruch 5:1–9

A reading from the Book of the Prophet Baruch

Jerusalem, take off your robe of **mourning** and **misery**;
    put on the **splendor** of **glory** from **God** forever:
Wrapped in the cloak of **justice** from God,
    bear on your head the **mitre**
    that **displays** the **glory** of the eternal name.
For God will show **all** the earth your **splendor**:
    you will be named by God **forever**
    the **peace** of **justice**, the **glory** of God's **worship**.

Up, Jerusalem! **stand** upon the heights;
    look to the east and **see** your children
gathered from the east and the west
    at the word of the Holy One,
    rejoicing that **they** are remembered **by God**.
Led away on foot by their enemies they left you:
    but **God** will bring them back to you
    borne aloft in **glory** as on royal thrones.
For God has **commanded**
    that **every lofty** mountain be made **low**,
and that the **age-old depths** and **gorges**
    be **filled** to **level ground**,
    that Israel may advance **secure** in the glory of God.

Slow down and emphasize the sentence beginning with "For God will show."

Deliver the second stanza in a joyful, exultant tone.

READING I | According to Jeremiah 36, Baruch worked as a scribe for Jeremiah. The setting of the book that bears Baruch's name is the Babylonian community of exiles from Judah. The book begins shortly after the terrible news of the destruction of Jerusalem by Babylonian soldiers has arrived in Babylon and been shared among the exiles (Baruch 1:1–3).

Baruch delivers an oracle to Jerusalem itself, desolate and emptied among the mountains. He addresses her like a mother informed that her kidnapped children have been freed: "Up, Jerusalem! Stand upon the heights; look to the east and see your children gathered from the east and the west" (Baruch 5:5). Just as eager as the exiles are to return is their city joyful to welcome them home.

The leveling of terrain—mountains lowered, valleys raised—to hasten the exiles home under God's protection is a familiar prophetic theme. Most well known may be Isaiah 40:3–4, which also speaks to the return of the exiles over rugged lands made into plains. Matthew, Mark, and Luke apply Isaiah's words of consolation to the ministry of John the Baptist, interpreting the verses to refer to John's preparation of "the way of the Lord," namely Jesus of Nazareth (Luke 3:4–6; also see Matthew 3:3 and Mark 1:2–3). John the evangelist places the same verses into the mouth of John the Baptist in his response to "priests and Levites" sent from Jerusalem to find out who he is (John 1:19–23).

The end of the exile, heralded by an oracle promising earth reordered, precedes the advent of the people of Jerusalem to their ancestral home. John the Baptist, preceding the advent of the Messiah, proclaims nothing less.

The **forests** and every **fragrant** kind of tree
　　have overshadowed Israel at God's command;
for **God** is leading **Israel** in **joy**
　　by the **light** of his **glory**,
　　with his **mercy** and **justice** for company.

READING II　Philippians 1:4–6, 8–11

A reading from the Letter of Saint Paul to the Philippians

Brothers and sisters:
I pray always with **joy** in my every **prayer** for all of you,
　　because of your **partnership** for the **gospel**
　　from the **first day** until **now**.
I am **confident** of this,
　　that the one who **began** a good work in you
　　will **continue** to complete it
　　until the day of **Christ Jesus**.
God is my **witness**,
　　how I **long** for **all** of you with the **affection** of Christ Jesus.
And **this** is my **prayer**:
　　that your **love** may **increase** ever more and more
　　in **knowledge** and every kind of **perception**,
　　to **discern** what is of **value**,
　　so that you may be **pure** and **blameless** for the day of Christ,
　　filled with the fruit of **righteousness**
　　that **comes** through **Jesus Christ**
　　for the **glory** and **praise** of God.

Make eye contact with the assembly as you proclaim the words "brothers and sisters."

Slow down and emphasize the words "I am confident of this," and pause after you deliver them. Do the same with "God is my witness."

READING II The Acts of the Apostles records that Paul came to Philippi, a Roman colony in Greek Macedonia, in response to a dream or vision he had of a Macedonian man entreating him to come (Acts 16:9–10). According to Acts, the earliest Philippian Church relied upon the patronage of Lydia, the first reported convert at Philippi and a merchant woman of some means. After her Baptism, she permitted Paul and his team to live and work out of her home (Acts 16:11–15). Although unwilling to take much (if anything) in the way of support from some Christian communities, Paul gratefully received aid from the Philippians in the early months of his European mission (Philippians 4:10–20). The warmth of Paul's opening words of thanksgiving in today's section testifies not only to the desire of an imprisoned man (Philippians 1:7, 13) to see loved ones, but also to the close relationship he already shared with this community: "For God is my witness, how I long for all of you with the affection of Christ Jesus" (Philippians 1:8).

In Philippians 1:9–10, Paul prays that the Philippians' "love may increase ever more and more in knowledge and every kind of perception, to discern what is of value so that you may be pure and blameless for the day of Christ." In this letter, Paul cites his own example, as well as those of Jesus and Epaphroditus, as one of self-sacrifice on behalf of others. The love Paul has in mind is not the love of one for another, but the love of all for all (see Philippians 2:1–4). Such a love demands people make use of their rational faculties of "knowledge" and all forms of "perception" in order "to discern what is of value." To use their hearts, Paul says, the Philippians must use their heads.

GOSPEL   Luke 3:1–6

A reading from the holy Gospel according to Luke

Proclaim each clause of the first stanza slowly, emphasizing the name of each person.

In the fifteenth year of the reign **of Tiberius Caesar**,
    when **Pontius Pilate** was governor **of Judea**,
    and **Herod** was **tetrarch** of **Galilee**,
    and his brother **Philip tetrarch** of the region
        of **Ituraea** and **Trachonitis**,
    and **Lysanias** was **tetrarch** of **Abilene**,
    during the high priesthood of **Annas** and **Caiaphas**,

Pause after the name "Caiaphas." Then slowly read "the word of God came to John," emphasizing "God."

the **word** of **God** came to **John** the son of **Zechariah**
    in the desert.
John went throughout the **whole** region of the Jordan,
    proclaiming a **baptism** of **repentance** for the **forgiveness**
        of **sins**,
    as it is **written** in the book of the words of the prophet **Isaiah**:

Proclaim the words of Isaiah clearly and strongly.

        A voice of one crying out in the desert:
        *"**Prepare** the way of the **Lord**,*
            *make straight his **paths**.*
        *Every valley shall be **filled***
            *and every mountain and hill shall be made **low**.*
        *The **winding** roads shall be **made straight**,*
            *and the **rough ways made smooth**,*
    *and **all** flesh shall see the salvation of **God**."*

GOSPEL "In the second year after the inauguration of Harry Truman, five years after the conclusion of the Second World War, when Frederick Moore Vinson was Chief Justice of the Supreme Court, the year the Yankees won the World Series . . . ."

It is much easier, of course, to write, "In 1950 . . . ." Such an option was not available to Luke, who lived in a world having neither a common calendar nor universally accepted means of dating historical events. Ancient historians who lived under the Roman Empire typically dated events, as

Luke does here, in relation to the year of an emperor's reign. We know that by modern reckoning Tiberius reigned from 14–37 AD. Fifteen years after Tiberius' imperial acclamation would place the events he describes in 29 AD. There are some problems with Luke's chronology, such as the mention of Annas and Caiaphas serving as high priest at the same time, but no more than one high priest served at any given time. Writing 50 to 90 years after the events he describes, it is a nice feat of research to have written so precisely.

Notice how Luke opens with a panoramic lens encompassing the whole Roman Empire, essentially the known world, then telescopes down to the regions of Palestine before closing in on Jerusalem and the Temple, and at last sharpening his focus on a single man, John the Baptist. Luke the historian is making a radical claim about the importance of the advent of Christ in the context of international events. What mattered to Luke about the fifteenth year of Tiberius' reign was that a lone prophet lived in the wilderness of an out-of-the-way region of the world.

3RD SUNDAY OF ADVENT

Lectionary #9

READING I   Zephaniah 3:14–18a

A reading from the Book of the Prophet Zephaniah

This is a joyful reading. Proclaim it as
such and give it a strong delivery.

Shout for joy, O daughter **Zion**!
    Sing joyfully, **O Israel**!
Be **glad** and **exult** with all your heart,
    O daughter **Jerusalem**!
The LORD has **removed** the judgment against you,
    he has **turned away** your enemies;
the **King of Israel**, the LORD, is in your midst,
    you have no further **misfortune** to fear.
On **that** day, it shall be said to Jerusalem:
    Fear not, O Zion, **be not** discouraged!
The LORD, your God, is in your midst,
    a mighty savior;
he will **rejoice** over you with **gladness**,
    and **renew** you in his **love**,
he will **sing** joyfully because of **you**,
    as one **sings** at **festivals**.

READING I   The conception of God as the king of Israel has deep roots in the political theology of Israelite religion. The rule of the human king from Jerusalem parallels and is supported by God's rule from heaven over the earth. If the earthly king acted in such a way as to invite God's disfavor, or ruled in such a way as to convince the people that God no longer favored him, the earthly king's political authority could quickly become a matter of doubt. This political theology explains why the prophetic charge of God's displeasure with kings and elites was greeted with such

hostility. The liturgical expression of this political theology is present in Psalm 118, which was probably composed for the celebration of the triumphant return from battle of a king of David's line.

An interesting use of Zephaniah 3 occurs in the first chapter of John. Jesus, having begun to collect his disciples, meets an initially skeptical Nathanael through Philip, whom Jesus has already called. Upon seeing Nathanael, Jesus remarks in language strongly reminiscent of Zephaniah 3:13: "Here is a true Israelite. There is no duplicity in him." "How do you know me?" Nathanael

asks, still skeptical. Jesus offers this cryptic reply: "Before Philip called you, I saw you under the fig tree." Nathanael answers, in language suggestive of Zephaniah 3:15: "Rabbi, you are the Son of God; you are the King of Israel" (John 1:45–49; also see John 12:15). In this antiphonal allusion to Zephaniah 3:13 and 15, the substance of Nathanael's testimony is parallel to that of John 1:1 and 1:18. Jesus is Son (John 1:49; also see 1:18) and Word (John 1:1), but also King (John 1:49) and God (1:1; also see 1:18).

READING II   Philippians 4:4–7

A reading from the Letter of Saint Paul to the Philippians

Make eye contact with the assembly as you proclaim the words "brothers and sisters."

Stress the word "rejoice" both times it occurs.

Brothers and sisters:
Rejoice in the Lord **always**.
I shall say it again: **rejoice**!
Your **kindness** should be known to **all**.
The **Lord** is **near**.
Have **no** anxiety at all, but in **everything**,
    by **prayer** and **petition**, with **thanksgiving**,
    make your **requests** known to **God**.
Then the **peace** of God that surpasses **all** understanding
    will guard your **hearts** and **minds** in Christ Jesus.

GOSPEL   Luke 3:10–18

A reading from the holy Gospel according to Luke

Proclaim John's answers to the questions asked powerfully. He's laying down the law!

The crowds asked John the Baptist,
    "**What** should we **do**?"
He said to them in reply,
    "Whoever has two cloaks
    should **share** with the person who has none.
And whoever has food should do likewise."
Even tax collectors came to be baptized and they said to him,
    "Teacher, **what** should we **do**?"

READING II If you ask individual members of a random group to point to the part of their body containing their mind, most will indicate their heads. Ancient people might not have. Some Greeks and Romans believed the head to be the seat of the mind, but not all did. And in the Old Testament, as in much of the ancient world, the heart—and not the head—is the seat of thought, cognition, and reason. When Paul tells the Philippians that "the peace of God that surpasses all understanding will guard your hearts and minds in Christ Jesus," he means that the peace of God will guard their thinking. The translation "hearts and minds," while accurate, permits a modern colloquial understanding of the heart as the organ of the emotions in contrast to the mind as the seat of reason. We might capture Paul's meaning with greater accuracy by replacing "hearts and minds" with "minds and thoughts." He means to say that God's peace will protect one's ability to reason and to think.

People who make daily prayer a habit and a priority typically know from experience that much peace and greater clarity of thought are two common byproducts that come from petitions and requests made known to God in gratitude (Philippians 4:6).

It is worth slowing down and meditating for a moment on this reading. Paul is in jail (Philippians 1:7, 13). He and the Philippians know death is possible, perhaps likely (Philippians 1:19–26), and yet he tells the Philippians to rejoice, not only in 4:4 (twice!), but also in 2:18 and 3:1. In 2:17, referring to his proximity to death, Paul himself rejoices and encourages the Philippians to do the same, while earlier even rejoicing in his imprisonment (1:18).

He answered them,
    "**Stop** collecting **more** than what is prescribed."
Soldiers also asked him,
    "And **what** is it that **we** should **do**?"
He told them,
    "**Do not** practice **extortion**,
    do not falsely accuse anyone,
    and be **satisfied** with your wages."

Now the people were filled with **expectation**,
    and all were asking in their hearts
    whether **John might** be the **Christ**.
John answered them **all**, saying,
    "I am **baptizing** you with **water**,
    but one **mightier** than I is **coming**.
I am **not** worthy to **loosen** the thongs of his sandals.
He will **baptize** you with the Holy Spirit and fire.
His winnowing fan is in his hand **to clear** his threshing floor
    and to **gather** the wheat into his barn,
    but the chaff he will **burn** with **unquenchable fire**."
Exhorting them in many other ways,
    he preached **good news** to the people.

Emphasize the words "I am not worthy to loosen the thongs of his sandals."

GOSPEL | While "What should we do?" is exactly the kind of question one expects people to ask of holy men and prophets, in what spirit do the crowds ask John this question? We will need to back up to 3:7–9. "You brood of vipers!" John roars at those coming to him for Baptism. "Who warned you to flee from the coming wrath? Produce good fruits as evidence of your repentance!" If that isn't enough to terrify, John declares that being Jewish offers no edge in the apocalypse to come, "for I tell you God can raise up children to Abraham from these stones!" Those

who do not produce good fruit "will be cut down and thrown into the fire." If the crowds find John at all convincing, "What should we do?" is a question they now ask in 3:10 with a great sense of urgency.

But after this fearsome build-up, the answers to this question, in the various ways the crowds, tax collectors, and soldiers pose it, are almost comical. John tells the crowds to share their abundance, the tax collectors to do an honest day's work, and the soldiers not to make evil use of their power. The production of good fruit appears to be a matter of basic morality, of doing

what everyone already knows is right. Crowds, tax collectors, and soldiers get no mystical answers from John. "What should we do?" they ask. "Behave!" he thunders.

All four Gospels stress that John the Baptist was not the Messiah. In Acts, the companion work to Luke's Gospel, John's prophecy of Jesus' Baptism comes to pass in the birth of the Church at the feast of Pentecost, the Holy Spirit rushing upon Jesus' followers and tongues of fire coming to rest over each one (Acts 2:1–4).

4TH SUNDAY OF ADVENT

Lectionary #12

READING I   Micah 5:1–4a

A reading from the Book of the Prophet Micah

Ephrathah = Ef-RAH-thah

Thus says the LORD:
You, **Bethlehem-Ephrathah**
  too small to be among the clans of **Judah**,
from **you** shall come forth for **me**
  one who is to be **ruler** in **Israel**;
whose **origin** is from of **old**,
  from **ancient** times.
Therefore the Lord will give them up, until the time
  when **she** who is to give birth has borne,
and the rest of his kindred shall **return**
  to the children of **Israel**.
He shall **stand firm** and **shepherd** his flock
  by the **strength** of the LORD,
  in the majestic name of the LORD, his **God**;
and they shall **remain**, for now his greatness
  shall reach to the **ends** of the **earth**;
  he shall be **peace**.

Pause before the words "he shall be
peace" and deliver this line slowly and
with emphasis.

READING I   Micah prophesied at about the same time as Isaiah, beginning in the late eighth century BC. But while Isaiah prophesied from the heart of Jerusalem as a member of the Temple establishment, Micah hailed from Moresheth, an insignificant village well south and west of Jerusalem. Few prophets denounce the greed of the wealthy with such force and so stridently attack the exploitation of the rural poor. Micah denounces rulers, the wealthy, priests, and prophets as corrupt. Because of them, "Zion shall be plowed like a field, and

Jerusalem reduced to rubble, and the mount of the Temple to a forest ridge" (Micah 3:12). Samaria, the capital of the north, does not come off much better. We learn from Jeremiah 26:16–19 that Micah was almost murdered for proclaiming the word of the Lord, but that his oracles also led to religious reforms under king Hezekiah of Judah (see 2 Kings 18:1–8).

We read from the book of Micah in Advent because it contains an oracle seeming to identify Bethlehem as the city of a yet-unborn ruler's birth. The earliest Christian text to connect this prophecy to Jesus is

Matthew's Gospel. Herod, "greatly troubled" by the arrival of Magi in Jerusalem asking questions about a "newborn king of the Jews," assembles the chief priests and scribes to learn that Bethlehem, based on Micah's oracle, is where the Messiah will come from (Matthew 2:1–6).

Similarly, there are few obvious reasons for us to think that Micah knew he prophesied the advent of Jesus of Nazareth. The principle of salvation history is that "more will be revealed."

READING II   Hebrews 10:5–10

A reading from the Letter to the Hebrews

Brothers and sisters:
When **Christ** came into the **world**, he said:
   "**Sacrifice** and **offering** you did not desire,
      but a **body** you **prepared** for me;
   in **holocausts** and **sin** offerings you took **no delight**.
   Then I said, 'As is **written** of me in the **scroll**,
      behold, I come to do **your** will, O **God**.'"

First he says, "**Sacrifices** and **offerings**,
      holocausts and **sin offerings**,
   you neither **desired** nor **delighted** in."
These are offered according to the **law**.
Then he says, "**Behold**, I come to do **your** will."
He takes away the **first** to establish the **second**.
By this "**will**," **we** have been consecrated
      through the offering of the **body** of **Jesus Christ** once for **all**.

Emphasize the words "but a body you prepared for me."

Proclaim the second stanza slowly. This is where the author explains the two passages he has just quoted.

Pause before the words "He takes away the first to establish the second" and pronounce them slowly.

READING II As the name suggests, Hebrews was probably written to Jewish Christians, although it names neither senders nor intended recipients and provides dubious information about the precise situation of each. The letter may have been written to persuade its recipients not to abandon Christianity. It is also possible that not all (or perhaps any) of the exhortations to steadfastness and warnings against falling away (see 2:1–3; 6:6, 11–12; 10:23–36) refer to such a situation. There is much we cannot know about the letter's author and its intended audience.

This reading is a piece of a lengthy and detailed theological argument in which the author assumes some basic similarities between Jesus and the cycle of sacrificial worship in the Jerusalem Temple. He assumes the similarities because one cannot compare things that are fundamentally different from one another. The goal of his comparison is to demonstrate that faith in Jesus is far superior to Temple Judaism.

The author assumes that Jesus and the high priest of the Temple are alike in that they offer sacrifices to atone for sins. There the similarity ends. While the high priest must make sacrifices year in and year out to atone for the sins of the people, Jesus himself atoned for all sin in perpetuity by the once-for-all sacrifice of himself on the cross. Jesus is both high priest and willing sacrificial victim.

In this reading, the author places bits of Psalm 40 into the mouth of Jesus upon his entry into the world. He refers the body "you prepared for me" to Jesus' physical body to be sacrificed upon the cross. In place of "sacrifice," "offering," "holocausts," and "sin offering," which are prescribed by law (see Leviticus 1:1—4:35; 5:14–26), Jesus volunteers himself, which, in the author's

GOSPEL   Luke 1:39–45

A reading from the holy Gospel according to Luke

Mary set out
    and **traveled** to the hill country in haste
    to a town of **Judah**,
    where she entered the house of **Zechariah**
    and greeted **Elizabeth**.
When **Elizabeth** heard Mary's greeting,
    the infant **leaped** in her womb,
    and Elizabeth, **filled** with the **Holy Spirit**,
    cried out in a loud voice and said,
    "**Blessed** are you among **women**,
    and **blessed** is the **fruit** of your **womb**.
And **how** does this happen to **me**,
    that the **mother** of my Lord should come to **me**?
For at the moment the sound of your greeting reached my ears,
    the infant in my womb **leaped** for joy.
Blessed are you who **believed**
    that what was **spoken** to you by the **Lord**
    would be **fulfilled**."

Elizabeth is prophesying. Deliver her words in the clear, forthright voice of a woman speaking under the power of the Holy Spirit.

Stress each occurrence of the word "Blessed."

---

understanding, makes him a superior sacrifice nullifying the need for any other.

GOSPEL In the first two chapters of Luke's Gospel alone, which concern the advents of Jesus and John the Baptist, the Holy Spirit is mentioned nine times. The angel Gabriel informs the priest Zechariah that his son, John, "will be filled with the Holy Spirit even from his mother's womb" (1:15). Elizabeth, John's mother, is filled with the Holy Spirit in today's reading as she proclaims a blessing on Mary (1:41–45). And Zechariah, when his powers of

speech are restored (1:18–20; 1:57–66), proclaims the canticle of 1:68–79 "filled with the Holy Spirit." This is a spirit-filled family in a spirit-filled Gospel.

In the Acts of the Apostles, the companion work to Luke's Gospel, the Holy Spirit brings the Church into existence at Pentecost (Acts 2:1–4) and is cause of its growth. But the Holy Spirit is also a bridge between the Church and Jesus' ministry, which Jesus begins "in the power of the Spirit" (Luke 4:14). And further back, an elder of Israel, Simeon, prophesies Jesus' mission at his presentation in the Temple: the Holy

Spirit rests "upon" Simeon, it has revealed that he will not die before the advent of the Messiah, and it leads him to the Temple to find the infant Jesus (Luke 1:25–27).

Thus, the Spirit provides continuity between Israel's prophetic tradition and Temple priesthood, and the Church. Linking them are the ministries of John the Baptist and Jesus. And while Jesus' ministry is much more than a mere link with the past, the past is very important to Luke as a writer of sacred history. He takes great care to show that the growth of the Church emerges in unbroken succession from the faith of Israel.

NATIVITY OF THE LORD: VIGIL

Lectionary #13

READING I   Isaiah 62:1–5

A reading from the Book of the Prophet Isaiah

Stress each occurrence of the word "not."

For **Zion's** sake I will **not be silent**,
    for **Jerusalem's** sake I will **not** be **quiet**,
until her **vindication** shines forth like the **dawn**
    and her **victory** like a burning **torch**.

Nations shall behold your **vindication**,
    and all the **kings** your **glory**;
you shall be called by a **new** name
    pronounced by the mouth of the LORD.
You shall be a **glorious crown** in the hand of the LORD,
    a royal diadem **held** by your **God**.

Stress the words "Forsaken," "Desolate," "My Delight," and "Espoused."

No more shall people call you "**Forsaken**,"
    or your land "**Desolate**,"
but you shall be called "**My Delight**,"
    and your land "**Espoused**."
For the LORD **delights** in you
    and makes your land his **spouse**.
As a young man **marries** a **virgin**,
    your Builder shall **marry you**;
and as a **bridegroom** rejoices in his **bride**
    so shall your **God rejoice** in **you**.

READING I When speaking of God's relation to the world, one often finds oneself speaking in metaphors: God is father, king, warrior, judge, friend, and so on. The Roman Catholic experience of God runs the gamut from transcendence to immanence, which is to say from doctrines of God's vast and inscrutable difference from all creation, to our lived experience of closeness with his divinity in the ordinary things of the world. Metaphor is neither accurate nor complete, but it gets the job done. In the Eucharist, ideas of transcendence and immanence commingle in a mystery well beyond human comprehension, which nevertheless enters our lives in the plainest of ways: we eat it and drink it together as a family at table. One also finds the tension between immanence and transcendence in Isaiah. God transcendent is the one before whom "all the nations are as nought, as nothing and void he accounts them" (Isaiah 40:17). But we encounter God immanent speaking to Jerusalem in today's reading: "As a young man marries a virgin, your builder shall marry you; and as a bridegroom rejoices in his bride so shall your God rejoice in you" (Isaiah 62:5).

The Catechism refers to the Incarnation as a "unique and altogether singular event" (Catechism, #464). While this is undoubtedly so, it is also possible to view the union of God with humanity in the second person of the Trinity as a lens through which myriad

A reading from the Acts of the Apostles

When **Paul** reached **Antioch** in **Pisidia** and entered
   the **synagogue**,
   he **stood** up, **motioned** with his hand, and **said**,
   "Fellow **Israelites** and you others who are **God-fearing**, **listen**.
The **God** of this people **Israel chose** our ancestors
   and **exalted** the people during their sojourn
   in the land of Egypt.
With **uplifted** arm he **led** them out of it.
Then he removed **Saul** and raised up **David** as king;
   of him he **testified**,
   'I have found **David**, **son of Jesse**, **a man** after my own **heart**;
   he will **carry** out my every wish.'
From **this man's** descendants **God**, according to his promise,
   has **brought** to Israel a **savior**, **Jesus**.
John heralded his coming by proclaiming a **baptism** of **repentance**
   to all the people of **Israel**;
   and as **John** was completing his course, he would say,
   '**What** do you **suppose** that **I** am? **I am not** he.
Behold, **one** is coming **after** me;
   I am **not** worthy to **unfasten** the **sandals** of his feet.'"

Antioch = AN-tee-ock
Pisidia = Pih-SIH-di-ah

Stress the words "Fellow Israelites," "you others who are God-fearing," and "listen." Pause after the word "listen."

Emphasize the words "this man's."

Stress and pause after the word "Behold."

examples of God's presence in the world stand out with greater clarity. The joy a bridegroom takes in a bride—and she in him—is a miraculous thing for the couple, of course, but also for the families, who recall squalling infancy, defiant adolescence, and finally, one hopes, happy and responsible adulthood. When we believe that God himself took on humanity in the infant Jesus, how much easier is it to see the sacramental joy of the divine bridegroom suffusing two families and a parish rejoicing in a couple in love?

READING II   Today's reading comes from a speech by Paul before the synagogue of Antioch in the region of Pisidia (Acts 13:14). This is a different Antioch than the Syrian city from which Paul and Barnabas set out on this, their first missionary journey (Acts 13:1–3). After Jerusalem, Syrian Antioch was the most important center of the Church in its early decades, the place where "the disciples were first called Christians" (Acts 11:26). Pisidian Antioch lay in southern Asia Minor, well west of Syrian Antioch. Why are there multiple Antiochs? Before the Romans took the eastern Mediterranean in the first century BC, much of the territory was under

Stress every part of the genealogy that departs from the basic "X became the father of Y" format. Examples are "Jacob the father of Judah *and his brothers*" and "David became the father of Solomon, *whose mother had been the wife of Uriah."* The reason for this is that the repetition can become a drone if you don't take advantage of breaks in the basic formula.

Abraham = AY-bra-ham

Perez = PER-rez

Hezron = Hez-RONE

Ram = RAHM

Amminadab = Ah-min-ah-DAB

Nahshon = Nah-SHONE
Salmon = Sal-MONE
Boaz = BO-az
Rahab = Rah-HAB
Obed = O-BAYD

Uriah = U-RI-yah

Rehoboam = Reh-ho-bo-AM

Abijah = Ah-bi-JAH

Asaph = Ah-SAF

Jehoshaphat = Jeh-ho-shah-FAT

Joram = Jo-RAM

Uzziah = U-ZI-yah

GOSPEL Matthew 1:1–25

A reading from the holy Gospel according to Matthew

The book of the genealogy of Jesus Christ,
  the son of David, the son of Abraham.

Abraham became the father **of Isaac**,
  Isaac the father of **Jacob**,
  Jacob the father **of Judah** and his **brothers**.
Judah became the father of **Perez** and **Zerah**,
  whose **mother** was **Tamar**.
Perez became the father of **Hezron**,
  Hezron the father of **Ram**,
  Ram the father of **Amminadab**.
Amminadab became the father of **Nahshon**,
  Nahshon the father of **Salmon**,
  Salmon the father of **Boaz**,
  whose **mother** was **Rahab**.
Boaz became the father of **Obed**,
  whose **mother** was **Ruth**.
Obed became the father of **Jesse**,
  Jesse the father of **David** the king.

David became the father of **Solomon**,
  whose **mother** had been the **wife** of **Uriah**.
Solomon became the father of **Rehoboam**,
  Rehoboam the father of **Abijah**,
  Abijah the father of **Asaph**.
Asaph became the father of **Jehoshaphat**,
  Jehoshaphat the father of **Joram**,
  Joram the father of **Uzziah**.

---

the sway of the Seleucid dynasty, a family of Macedonian origin, which produced eight rulers named Antiochus in roughly 250 years (see Commentary I, November 11, 2007). Seleucid kings, like many rulers, enjoyed having towns and cities named after them.

In 1 Corinthians, Paul claims that he has striven in the course of his travels to bring the Gospel to people as they are, on their terms, not his. "To the Jews I became like a Jew to win over Jews." To those under law, outside the law, and "the weak," Paul claims to have become as they for his Gospel's sake. "I have become all things to all, to save at least some" (1 Corinthians 9:20–23). In Acts, the author shows Paul doing something like this. In Acts 17, Paul preaches to a crowd of Greeks inclined to philosophy in a way designed to make the Gospel comprehensible to them. In today's reading, Paul preaches to a synagogue crowd and stresses the salvation history of Israel in Egypt, the people's entry into Canaan, the rule of judges, the reign of Saul, and the accession of David. By highlighting Jesus' Israelite and Davidic heritage, Paul proclaims him as Messiah according to criteria important to his audience.

Jotham = Jo-THAM
Ahaz = Ah-HAZ
Hezekiah = Heh-zeh-KI-yah
Manesseh = Mah-nah-SHE

Jechoniah = Jeh-cho-NI-yah

Shealtiel = She-al-ti-EL
Zerubbabel = Zeh-rub-bah-BEL
Abiud = Ah-bi-UD
Eliakim = El-i-yah-KEEM
Azor = Ah-ZOR
Zadok = Zah-DOK
Achim = Ah-CHEEM
Eliud = El-i-YUD
Eleazar = Eleazar
Matthan = Mat-TAN

Slow down to read the final tally of the three sets of 14.

Uzziah became the father of **Jotham**,
   Jotham the father of **Ahaz**,
   Ahaz the father of **Hezekiah**.
Hezekiah became the father of **Manasseh**,
   Manasseh the father of **Amos**,
   Amos the father of **Josiah**.
Josiah became the father of **Jechoniah** and his **brothers**
   at the time of the **Babylonian exile**.

After the **Babylonian exile**,
   Jechoniah became the father of **Shealtiel**,
   Shealtiel the father of Zerubbabel,
   Zerubbabel the father of **Abiud**.
Abiud became the father of **Eliakim**,
   Eliakim the father of **Azor**,
   Azor the father of **Zadok**.
Zadok became the father of **Achim**,
   Achim the father of **Eliud**,
   Eliud the father of **Eleazar**.
Eleazar became the father of **Matthan**,
   Matthan the father of **Jacob**,
   Jacob the father of **Joseph**, the **husband** of **Mary**.
Of her was born **Jesus** who is called the **Christ**.

Thus the total number of **generations**
   from **Abraham** to **David**
   is **fourteen** generations;
   from **David** to the **Babylonian** exile,
   fourteen generations;
   from the **Babylonian exile** to the **Christ**,
   fourteen generations.

GOSPEL | Two of the four Gospels have genealogies of Jesus. We find Luke's genealogy wedged between Jesus' Baptism and his temptation in the desert (Luke 3:23–38). Luke begins with Jesus and extends his male line back to Adam, and through Adam even to God. Matthew's genealogy begins his Gospel. It commences with Abraham and concludes with Jesus. One way to assess the difference between Matthew's genealogy and Luke's is that Matthew's suggests a primary concern with Jesus' Jewish heritage, while Luke's reveals Jesus' fraternity with all humanity.

It is often helpful to compare the beginnings of the four Gospels. The earliest of the four is probably Mark's. After a succinct introduction ("the beginning of the Gospel of Jesus Christ, the Son of God"), Mark hastens from John the Baptist to Jesus' ministry in a mere 13 verses. He offers no account of Jesus' birth, infancy, or childhood. In Matthew, a genealogy beginning with Abraham, the father of Israel, begins the Gospel. In Luke, the Gospel's beginning is not so much temporal as spatial. The setting of the narrative commences where it concludes—in the Temple (Luke 1:8; 24:53). John, like Mark, starts with a "beginning." But John's beginning is not the beginning of the "gospel," but a beginning even before the Creation (1:1–5).

Now **this** is how the **birth** of **Jesus Christ** came about.
When his mother **Mary** was betrothed to **Joseph**,
    but **before** they lived together,
    she was **found** with **child** through the **Holy Spirit**.
Joseph her **husband**, since he was a **righteous** man,
    yet unwilling to expose her to shame,
    decided to divorce her quietly.
Such was his intention when, **behold**,
    the angel of the Lord appeared to him in a dream and said,

Read the angel's words to Joseph in his dream in a clear, strong voice.

    "Joseph, son of David,
    do **not** be afraid to take Mary your wife into your home.
For it is through the Holy Spirit
    that this child has been conceived in her.
She will bear a son and you are to name him **Jesus**,
    because he will **save** his people from their **sins**."
All this took place to fulfill
    what the Lord had said through the prophet:
    *Behold, the virgin shall **conceive** and **bear** a son,*
        *and they shall name him **Emmanuel**,*
    which means "***God is with us***."
When Joseph awoke,
    he did as the angel of the Lord had commanded him
    and took his **wife** into his home.
He had no relations with her until she bore a son,
    and he named him **Jesus**.

[Shorter: Matthew 1:18–25]

NATIVITY OF THE LORD: MIDNIGHT

Lectionary #14

READING I   Isaiah 9:1–6

A reading from the Book of the Prophet Isaiah

The line beginning with the words "The people who walked" is parallel to the line beginning with the words "upon those." The second line repeats, reflects, or in some way completes the first. Such parallelism characterizes much of this reading. Pause between your deliveries of each line that is parallel to another.

> The people who walked in **darkness**
>   have seen a **great light**;
> upon those who **dwelt** in the **land** of **gloom**
>   a **light** has **shone**.
> You have brought them **abundant joy**
>   and **great rejoicing**,
> as they **rejoice** before you as at the **harvest**,
>   as people **make merry** when **dividing spoils**.
> For the **yoke** that **burdened** them,
>   the **pole** on their **shoulder**,
> and the **rod** of their **taskmaster**
>   you have **smashed**, as on the day of **Midian**.
> For every boot that tramped in **battle**,
>   every cloak rolled in **blood**,
>   will be **burned** as fuel for flames.
> For a **child** is **born** to **us**, a **son** is **given us**;
>   upon **his** shoulder **dominion** rests.
> They name him **Wonder-Counselor**, **God-Hero**,
>   **Father-Forever**, **Prince of Peace**.
> His dominion is **vast**
>   and forever **peaceful**,

Midian = MIH-di-an

Stress the titles "Wonder-Counselor," "God-Hero," "Father-Forever," and "Prince of Peace."

READING I   Today's reading in its original historical context probably celebrated the birth of a son to a king of Judah. Many scholars identify the baby with the Immanuel child of Isaiah 7:14 and 8:8. The birth of the child would have been greeted with public festivities, sacrifices, and liturgies of thanksgiving in the Temple. Isaiah 9 may have originally been composed for such a celebration. We cannot be certain, but the child was perhaps Hezekiah, the son and heir of King Ahaz of Judah.

Among the kings of Judah, Hezekiah stands out as an extraordinary example of piety (2 Kings 18:1–8). Matthew 4:15–16 quotes Isaiah 8:23 — 9:1 directly. The evangelist interprets the prophecy to refer not to the birth of a son to a king in the distant past, but to Jesus' residence in the village of Capernaum, an area within or near the ancestral territory of the Israelite tribes of Zebulun and Naphthali (Isaiah 8:23).

READING II   Jesus was a Jew and led a movement predominately, perhaps exclusively, composed of Jews. This movement neither broke with Judaism during Jesus' lifetime, nor for many years afterward. When the break came, it did not occur in the same way and at the same time in every place. But by the end of the first century, 70 years after Jesus' execution, his movement had become a religion made up of Churches, soon to be called in many places *the* Church, which were primarily

from David's **throne**, and over his **kingdom**,
    which he **confirms** and **sustains**
by **judgment** and **justice**,
    both **now** and **forever**.
The zeal of the LORD of hosts will do this!

READING II   Titus 2:11–14

A reading from the Letter of Saint Paul to Titus

Pause after the word "Beloved" and make eye contact with the assembly.

Beloved:
The **grace** of God has appeared, saving **all**
    and training us to **reject godless ways** and **worldly desires**
    and to live **temperately**, **justly**, and **devoutly** in this age,
    as we await the **blessed hope**,
    the appearance of the **glory** of our great **God**
    and savior **Jesus Christ**,
    who **gave himself** for **us** to **deliver us** from **all** lawlessness
    and to **cleanse** for **himself** a people as his **own**,
    eager to do what is **good**.

Emphasize the words "temperately, justly, and devoutly."

GOSPEL   Luke 2:1–14

A reading from the holy Gospel according to Luke

In those days a **decree** went out from **Caesar Augustus**
    that the **whole world** should be enrolled.
This was the first enrollment,
    when **Quirinius** was governor of **Syria**.

Quee-RIN-nee-us

Gentile in composition. Aramaic, the language of the movement, had been traded for Greek. The Galilean countryside, where Jesus called his first disciples, healed, taught, prophesied, and performed miracles, no longer held the bulk of his followers. They now lived in Rome, Corinth, Ephesus, Pergamon, and many other cities of the Mediterranean basin. Accompanying these changes of ethnicity, institutions, language, geography, and society came different ways to conceive of the advent of Jesus Christ under the influence of the wider culture of the Church.

In Titus 2:11, the author writes that God's grace "has appeared," and in 2:13 that "we await the blessed hope, the appearance of the glory of the great God and of our savior Jesus Christ." The two advents of Christ are described as "appearances," for which the author uses the technical religious terminology of Greek religion. The verb *epiphainō* and the noun *epiphaneia*, the origin of the English word "epiphany," define the appearance of a god in all his or her divine power and strength. The Transfiguration of Jesus, for example, strongly resembles a Greek epiphany (see

Matthew 17:1–7; Mark 9:2–8; Luke 9:28–36). The Jewish apocalyptic idea of the glorious return of the Son of Man (Daniel 7:13; Matthew 26:64; Mark 14:62; Revelation 1:7) Titus describes as an epiphany, an appearance of Jesus in his divine glory, a religious concept doubtless quite familiar to the letter's presumed Gentile addressees.

GOSPEL   In Luke 2:1–16, we see another example of Luke's "backward" history (see Gospel Commentary, December 10, 2006). The passage begins

Pause between the words "each to his own town" and "And Joseph too." Galilee = GAL-li-lee

So all went to be enrolled, each to his own town.
And **Joseph** too went up from **Galilee** from the town of **Nazareth**
    to Judea, to the city of **David** that is called **Bethlehem**,
    because he was of the house and family of **David**,
    to be enrolled with **Mary**, his betrothed, who was with **child**.
While they were there,
    the time came for her to have her **child**,
    and she gave birth to her **firstborn son**.
She wrapped him in **swaddling clothes** and laid him in a **manger**,
    because there was **no room** for them in the **inn**.

Now there were **shepherds** in that region living in the **fields**
    and keeping the **night watch** over their **flock**.
The **angel of the Lord** appeared to them
    and the **glory of the Lord** shone around them,
    and they were struck with **great fear**.

Pause before the angel's words. Deliver them clearly and strongly.

The angel said to them,
    "**Do not be afraid**;
    for behold, I proclaim to you **good news** of **great joy**
    that will be for **all the people**.
For **today** in the city of **David**
    a **savior** has been born for you who is **Christ** and **Lord**.
And this will be a **sign** for you:
    you will find an **infant** wrapped in **swaddling clothes**
    and lying in a manger."
And suddenly there was a **multitude** of the **heavenly host**
    with the **angel**,
    praising God and **saying**:
        "**Glory to God in the highest**
            and on earth **peace** to those **on whom his favor rests**."

with a proper subject for a serious work of history, an emperor, the great Augustus (31 BC–14 AD). Luke follows with another suitable figure—someone called Quirinius, an imperial legate to Syria (6 AD). So far so good. But by the fourth verse we suspect that we are going to learn no decent history at all. We shortly discover that we will learn nothing about Augustus, nothing about Quirinius, and nothing really about the census, but rather that someone called Joseph from the Galilee traveled to Bethlehem with his pregnant wife, who delivered her baby in a stable there, and that the child's first visitors were some shepherds who showed up because they thought some angels told them to.

Kings, generals, wars, rebellions, and famines are appropriate subjects for a history. Luke knows his account will not qualify for many people, a fact to which he himself draws attention by mentioning Caesar Augustus only to ignore him. The ancient world is not so foreign that we cannot imagine how a book seeming to be history, but instead concerning a child born in a stable surrounded by shepherds, might have been considered absurd.

It *is* absurd in many ways: that God should have been born as a common child in a little backwater village among livestock is just as ridiculous as the news that this God grew up, went about teaching and healing other nobodies, and died. But most absurd of all is the rest of the news: that God, born in a stable and killed on a cross, was also raised from the dead and still lives in power among his followers.

NATIVITY OF THE LORD: DAWN

Lectionary #15

READING I   Isaiah 62:11–12

A reading from the Book of the Prophet Isaiah

Emphasize the word "savior."

See, the LORD proclaims
    to the **ends** of the **earth**:
say to daughter **Zion**,
    your **savior** comes!
Here is his **reward** with him,
    his **recompense** before him.
They shall be called the **holy people**,
    the **redeemed** of the LORD,

Emphasize the word "Frequented."

and you shall be called "**Frequented**,"
    a city that is **not forsaken**.

READING I In a letter attributed to Ignatius of Antioch, who purportedly wrote it on his way to martyrdom, readers are urged to make themselves worthy of their name. The name is "Christian." No one going by another name, the letter reads, can belong to God. A person who does not go by this name has not yet understood that the words of Isaiah 62:2 ("You shall be called by a new name pronounced by the mouth of the Lord") and 62:12 ("They shall be called the holy people") refer to the Church. He backs up his reading with Acts 11:26: "it was in Antioch that the disciples were first called Christians." The "new name" means this prophecy is Christian property, not Jewish.

The Catechism declares that the task of reading scripture in and with the Roman Catholic Church requires that one try to discern its human and divine authors' intentions (Catechism, #109). On the basis of what evidence might one say that the human author of Isaiah 62:11–12, a Jew, meant to tell his readers that their descendants would not belong to God? On what grounds might one argue that God is pleased to deny Jews and Muslims the promises contained in their sacred writings?

READING II In Titus 3:8, we find a phrase: "This saying is trustworthy." It immediately follows this reading, like a stamp of approval. There are other instances worth looking at in 1 Timothy and 2 Timothy, two letters closely related to Titus and that, together with it, form a trio often called the "Pastoral Epistles." In 2 Timothy 2:11, we find "this saying is trustworthy"

Stress the word "Beloved" and make eye contact with the assembly as you do.

Stress "not" and "his mercy."

READING II   Titus 3:4–7

A reading from the Letter of Saint Paul to Titus

Beloved:
When the **kindness** and **generous love**
    of **God our savior** appeared,
not because of any righteous deeds **we** had done
    but because of **his mercy**,
he saved us through the **bath** of **rebirth**
    and **renewal** by the **Holy Spirit**,
whom he **richly** poured out on us
    through **Jesus Christ** our **savior**,
so that **we** might be **justified** by his **grace**
    and become **heirs** in **hope** of eternal life.

immediately before another sentence, 2 Timothy 2:11–13. New Testament scholars often call this passage a hymn. Another passage where the same introductory phrase appears is 1 Timothy 1:15. In Timothy 4:9, "this saying is trustworthy," like Titus 3:8, most likely follows the sentence it approves. There remains one ambiguous case, 1 Timothy 3:1, where it is not clear if "this saying is trustworthy" supports what went before or what comes after.

It appears that the author of these three letters used "this saying is trustworthy" to highlight material of particular importance, perhaps calling attention to its traditional character. In the case of Titus 3:4–7 and 2 Timothy 2:11–13, there is at least a good chance that the saying highlights text used in liturgical settings. In Titus 3:4–7, judging from the content, that setting was most likely baptismal. As with Galatians 3:26–28, we may here have a shard of an early Christian baptismal liturgy.

Salvation in this reading is a matter God's mercy, not the righteousness of the baptized. Salvation is not earned, but offered. Notice also that there is no mention of sharing in Christ's death through Baptism. Instead, Baptism is conceived as rebirth and renewal (see, in contrast, Romans 6:1–11). The understanding of renewal in the spirit resembles Paul's thinking in 2 Corinthians 5:1–11, although the context is somewhat different.

GOSPEL   Luke 2:15–20

A reading from the holy Gospel according to Luke

When the **angels** went away from them to **heaven**,
    the **shepherds** said to one another,
    "**Let us go**, then, to **Bethlehem**
    to see this thing that has taken place,
    which the **Lord** has **made known** to us."
So they went in haste and found **Mary** and **Joseph**,
    and the **infant** lying in the **manger**.
When they saw this,
    they **made known** the message
    that had been told them about this child.
All who heard it were **amazed**
    by what had been told them by the shepherds.
And **Mary kept all** these things,
    reflecting on them **in her heart**.
Then the shepherds returned,
    glorifying and **praising God**
    for **all** they had **heard** and **seen**,
    just as it had been **told** to them.

Slow down and emphasize the shepherds' words.

Pause before the final stanza, slow down when you deliver it, and stress the name "Mary." Pause before delivering the final sentence. Emphasize Mary's reaction and experience.

GOSPEL A Christmas crèche is hardly a Christmas crèche without shepherds and wise men in motionless adoration of the infant Jesus. The crèche is an icon, a visual representation of the combination of the two accounts of Jesus' nativity in the Gospels. Matthew supplies the star and the wise men; Luke provides the shepherds.

In previous commentaries, the "backward" history of the Gospel of Luke has been noted (see Gospel commentaries for Christmas Midnight 2006 and December 10, 2006). Whom might one expect to be called to the crib of a newborn king? Members of the royal family, perhaps, might come to honor their new relative. Courtiers might celebrate the news from a respectful distance. Sages and seers, having searched the heavens and astrological charts, might offer reports of the miraculous portents (true or not) heralding the child's birth. Who are those called to Jesus' crib? Shepherds. There are not too many rungs beneath "shepherd" on the ladder of ancient employment.

The call of the shepherds to the stable continues Luke's "backward" history. Their call is also an early sign of the kind of king that Luke will depict Jesus to be: a king who includes the poor and outcast, those pushed aside, stepped over, and forgotten, as first among the members of his kingdom.

NATIVITY OF THE LORD: DAY

Lectionary #16

READING I   Isaiah 52:7–10

A reading from the Book of the Prophet Isaiah

This is a joyful reading. Proclaim it in a strong tone, emphasizing the words "beautiful," "peace," and "salvation."

How **beautiful** upon the mountains
  are the **feet** of him who brings **glad tidings**,
announcing **peace**, bearing **good news**,
  announcing **salvation**, and saying to **Zion**,
  "**Your God is King!**"

Proclaim the words "Your God is King" slowly, pausing before moving on to the next stanza.

Hark! Your sentinels raise **a cry**,
  together they shout for **joy**,
for they **see** directly, before their **eyes**,
  the LORD restoring Zion.
Break out together in **song**,
  O **ruins** of **Jerusalem**!
For the LORD **comforts** his people,
  he **redeems Jerusalem**.
The LORD has **bared** his **holy** arm
  in the **sight** of all the nations;
all the ends of the earth will **behold**
  the **salvation** of our **God**.

READING I Ancient Israelites conceived of God as being surrounded by a heavenly cohort of divine beings. Sometimes these divine beings are referred to as spirits, sometimes as angels, and sometimes they are called by other names. The term scholars typically use for this conception of God and his attendants is the divine council. The council is a way of imagining or conceiving of God's rule and authority that Israelite religion shared with a number of the religions in close proximity to it in the Ancient Near East. In today's reading, we see a characteristic figure of the divine council, the angelic herald who announces the message of the council. Here the herald bears good news of Jerusalem's restoration and the bearing of God's "holy arm." God, the herald announces, has acted with strength on Israel's behalf.

Chapter 52 belongs to a portion of the book of Isaiah concerning the end of Israel's captivity in Babylon. It offers a theological interpretation of the war and geopolitics that led to many of the exiles returning to Judah and eventually reconstructing both Jerusalem and the Temple. The bearing of God's arm likely refers to the war on Babylon by Cyrus of Persia. In Isaiah 45:1, Cyrus is called the Lord's "anointed." In

READING II   Hebrews 1:1–6

A reading from the Letter to the Hebrews

Brothers and sisters:

In times past, **God spoke** in **partial** and **various** ways
   to our **ancestors** through the **prophets**;
   in these last days, he has spoken to **us** through **the Son**,
   whom he made **heir** of **all** things
   and **through whom** he **created** the universe,
      who is the **refulgence** of his **glory**,
      the very **imprint** of his **being**,
      and who **sustains all things** by his **mighty word**.
   When he had accomplished **purification** from **sins**,
      he took his **seat** at the **right hand** of the **Majesty** on high,
      as **far superior** to the **angels**
      as the **name** he has **inherited** is **more excellent** than **theirs**.

For to which of the **angels** did **God ever say**:
   You are my **son**; this day **I** have begotten **you?**
Or again:
   I will be a **father** to **him**, and **he** shall be a **son** to **me?**
And again, when he leads the firstborn into the world, he says:
   Let **all the angels** of **God worship him.**

Isaiah 45:4–5, God speaks to Cyrus, declaring that God calls and arms him, "though you know me not." Other passages suggesting the likelihood of Cyrus' ultimate victory over Babylon are Isaiah 43:14–17; 47:1–15; and 48:14. Cyrus has become God's instrument, according to the text, and the means by which God has chosen to force the surrender of Israel's enemies, end the exile, and bring the people home to Judah.

READING II Hebrews contains no sender, no addressee(s), and no greeting—three things one expects of a letter. For this reason, some biblical scholars have, with good reason, doubted whether Hebrews was composed as a letter in the first place, supposing that it was instead either a homily or a theological treatise intended for circulation.

From the first two verses of this letter we learn that, while God formerly spoke to "our ancestors through the prophets," "in these last days, he spoke to us through a son." The son is the "heir of all things" and helped to create the universe (1:1–2). In these first two verses, the author establishes his conviction that Jesus not only is the recent successor of the prophets, but also one who participated with God at the Creation. Jesus is present at both time's beginning and end.

GOSPEL   John 1:1–18

A reading from the holy Gospel according to John

In the **beginning** was the **Word**,
  and the **Word** was **with God**,
  and the **Word was God**.
He **was** in the **beginning with God**.
All things came to be through **him**,
  and **without him nothing came to be**.
What **came to be** through him was **life**,
  and this **life** was the **light** of the human race;
  the **light** shines in the **darkness**,
  and the **darkness** has **not overcome** it.
A man named **John** was **sent** from **God**.
He **came** for **testimony**, to **testify** to the **light**,
  so that **all** might **believe** through him.
He was **not** the **light**,
  but came to **testify** to the **light**.
The **true light**, which enlightens everyone,
  was coming into the **world**.
He was **in** the world,
  and **the world** came to be through **him**,
  but the world **did not know** him.
He came to what was his **own**,
  but his **own people did not** accept him.

The comparison between Jesus and the angels has intrigued many biblical scholars. Some have interpreted it to mean that the intended recipients of this letter were worshipping angels. A second-century writing called *The Shepherd of Hermas* suggests that such an "angelic" Christology did exist among some Christians, but there is no solid evidence that the author of Hebrews was responding to such views. The main thrust of the comparison, which the author develops in subsequent verses, is that while angels are indeed exalted, Jesus is even more so, due both to his proximity to God and his humanity. The author's reasoning probably works like this: if it is true, as all agree, that angels are rightly honored, then how much more rightly honored is Christ, who is closer than they *both* to humans *and* to God!

GOSPEL   "No one has ever seen God. The only Son, God, who is at the Father's side, has revealed him" (John 1:18). John 1:18 is one of a handful of New Testament passages in which Jesus is called God. Some early manuscripts, however, substitute the Greek word for "son" *(huios)* for "God" *(theos)* the second time "God" appears above.

How do Bible translators make decisions about what to print in such a situation? Copying a text by hand with precise accuracy is hard. Sometimes scribes made mistakes. A scribe might misread or misspell a word, jumble the words of a verse, or leave out a word or even a whole line.

But to those who **did** accept him
    he gave **power** to become **children of God,**
    to those who **believe** in his **name,**
    who were **born not** by **natural** generation
    nor by **human** choice **nor** by **a man's** decision
    but of **God.**
    And the **Word** became **flesh**
        and made his **dwelling** among **us,**
        and **we saw** his **glory,**
        the **glory** as of the **Father's** only **Son,**
        full of **grace** and **truth.**
    John **testified** to him and cried out, saying,
    "This was he of whom I said,
    'The one who is coming **after** me **ranks ahead** of **me**
    because he existed **before** me.'"
From his **fullness** we have all received,
    grace in place of **grace,**
    because while the **law** was **given** through **Moses,**
    grace and **truth came** through **Jesus Christ.**
No one has ever seen **God.**
The **only Son**, **God**, who is **at** the **Father's side,**
    has **revealed** him.

[Shorter: John 1:1–5, 9–14]

Proclaim the words "No one has ever seen God" slowly and with reverence.

Sometimes one scribe would make a note to himself in the margin and a later scribe would insert the note into the text, thinking he was correcting an earlier mistake. Most of these errors were unintentional, but occasionally scribes "edited for content." John 1:18 is a verse that was edited in this way.

We cannot know when or why a scribe substituted the word "son" for "God." But we can be reasonably certain that "God" is the most likely original reading. The particular manuscripts and other "textual witnesses" that contain "God" instead of "son" are of far better quality. Also, it is the most "difficult" of the available readings. Translators reason that less difficult readings are attempts to smooth over a theological rough spot. One reason this is the most difficult reading is that John often calls Jesus "son," but only "God" here and in 20:28.

Why would a scribe have made this change? Perhaps he was confused by the word "God" used twice in such close proximity for different persons. Perhaps he read John 3:16 and wanted to square 1:18 with it. We cannot know. But we can say the RNAB used the most likely original reading of John 1:18.

HOLY FAMILY OF JESUS, MARY, AND JOSEPH

Lectionary #17

READING I   1 Samuel 1:20–22, 24–28

A reading from the first Book of Samuel

In those days **Hannah conceived**, and at the end of her term
　bore a son
　whom she called **Samuel**, since she had **asked** the LORD
　for him.
The next time her husband **Elkanah** was going up
　with the rest of his household
　to offer the customary **sacrifice** to the Lord and to **fulfill**
　his vows,
　Hannah did **not** go, explaining to her husband,
　"Once the child is weaned,
　I will **take** him to **appear** before the LORD
　and to **remain** there **forever**;
　I will **offer** him as a **perpetual nazirite**."

Once Samuel was weaned, Hannah **brought him up** with her,
　along with a three-year-old bull,
　an ephah of flour, and a skin of wine,
　and **presented** him at the **temple** of the LORD in **Shiloh**.
After the boy's father had **sacrificed** the young bull,
　Hannah, his mother, approached **Eli** and said:
　"**Pardon, my lord**!
As you live, my lord,
　I am the **woman** who stood near you here, **praying** to the LORD.

Elkanah = El-kah-NAH

Deliver Hannah's lines slowly.

Shiloh = SHI-loh

Eli = AY-lee

There is a choice of first readings today. Speak with the liturgy coordinator or homilist to find out which reading will be used.

READING I **1 SAMUEL.** Taken together, the books of Joshua, Judges, 1 and 2 Samuel, and 1 and 2 Kings comprise the "deuteronomistic history." The books are a "history" in the sense that they cover events taking place in rough chronological order, from the tribal conquest of Canaan to the fall of the independent kingdom of Judah before the might of Babylon. They are "deuteronomistic" in the sense that the theology of its multiple authors and editors seems generally to reflect the radically monotheistic theology of the book of Deuteronomy.

Shiloh was an important religious site in Israel. Bear in mind that the Temple has not yet been built, Jerusalem is not in Israelite hands, and there is not yet a king in Israel. The Ark of the Covenant resides in a shrine or sanctuary in Shiloh, but it does not, as such, have the kind of permanent home that the Temple will one day provide it. As 1 Samuel 4:3 shows, the mobility of the Ark is still taken for granted. As one would expect of a loose confederation of tribes, there are multiple shrines and holy places in the land, many of which could (and did) provide homes for the Ark.

Samuel is born and sent to live at Shiloh during an important period of political transition in Israel. Probably due largely to hostilities with the Philistines, the institution of the monarchy will soon arise as a more efficient means of waging war and providing for an adequate defense. The development of a "national" consciousness in Israel

"I **prayed** for this child, and **the Lord granted** my request.
Now **I**, in turn, give **him** to the LORD;
    as **long** as he **lives**, he shall be **dedicated** to the LORD."
Hannah left Samuel there.

Or:

A reading from the Book of Sirach

God **sets** a father in **honor** over his children;
    a mother's **authority** he **confirms** over her sons.
Whoever **honors** his father **atones** for sins,
    and **preserves** himself from them.
When he **prays**, he is heard;
    he **stores up** riches who **reveres** his mother.
Whoever **honors** his **father** is gladdened by children,
    and, when he **prays**, is heard.
Whoever **reveres** his father will live a long life;
    he who **obeys** his father brings **comfort** to his mother.

My son, **take care** of your father when he is **old**;
    grieve him not as long as he lives.
Even if his **mind fail**, be **considerate** of him;
    revile him not all the days of his life;
kindness to a **father** will **not** be **forgotten**,
    firmly planted against the **debt** of your **sins**
    —a house raised in **justice** to you.

Pause briefly before reading the second stanza.

probably received a huge boost due to the tribes' perception of Philistia as their common enemy. It was a powerful incentive to establish new bonds among themselves.

It will be a help to your proclamation of these verses if you read the entirety of 1 Samuel 1. (For the levitical rules concerning *nazirites,* see Numbers 6.) It makes for good reading and telling.

SIRACH. As "the original cell of social life," the family is of obvious importance (Catechism, #2207). But the choice between the family and community, between the family and government, or between the family

and society are ultimately false choices. The well-being of the family is the foundation of the well being of all other social institutions. In recognition of this fact, the Catechism teaches, "where families cannot fulfill their responsibilities, other social bodies have the duty of helping them and of supporting the institution of the family" (Catechism, #2209).

Sirach was originally composed in Hebrew at the beginning of the second century BC and later translated into Greek by the author's grandson. It is fitting to consider the facts of the book's translation in light of

today's reading. The laborious work of translating his grandfather's writing suggests that the grandson understands the duties of which his grandfather wrote.

As Catholic Christians, we are likely accustomed to thinking in family terms beyond those of our "biological families" or "families of origin." For the Church conceives of itself as a family. A few of the scriptural warrants for this conception are the frequent address of Paul in his letters to his "brothers and sisters," Jesus' statement that his mother and brothers are those who do God's will (Matthew 12:46–50; Mark 3:31–35;

Stress each occurrence of the word "Beloved" and pause after delivering it.

READING II   1 John 3:1–2, 21–24

A reading from the first Letter of Saint John

Beloved:
See what **love** the **Father** has **bestowed** on us
      that we may be called the **children of God**.
And **so we are**.
The reason the **world does not know us**
      is that **it did not know him**.
Beloved, we are God's **children now**;
      what we **shall** be has **not yet** been **revealed**.
We do **know** that when it is **revealed** we shall be **like** him,
      for **we** shall **see** him **as he is**.

Beloved, if our **hearts do not condemn** us,
      we have **confidence** in **God** and **receive** from him
            whatever we **ask**,
      because we **keep** his **commandments** and **do** what **pleases** him.
And his **commandment** is **this**:
      we should **believe** in the name of his Son, Jesus Christ,
      and **love** one another just as he **commanded** us.
Those who **keep** his **commandments remain** in him, and he
            in them,
      and the way we **know** that he **remains** in us
      is from the **Spirit** he **gave** us.

Or:

Luke 8:19–21), and Jesus' designation of his disciples as "my brothers" (John 20:17). We are also perhaps accustomed to speaking in terms of the "human family." If we are serious and mean what we say, then we must admit, at the very least, that our duty to mother and father extends well beyond the people who brought us into the world.

READING II   **1 JOHN.** "And it was night." These ominous words conclude the episode of Judas' departure to betray Jesus in John's Gospel (13:30). Like

much else in John, the sentence contains multiple meanings. It is, on one level, a statement of fact: night falls as Judas leaves. On another level, night describes the world's ignorance about Jesus, an ignorance that will prove fatal. Nicodemus, the sympathetic Pharisee, comes to Jesus at night, which again describes not only when he comes, but in what condition (3:1–12; 19:39). Night is the time when the unenlightened stumble (11:10), when Jesus implies that even he cannot work (9:4).

In 1 John 3:1, the cause of the world's ignorance of the Church is prior ignorance of God. The author sees his Church as the evangelist sees Jesus: in danger from the world due to its fatal ignorance and darkened mind.

And yet the Church endures despite the ignorance of the world. Immediately after Judas' departure, Jesus gives his disciples the love command: "I give you a new commandment: love one another" (John 13:34). As the following verse makes clear, love is the sign by which Jesus' disciples shall be recognized. In 1 John 3:23, the love command recurs: "We should believe in the

READING II   Colossians 3:12–21

A reading from the Letter of Saint Paul to the Colossians

Brothers and **sisters**:
Put on, as God's chosen ones, **holy** and **beloved**,
    heartfelt **compassion**, **kindness**, **humility**, **gentleness**,
      and **patience**,
    bearing with one another and **forgiving** one another,
    if one has a **grievance** against another;
    as the Lord has **forgiven you**, **so must you also do**.
And over all these put on **love**,
    that is, the bond of **perfection**.
And let the **peace** of **Christ control** your **hearts**,
    the **peace** into which you were also called in **one body**.
And be **thankful**.
Let the word of Christ **dwell** in you **richly**,
    as in all **wisdom** you **teach** and **admonish** one another,
    singing **psalms**, **hymns**, and **spiritual songs**
    with **gratitude** in your **hearts** to God.
And whatever you do, in **word** or in **deed**,
    do **everything** in the name of the **Lord Jesus**,
    giving **thanks** to **God** the **Father** through **him**.

Wives, be subordinate to your **husbands**,
    as is proper in the Lord.
Husbands, love your **wives**,
    and avoid any **bitterness** toward them.

Look at the assembly as you say the words "Brothers and sisters."

Pause briefly before reading this last stanza.

---

name of [God's] son, Jesus Christ, and love one another just as he commanded us."

To be Christian, in the opinion of our author, is to love actively. In a culture where "Christian" brands everything from music to programs of weight loss, the need to learn Christianity by doing love in works of mercy and service is perhaps harder to see, but no less urgent.

For a discussion of the technical use of the phrase "children of God" in 1 John and the Gospel of John, see Commentary II, November 1, 2007.

COLOSSIANS. In this reading from Colossians, the author exhorts his addressees about how members of the Church are to conduct themselves toward one another and toward members of their own family.

On one level, the morality of this reading is very conventional for its time and place. The list of virtues in 3:12 is typical of Greco-Roman social ethics. Distinctly Christian, however, is the *basis* for some of this instruction. People are not to forgive one another just because it's the decent thing to do, although forgiveness is clearly that. No, people are to forgive one another because Christ has forgiven them. In other words, to forgive someone conforms a person to the example set by Christ. The ethics may be conventional, but their foundation is not.

As in the case of the social ethics of the Church, in 3:18—4:1 we have another conventional description. The free Greco-Roman household, outlined by Aristotle and others, was organized as a hierarchy. At the top was the father. To his authority all members of the household, including his slaves,

Children, obey your **parents** in everything,
> for this is **pleasing** to the Lord.
Fathers, do not provoke your **children**,
> so they may not become **discouraged**.

[Shorter: Colossians 3:12–17]

GOSPEL   Luke 2:41–52

A reading from the holy Gospel according to Luke

Each year Jesus' parents went to **Jerusalem** for the feast
> of **Passover**,
>> and when he was twelve years old,
>> they went up according to festival **custom**.
After they had completed its days, as they were returning,
>> the boy **Jesus** remained behind in **Jerusalem**,
>> but his parents did not know it.
Thinking that he was in the caravan,
>> they **journeyed** for a day
>> and looked for him among their relatives and acquaintances,
>> but **not finding** him,
>> they **returned** to **Jerusalem** to look for him.
After **three days** they **found** him in the **temple**,
>> **sitting** in the **midst** of the **teachers**,
>> **listening** to them and **asking** them questions,
>> and all who heard him were **astounded**
>> at his **understanding** and his **answers**.

---

were subject. In actual practice, family structures were far more complicated and diverse than this model suggests, but the acceptance of male authority over the family was pretty nearly universal in antiquity.

We must not assume, however, that the families the author considers were families entirely composed of Christians. A wife or a slave might well have been the only Christian in a household.

GOSPEL This reading is the only piece of the four Gospels to depict any time in Jesus' life between his infancy and adulthood. Some early Christians, however, were sufficiently intrigued by this gap in Jesus' life to expand upon it in works of imaginative fiction. The infancy stories of Thomas, probably composed around the middle of the second century, recount amazing deeds that Jesus performed between the ages of 5 and 12. Among other things, the young Jesus brings dead birds back to life,

performs miracles in Joseph's workshop, and outsmarts his teachers. The concluding episode of these stories closely follows today's Gospel selection. Perhaps the most significant difference between the story and our text is that the teachers in the Temple inform Mary of what an unusual child she has. For Christians who knew Luke's account, this would be a plausible fiction, for the implication of Luke 2:50 is that Joseph and Mary, by their son's twelfth year, have not

Keep in mind that Mary is frantic. Deliver her words like a mother would in her situation.

Nazareth = NAH-za-reth

When his **parents** saw him,
    they were **astonished**,
    and his **mother** said to him,
    "**Son**, **why** have you done this to **us**?
Your father and **I** have been **looking** for you with **great anxiety**."
And **he** said to **them**,
    "**Why** were you looking for **me**?
Did you not know that I must be in **my Father's house**?"
But they did not **understand** what he said to them.
He went down with them and came to **Nazareth**,
    and was **obedient** to them;
    and his mother **kept all these things** in her **heart**.
And **Jesus advanced** in **wisdom** and **age** and **favor**
    before **God** and **man**.

yet fully comprehended his extraordinary connection to his Father in heaven.

With Luke 2:51, Luke's infancy story comes to an end. "Son of the Most High" (1:32), "Son of God" (1:35), "Lord" (1:43; 2:11), "savior" (2:11), "Messiah" (2:11), and "salvation" (2:30) are all titles or designations of Jesus in these chapters. If you go back and check, you will notice that all of these terms are applied to Jesus by divine beings or people under the Spirit's influence. No one comes to knowledge of Jesus' full identity except by means of God's revelation. Luke is trying to make clear that Jesus' divinity, while apparent from the time of his birth, may be perceived only with God's help—the gift of faith.

MARY, MOTHER OF GOD

Lectionary #18

READING I   Numbers 6:22–27

A reading from the Book of Numbers

The LORD said to **Moses**:
"Speak to **Aaron** and his **sons** and **tell** them:
   This is how you shall **bless** the **Israelites**.
Say to them:
   The LORD **bless** you and **keep** you!
   The LORD **let** his **face shine** upon you,
      and be **gracious** to you!
   The LORD **look** upon you **kindly**
      and **give** you **peace**!
So shall they **invoke** my name upon the **Israelites**,
   and I will **bless** them."

In the text of the blessing, stress the words "bless," "keep," "shine," "grace," and "peace."

READING I — We live in a period of Bible translation. Publishers offer their dizzying variety of versions to consumers with one eye firmly on the market: some people want an "accurate" or "literal" translation, some want a translation contemporary in language and tone, and some require a translation favored by their tradition. The first major period in the history of the Bible's translation occurred after the reign and conquests of Alexander the Great (336 BC–323 BC) made Greek the common language of much of the Mediterranean. Around 250 BC, parts of the Old Testament were translated from Hebrew into Greek. The result was the Septuagint.

Take this reading for instance. The Hebrew word for what Moses instructs Aaron and his sons to do is *barach*. It is usually translated by the word "bless." The counterpart to the blessing is the curse. A blessing's power comes from God, although it is made effective by the person who offers it. Isaac's blessing of Jacob in Genesis 27, for example, is an effective act that cannot be revoked, even when Jacob's deception is exposed.

The Greek word translating *barach* in today's reading is *eulogeō*. In secular Greek it means "speak well of" or "praise." While this communicates the verbal sign that accompanies a blessing, it cannot capture the full power of a blessing and its effective nature beyond the verbal act and the individual offering it.

Aaron and his sons the priests are instructed to do something more than praise or speak well of God and the people. They are, in cooperation with God, calling benevolent power down on the people of Israel.

READING II   Galatians 4:4–7

A reading from the Letter of Saint Paul to the Galatians

Brothers and **sisters:**
When the fullness of time had come, **God** sent his **Son,**
    born of a **woman, born** under the **law,**
    to **ransom** those **under** the **law,**
    so that **we** might **receive adoption** as **sons.**

As **proof** that you are **sons,**
    God sent the **Spirit** of his **Son** into our **hearts,**
    crying out, "**Abba, Father!**"
So you are **no longer** a **slave** but a **son,**
    and **if** a **son then** also an **heir,** through **God.**

Pause between "born of a woman" and
"born under law."

Stress the words "slave," "son," and "heir."

READING II   The situation Paul dealt with in his letter to the Church of Galatia was not terribly complicated, although it had profound implications for the development of Christianity as a religion distinct from Judaism. It appears some Christian missionaries have come to the Church of Galatia and informed the men that they have to get circumcised if they want to have a proper relationship with God through Christ. Galatians is Paul's elaborate and carefully argued response.

By the time we get to today's reading, Paul has already argued that God, not any human being, made him into an apostle, but that even so he still received the approval of the reputable members of the Church in Jerusalem (1:1—2:10). He has charged Peter with hypocrisy concerning table fellowship with Gentiles (2:11–14). And he has argued that *justification,* the establishment of a proper relationship with God (see Catechism, #1987–1995), happens not through law but through faith in Jesus Christ (2:15—3:29). In today's reading, Paul tries to sort out how law and faith relate to one another.

Paul's discussion is theological in nature, but its guiding metaphor is social and cultural. As we know from Aristotle and other sources, the ancient household was under the authority of the father and, if the family was wealthy, designated slaves. The law, Paul writes in 3:24–25, was once a "disciplinarian." The word "disciplinarian" translates is *paidagōgos,* which is the job description of a slave charged with getting a child to and from school. Formerly, the law was necessary, for it guarded people in their metaphorical infancy and childhood. But now, with the advent of Christ and the

GOSPEL Luke 2:16–21

A reading from the holy Gospel according to Luke

The shepherds went **in haste** to Bethlehem
   and found **Mary** and **Joseph**,
   and the **infant** lying in the **manger**.
When they saw this,
   they **made known** the message
   that had been **told** them about this **child**.
All who heard it were **amazed**
   by what had been **told** them by the shepherds.
And Mary **kept all these things**,
   reflecting on them in her **heart**.
Then the shepherds **returned**,
   glorifying and **praising** God
   for all they had **heard** and **seen**,
   just as it had been **told** to them.

When eight days were **completed** for his circumcision,
   he was named **Jesus**, the name given him by the **angel**
   before he was **conceived** in the **womb**.

Pause before and after the sentence beginning with "And Mary kept."

arrival of maturity, the law is no longer necessary. Just as a child reaches an age of accountability and inheritance, so have the Galatians left their own spiritual submission behind (4:1–3) and become, with Christ, God's own heirs.

GOSPEL It has often been observed that Luke portrays Mary as the first believer in Jesus. There is merit to this view, but what kind of believer was she? How did she come to believe?

Luke presents Mary as a thoughtful person (Luke 2:19), but her interior life, what little we read of it, is very private. On first meeting Gabriel and hearing his salutation, "Hail, favored one! The Lord is with you!" Mary does not answer immediately. Luke reports that Mary, very troubled, first "pondered what sort of greeting this might be." Furthermore, she asks a clarifying question of Gabriel (1:34), which is a lot like the question Zechariah was struck dumb for asking (1:18–20).

Elizabeth testifies that Mary believes what Gabriel says in 1:45. And Luke tells us that Mary stores up in her heart what she sees and hears about her son (2:19; 2:51). But what did she make of the information?

Having missed their son among the members of the caravan back to Nazareth, Jesus' parents return to find him among teachers in the Temple. To their frantic question, "Son, why have you done this to us?" Jesus replies, "Did you not know that I must be in my Father's house?" Luke goes on to say, "But they did not understand what he said to them."

EPIPHANY OF THE LORD

Lectionary #20

READING I   Isaiah 60:1–6

A reading from the Book of the Prophet Isaiah

Rise up in **splendor**, **Jerusalem**! Your **light** has come,
    the **glory** of the LORD **shines** upon you.
See, **darkness** covers the **earth**,
    and **thick clouds** cover the **peoples**;
but upon **you** the LORD **shines**,
    and over **you appears** his **glory**.
Nations shall walk by your **light**,
    and **kings** by your **shining radiance**.
Raise your **eyes** and **look** about;
    they all **gather** and **come** to **you**:
your **sons** come from afar,
    and your **daughters** in the arms of their nurses.

Then you shall be **radiant** at what you **see**,
    your **heart** shall **throb** and **overflow**,
for the **riches** of the **sea** shall be **emptied** out before **you**,
    the **wealth** of **nations** shall be **brought** to **you**.
Caravans of **camels** shall fill you,
    dromedaries from **Midian** and **Ephah**;
all from **Sheba** shall come
    bearing **gold** and **frankincense**,
    and proclaiming the **praises** of the LORD.

Stress the words "sons" and "daughters"

Pause before the words "Raise your eyes."

Midian = MIH-dee-an
Ephah = EF-ah
Sheba = SHE-bah

READING I "Nations shall walk by your light, and kings by your shining radiance." Isaiah's image of Jerusalem as a gleaming beacon to the nations and their rulers appears in the Lectionary at Epiphany due to the Church's traditional understanding of itself as the means of the world's enlightenment. Although Rome was but one among the important Christian dioceses of antiquity, its relative importance grew as the Muslim world expanded to incorporate lands once Christian and the Western Church had split from the Eastern. This is not to say, however, that the Roman Catholic Church was simply the accidental victor of circumstances. Its primacy was (and is) the result of painstaking work over the centuries by missionaries, scholars, officials, and laypeople dedicated to its service and improvement.

Today's reading does not specify why the nations will join the throngs of Jerusalem's sons and daughters. Are they attracted? Are they invited? Does the prophet assume that the glory of Jerusalem is such that the peoples of the world will be drawn to it irresistibly?

To the degree that the Roman Catholic Church understands this scripture to prophesy its mission to the world, it is good to ask whether or not we are fulfilling that mission. A Church that is truly universal shares among all of its members the responsibility for its own well-being, as well as a responsibility to the well-being of those who have yet to see clearly the light in the Church amid so much darkness in the world.

Pause after the words "brothers and sisters" and make eye contact with the assembly.

Stress the word "now."

Pause between the words "prophets by the Spirit" and "that the Gentiles." Slow down to emphasize everything after the word "that."

READING II   Ephesians 3:2–3a, 5–6

A reading from the Letter of Saint Paul to the Ephesians

Brothers and **sisters**:
You have heard of the stewardship of **God's grace**
    that was **given** to **me** for your benefit,
        namely, that the **mystery** was **made known** to me
            by **revelation**.
It was **not made known to people in other generations**
    as it has **now** been revealed
    to his **holy apostles** and **prophets** by the **Spirit**:
        that the **Gentiles** are **coheirs**, members of the **same body**,
        and **copartners** in the **promise** in **Christ Jesus**
            through the **gospel**.

GOSPEL   Matthew 2:1–12

A reading from the holy Gospel according to Matthew

When **Jesus** was born in **Bethlehem** of **Judea**,
    in the days of King **Herod**,
        behold, **magi** from the **east** arrived in **Jerusalem**, saying,
        "**Where** is the **newborn king** of the **Jews**?
We **saw** his star at its **rising**
    and **have come** to do him **homage**."

Herod = HAIR-rud

READING II In today's reading, the author speaks of a "mystery" revealed to him and to "holy apostles and prophets by the Spirit." The mystery is "that the Gentiles are coheirs, members of the same body, and copartners in the promise in Christ Jesus through the Gospel." In other words, Jews and Gentiles have an equal share in what Christ offers (Ephesians 3:5–6).

We encounter a few passages in the New Testament suggesting that Gentiles were not part of the focus of Jesus' movement. Matthew 10:5 and 23 are pretty clear that Jesus wanted his disciples to focus exclusively on Israel. Against this, however, is the commission by revelation in Matthew 28:16–20, where the risen Jesus sends the remaining 11 disciples out to "make disciples of all nations." Among the evangelists one should add Luke's voice. Luke 24:47–49 specifies that Jerusalem is the beginning of a mission to "all nations." In Acts, Jerusalem is the commencement of a mission "throughout Judaea and Samaria, and to the ends of the earth" (Acts 1:8). John's commission to the disciples is brief and mentions no particular nations or regions (John 20:21). Mark includes no commission by the risen Jesus as in the other three Gospels, although he includes an extensive ministry by Jesus in Gentile territory (Mark 7:24—8:26).

Galatians 1 and 2 is the most extensive section concerning Paul's divine commission to preach the Gospel to the Gentiles. From Galatians 2:1–10 we learn that Paul contended that leaders of the Church in Jerusalem agreed to a division of authority: Paul to the Gentiles, Peter to the Jews. This does not exactly square with the picture of Acts, in which Peter begins the Gentile mission (Acts 10 and 11), and Paul, despite his

Pause before reading the quotation
of Micah.

When **King Herod heard** this,
  he was **greatly** troubled,
  and all **Jerusalem** with him.
Assembling all the chief **priests** and the **scribes** of the people,
  he **inquired** of them where **the Christ** was to **be born**.
They said to him, "In Bethlehem of Judea,
  for thus it has been **written** through the **prophet**:
    *And you, **Bethlehem**, land of **Judah**,
      are **by no means least** among the **rulers of Judah**;
      since from **you** shall come a **ruler**,
      who is to **shepherd** my people **Israel**.*"
Then Herod called the **magi secretly**
  and ascertained from them the **time** of the star's **appearance**.
He **sent** them to **Bethlehem** and said,
  "**Go** and **search** diligently for the **child**.
When you have **found** him, **bring** me word,
  that I too may go and do him **homage**."
After their audience with the king they **set out**.
And **behold**, the star that they had **seen** at its rising
    preceded them,
  until it **came** and **stopped** over the **place** where the **child was**.
They were **overjoyed** at **seeing** the **star**,
  and on **entering** the house
  they **saw** the **child** with **Mary** his **mother**.
They **prostrated** themselves and did him **homage**.
Then they opened their **treasures**
  and offered him **gifts** of **gold**, **frankincense**, and **myrrh**.
And having been **warned** in **a dream not** to return to Herod,
  they **departed** for their country by **another** way.

testimony of 13:44–47, continues to work in synagogues (14:1; 17:1–2, 10; 18:4; 19:8).

GOSPEL Simon Magus, the hapless magician of Acts 8:9–25, initially sees the apostles' power as a business opportunity. Soon, however, we see him acknowledging Peter's superiority, even begging Peter to intercede with Jesus in order to keep a curse from falling on him for his attempt to purchase the apostles' power with money.

The Magi of Matthew 2:1–12 are of a different sort. For one thing, Matthew portrays them positively. They worship and offer gifts to the infant Jesus without seeking anything in exchange. Ancient readers might have recognized them as stock literary types, for the eastern man of wisdom can often be found wandering through Greco-Roman literature.

It is an important point that the Magi first visit Herod in order to inquire about the birth of the Jews' newborn king. Calling together his court intellectuals, we find that Herod and his court already have all the information they need to determine that the Messiah will come from Bethlehem. But instead of coming with the Magi to offer his own gifts and worship with them, Herod starts scheming. The plan he ultimately hatches will come to bloody, if ultimately unsuccessful completion in Matthew 2:16.

Just as Luke's infancy narrative repeatedly stresses the divinity of Jesus from the earliest mention of him (see Gospel Commentary, December 31, 2006), Matthew also has a persistent refrain: the intervention of the supernatural in Jesus' birth. Note the role of the Holy Spirit, the fulfillment of prophetic oracles, and the importance of dreams in the unfolding of the story of Matthew 1:18—2:23.

BAPTISM OF THE LORD

Lectionary #21

READING I Isaiah 40:1–5, 9–11

This is a joyful reading. Proclaim it as such.

Pause after the first occurrence of the word "Comfort." Stress the word each time you pronounce it.

A reading from the Book of the Prophet Isaiah

Comfort, give **comfort** to my people,
    says your God.
Speak **tenderly** to Jerusalem, and **proclaim** to her
    that her **service** is at an **end**,
    her **guilt** is **expiated**;
indeed, she has **received** from the **hand** of the LORD
    double for all her sins.

A voice cries out:

Proclaim in a strong clear voice beginning with the words "In the desert."

In the desert **prepare** the **way** of the LORD!
    Make **straight** in the wasteland a **highway** for our **God**!
Every valley shall be **filled** in,
    every mountain and hill shall be **made low**;
the **rugged** land shall be made a **plain**,
    the **rough** country, a **broad** valley.
Then the **glory** of the LORD shall be **revealed**,
    and **all people** shall see it together;
    for the **mouth** of the LORD has **spoken**.

There is a choice of first and second readings today. Speak with the liturgy coordinator or homilist to find out which reading will be used.

READING I ISAIAH 40. God's commands to "comfort," "speak," and "proclaim" are all plural verbs in Hebrew. Some scholars have contended that this text was originally composed as an account of the prophet's call, similar to Isaiah 6 or Ezekiel 1 and 2. The plural verbs make this

unlikely. Perhaps God commissions members of the heavenly court (see Luke 2:8–14) or a community of prophets to proclaim the joyful message. Either option is possible. In any case, the rough historical context in which this oracle was originally given is the period in the sixth century BC of Babylon's defeat by Cyrus of Persia and the end of the exile. The exile is the "service" of Jerusalem that is "at an end" (Isaiah 40:2).

In a previous commentary, the attendance of the shepherds at Jesus' nativity was offered as evidence of Luke's "backward" history (Gospel Commentary, Christmas

Dawn). The curious thing about shepherds is that while they lived on the spatial and social margins of society, they were symbols of selfless love and benevolence in pastoral poetry, literature, and art. The image of God as a shepherd in Isaiah 40:9–11 emerges from this pastoral theme, as does Luke's parable of the lost sheep (Luke 15:1–7; see Matthew 18:12–14), and John's depiction of Jesus as the good shepherd (John 10:11–16). Perhaps the most common artistic depiction of Jesus in the first four centuries

Go up on to a **high** mountain,
　Zion, **herald** of glad tidings;
cry out at the **top** of your **voice**,
　Jerusalem, **herald** of good news!
Fear not to cry out
　and say to the cities of Judah:
　Here is your **God**!
Here comes with **power**
　the Lord GOD,
　who **rules** by his **strong arm**;
here is his **reward** with him,
　his **recompense** before him.
Like a **shepherd** he **feeds** his **flock**;
　in his **arms** he **gathers** the **lambs**,
carrying them in his **bosom**,
　and **leading** the **ewes** with care.

Or:

of the Church was as the Good Shepherd. We find the image on Christian sarcophagi and catacomb walls depicted in a manner virtually indistinguishable from similar pastoral depictions in Greco-Roman art.

Words from Isaiah 40:3–5 describe the function of John the Baptist as Jesus' forerunner and interpret that function in the light of prophetic tradition. In John's Gospel, these words come from the Baptist's own mouth (Matthew 3:3; Mark 1:2–3; Luke 3:4–6; John 1:23).

ISAIAH 42. The reading for today comes from a portion of Isaiah biblical scholars commonly designate second Isaiah (Isaiah 40—55). The core material of these chapters was likely composed at the time of the fall of the Babylonian empire to Cyrus of Persia and the close of the period of Israel's captivity in Babylon. Sometimes called the "Book of Consolation," Isaiah 40—66 is often universal in outlook, foreseeing a world in which Israel has a central role to play in the mediation of God to the human race.

In Isaiah 42, God addresses a servant fashioned for the task of being "a covenant of the people, a light for the nations." Sight to the blind, freedom for the imprisoned, and the work of the servant formed and commissioned by God is God's a gift to the entire world.

Who is this servant? Was he, in the original historical context of the book's composition, the same figure as in 52:13—53:12? Is he a particular historical figure, perhaps a prophet or a member of David's

READING I   Isaiah 42:1–4, 6–7

A reading from the Book of the Prophet Isaiah

Thus says the LORD:
Here is my **servant** whom I **uphold**,
  my **chosen one** with whom I am **pleased**,
upon whom I have put my **spirit**;
  he shall bring forth **justice** to the **nations**,
not crying out, **not shouting**,
  not making his **voice heard** in the street.
A bruised **reed** he shall not **break**,
  and a smoldering **wick** he shall **not quench**,
until he establishes **justice** on the earth;
  the coastlands will wait for his **teaching**.

I, the LORD, have called **you** for the **victory of justice**,
  I have grasped **you** by the **hand**;
I formed **you**, and set **you**
  as a **covenant** of the **people**,
  a **light** for the **nations**,
to **open** the **eyes** of the **blind**,
  to **bring out prisoners** from **confinement**,
  and from the **dungeon**, those who live in **darkness**.

Pause briefly before beginning the second stanza.

---

household? Is the servant Cyrus of Persia (see Isaiah 45)? Or is the servant meant to stand for Israel itself? The text is not clear. It should not surprise us, however, that the early Church understood the prophecy to refer to Jesus Christ. The echo of Isaiah 42:1 resounds in the accounts of Jesus' baptism in Matthew 3:17, Mark 3:11, and Luke 3:22.

In Isaiah 42:5, God recalls his earlier acts of creation in the service of proclaiming new promises. This is the prophet's way of reminding his audience that the God who now promises big things has a proven track record of tremendous deeds.

READING II   TITUS. Not only has the appearance of grace brought salvation, says Titus 2:11, but it has also schooled believers to whom it has come "to reject godless ways and worldly desires and to live temperately, justly, and devoutly in this age." Before we rejoice in the fact that grace offers a course in moral instruction, consider what it might mean to actually take such instruction to heart. What "godlessness" and "worldly desires" are we not only unwilling to reject, but totally committed to keeping? Can one really say that, deep down, one wants to live "temperately, justly, and devoutly"? Are the lessons of grace the sort of lessons we are happy, or even willing, to learn? God may give grace freely, but it can be a difficult gift to accept.

READING II   Titus 2:11–14; 3:4–7

A reading from the Letter of Saint Paul to Titus

Pause after the word "Beloved.

Beloved:
The **grace** of **God** has appeared, **saving all**
    and **training** us to **reject godless** ways
        and **worldly** desires

Slow down to stress the words "temperately, justly, and devoutly."

and to live **temperately**, **justly** and **devoutly** in **this** age,
as we await the **blessed hope**,
the **appearance** of the **glory** of our great **God**
and **savior Jesus Christ**,
who **gave himself** for **us** to deliver **us** from **all lawlessness**
and to **cleanse** for **himself** a **people** as his **own**,
eager to do what is **good**.

When the **kindness** and **generous love**
    of **God** our **savior** appeared,

Emphasize the words "not" and "mercy."

not because of any **righteous deeds** we had done
    but because of his **mercy**,
he saved us through the **bath** of **rebirth**
    and **renewal** by the **Holy Spirit**,
whom he **richly** poured out on us
    through **Jesus Christ** our **savior**,
so that we might be **justified** by his **grace**
    and become **heirs** in **hope** of eternal life.

Or:

"This age" calls attention to the way in which our author conceives of time. For him to "await the blessed hope," which, here, as in much early Christian literature, refers to the Resurrection, is to live with his eyes fixed firmly on a future much of his world does not imagine. He sees himself as an amphibian: mortal now, immortal then; at work now, at rest then.

Learning to live "in this age" while awaiting "the blessed hope" can be both an ordeal of pain and a wash of joy. Grace schools us to teach one another how to live

with both. Neither is particularly easy, any more than is the surrender of the godlessness of self for God alone easy, or is the desire for "the blessed hope" in exchange for "worldly desires" easy.

ACTS. Peter's speech in today's reading has been building during the entire tenth chapter of Acts. A certain Cornelius, a Roman centurion residing in the harbor city of Cesarea, receives a dream vision in which an angel tells him to send for someone named Simon, also called Peter, staying

in nearby Joppa. Cornelius, who is also a Gentile patron of Judaism and the Jews, obeys (Acts 10:1–8).

The next day in Joppa, Peter climbs up on his friend's roof to pray. At the conclusion of his prayers, he finds himself hungry. At that moment Peter himself has a vision, in which a smorgasbord of animals considered unclean by Jews is repeatedly presented to him. Although instructed to kill and eat them, Peter resists, saying that he has never in his life eaten anything unclean. He is told, however, that what God has made clean he

READING II   Acts 10:34–38

A reading from the Acts of the Apostles

Peter proceeded to speak to those gathered
  in the house of **Cornelius**, saying:
"In **truth**, I see that God shows **no partiality**.
Rather, in **every** nation **whoever fears** him and **acts uprightly**
  is **acceptable** to him.
You know the word that he sent to the **Israelites**
  as he proclaimed **peace** through **Jesus Christ**, who is **Lord** of **all**,
  what has **happened all over Judea**,
  beginning in **Galilee** after the **baptism**
  that **John preached**,
  how God **anointed Jesus** of **Nazareth**
  with the **Holy Spirit** and **power**.
He went about doing **good**
  and **healing** all those **oppressed** by the **devil**,
  for **God** was **with him**."

Pause very briefly before you begin to proclaim the words of Peter.

may not consider unclean. At the conclusion of his vision, Peter learns that Cornelius' men are waiting for him. Peter leaves with the men for Cesarea, where the divine plan in which he and Cornelius have up to now played unwitting parts is finally made clear to both (10:9–43).

Cornelius, a Roman centurion of the Italian cohort, and Peter, a Jewish fisher-man from Galilee, are an unlikely pair. But Acts brings them together for a reason. From the Temple the Church has expanded into Jerusalem, Judea, Samaria, and as far away as Antioch. Now the Church expands beyond the bounds of ethnic and religious Israel to include even Gentiles. In Acts 10, the story of the Church takes a long stride toward catholicity.

GOSPEL   All four evangelists, in different ways and to different degrees, make clear that Jesus was superior to John the Baptist. And, therefore, an issue they had to confront was the fact that Jesus had been baptized by John, and not the

other way round. Matthew 3:13–17 records a conversation that goes right to the heart of this issue. John says, "I need to be baptized by you, and yet you are coming to me?" Jesus gives John permission to go ahead with it, despite his misgivings (Matthew 3:14–15). Mark 1:9–11 simply records the event of John's Baptism by Jesus without any conversation. In the Gospels of Luke and John, Jesus' Baptism by John is not depicted. While John 1:29–34 contains many elements found in the other Gospels, John the Baptist

GOSPEL   Luke 3:15–16, 21–22

A reading from the holy Gospel according to Luke

The **people** were filled with **expectation**,
    and **all** were **asking** in their **hearts**
    whether **John** might be the **Christ**.
John **answered** them all, saying,
    "**I** am **baptizing** you with **water**,
    but **one mightier** than I is coming.
I am **not worthy** to **loosen** the **thongs** of his **sandals**.
He will **baptize** you with the **Holy Spirit** and **fire**."

After **all** the **people** had been **baptized**
    and **Jesus** also had been **baptized** and was **praying**,
    heaven was **opened** and the **Holy Spirit**
        descended upon him
    in **bodily form** like a **dove**.
And a **voice** came from **heaven**,
    "**You** are my **beloved Son**;
    with **you** I am well **pleased**."

Remember that John is a fiery preacher. Proclaim his speech with strength.

Slow down to read the words "You are my beloved Son; with you I am well pleased."

never performs the rite in this Gospel. John's Gospel also contains strong statements by John the Baptist concerning Jesus' superiority (John 1:19–20; 3:25–30). Luke 3:19–20 mentions John's imprisonment by Herod Antipas, tetrarch of Galilee, and immediately afterward reports Jesus' Baptism.

John himself offers the main distinction between his Baptism and that of Jesus. "I am baptizing you with water, but one mightier than I is coming." "He will baptize you with the Holy spirit and fire" (Luke 3:11; see Matthew 3:11; Mark 1:7–8; John 1:26). In Acts, Jesus' Baptism by spirit and fire occurs first at Pentecost (2:1–4) and occurs many times subsequently as the Church grows to include Gentiles and other surprising elements.

Whatever the precise relationship between Jesus and John the Baptist, it is clear that Jesus' ministry begins only after his Baptism by him. John's Gospel reports the very interesting information that Jesus drew his first disciples from John's followers (John 1:35–51). Andrew, Peter's brother, is the first. To Andrew's question, "where are you staying?" Jesus answers, "Come and see," inviting Andrew and other seekers to join him.

2ND SUNDAY IN ORDINARY TIME

Lectionary #66

READING I   Isaiah 62:1–5

A reading from the Book of the Prophet Isaiah

Stress the word "not" in the first two lines.

For **Zion's sake** I will **not** be **silent**,
    for **Jerusalem's sake** I will **not be quiet**,
until her **vindication shines** forth like the **dawn**
    and her **victory** like a **burning torch**.

Nations shall **behold** your **vindication**,
    and all the kings your **glory**;
you shall be **called** by a **new name**
    pronounced by the **mouth** of the LORD.
You shall be a **glorious crown** in the **hand** of the LORD,
    a **royal diadem** held by your **God**.

Stress the words "Forsaken," "Desolate,"
"My Delight," and "Espoused."

No more shall people call you "**Forsaken**,"
    or your land "**Desolate**,"
but you shall be called "**My Delight**,"
    and your land "**Espoused**."
For the LORD **delights** in you
    and makes your land his **spouse**.
As a **young man marries a virgin**,
    your **Builder** shall **marry you**;
and as a **bridegroom rejoices** in his **bride**
    so shall your **God rejoice** in **you**.

READING I   Most scholars, though certainly not all, have dated the oracles of Isaiah 56—66 to the time of the Babylonian exiles' return to Judah (after 536 BC). They distinguish these chapters from chapters 40 to 55, which appear to describe an earlier time in Babylon near the exile's end (ca. 538 BC). Still earlier is much of the material in chapters 1 to 39, some of which dates to the period before the fall of the northern kingdom in 721 BC.

Today we read of Jerusalem's new name of "My Delight" following its vindication. Even if we agree that today's reading comes from the period of the exiles' return and the reconstruction of Jerusalem, it is also true that 62:1–5 has probably been composed with an eye on other prophecies contained within the book of Isaiah. In Isaiah 1:26, for example, we also read of Jerusalem renamed "city of justice, faithful city" after God's destruction of its enemies and the restoration of ancient institutions. Whatever the precise history and editing of Isaiah's oracles, the book's final form has been shaped with an eye on both exile and return.

What is the significance of renaming Jerusalem? For one thing, it underscores the hope that Jerusalem restored after the exile will be a different kind of city. A consistent theme among the various theologies of the authors is that Judah's and Jerusalem's sins brought the exile on themselves, at least in part (see, for example, Isaiah 40:2). But this is not a "clean break" with the past. The experience of the restoration is understood as mercy on the order of the Exodus (43:16–20), the covenant after the flood (Isaiah 54:9), and even the Creation of heaven and earth (65:17–25).

READING II 1 Corinthians 12:4–11

A reading from the first Letter of Saint Paul to the Corinthians

Brothers and **sisters**:
There are **different** kinds of **spiritual gifts** but the **same Spirit**;
    there are **different** forms of **service** but the **same Lord**;
    there are **different** workings but the **same God**
    who **produces all** of them in **everyone**.
To **each** individual the **manifestation** of the **Spirit**
    is **given** for some **benefit**.
To **one** is given through the **Spirit** the expression of **wisdom**;
    to **another**, the expression of **knowledge** according
        to the same **Spirit**;
    to **another**, **faith** by the same **Spirit**;
    to **another**, **gifts** of **healing** by the **one Spirit**;
    to **another**, mighty **deeds**;
    to **another**, **prophecy**;
    to **another**, **discernment** of **spirits**;
    to **another**, **varieties** of **tongues**;
    to **another**, **interpretation** of **tongues**.
But **one** and **the same Spirit** produces **all** of these,
    distributing them **individually** to **each** person as **he wishes**.

GOSPEL John 2:1–11

A reading from the holy Gospel according to John

There was a **wedding** in **Cana** in **Galilee**,
    and the **mother** of **Jesus** was there.
Jesus and his **disciples** were also invited to the wedding.

Pause between each occurrence of the word "another" and the phrase to follow.

Pause before the final stanza. Read it slowly, emphasizing the words "one and the same."

Cana = CAY-nah
Galilee = GAL-i-lee

READING II The assembly at Corinth, Paul makes plain at the outset of this letter, is a divided community (1:10–17). It appears from 1:12 that these divisions were expressed in the recognition—and lack of the same—given to certain religious authorities. The rest of the letter reveals these divisions to be quite complicated and deep-seated, extending well beyond problems of authority. Effects of class and social status difference divided the Church at Corinth as well.

About some issues at Corinth, Paul brooks no compromise. Thus, the man married to, or perhaps just sleeping with, his stepmother is to be expelled post haste (1 Corinthians 5:1–5). Concerning other issues such as marriage (chapter 7) and eating meat offered to idols (chapters 8 to 10), Paul tolerates a wide variety of behavior, provided no harm can come to the community or its individual members because of it.

Note that it is the *difference* of gifts in the Corinthian community that argues for its unity—at least when one considers their divine source. The refrain of a unity that underlies the diversity of roles, tasks, and gifts in the community sounds throughout 12:4–11. Just as a resounding "No!" to Paul's first rhetorical question in 1:13 ("Is Christ divided?") convicts the Corinthians of divisiveness and demands them to heal their rifts, the variety of spiritual gifts must not be a basis for division. And while Paul clearly appreciates some spiritual gifts more than others (see 14:1–33), the existence and diversity of these gifts, service, and workings speak to the unity within the one who provided them—a unity that must also characterize the Church called together by him.

Pause between Jesus' part and Mary's.

When the **wine** ran **short**,
    the **mother** of **Jesus** said to him,
    "They have no **wine**."
And **Jesus** said to her,
    "**Woman**, how does your concern affect **me**?
My **hour** has **not yet come**."
His mother said to the servers,
    "**Do whatever** he tells you."
Now there were **six** stone water jars there for Jewish
    ceremonial washings,
    each holding twenty to thirty gallons.
Jesus told them,
    "**Fill** the jars with **water**."
So they **filled** them to the **brim**.
Then he told them,
    "**Draw** some **out now** and **take** it to the **headwaiter**."
So they took it.
And when the **headwaiter** tasted the **water** that had become
    wine,
    without knowing where it came from
    —although the **servers** who had drawn the water **knew**—
    the **headwaiter** called the **bridegroom** and said to him,
    "**Everyone** serves **good wine first**,
    and then when **people** have **drunk freely**, an **inferior** one;

Pause after the words "good wine until now." Read the final stanza slowly.

    but **you** have **kept** the **good wine** until **now**."
Jesus did this as the **beginning** of his **signs** at **Cana** in **Galilee**
    and so **revealed** his **glory**,
    and his disciples **began** to **believe** in him.

GOSPEL | Knowing and accepting where Jesus comes from and where he is going are important elements of the Christology of John's Gospel. In John 8:14, Jesus addresses a group of people who have challenged the truth of his speech on the grounds that he offers no one else to back it up. Jesus replies, "Even if I do testify on my own behalf, my testimony can be verified, because I know where I came from and I know where I am going. But you do not know where I come from or where I am going." From John's perspective, Jesus comes from heaven and will return

there. To be ignorant of this is neither to know nor accept him.

Elsewhere in John we see the subject of the origin and destiny of Jesus used similarly. Nicodemus has evidence of the spirit, but does not know where it comes from or where it goes (3:8). The Jerusalemites in the Temple precincts think they know where Jesus is from, but in fact they haven't got a clue. And Pilate, during Jesus trial, asks the now familiar question found in 19:9: "Where are you from?"

Knowledge of the origins of things coming from Jesus also matters to John's Christology. This is true of the Samaritan woman's ignorance of the source of "living water" (4:11) and the disciples' ignorance of the source of food for the multitudes (6:5–9). And it is also the case with the wine in today's reading (2:9). Jesus is the source. The headwaiter is ignorant, but those working under him are not. Jesus is the source of living water (Baptism), as well as the bread and wine (Eucharist), though it is not apparent to everyone.

3RD SUNDAY IN ORDINARY TIME

Lectionary #69

READING I   Nehemiah 8:2–4a, 5–6, 8–10

A reading from the Book of Nehemiah

Ezra the **priest** brought the **law** before the **assembly**,
    which consisted of **men**, **women**,
    and those **children** old enough to **understand**.
Standing at one end of the open place that was before
        the Water Gate,
    he read out of the **book** from **daybreak** till **midday**,
    in the **presence** of the **men**, the **women**,
    and those **children** old enough to **understand**;
    and **all** the **people listened** attentively to the **book** of **the law**.
Ezra the **scribe** stood on a wooden platform
    that had been made for the occasion.
He **opened** the **scroll**
    so that **all** the **people** might see it
    —for he was standing higher up than any of the people—
    and, as he opened it, **all** the people **rose**.
Ezra blessed the LORD, the great **God**,
    and **all** the **people**, their **hands** raised **high**, **answered**,
    "**Amen, amen**!"
Then they **bowed** down and **prostrated** themselves
        before the LORD,
    their faces to the ground.
Ezra read plainly from the **book** of the **law** of **God**,
    interpreting it so that **all** could **understand** what was **read**.

This reading is long, but proclaim it slowly so that all of the details of the narrative sink in. A fairly complicated and involved liturgical scene is being narrated.

READING I Torah is a Hebrew word meaning "law" or "instruction." In Judaism, the word refers to the five books of Genesis, Exodus, Leviticus, Numbers, and Deuteronomy. They are also sometimes called the "books of the Law," or just "the Law." They are also commonly called "the five books of Moses" due to Jewish and Christian tradition that Moses was their inspired author. But some biblical scholars, even as far back as the Middle Ages, disputed whether or not Moses could reasonably be supposed to have written them. One of the most important pieces of evidence against Moses' authorship is the fact that Deuteronomy 34 depicts his death and burial. Many Jews and Christians demonstrated themselves capable of working around the problem, but it remains an important point.

There is not, at present, widespread agreement about how the Torah was composed. For much of the twentieth century, university and seminary students learned that the Torah was a combination of four major strands, designated J, E, P, and D. Each strand was believed to have been composed by an author or authors distinguishable from the other three due to their interest in particular themes, such as prophecy (D) and the Temple liturgies (P), as well

Then **Nehemiah**, that is, His **Excellency**, and **Ezra**
    the **priest-scribe**
 and the **Levites** who were **instructing** the **people**
 said to **all** the **people**:
 "**Today** is **holy** to the LORD your **God**.
Do **not** be **sad**, and do **not weep**"—
 for **all** the **people** were **weeping** as they **heard** the **words**
    of the **law**.
He said further: "**Go**, **eat** rich foods and **drink** sweet drinks,
 and **allot portions** to those who had **nothing** prepared;
 for **today** is **holy** to our LORD.
Do **not** be **saddened** this **day**,
 for **rejoicing** in the LORD must be your **strength**!"

READING II   1 Corinthians 12:12–30

A reading from the first Letter of Saint Paul to the Corinthians

Brothers and **sisters**:
As a **body** is **one** though it has **many** parts,
 and **all** the parts of the **body**, though **many**, are **one** body,
 so also **Christ**.
For in **one Spirit** we were **all baptized** into **one** body,
 whether **Jews** or **Greeks**, **slaves** or **free** persons,
 and **we** were **all** given to **drink** of **one Spirit**.

Stress the words "we" and "one." Awareness of the collective unity of the body's members is the metaphorical antidote to the divisions of Corinth.

as their names for God (J and E). Many additional reasons for this hypothesis were also offered. In more recent years, the hypothesis has unraveled somewhat as scholars and others have questioned many of its findings and basic assumptions.

If "the book of the Law of Moses" Ezra reads before the people is a version of the Torah, and if our text contains the accurate historical recollection that Ezra had one, then it is quite likely that the Babylonian exile, despite its many hardships, was a fertile period in the composition and editing of scripture.

READING II In 1 Corinthians 6:13, Paul writes that "the body" is "for the Lord." What Paul means by "body" in 6:13 becomes clearer in the light of today's reading. It is not the body of the individual believer, but rather the body of the whole Church.

In composing 1 Corinthians 12:12–30, Paul made use of a metaphor common in Greek political writing: the human body as the body of the city-state. The Greek orator Dio Chrysostom, in his third speech on kingship, makes use of the same metaphor when comparing the utility of a network of friends to the parts of a man's body (Dio Chrysostom, 3.104–108). In 1 Corinthians 12:4–11, Paul

Emphasize the pronoun "I" throughout. It will call attention to the irresponsible individualism against which Paul is arguing.

Now the **body** is not a **single part**, but **many**.
If a **foot** should say,
    "**Because I** am **not** a **hand I** do **not belong** to the **body**,"
    it does **not** for this reason **belong any less** to the body.
Or if an **ear** should say,
    "**Because I** am **not** an **eye I** do **not belong** to the **body**,"
    it does **not** for this reason **belong any less** to the body.
If the **whole body** were an **eye**, where would the **hearing** be?
If the **whole body** were **hearing**, where would the **sense**
        of **smell** be?
But as it is, **God** placed the **parts**,
    each one of them, in the **body** as he intended.
If they were **all** one part, **where** would the body be?
But as it is, there are **many** parts, yet **one** body.
The **eye** cannot say to the **hand**, "I do not **need** you,"
    nor again the **head** to the **feet**, "I do not **need** you."
Indeed, the **parts** of the body that seem to be **weaker**
    are **all** the more **necessary**,
        and those **parts** of the **body** that we consider less **honorable**
        we surround with **greater honor**,
        and our less presentable parts are treated with **greater propriety**,
        whereas our more presentable parts do not need this.
But **God** has so **constructed** the **body**
    as to give **greater honor** to a part that is **without** it,
    so that there may be **no division** in the body,
        but that the **parts** may have the **same concern** for **one another**.
If **one** part **suffers**, **all** the parts **suffer** with it;
    if **one** part is **honored**, **all** the parts **share its joy**.

conceives of the Corinthian assembly as a collection of diverse gifts and ministries united by one spirit. In 12:12–30, Paul describes how variety suffused by a deeper unity works out in actual practice.

   While all parts of the body are useful, some are more useful or important than others. It follows from the metaphor that some gifts and ministries are more important than others. Paul offers what is one of the earliest Church hierarchies in a Christian text. At the top of the list one finds a triumvirate in descending order of importance of apostles, prophets, and teachers.

   This hierarchy, given the youth of the Church and the Corinthian assembly, probably did not describe a set of well-defined offices. Take the case of "apostle." The basic meaning of apostle is "envoy." But for Paul an apostle was someone who, like him, could claim to have been assigned a mission by God. Not all early Christians, however, understood the word as Paul did. Indeed, Paul's use of the term was very much bound up in his own experience and work. In any case, Paul's main point is that the Corinthians need all the gifts and services, but that each person does not have, and cannot do, all of them.

Now **you** are **Christ's body**, and **individually** parts of it.
Some people **God** has designated in the **church**
  to be, **first**, **apostles**; **second**, **prophets**; **third**, **teachers**;
  then, **mighty deeds**;
  then **gifts** of **healing**, **assistance**, **administration**,
  and **varieties** of tongues.
Are all **apostles**? Are **all prophets**? Are **all teachers**?
Do **all** work **mighty deeds**? Do **all** have **gifts** of **healing**?
Do **all** speak in **tongues**? Do **all interpret**?

[Shorter: 1 Corinthians 12:12–14, 27]

GOSPEL   Luke 1:1–4; 4:14–21

A reading from the holy Gospel according to Luke

Since **many** have **undertaken** to **compile** a **narrative** of the **events**
  that have been **fulfilled** among us,
  just as those who were **eyewitnesses** from **the beginning**
  and **ministers** of the **word** have **handed them down** to **us**,
  I too have **decided**,
  after investigating **everything** accurately **anew**,
  to **write** it down in an **orderly sequence** for you,
  most **excellent Theophilus**,
  so that you may **realize** the **certainty** of the teachings
  you have received.

Jesus returned **to Galilee** in the power of the **Spirit**,
  and **news** of him **spread** throughout the **whole** region.
He **taught** in their **synagogues** and was **praised** by all.

Theophilus = Thee-AH-fil-us

Emphasize the clause including "certainty," and let special stress fall on that word.

GOSPEL   One of the strongest pieces of evidence in support of the case that the author of Luke and the author of Acts are one in the same concerns the strong similarity between the prologues to each work. Compare Luke 1:1–4 and Acts 1:1–2 and you will quickly see the likeness between them. In form, the introduction to the Gospel of Luke differs little from introductions composed by Greek historians and biographers.

One of the most intriguing statements of Luke's prologue is his statement that "many" have already tried their hand at writing "a narrative of the events that have been fulfilled among us" (Luke 1:1). This must mean that Luke knows of other Gospels, perhaps other accounts of the Church like Acts, perhaps both. It is quite likely that Luke made extensive use of Mark's Gospel

in writing his own, and that he had access to a source unknown to Mark but also used by Matthew. Luke used other written sources as well, although it is hard to say too much about them. Perhaps some of these sources were composed by the people he calls "eyewitnesses from the beginning and ministers of the word." In any case, Luke is telling Theophilus, the person to whom he addresses both Luke and Acts, that he has done his

He came to **Nazareth**, where he had grown up,
  and went according to his **custom**
    into the **synagogue** on the **sabbath** day.
He stood up to read and was handed **a scroll** of the prophet **Isaiah**.
He **unrolled** the **scroll** and found the passage where it was **written**:
  *The **Spirit** of the **LORD** is upon me,*
    *because he has **anointed me***
      *to bring **glad tidings** to the **poor**.*
  *He has sent **me** to **proclaim liberty** to **captives***
    *and **recovery** of **sight** to the **blind**,*
    *to let the **oppressed** go **free**,*
    *and to **proclaim** a year **acceptable** to the **Lord**.*
Rolling up the **scroll**, he handed it back to the attendant and
    sat down,
  and the **eyes** of **all** in the **synagogue** looked **intently** at **him**.
He said to them,
  "**Today** this **Scripture** passage is **fulfilled** in your **hearing**."

Pause before delivering the prophecy of Isaiah. Read it slowly.

research. Indeed, Luke's claim to have made an accurate study of "everything anew" is the warrant for his Gospel.

One of the items Luke has to offer is stylish and elegant Greek. This is clear in his prologue, which is a single Greek sentence. The sentence concludes with a clause containing the purpose of Luke's composition for Theophilus ("so that you may realize") and ending with the word "certainty" *(asphaleia)*. Luke has been building toward certainty from the first word of the prologue. His description of his research and sources in comparison with the work of prior authors is all designed to make the case for the certainty of what follows.

4TH SUNDAY IN ORDINARY TIME

Lectionary #72

See Galatians 1:15. There, Paul draws on Jeremiah's description of his call to prophesy in his description of his apostolate to the Galatian Church.

READING I   Jeremiah 1:4–5, 17–19

A reading from the Book of the Prophet Jeremiah

The **word** of the LORD came to me, saying:
  Before I **formed** you in the **womb** I **knew you**,
    before you were **born** I **dedicated you**,
    a **prophet** to the **nations** I appointed you.

Note the extended military metaphor. It foreshadows what will be an extremely challenging career.

But do you **gird** your loins;
    stand up and **tell** them
    all that I **command** you.
Be **not crushed** on their account,
    as **though** I would leave you **crushed** before **them**;
for it is **I** this day
    who have made **you** a **fortified city**,
a **pillar** of **iron**, a **wall** of **brass**,
    against the **whole** land:
against Judah's kings and **princes**,
    against its **priests** and **people**.
They will fight against **you** but **not prevail** over you,
    for **I** am **with you** to deliver you, says the LORD.

READING I   After the reign of Solomon, son of David by Bathsheba, the kingdom of Israel split in two. The southern tribal territory of Judah and Benjamin became the kingdom of Judah, while the remaining tribes of central Israel and the Galilee were known as the kingdom of Israel. In 721 BC, these northern tribes fell before the might of the Assyrian Empire, their members killed, enslaved, dispersed, and absorbed by the invaders and the settlers who followed them. In the following century

the Babylonian Empire arose to challenge Assyria. It was in this period of Babylonian expansion that Jeremiah lived. The southern kingdom of Judah was all that remained of David's realm by Jeremiah's day.

If ever there was a thankless task, it fell to the prophet Jeremiah. He was commanded, as the saying goes, "to speak truth to Power." And Power wanted nothing from him except what he could not provide—a still tongue. Jeremiah was as unpopular as he was because he spoke out against the injustice and faithlessness of Judah's rulers and wealthy citizens. He promised calamity

if they did not change their ways. As in our own time, serious criticism of powerful people is one of the quickest routes to public condemnation. But Jeremiah kept at it. His prophetic commission allowed him to do nothing else. And today we do not remember the names of the court prophets who spoke soothing words to Judah's kings, princes, priests, and people. We remember the suffering prophet who answered God's call and tried to draw his people back from the precipice of disaster.

READING II   1 Corinthians 12:31—13:13

A reading from the first Letter of Saint Paul to the Corinthians

Brothers and **sisters**:
Strive eagerly for the **greatest** spiritual gifts.
But I shall show you a **still more excellent** way.

Pause briefly between stanzas.

If I speak in **human** and **angelic** tongues,
    but do not have **love**,
    I am a resounding **gong** or a clashing **cymbal**.
And if I have the gift of **prophecy**,
    and **comprehend all mysteries** and **all knowledge**;
    if I have **all faith** so as to move mountains,
    but do **not have love**, I am **nothing**.
If I give away **everything** I own,
    and if **I hand** my **body over** so that I may **boast**,
    but do **not have love**, I gain **nothing**.

Love is **patient**, love is **kind**.
It is not **jealous**, it is not **pompous**,
    it is not **inflated**, it is not **rude**,
    it does not seek its own **interests**,
    it is not **quick-tempered**, it does not **brood** over **injury**,
    it does not **rejoice** over **wrongdoing**
    but **rejoices** with the **truth**.
It **bears all** things, **believes all** things,
    hopes all things, **endures all** things.

Love **never** fails.
If there are prophecies, they will be brought to **nothing**;
    if tongues, they will **cease**;
    if knowledge, it will be **brought** to **nothing**.

READING II So often is this text read at weddings that some may be surprised to learn these words of Paul do not concern marriage specifically. It is in the seventh chapter of 1 Corinthians, not here that Paul takes up the issue of marriage. In chapter 13 the specific issue is love in relation to the receipt and use of spiritual gifts, particularly the gift of tongues ("glossalalia"). Why does Paul contrast "human and angelic tongues" with love?

The Church at Corinth, as a reader learns at the letter's very beginning (see 1:10–13), is a Church divided. Biblical scholar Margaret M. Mitchell *(Paul and the Rhetoric of Reconciliation)* has argued that Paul composed and sent this letter to Corinth to encourage the Church to reunify. Paul's love is no gooey pop-song sentiment. For Paul, as for many Greek writers on politics and philosophy before him, love is social cement building up friendship and the common life of society. In contrast to love's constructive

and unifying power, the gift of tongues, in Paul's opinion, has been destructive and divisive, a source of pride for its recipients, and a cause of resentment in others.

The Greek word Paul uses here for love is *agapē*. Latin translates this word as *caritas,* from which comes our English word "charity." With faith and hope, charity, according to Roman Catholic teaching, is one of the theological virtues, which have God as their source, cause, and ultimate

For we **know partially** and we **prophesy partially**,
> but when the **perfect** comes, the **partial** will pass away.
When I was a **child**, I used to **talk** as a **child**,
> **think** as a **child**, **reason** as a **child**;
> when I became a **man**, I put aside **childish** things.
At **present** we see **indistinctly**, as in a **mirror**,
> but **then face to face**.
At **present** I know **partially**;
> **then** I shall know **fully**, as I am **fully known**.
So **faith**, **hope**, **love** remain, these three;
> but the **greatest** of these is **love**.

[Shorter: 1 Corinthians 13:4–13]

The "at present" and "then" of this passage refer to the present age before the return of Christ and the time after. See also 1 Corinthians 7:31, 15:20–28.

GOSPEL   Luke 4:21–30

A reading from the holy Gospel according to Luke

Jesus began speaking in the **synagogue**, saying:
> "Today this **Scripture** passage is **fulfilled** in your **hearing**."
And **all** spoke **highly** of him
> and were **amazed** at the **gracious** words that came
> > from his **mouth**.
They **also** asked, "Isn't this the **son** of **Joseph**?"
He said to them, "**Surely** you will quote me this proverb,
> '**Physician**, **cure** yourself,' and say,
> 'Do **here** in your **native place**
> the things that we **heard** were **done** in **Capernaum**.'"

---

aim. "The practice of all the virtues," says the Catechism, "is animated and inspired by charity" (#1827). Love is the live crackle in the wiring of Church, energizing our common life of service to one another, to our world, and to God.

GOSPEL What is it that has been fulfilled in the presence of Jesus' hometown assembly? The Lectionary, beginning with Luke 4:21, does not say. But back in 4:18, Jesus reads aloud before the Nazareth synagogue the words of the prophet Isaiah that the Spirit of the Lord is upon him and that he has been anointed to bring Good News to the poor, proclaim release to captives, sight to the blind, to set free the oppressed, and to proclaim an acceptable year of the Lord see (see Isaiah 61:1–2; 58:6).

In 4:25–27 Jesus refers to two miracles by Old Testament prophets, one by Elijah (1 Kings 17:1–16) and one by Elijah's disciple, Elisha (2 Kings 5:1–14). Both miracles were performed to the advantage of Gentiles. The widow came from the region of Sidon, which was a coastal region to the northwest of Israel in Elijah's time. Naaman was not only a Syrian, but also a military commander of Aram, which in Elisha's day was a kingdom periodically at war with Israel. For a poor Sidonian widow and an officer in an army sometimes at war with the kingdom of Israel, Jesus reminds us, the prophets performed miracles. The prophecies of good

See 1 Kings 17:1–16.

See 2 Kings 5:1–14.

And he said, "**Amen**, I say to you,
  no **prophet** is accepted in his own **native place**.
Indeed, I tell you,
  there were many **widows** in **Israel** in the days of **Elijah**
  when the **sky** was **closed** for **three** and a **half years**
  and a severe **famine** spread over the entire **land**.
It was to none of these that **Elijah** was **sent**,
  but only to a widow in **Zarephath** in the land of **Sidon**.
Again, there were **many lepers** in Israel
  during the time of **Elisha** the prophet;
  yet not one of them was **cleansed**, but only **Naaman**
    the **Syrian**."
When the people in the **synagogue** heard this,
  they were all **filled** with **fury**.
They **rose** up, **drove** him out of the town,
  and **led** him to the brow of the hill
  on which their town had been built,
  to **hurl** him down headlong.
But Jesus **passed through** the **midst** of them and went away.

news, release, and liberation that Jesus claims fulfilled (we do not yet know how) is seemingly not a message for his Jewish hometown crowd.

Many of those hearing or reading this passage will perhaps identify with Jesus without a second thought. But there is some profit in putting oneself in the position of the citizens of Nazareth. What angers them? Is it not Jesus' suggestion that scripture proclaims Good News to strangers outside their fold? In a Church that often reflects the divisions of race, class, and belief that mar God's earth, each one of us does well to remember that Jesus belongs not to *our* group, *our* set, *our* clique. He is not property. He came, of God's own choosing, for the world's sake, nothing less.

5TH SUNDAY IN ORDINARY TIME

Lectionary #75

READING I   Isaiah 6:1–2a, 3–8

A reading from the Book of the Prophet Isaiah

In the year King **Uzziah** died,
    I **saw** the LORD **seated** on a **high** and **lofty** throne,
    with the **train** of his **garment** filling the **temple**.
Seraphim were stationed above.

They cried one to the other,
    "**Holy**, **holy**, **holy** is the LORD of hosts!
All the **earth** is filled with his **glory**!"
At the sound of that cry, the frame of the door **shook**
    and the house was **filled** with **smoke**.

Then I said, "**Woe** is me, I am **doomed**!
For I am a man of **unclean** lips,
    living among a **people** of **unclean** lips;
    yet my **eyes** have **seen** the **King**, the LORD of hosts!"
Then one of the **seraphim** flew to me,
    holding an ember that he had taken with tongs from the altar.

He **touched** my **mouth** with it, and said,
    "**See**, now that this has **touched** your lips,
    your **wickedness** is **removed**, your **sin purged**."

Then I heard the voice of the LORD saying,
    "**Whom** shall I **send**? **Who** will **go** for us?"
    "**Here I** am," I said; "**send me**!"

Visions of God's throne are important elements of later prophetic and apocalyptic texts. See Ezekiel 1, Daniel 7, and Revelation 4.

The three holies are sometimes called the Trisagion (see Revelation 4:8). The cry of the crowds upon Jesus' triumphal entry into Jerusalem (Psalm 118:25; Matthew 21:9; Mark 11:9; Luke 19:38; John 12:13) and the Trisagion comprise the Sanctus in the Eucharistic liturgy.

READING I   This passage is what biblical scholars call a prophetic call narrative (see Reading I from January 28). It is the prophet Isaiah's account of how he was selected to speak God's word.

In order to understand this breathtaking scene in greater depth, a few facts are helpful. In the religion of Israel, as it is has come down to us in scripture (see Deuteronomy 18:9–22), a prophet was someone designated to speak God's own words. Perhaps a worker of miracles (like Elijah and Elisha), or a performer of shocking symbolic public acts (see, for example, Jeremiah 19 or 27), or a preacher, a prophet was something more. The prophet was believed to stand in the presence of God, who sat enthroned among the angelic host of heaven, in order to hear the deliberations of the council of heaven. The prophet would then report God's decisions and decrees, typically introducing his prophecy with the phrase "Thus says the Lord."

In this reading, the prophet Isaiah is visited in the Jerusalem Temple by God and the angelic host. The host is composed of beings called "Seraphim," a Hebrew word meaning something like "burning ones." The prophet's "unclean lips," unfit to speak God's words, are cauterized like a wound. Cleansed, Isaiah is now fit to stand in the presence of God and the heavenly council, hear its deliberations, and bring tidings to Israel.

READING II 1 Corinthians 15:1–11

A reading from the first Letter of Saint Paul to the Corinthians

I am reminding you, **brothers** and **sisters**,
    of the **gospel** I preached to you,
    which you indeed **received** and in which you also **stand**.
Through it you are also being **saved**,
    if you hold fast to the word I **preached** to you,
    unless you **believed** in **vain**.
For I handed on to you as of **first importance** what I also received:
    that **Christ** died for our **sins** in accordance with the **Scriptures**;
    that he was **buried**;
    that he was **raised** on the **third day**
      in accordance with the **Scriptures**;
    that he **appeared** to **Cephas**, then to the **Twelve**.
After that, Christ appeared to **more**
    than **five hundred** brothers **at once**,
    most of whom are still **living**,
    though some have **fallen asleep**.
After that he appeared to **James**,
    then to **all the apostles**.
Last of all, as to one born **abnormally**,
    he appeared to **me**.
For I am the **least** of the apostles,
    not fit to be called an apostle,
    because I **persecuted** the church of God.
But by the **grace** of God **I am** what **I am**,
    and his **grace** to me has **not** been ineffective.

The early post-Resurrection appearances of Jesus were an important element in the creation of early Christian ideas of authority.

An account of Christ's appearance to Paul is found in Acts 9. He himself mentions or alludes to it in Corinthians 9:1, 15:8; 2 Corinthians 4:6; and Galatians 1:16. Paul gives us bits of his pre-Christian biography in several places, most notably 2 Corinthians 11:22; Galatians 1:13–14; and Philippians 3:5–6.

The Roman Catholic Church incorporates the Seraphim's cries into the Sanctus, a hymn of praise of the Eucharistic liturgy. The belief that the Sanctus is part of the liturgy of heaven comes from this reading as well as Revelation 4:1–11. The place of the Sanctus in the Eucharistic liturgy testifies to Roman Catholic belief that the Mass parallels the heavenly liturgy.

READING II There is no reason to imagine that Paul always described "the gospel" and its contents in the same way. He wrote letters to particular people in response to particular situations. He worked on the fly. But some elements appear multiple times in his letters. The Gospel's general outline is found here in 1 Corinthians 15:1–11: Jesus Christ died on a cross for our sins in accordance with the scriptures; he was raised from the dead, also in accordance with the scriptures; He appeared to some after he was raised; he will return (not in 1 Corinthians 15:1–11, but see 15:20-28).

Why is the claim that Jesus died and rose in accordance with the scriptures important to Paul? Searching the texts of the religion of Israel for predictions of Jesus' death

Indeed, I have **toiled** harder than **all** of them;
    not I, however, but the **grace** of **God** that is with me.
Therefore, whether it be I or they,
    so we **preach** and so you **believed**.

[Shorter: 1 Corinthians 15:3–8, 11]

GOSPEL   Luke 5:1–11

A reading from the holy Gospel according to Luke

While the crowd was pressing in on **Jesus** and listening
    to the word of **God**,
  he was standing by the **Lake** of **Gennesaret**.
He saw two boats there alongside the **lake**;
  the **fishermen** had **disembarked** and were **washing** their nets.
Getting into one of the boats, the one belonging to **Simon**,
  he asked him to put out a **short distance** from the **shore**.
Then he sat down and **taught** the crowds from the boat.
After he had finished speaking, he said to **Simon**,
  "Put out into **deep water** and **lower** your nets for a **catch**."
Simon said in reply,
  "**Master**, we have worked hard **all night** and have
    caught **nothing**,
  but at your command I will **lower** the nets."
When they had done this, they caught a **great number** of fish
    and their **nets** were **tearing**.

"Lake of Gennesaret" is another name for the Sea of Galilee, a body of fresh water in the region of the Galilee.

This is a conversation. Let your delivery reflect that there are several speakers: Peter, Jesus, and the narrating voice of the text.

and Resurrection was among the principle tasks of earliest Christianity. In Luke 24:25–27,44–47, the evangelist reports that the resurrected Christ himself, before his Ascension, showed his disciples how the scriptures predicted his death and Resurrection.

Judaism, even in Jesus' day, was already an ancient religion. Roman law, for example, at times overlooked Judaism's seemingly antisocial features, such as monotheism, due to its venerable age. Christians,

finding Jesus in the pages of scripture, laid claim to ancient texts and traditions. Later Christian apologists, facing opposition, used this claim to refute the charge that their religion was something brand new.

For Paul, the Gospel is not just a report about something marvelous in the recent past. It is the culmination of things written long ago, but not understood until made plain by the death and rising of Jesus Christ.

GOSPEL "Woe is me, I am doomed!" says the prophet Isaiah, suddenly and terribly aware of his impurity in the presence of God. "Depart from me, Lord, for I am a sinful man!" says Simon Peter, on his knees, less grateful than afraid of his nets bulging with fish. The reaction of both men before God is the same: fear and the awareness of sin.

Fear, often of death, frequently attends human beings who meet with divine beings in scripture. "No one sees me," God tells

They signaled to their partners in the other boat
   to come to help them.
They came and **filled** both boats
   so that the boats were in danger of **sinking**.
When **Simon Peter** saw this, he **fell** at the knees of Jesus and said,
   "**Depart** from me, **Lord**, for I am a **sinful man**."
For **astonishment** at the catch of fish they had made **seized** him
   and **all** those with him,
     and **likewise James** and **John**, the sons of **Zebedee**,
   who were **partners** of **Simon**.
Jesus said to **Simon**, "Do **not** be **afraid**;
   from **now** on you will be **catching men**."
When they brought their **boats** to the **shore**,
   they **left everything** and **followed him**.

Moses, "and still lives" (Exodus 33:20). That he did see God and lived, Jacob thinks, is worthy of some memorial (Genesis 32:31). Moses fears to look upon God at the burning bush (Exodus 3:6). Fear grips Zechariah, the father of John the Baptist, when the angel of the Lord meets him, like Isaiah, alone in the Temple (Luke 1:12). And Mary, disturbed by the appearance of the angel Gabriel, is told not to fear (1:30). Fear is the normal human response to an encounter with divinity in scripture.

When reading this Gospel passage, give particular attention to the delivery of the line beginning "Depart from me." Here, Simon Peter speaks for all of us who, in those moments when we have drawn close to God, have also come face to face with the certain knowledge that our willful sin provides solid reason for our tragic separation.

"All of human history as seen by the Bible," wrote the biblical scholar Abraham J. Heschel, "is the history of *God in search of man.*" Though he begs Jesus to leave, the passage concludes with Simon Peter, James, and John leaving "everything" behind to follow. Harder than the search for God, perhaps, is the fear that God may find us, ask us to cast aside our tasks, and follow.

6TH SUNDAY IN ORDINARY TIME

Lectionary #78

READING I   Jeremiah 17:5–8

Let your reading reflect that the two halves of this reading have very different tones.

A reading from the Book of the Prophet Jeremiah

Thus says the LORD:
Cursed is the one who **trusts** in **human beings**,
    who **seeks** his **strength** in **flesh**,
    whose **heart** turns **away** from the LORD.
He is like a **barren bush** in the **desert**
    that **enjoys no change** of season,
but **stands** in a **lava** waste,
    a **salt** and **empty** earth.
Blessed is the one who **trusts** in the LORD,
    whose **hope** is the LORD.
He is like a **tree** planted beside the **waters**
    that stretches out its **roots** to the **stream**:
It fears not the **heat** when it comes;
    its leaves stay **green**;
in the year of **drought** it shows **no distress**,
    but still bears **fruit**.

READING I When reading this text, bear in mind the very different tone and subjects of its two halves. Be sure also to mark the transition between the two halves, perhaps with a pause of a few moments.

It is worth asking why the prophet considers trust in human beings to be such a negative thing. Does this pose a problem for Catholics? Does not the very adjective "catholic," which comes from Greek and means "universal," assume some level of trust in one another? Corporate worship is essential to our sacramental life. Can't we

trust in our brothers and sisters in Christ to attend to our physical needs when we encounter severe misfortune or to lift us up in prayer when our spirits flag?

The Greek translation of the Old Testament is called the Septuagint. When New Testament writers, such as Paul, cite scripture and discuss "the Scriptures," they almost always mean the Septuagint. The Septuagint's translation of the Hebrew word "trust" or "rely" *(batah)* is the phrase "have hope." According to Catholic teaching, hope, along with faith and love, is one of the three theological virtues. "Hope," the Catechism

instructs, "is the theological virtue by which we desire the kingdom of heaven and eternal life as our happiness, placing our trust in Christ's promises and relying not on our own strength, but on the help of the Holy Spirit" (Catechism, #1817).

Our brothers and sisters in Christ are God's resources on earth, those upon whom God has poured out the Holy Spirit and anointed for service to the world. If we will not trust and rely upon our brothers and sisters, loving one another in relationships of mutual aid, we choose a life of separation from God.

READING II   1 Corinthians 15:12, 16–20

A reading from the first Letter of Saint Paul to the Corinthians

Brothers and **sisters**:
If **Christ** is **preached** as **raised** from the **dead**,
    how can some among you say there is **no resurrection**
        of the dead?
If the **dead** are not **raised**, neither has **Christ** been **raised**,
    and if **Christ** has not been **raised**, your **faith** is **vain**;
        you are **still** in your **sins**.
Then those who have **fallen asleep** in Christ have **perished**.
If for this life only we have **hoped** in **Christ**,
    we are the **most pitiable people** of all.

But now **Christ** has been **raised** from the **dead**,
    the **firstfruits** of those who have **fallen asleep**.

When Paul writes "fallen asleep," he means "died." Compare 1 Thessalonians 4:13–18.

GOSPEL   Luke 6:17, 20–26

A reading from the holy Gospel according to Luke

Jesus came down with the **twelve**
    and stood on a stretch of **level ground**
    with a **great** crowd of his **disciples**
    and a **large** number of the **people**
    from all **Judea** and **Jerusalem**
    and the coastal region of **Tyre** and **Sidon**.

Luke's "Sermon on the Plain" shares a great deal of material in common with Matthew's "Sermon on the Mount" (Matthew 5:1–12).

The geographical regions given are both largely Gentile (Tyre, Sidon) and largely Jewish (Judea, Jerusalem).

READING II The theme of hope in eternal life continues into the second reading. Here, Paul picks up the thread he began in last Sunday's second reading. Recall that there he spelled out to the Corinthians what "the gospel" is. He described it as composed of a report about the Crucifixion and Resurrection of Jesus in accord with the witness of scripture (1 Corinthians 15:1–4).

But the Gospel contains more witnesses than the witness of scripture alone. Paul also called upon human witnesses, people (including himself) who witnessed the risen Christ with their own eyes and are therefore able to authenticate the claim of Jesus' Resurrection (1 Corinthians 15:5–8).

By a parade of textual and human witnesses, Paul attempts to prove the fact of Christ's Resurrection. Having done so, Paul now tries to convince the Corinthians that Christ's Resurrection necessarily implies the Resurrection of those who believe in him. Imagine, he suggests, the consequences if Christ has *not* been raised: still shrouded in sin, the Corinthians' "faith is in vain." Because this is not true, Paul reasons, Christ must have been raised. And if Christ has been raised, then, despite the disagreement of some members of the Corinthian assembly, there is also a resurrection of the dead.

Antiquity was filled with stories of gods and heroes who died and rose again. One thing that distinguishes Paul's story from these others is the conviction that Christ's Resurrection has decisively altered the fabric of human existence. Using a sacrificial and agricultural metaphor, Paul calls Christ "the first fruits of those who have fallen asleep" and assures his able and intelligent questioners in Corinth that Christ has bound their fortunes to his own.

And raising his eyes toward his disciples he said:
     "**Blessed** are you who are **poor**,
          for the **kingdom** of God is **yours**.
     Blessed are you who are now **hungry**,
          for you will be **satisfied**.
     Blessed are you who are now **weeping**,
          for you will **laugh**.
     Blessed are you when people **hate** you,
          and when they **exclude** and **insult** you,
          and **denounce** your name as **evil**
          on account of the **Son** of **Man**.
Rejoice and **leap** for **joy** on that **day**!
Behold, your **reward** will be **great** in heaven.
For their **ancestors** treated the **prophets** in the same way.
     But **woe** to you who are **rich**,
          for you have received your **consolation**.
     Woe to you who are **filled** now,
          for you will be **hungry**.
     Woe to you who **laugh** now,
          for you will **grieve** and **weep**.
     Woe to you when **all speak well** of you,
          for their **ancestors** treated the **false prophets** in this way."

The title "Son of Man" was an important one in apocalyptic literature (see, for example, Daniel 7:13). It is an important messianic title of Jesus in the Gospels. The title appears only on Jesus' lips in Luke (9:18, 44; 18:31–33; 21:36).

GOSPEL | Like the first reading, this passage from Luke offers more than blessing. Balancing Jesus' blessing on the poor, to whom is promised the kingdom of God, is a word of woe to the rich. The consolations of power, money, possessions, and privilege, Jesus says, are already theirs. One of Luke's special emphases distinguishing his Gospel from the other three is his portrayal of Jesus' special concern for social outcasts, particularly the poor.

Some may point to a parallel passage in Matthew 5:3, "Blessed are the poor in spirit," and argue that Luke's poor are not limited to people enduring poverty. This is not likely. Luke's Jesus pronounces blessing on the poor and woe to the rich without further qualification.

The balancing of blessings and woes continues. Blessings upon the hungry and those who weep are balanced by woe to those filled and those who laugh: their situations, Jesus says, shall be reversed. They are blessed who endure hatred and contempt, as were the prophets, for Jesus' sake, while woe is promised to the popular. And as woe came to the false prophets of Israel's past, yes-men who blabbed whatever the king wanted to hear, woe will come to those who, like the false prophets of old, enjoy public acclaim.

The blessed life, according to Luke, is not lived amid pomp, power, and popularity. This is an important message to proclaim in North America, where some religious yes-men of startling variety assure our most powerful citizens of God's approval; where wealth and celebrity are objects of worship; where the poor, when they are not being lectured or criticized, are all but forgotten.

7TH SUNDAY IN ORDINARY TIME

Lectionary #81

READING I   1 Samuel 26:2, 7–9, 12–13, 22–23

A reading from the first Book of Samuel

In those days, **Saul** went down to the desert of **Ziph**
   with three thousand picked men of **Israel**,
to search for **David** in the desert of **Ziph**.
So **David** and **Abishai** went among **Saul's soldiers** by night
   and found **Saul** lying asleep within the barricade,
with his **spear** thrust into the **ground** at his head
and **Abner** and his men sleeping around him.

Abishai whispered to **David**:
   "**God** has delivered your **enemy** into your **grasp** this day.
Let me **nail** him to the ground with one **thrust** of the **spear**;
   I will **not need** a second thrust!"
But **David** said to **Abishai**, "**Do not** harm him,
   for **who** can lay hands on the LORD'S **anointed**
     and remain **unpunished**?"
So **David** took the **spear** and the **water jug** from their place
   at Saul's head,
and they got away **without** anyone's **seeing** or **knowing**
   or **awakening**.
All remained **asleep**,
   because the LORD had put them into a **deep slumber**.

Going across to an opposite slope,
   David stood on a remote **hilltop**
   at a **great distance** from **Abner**, son of **Ner**, and the **troops**.

Abishai = AH-bi-shai

"Anointed" is a common designation of kings of Israel and Judah in the Old Testament.

READING I Today's reading comes from a section of the Bible commonly called the "deuteronomistic history" by biblical scholars. Scholars who use this designation usually agree that the books of Joshua, Judges, 1 and 2 Samuel, 1 and 2 Kings together form a single narrative outlining the period from Israel's conquest of Canaan to the end of the kingdom of Judah. The narrative is called the deuteronomistic history because its contributors' theological interpretations of Israel's history appear to reflect theological themes of the book of Deuteronomy.

If one were to summarize the contents of 1 Samuel in a phrase, one might reasonably say that 1 Samuel is the story of the rise of monarchy in Israel, or perhaps the rise and fall of Saul, son of Kish. Anointed king by Samuel (1 Samuel 10:1), Saul proved himself a capable military leader against Israel's neighbors, the Philistines. But he was consumed with jealousy for David, his younger contemporary, whose military successes and popularity at first rivaled and then surpassed his own. Saul's jealousy only increased with time, hurling him past the point of madness. He and his sons died pursuing his vain vendetta against David. Saul is without doubt among the Bible's most tragic figures.

He said: "**Here** is the king's **spear**.
Let an attendant come over to get it.
The **LORD** will reward each man for his **justice** and **faithfulness**.
Today, though the **LORD delivered** you into my **grasp**,
　I would **not** harm the **LORD'S anointed**."

READING II　1 Corinthians 15:45–49

A reading from the first Letter of Saint Paul to the Corinthians

Brothers and **sisters**:
It is **written**, *The first man*, **Adam**, *became a* **living being**,
　the last **Adam a life-giving spirit**.
But the **spiritual** was not **first**;
　rather the **natural** and **then** the **spiritual**.
The **first man** was from the **earth**, **earthly**;
　the **second man**, from **heaven**.
As was the **earthly one**, so also are the **earthly**,
　and as is the **heavenly one**, so also are **the heavenly**.
Just as we have borne the **image** of the **earthly one**,
　we shall also bear the **image** of the **heavenly one**.

"Brothers and sisters" (in Greek, *adelphoi*) is a typical form of address in early Christian correspondence. Pause and look at the assembly as you proclaim these words.

Today's reading shows David presented with the opportunity to slaughter Saul together with his whole battalion. And it is not out of respect for Saul that David does not. What stays David's hand is his belief that Saul is under God's protection (Saul is an "anointed" king, and to kill one of God's anointed would truly be an offense against God) and, despite Saul's relentless campaign of violence against him, worthy of respect.

READING II For the last three weeks the second reading has come from 1 Corinthians 15. Last week Paul was arguing that the truth of Christ's Resurrection, for which he claimed both textual and eye-witness support, implies the Resurrection of the dead. Some in Corinth, it seems, did not believe in the general Resurrection (15:12). Paul intends 1 Corinthians 15 to settle the question and get the Corinthians, as he urges at the letter's beginning, to end their divisions (1:10).

Throughout Paul's letters, there is ample evidence that he received a basic education in the rhetorical arts. In today's selection, Paul compares Adam with Christ. The comparison (*synkrisis* in Greek) was a common rhetorical technique used by ancient Greek orators and writers. First, Paul cites scripture describing the creation of the first man (Genesis 2:7). Playing on the Hebrew word *adam*, which means "human being," Paul places the first man, Adam, in opposition to

GOSPEL   Luke 6:27–38

A reading from the holy Gospel according to Luke

Jesus said to his disciples:
"To you who **hear** I say,
   love your **enemies**, do **good** to those who **hate** you,
   bless those who **curse** you, **pray** for those who **mistreat** you.
To the person who **strikes** you on **one cheek**,
   offer the **other** one as **well**,
   and from the person who **takes** your cloak,
   do not **withhold** even your tunic.
Give to **everyone** who **asks** of you,
   and from the one who **takes** what is yours **do not demand**
      it back.
Do to **others** as **you** would have **them** do to **you**.
For if you **love** those who **love** you,
   what **credit** is that to you?
Even **sinners love** those who **love** them.
And if you do **good** to those who do **good** to you,
   what **credit** is that to you?
Even **sinners** do the same.
If you **lend money** to those from whom you **expect** repayment,
   what **credit** is that to you?
Even **sinners** lend to **sinners**,
   and get back the **same** amount.

---

the second man, Christ. The first is "natural" and "earthly," the second "spiritual" and "heavenly." Christ is of a different character entirely than Adam.

But as ancient rhetorical specialists agreed, a good *synkrisis* compares things that share some fundamental similarity. Paul's argument about Christ and Adam, in other words, is not apples and oranges. The similarity of Adam and Christ is that the Corinthians bear the "image" (in Greek, *eikōn*) of each. As it has been for us with the earthly man, Paul is saying, so now it is for us with the heavenly man.

Beginning in the Middle Ages, European artists often painted a skull at the foot of Christ's cross. The skull represents Adam's mortality and death conquered by the Savior nailed above it. The scene, repeated many thousands of times over the centuries, translates the substance of Paul's comparison into a powerful image testifying to what Christ accomplished for the human race.

GOSPEL Luke's sermon on the plain (6:20–49) is far shorter than Matthew's sermon on the mount (5:1—7:29). They share a great deal in common (beatitudes, ethical instruction, similar conclusions) and likely originate from the same written source. Biblical scholars usually call this source Q, from the German word *Quelle* ("source"). Try comparing Jesus' sermon in Luke with that in Matthew and note the similarities and differences.

But rather, **love** your **enemies** and do **good** to them,
and **lend** expecting **nothing** back;
then your **reward** will be great
and you will be **children** of the **Most High**,
for he himself is kind to the **ungrateful** and the **wicked**.
Be **merciful**, just as your Father is **merciful**.

"**Stop judging** and you will **not** be **judged**.
Stop condemning and you will **not** be **condemned**.
Forgive and you will be **forgiven**.
Give and gifts will be **given** to you;
a good measure, packed together, shaken down,
and overflowing,
will be **poured** into your lap.
For the **measure** with which you **measure**
will in return **be measured** out to you."

These words are a promise. Proclaim them as such.

Jesus does not say, "Make friends of your enemies." His instruction is much harder than this. There can be no question, according to Jesus, that his disciples must love those having their worst interests at heart. In his biography of Saint Francis of Assisi, G. K. Chesterton writes that "it is true that there is not, as pacifists and prigs imagine, the least inconsistency between loving men and killing them, if we fight them fairly and for a good cause." This may be true and in the spirit of Luke 6:31, although the preceding three verses severely limit what sort of cause we may call "good." The tendency of these verses is toward pacifism.

These verses contain what are simply some of the hardest teachings of the Christian religion. The morality Jesus demands of his disciples is not merely ratcheted up a few degrees beyond what they are used to. The distance from "Love your neighbors" to "Love your enemies" is infinite. The cross alone can bridge it.

ASH WEDNESDAY

Lectionary #219

READING I   Joel 2:12–18

A reading from the Book of the Prophet Joel

Even now, says the LORD,
    return to me with your **whole heart**,
    with **fasting**, and **weeping**, and **mourning**;
Rend your hearts, **not** your **garments**,
    and **return** to the LORD, your **God**.
For **gracious** and **merciful** is he,
    slow to **anger**, **rich** in **kindness**,
    and **relenting** in **punishment**.
Perhaps he will again **relent**
    and leave behind him a **blessing**,
Offerings and **libations**
    for the LORD, your God.

Blow the trumpet in **Zion**!
    proclaim a fast,
    call an assembly;
Gather the people,
    notify the congregation;
Assemble the elders,
    gather the children
    and the infants at the breast;
Let the **bridegroom quit** his room,
    and the **bride** her chamber.

Fasting, weeping, and the tearing of garments are outward signs of repentance.

READING I Little is known about the life of the prophet Joel. One potential clue to his identity is his use of cultic language in today's reading. The term "cultic" does not describe attributes of a religious splinter group or sect, which are what most of us probably imagine when we read or hear the words "cult" and "cultic." Cult, in the study of religion, refers to the practice of worship. Cultic language is the language of worship. Perhaps Joel's employment of such language (see 2:14–17) means that he was, like the prophets Isaiah and Ezekiel, a priest of the Temple at Jerusalem in addition to being a prophet.

The principal theme of Joel is the day of the Lord. This day was conceived in various ways in ancient Israelite religion, but it was typically understood as a day on which God would judge the people of Israel. The idea pervades the books of the prophets. In apocalyptic Jewish and Christian writings of subsequent centuries, the day of the Lord assumes much greater importance. In these texts the day of the Lord is often seen as a time of great upheaval, even including the alteration of the physical universe, when God, with the assistance of the angelic host, punishes the wicked and rewards the good.

Note the intercessory function of the priests. The intercessory, priestly function of Christ is important in the letter to the Hebrews (see 2:17; 3:1; 4:15; and 5:5–10). Christ's intercession is found also in Romans 8:34.

Between the **porch** and the **altar**
    let the priests, the ministers of the LORD, **weep**,
And say, "**Spare**, O LORD, your **people**,
    and make not your **heritage** a **reproach**,
    with the **nations ruling** over them!
Why should they say among the **peoples**,
    '**Where** is their **God**?'"

Then the LORD was **stirred** to **concern** for his **land**
    and took **pity** on his **people**.

READING II   2 Corinthians 5:20—6:2

A reading from the second Letter of Saint Paul to the Corinthians

Brothers and **sisters**:
We are **ambassadors** for **Christ**,
    as if **God** were appealing through **us**.
We **implore** you on behalf of **Christ**,
    be **reconciled** to **God**.
For our sake he made him to **be sin**
    who did **not** know **sin**,
    so that **we** might become the **righteousness**
    of **God** in **him**.

The notion that God made Christ "to be sin" for the sake of believers is similar to the idea in Galatians 5:13 that Christ became a curse himself in order to remove believers from the curse of the law.

It is in preparation for the judgment to accompany the day of the Lord that God, through Joel, begs the people of Israel to gather together in penitential worship. It is appropriate, therefore, that the Church reads this text on Ash Wednesday. On Ash Wednesday Roman Catholics around the world commence the season of Lent, calling to mind when (not if!) our thought and action have opposed what God desires for us. Today the Lord entreats us: "return to me with your whole heart, with fasting weeping, and mourning."

READING II Paul's relations with the Corinthian assembly were rocky. In his letters to it he is by turns comforting and insulting, loving and exasperated, friendly and angry, serious and clowning. Part of Paul's trouble was that the Corinthians, as a group, were clearly thoughtful people, asked excellent questions, and did not always bow to Paul's authority when they were displeased with him.

Second Corinthians, while it comes to us in our New Testament as a single letter, is probably composed of fragments of several letters that Paul wrote. The earliest of these fragments (2:14—6:13 and 7:2–4) contains today's selection.

Not long after Paul wrote the letter we call 1 Corinthians, some Christian missionaries showed up in Corinth and challenged Paul's authority there. These missionaries seem to have brought with them letters of

Working together, then,
    we appeal to you **not** to receive the **grace**
        of **God** in **vain**.
For he says:

    *In an **acceptable time** I **heard** you,*
        *and on the **day** of **salvation** I **helped** you.*

Behold, **now** is a very a**cceptable time**;
    behold, **now** is the **day** of **salvation**.

Here Paul quotes Isaiah 49:8.

GOSPEL   Matthew 6:1–6, 16–18

A reading from the holy Gospel according to Matthew

Jesus said to his disciples:
    "Take care not to **perform righteous deeds**
    in order that people may **see** them;
    otherwise, you will have **no recompense**
        from your **heavenly Father**.
When you **give** alms,
    do not **blow** a **trumpet** before you,
    as the **hypocrites** do in the **synagogues**
        and in the streets
    to **win** the **praise** of others.
Amen, I say to you,
    they have **received** their reward.
But when **you** give alms,
    do **not** let your **left** hand know what your **right** is doing,
    so that your **almsgiving** may be **secret**.
And your Father who **sees** in **secret** will **repay** you.

As on last Sunday, Jesus is calling for a level of morality and religious behavior that, in comparison with believers' environments, is ratcheted up a few notches.

Note that Jesus says "*when* you give alms," not "*if*" you give them.

---

recommendation, perhaps from influential and well-known members of the Christian communities in Palestine. They probably led the Corinthians to wonder why Paul did not have similar credentials. Paul defends himself by saying, in general, that he needs no letters of recommendation, because God, through his apostolate, recommends him (see 3:1–6; 5:12).

This is the tense backdrop for the words of reconciliation comprising today's reading. Paul selects his terms carefully. The Greek word *presbeuein* in 5:20, which

means to act in the capacity of an ambassador, signifies that Paul claims to speak for God just as an ambassador speaks for his sovereign. It follows from this argument that the Corinthians, if they would be reconciled with God, must do so through Paul, God's ambassador, by once again accepting his authority as an apostle.

Christians everywhere should be grateful to the Corinthians. Our texts are the richer for their intelligence and obstinacy.

GOSPEL   While the prophet Joel in the first reading urges the celebration of a public liturgy of penance attended by all the people and presided over by priests, Jesus cautions that public religious acts may add up to hypocrisy. Why are these seemingly contradictory texts placed together in the liturgy of Ash Wednesday?

The first point to make is that the reading from Joel is not so far from the Gospel selection (which comes from the "Sermon on the Mount" in Matthew's Gospel) as it

"**When** you **pray**,
do **not** be like the **hypocrites**,
who **love** to **stand** and **pray** in the **synagogues**
and on **street corners**
so that **others** may **see** them.
Amen, I say to you,
they have **received** their reward.
But when **you** pray, **go** to your **inner room**,
close the door, and **pray** to your Father in **secret**.
And your **Father** who **sees** in **secret** will **repay** you.

"**When** you **fast**,
do **not** look **gloomy** like the **hypocrites**.
They **neglect** their appearance,
so that they may **appear** to others to be **fasting**.
Amen, I say to you, they have **received** their reward.
But when **you** fast,
anoint your **head** and wash your **face**,
so that you may **not appear** to be **fasting**,
except to your **Father** who is **hidden**.
And your **Father** who **sees** what is **hidden**
will **repay** you."

might at first seem. "Rend your hearts, not your garments," the prophet says, implying that the inward disposition of the repentant sinner is what rightly orients him or her toward God, not the dramatic outward display of tearing one's clothes. Likewise, Jesus encourages the crowd to give alms, pray, and fast in secret because it is the only way to be sure that one performs these acts with an intention completely free from hypocrisy. Both readings demand that the practice of one's religion be genuine.

Many Christians will spend much of Ash Wednesday signed with ashes, which is obviously a very public religious display. It may be appropriate to call attention to this in relation to Jesus' command that his followers pray in secret. If today's Gospel tells us anything, it is that our motives matter. They are not *all* that matter when deciding either to act or not to act in particular situations. But they matter. We who elect to continue wearing the ashes after the liturgy should perhaps examine our consciences in order to see if our decision has to do with adherence to tradition, a desire to draw attention to our piety, or some other reason entirely.

1ST SUNDAY OF LENT

Lectionary #24

READING I   Deuteronomy 26:4–10

A reading from the Book of Deuteronomy

Moses spoke to the people, saying:
   "The **priest** shall receive the basket from you
   and shall set it in front of the **altar** of the LORD, your **God**.
Then you shall **declare** before the LORD, your **God**,
   'My **father** was a **wandering Aramean**
   who went down to **Egypt** with a small household
   and lived there as an **alien**.
But there he became **a nation**
   great, **strong** and **numerous**.
When the **Egyptians maltreated** and **oppressed** us,
   imposing **hard labor** upon us,
   we cried to the LORD, the **God** of our fathers,
   and he heard our **cry**
   and saw our **affliction**, our **toil** and our **oppression**.
He brought us out of **Egypt**
   with his **strong** hand and **outstretched** arm,
   with **terrifying power**, with **signs** and **wonders**;
   and **bringing** us into this **country**,
   he gave us this **land** flowing with **milk** and **honey**.

The "wandering Aramean" is Jacob (Israel).

"Aramean" is an ethnic designation somewhat broader that "Israelite," probably referring to the Mesopotamian roots of Jacob's family. One must admit, however, that what the author means by the term is not precisely clear.

READING I   The modern west is unusual in many respects when compared with the ancient Mediterranean world. The rhythm of the agricultural cycle upon which human life depends is not a subject of much concern to many present-day urbanites. That was not true of ancient people, nor is it true of rural people today. The majority of people under the Roman Empire worked the land to live. All people, rural and urban, lived with the possibility of famine if even minor problems afflicted the harvest. It is fitting that the expression of gratitude to God for the harvest in today's reading accompanies a commemoration of God's saving acts in history. One year's gathered harvest was, like the Exodus, nothing less that the gift of life.

What we have in today's reading are instructions for the performance of a religious rite. Much as there are rubrics and liturgical guides for the celebration of the sacraments, so also do the pages of the Bible, in this case the book of Deuteronomy, contain instructions for the worship of God. This feature of the text has led some biblical scholars to suggest that this passage emerged from the liturgical life of ancient Israel's annual festivals.

The spoken portion of the rite is a recitation of "salvation history," a theological term referring to the historical sequence of God's deliverance of Israel and its descendant the Church.

Therefore, I have now brought you **the firstfruits**
  of the **products** of the **soil**
  which you, O LORD, have **given** me.'
And having set them before the LORD, your **God**,
  you shall **bow** down in his **presence**."

READING II   Romans 10:8–13

A reading from the Letter of Saint Paul to the Romans

Brothers and **sisters**:
What does **Scripture** say?
*The word is **near** you,*
  *in your **mouth** and in your **heart***
  —that is, the **word of faith** that we **preach**—
  for, if you **confess** with your **mouth** that Jesus is **Lord**
  and **believe** in your **heart** that **God** raised him from the **dead**,
  you will be **saved**.
For one **believes** with the **heart** and so is **justified**,
  and one **confesses** with the **mouth** and so is **saved**.
For the **Scripture** says,
  No** one who **believes** in him will be put to **shame.
For there is no distinction between **Jew** and **Greek**;
  the same **Lord** is **Lord** of all,
  enriching **all** who call upon him.
For "**everyone** who calls on the name of the Lord will be saved."

It worth stressing the simplicity of Paul's conviction concerning salvation's requirements.

Christ eliminates theological distinction between Jew and Greek as a *solution* to the common *problem* of sin (see Romans 3:21–26 especially). The elimination in the Church of worldly distinction is also a theme of Galatians 3:26–28.

The "wandering Aramean," who took his family to Egypt in a time of famine is Jacob, also called Israel (see Genesis 32:29), who brought his family to Egypt when famine consumed the land of Canaan (Genesis 46:1–7). This rite of thanksgiving for the harvest calls to mind not only the events of the Exodus and the Israelites' conquest of Canaan, but the famine that took the Israelites to Egypt in the first place.

It is fitting, when meditating upon this passage, to consider the elements of salvation history present in Roman Catholic worship. The Nicene Creed contains a recitation of selected historical events from the life of Jesus. And doubtless we can recall times in our own lives when God has delivered us from circumstances well beyond our ability to control. Personal stories of God's work in our lives are narratives of salvation history as well. They also are worth reciting.

READING II "The word is near you, in your mouth and in your heart." Paul follows this quotation of Deuteronomy 30:14 with a promise: *salvation*

(God's rescue of believers from the desolation of the effects of sin) and *justification* (the process by which believers cooperate with God's grace and enter into a right relationship with God) belong to those confessing and believing two things: 1) that Jesus is Lord and 2) that God raised him from the dead.

If Paul is such a scripture scholar, then what have these words from Deuteronomy to do with salvation and justification? When Paul quotes scripture, much of the time he has more of the text in mind than he actually quotes. The passage from Deuteronomy

GOSPEL Luke 4:1–13

A reading from the holy Gospel according to Luke

Filled with the **Holy Spirit**, **Jesus** returned from the **Jordan**
and was led by the **Spirit** into the desert for **forty** days,
to be **tempted** by the **devil**.
He ate **nothing** during those days,
and when they were over he was **hungry**.
The **devil** said to him,
"**If** you are the **Son** of **God**,
command this **stone** to become **bread**."
Jesus answered him,
"It is **written**, *One does not **live** on bread **alone**.*"
Then he took him up and **showed** him
all the kingdoms of the world in a single instant.
The **devil** said to him,
"I shall **give** to you all this **power** and **glory**;
for it has been **handed over to** me,
and **I** may give it to **whomever** I wish.
All this will be **yours**, **if** you **worship** me."
Jesus said to him in reply,
"It is **written**:
*You shall **worship** the **Lord**, your **God**,
and him **alone** shall you **serve**.*"

Compare Matthew 4:1–11. What's different here?

See Deuteronomy 8:3.

See Deuteronomy 6:13 and 10:20.

comes from a chapter in which Moses discusses God's mercy on Israel. While Israel's good fortune, Moses says, depends on its obedience to the terms of its special relationship with God, God still extends mercy if and when Israel violates the terms of that relationship. In Deuteronomy 30:11, Moses says that God's command, which is "the word" in Paul's quotation of 30:14, is not complicated or hard to understand. It is a simple (if not exactly easy) matter of Israel's

acceptance (or refusal) of a good life on the land in exchange for fidelity to God. Paul sees Deuteronomy 30, as he does many of the Old Testament passages he quotes, through the lens of the cross and Resurrection of Jesus. The word in Paul's mouth and heart is "Jesus is Lord."

GOSPEL Today's reading from Luke's Gospel is often called "The Temptation." This title comes from the statement of the second verse that Jesus "was

led by the Spirit into the desert for forty days to be tempted by the devil." In the New Testament, Matthew (4:1–11), Mark (1:12–13), and probably the letter to the Hebrews (2:14–18; 4:15) know this tradition.

"Temptation" does not fully and accurately capture Luke's meaning. The Greek word Luke uses to describe what was done to Jesus by the devil is *peirazō*. In the passive voice, which is how Luke uses it here, the verb means "to be put to the test" in addition to "to be tempted." The Greek word

See Psalm 91:1, 12.

Then he led him to **Jerusalem**,
    made him **stand** on the **parapet** of the **temple**, and said to him,
"**If** you are the **Son** of **God**,
    throw yourself **down** from here, for it is **written**:
        *He will **command** his **angels** concerning you, to **guard** you,*
    and:
        *With their **hands** they will **support** you,*
        *lest you **dash** your foot against a **stone**."*
Jesus said to him in reply,
    "It **also** says,
    *You shall **not** put the **Lord**, your **God**, to the **test**."*

See Deuteronomy 6:16.

When the **devil** had **finished** every **temptation**,
    he departed from him **for a time**.

---

has a wider range of meaning, in other words, than we are able to capture with a single word in English.

The difference in meaning between testing and tempting at first may not seem especially significant. But here we need to inquire into why Luke describes this scene as he has. The word *peirazō* is used in the Septuagint, which is the Greek translation of the Old Testament used by the early Church, of God's testing of Israel. It is also used of Israel's testing of God. The 40 days

of Jesus' testing in the wilderness call to mind Israel's journey of 40 years in the wilderness. God intended the hardships of this desert odyssey, as Deuteronomy 8:2 makes clear, to test Israel's mettle. The 40 days of Jesus' fasting also calls to mind the 40 days Moses himself fasted before writing down Israel's covenantal laws (Exodus 34:28). One might think also of the prophet Elijah, whose 40-day journey to the mountain where Moses received the laws was a symbolic reenactment of the Exodus (1 Kings 19:8).

In this reading, we encounter a chapter or more of scripture submerged like an iceberg beneath the tiny protrusion of a single quoted sentence. In this Gospel passage, the study of a few words discloses how Luke has tied his scene to multiple events in Israel's sacred history.

2ND SUNDAY OF LENT

Lectionary #27

READING I   Genesis 15:5–12, 17–18

A reading from the Book of Genesis

The Lord GOD took Abram outside and said,
  "Look up at the sky and count the stars, if you can.
Just so," he added, "shall your descendants be."
Abram put his faith in the LORD,
  who credited it to him as an act of righteousness.

Pause briefly before beginning the second stanza.

He then said to him,
  "I am the LORD who brought you from Ur of the Chaldeans
  to give you this land as a possession."
"O Lord GOD," he asked,
  "how am I to know that I shall possess it?"
He answered him,
  "Bring me a three-year-old heifer, a three-year-old she-goat,
  a three-year-old ram, a turtledove and a young pigeon."
Abram brought him all these, split them in two,
  and placed each half opposite the other;
  but the birds he did not cut up.
Birds of prey swooped down on the carcasses,
  but Abram stayed with them.
As the sun was about to set, a trance fell upon Abram,
  and a deep, terrifying darkness enveloped him.

READING I In today's Old Testament reading, God makes an extraordinary claim to Abram. The multitude of Abram's descendants, God says, will be like the stars of the night sky. If you have ever seen a night sky unaffected by artificial light or much pollution, where innumerable pinpricks of light turn the blackness to gray, then you know how extraordinary this claim is. How does Abram respond? "Abram put his faith in the Lord, who credited it to him as an act of righteousness."

The Hebrew root for "put faith in" *(aman)* has entered Greek and English in a different form and with a different but related meaning. We know it as the word "amen" with which we conclude prayers. The original meaning of amen is captured in some translations of the Bible by the word "truly." Amen is at one and the same time both wish and testimony that a prayer has solid support from both God and the person offering it up.

The reason for this information has to do with the meaning of "belief" in God. Abram's belief in God is not blind. By this point in Genesis Abram has experience with God. He has been promised much (see Genesis 12:2–3, 7; 13:14–18), but God has also helped his wife Sarai and him when they needed it (see Genesis 12:10–20). Abram's faith in God's words has to do, in part, with what God has already done for him.

When the sun had set and it was dark,
   there **appeared** a smoking fire pot and a flaming torch,
   which **passed between** those pieces.

It was on **that** occasion that the LORD made a **covenant**
   with **Abram**,
   saying: "To your **descendants** I **give** this **land**,
   from the Wadi of **Egypt** to the Great River, the **Euphrates**."

This is indeed broad territory, much broader than anything Israel ever held. Locate the Euphrates River on a map to get a sense of how large an area this is.

READING II   Philippians 3:17—4:1

A reading from the Letter of Saint Paul to the Philippians

Join with others in being **imitators** of me, brothers and sisters,
   and **observe** those who thus **conduct** themselves
   according to the **model** you have in us.
For many, as I have **often** told you
   and now tell you even in **tears**,
   conduct themselves as **enemies** of the cross of Christ.
Their end is **destruction**.
Their God is their **stomach**;
   their glory is in their "**shame**."
Their minds are occupied with **earthly** things.
But our **citizenship** is in **heaven**,
   and from it we also await a **savior**, the Lord **Jesus Christ**.
He will **change** our **lowly** body
   to **conform** with his **glorified** body
   by the **power** that enables him also
   to bring **all** things into **subjection** to himself.

Scholars are divided over whether Paul is referring to specific people inside the Christian movement (perhaps those people who preach Christ out of poor motives in 1:15–17), specific antagonists outside of it, or non-specific opponents imagined for the sake of argument.

Paul uses Greek political language to describe believers' membership in heaven. See also Philippians 1:27.

Abram's faith in God became a much-debated model of Christian faith in early Christianity (see Romans 4:1–25; Galatians 3:1–29; 4:21–31; James 2:18–26). It is important to understand that Christian faith, like the faith of Abram, is based in part on experience. As a community, what we know of Jesus is based on the eyewitness testimony of our early members (Luke 1:1–4; John 1:14; 19:35; 20:30–31; 21:24–25; 1 Corinthians 15:3–11). As individuals, what we have experienced of God is more personal, but no less real.

READING II "Join with others in being imitators of me, brothers and sisters," urges Paul, "and observe those who thus conduct themselves according to the model you have in us." Modeling oneself on the venerable example of a predecessor was an important dimension of Greek philosophical education. When Paul tells the Philippians to imitate him, he is drawing on Greek philosophical and educational traditions that the Philippians, who resided in Macedonia, would have likely understood.

In what specific ways does Paul want the Philippians to imitate him? This question requires a somewhat closer look at the letter to the Philippians. Paul writes it from prison (1:12–14) where he may face a death sentence (1:20–26). But he is happy, he says, that his incarceration has served the advancement of the Gospel (1:12–14). And while Paul claims some people proclaim the Gospel for reasons that he does not approve, he nevertheless rejoices that Christ is preached (1:15–18). In other words, Paul models self-sacrifice and the setting aside of personal considerations for the common good.

Therefore, my **brothers** and **sisters**,
  whom I **love** and **long for**, my **joy** and **crown**,
  in this way **stand firm** in the **Lord**.

[Shorter: Philippians 3:20—4:1]

A reading from the holy Gospel according to Luke

Jesus took **Peter**, **John** and **James**
  and went up the mountain to **pray**.
While he was **praying**, his face **changed** in appearance
  and his clothing became **dazzling white**.
And **behold**, two men were conversing with him, **Moses**
    and **Elijah**,
  who **appeared** in **glory** and spoke of his **exodus**
  that he was going to **accomplish** in **Jerusalem**.
Peter and his companions had been **overcome** by **sleep**,
  but becoming fully **awake**,
  they saw his **glory** and the two men standing with him.
As they were about to part from him, **Peter** said to **Jesus**,
  "Master, it is **good** that we are here;
  let us make **three** tents,
  one for **you**, one for **Moses**, and one for **Elijah**."
But he did **not** know what he was saying.

The word translated here as "accomplish" (in Greek, *plēroō*) also means "complete" or "fulfill." All four evangelists understand Jesus' death and Resurrection as the fulfillment of scripture, which may be the way Luke wants us to see verse 31.

And in setting aside personal considerations, Paul attempts to show that he is himself an imitator of Christ. In the so-called Philippians' hymn (2:6–11), Christ forgoes grasping after equality with God, but rather accepts both lowly human form and obedience to the point of suffering a painful and humiliating public execution. In a day of denominational disunity within the Christian family, the examples of Paul and Christ are worth giving serious attention.

GOSPEL A bright idea, seemingly out of nowhere, or a sudden realization is typically called an "epiphany." The word "epiphany" comes to us directly from Greek *(epiphaneia)* and means "appearance" or "manifestation." But in antiquity, the word often has a technical definition of a god's self-revelation in all his or her divine glory. The Transfiguration of Jesus on the mountain is a Christian instance of a religious phenomenon found throughout the religions of the Greco-Roman world. It is Jesus' revelation of his divine identity to a select group of his disciples.

After Jesus has been transformed, his disciples witness him speaking with Moses and Elijah about his *"exodus."* The Greek word *exodos* is used in the Septuagint, the Greek translation of the Old Testament, to describe the Israelites' journey from Egyptian

While he was still speaking,
a cloud **came** and **cast** a **shadow** over them,
and they became **frightened** when they entered the cloud.
Then from the cloud came a voice that said,
"**This** is my **chosen Son; listen** to him."
After the voice had spoken, **Jesus** was found **alone**.
They fell **silent** and did not at that time
tell **anyone** what they had **seen**.

slavery into freedom. Here it likely refers to Jesus' journey to Jerusalem, which begins in earnest in 9:51 and takes a meandering course through much of the rest of Luke's Gospel. This may be useful information to stress in the Lenten context, since the readings of Lent culminate in Jerusalem during Holy Week, bracketed by Jesus' triumphal entry into Jerusalem on Palm Sunday and his Crucifixion just outside the city walls on Good Friday.

It is important to note that this epiphany of Jesus, the appearances of Moses and Elijah, and the voice from heaven are not enough for the disciples to understand Jesus' true identity as the Son of Man (see 9:44–45).

Peter's offer to make tents for Jesus, Moses, and Elijah is one of the most endearing depictions of the apostle in the Gospels. He simply cannot comprehend the scene before his eyes. Who can blame him?

3RD SUNDAY OF LENT

Lectionary #30

READING I   Exodus 3:1–8a, 13–15

A reading from the Book of Exodus

Moses was tending the flock of his father-in-law **Jethro**,
   the priest of **Midian**.
Leading the flock across the desert, he came to **Horeb**,
   the mountain of **God**.
There an **angel** of the LORD **appeared** to **Moses** in **fire**
   flaming out of a **bush**.
As he looked on, he was **surprised** to see that the **bush**,
   though on fire, was **not** consumed.
So **Moses** decided,
   "I must go over to **look** at this **remarkable sight**,
   and see **why** the **bush** is **not** burned."

When the LORD saw him **coming** over to look at it more closely,
   God called out to him from the bush, "**Moses! Moses!**"
He answered, "**Here** I am."
God said, "Come no nearer!
Remove the sandals from your feet,
   for the place where you stand is **holy** ground.
I am the **God** of your **fathers**," he continued,
   "the God of **Abraham**, the God of **Isaac**, the God of **Jacob**."
Moses hid his face, for he was **afraid** to look at God.
But the LORD said,
   "I have **witnessed** the **affliction** of **my people** in Egypt

Tradition identifies "Horeb" with "Sinai." Exodus was composed by a number of different writers and editors with different names and traditions for the elements of the story.

On the Third, Fourth, and Fifth Sundays of Lent in Years B and C, there are two sets of readings assigned by the Church and therefore two sets in the *Workbook.* If the parish has catechumens and people elected for initiation or full communion at the Easter Vigil, it's likely that you will use the readings from Year A. Check with the person who coordinates the schedule of readers to find out which readings to prepare.

READING I   Other than the spectacle of a bush not consumed by the flames engulfing it, perhaps the most curious feature of this passage is God's reply to Moses' question about God's name. God's answer of "I am who I am" does not initially read like much of an answer at all. Perhaps it is significant that Moses does not respond to the Lord by saying "Well, thank you very much for clearing *that* up."
   In Hebrew, God's proper and personal name is Yahweh. Many Jews consider the name too sacred to pronounce (a practice non-Jews would do well to respect around Jewish friends and associates). The name most likely comes from a form of the Hebrew verb "to be." God's wordplay on his name in his answer to Moses' question may have been intended to signify something about God's own being and life. "I am who I am," "I am he who exists," and "I am the one who endures" are all possible meanings for God's reply. "I am who I am" was

and have **heard** their cry of **complaint** against their
slave drivers,
so I **know well** what they are **suffering**.
Therefore **I have come down** to **rescue** them
from the hands of the Egyptians
and **lead** them out of that land into a **good** and **spacious** land,
a land flowing with **milk** and **honey**."

This refers to Canaan.

Moses said to God, "But when I go to the **Israelites**
and say to them, 'The **God** of your **fathers** has **sent** me to you,'
if they ask me, '**What** is his **name**?' **what** am I to **tell** them?"
God replied, "**I am who am**."
Then he added, "**This** is what you shall **tell** the **Israelites**:
I AM sent **me** to **you**."

God spoke further to **Moses**, "Thus shall you **say**
to the **Israelites**:
The LORD, the God of your **fathers**,
the God of **Abraham**, the God **of Isaac**, the God of **Jacob**,
has **sent me** to **you**.

"This is my name **forever**;
thus am I to be remembered through **all generations**."

READING II   1 Corinthians 10:1–6, 10–12

A reading from the first Letter of Saint Paul to the Corinthians

I do **not** want you to be unaware, **brothers** and **sisters**,
that our ancestors were all under the **cloud**
and all passed through the **sea**,

also the choice of one of the more influential and prolific biblical scholars in history, Origen of Alexandria. Origen, like many intellectuals in the early Church, was influenced by Platonic philosophy. He believed that God was a being who truly and purely existed in such a way that all Creation derived existence by participation this divine life (*On First Principles* I.3). "I am who I am" was a translation that made good philosophical and theological sense to Origen. More modern biblical scholars, such as Frank

Moore Cross, have suggested that the name Yahweh may have originally referred to God's creative power *(I call into being what I call into being; I create what I create)*.

These topics are worth delving into because they are simply too intriguing to ignore. But our searching should not lead us to lose sight of the inscrutability of God's answer to Moses, however we choose to analyze it. Even in the moment of personal disclosure, God remains mystery.

READING II   Today's reading is an example of how the early Church read the Old Testament through the lens of its proclamation about Christ. First Corinthians 8—10 is a quite moving section of the letter. In 1 Corinthians 10:4, Paul refers to a rock in the wilderness that gave the Israelites water as they journeyed through the desert (Exodus 17:1–7; Numbers 20:7–13; Deuteronomy 8:15). And he appears to know a tradition also found in later Jewish writings that the rock was mobile, following the people as they

See Numbers 14 and 16.

Paul firmly believed that Christ's Resurrection meant that God was very soon coming to intervene directly in the world.

and **all** of them were **baptized** into **Moses**
in the **cloud** and in the **sea**.
All **ate** the **same spiritual** food,
and all **drank** the **same spiritual** drink,
for they **drank** from a **spiritual rock** that **followed** them,
and the **rock** was the **Christ**.
Yet God was **not** pleased with **most** of them,
for they were **struck down** in the desert.

These things **happened** as **examples** for **us**,
so that **we** might not **desire** evil things, as **they** did.
Do not **grumble** as some of **them** did,
and **suffered death** by the **destroyer**.
These things **happened** to **them** as an **example**,
and they have been **written down** as a **warning** to **us**,
upon whom the **end** of the **ages** has **come**.
Therefore, whoever **thinks** he is standing **secure**
should **take care** not to **fall**.

GOSPEL Luke 13:1–9

A reading from the holy Gospel according to Luke

Some people told **Jesus** about the **Galileans**
whose **blood Pilate** had mingled with the **blood**
of their **sacrifices**.
Jesus said to them in reply,
"Do you **think** that because these Galileans **suffered**
in this way
they were **greater sinners** than **all other** Galileans?

traveled. "And the rock," Paul adds, "was the Christ." The rock, in other words, is an *allegory*. The true and spiritual significance of the rock lies at a level deeper than what one gets from a plain reading of the text. This deeper level of meaning is that Christ's saving work predates his cross and Resurrection, extending far back into Israel's sacred history.

What is more, Paul sacramentally interprets the cloud that led the Israelites in the wilderness (Exodus 13:21) and the sea through which they escaped from the Egyptian army

(Exodus 14—15). On Paul's reading, these details prefigure the sacrament of Baptism. Similarly, the spiritual food and drink refer to God's gifts of quail and manna to the Israelites (Exodus 16:4–36), as well as the water from the rock. But Paul sees these as more than stories from Israel's past. Their deeper meaning prefigures the Eucharist.

This kind of interpretation, moreover, does not belong solely to the distant past. The Catechism cites 1 Corinthians 10:4 specifically as containing biblical symbolism of the Holy Spirit. Water "welling up from

Christ crucified as its source and welling up in us to eternal life" symbolizes the role of the Holy Spirit in Baptism (Catechism, #694).

GOSPEL The questions Jesus poses in today's Gospel highlight this issue of the relationship between sin and tragedy. The contemporary tragedies Jesus mentions do *not*, he says, mean that the people who suffered them were worse sinners than their neighbors who were

This is often pronounced "Si-LOAM,"
although in Hebrew it is pronounced
"Shi-lo-AM."

By no means!
But I tell **you**, if **you** do not repent,
   you will all **perish** as **they** did!
Or those eighteen people who were **killed**
   when the tower at **Siloam fell** on them—
   do you **think** they were **more** guilty
   than **everyone else** who lived in **Jerusalem**?
By no means!
But I tell **you**, if **you** do not repent,
   you will all **perish** as **they** did!"

And he told them this parable:
   "There once was a person who had a **fig tree** planted
      in his orchard,
   and when he **came** in search of fruit on it but found **none**,
   he said to the gardener,
   'For **three years** now **I have come** in search of **fruit**
      on this fig tree
   but have found **none**.
So **cut** it **down**.
Why should it **exhaust** the **soil**?'
He said to him in reply,
   '**Sir**, **leave** it for this year **also**,
   and I shall **cultivate** the ground around it and **fertilize** it;
   it **may** bear **fruit** in the **future**.
If not you can **cut** it **down**.'"

spared. The point Jesus makes to those bringing him the grisly news of Pilate's outrageous deed is that the effects of sin without repentance are every bit as dangerous. Do not muse so much on the murdered Galileans, Jesus says, but worry rather about the slow suicides of your unrepentant souls.

Lent is a time to call to mind one's own sins and the sins of one's community, society, nation, and Church. It helps no one to ignore that sin risks eternal separation from God. But neither does it help to withhold discussion of the restorative powers of repentance on a contrite soul. The awareness of sin is well and good, but only if that awareness leads to contrition, confession, and (if possible or useful) restitution for harm done. Maturity demands living responsibly and being accountable for what one does and does not do. A mature faith requires nothing less.

Are we to interpret God as the owner of the field and Jesus as the gardener? Maybe this pushes the story too hard. Perhaps its purpose is to tell of God's long forbearance concerning of human sin. In any case, to speak only of God's forbearance leaves the story incomplete. One must also speak of a God who desires relationships with all members of Creation that are unencumbered by any cause for separation.

3RD SUNDAY OF LENT, YEAR A

Lectionary #28

READING I   Exodus 17:3–7

A reading from the Book of Exodus

In those days, in their **thirst** for water,
    the people **grumbled** against **Moses**,
    saying, "**Why** did you ever make us leave **Egypt**?
Was it just to have us **die** here of **thirst**
    with our **children** and our **livestock**?"
So **Moses** cried out to the LORD,
    "**What** shall **I do** with this **people**?
A little **more** and they will **stone** me!"
The LORD answered **Moses**,
    "Go over there in **front** of the **people**,
    along with **some** of the **elders** of **Israel**,
    holding in your **hand**, as you go,
    the **staff** with which you **struck** the river.
I will be **standing** there in **front** of you on the **rock** in **Horeb**.
Strike the rock, and the **water** will **flow** from it
    for the **people** to **drink**."
This **Moses** did, in the presence of the **elders** of **Israel**.
The place was called **Massah** and **Meribah**,
    because the **Israelites quarreled** there
    and **tested** the LORD, saying,
    "**Is** the LORD in our midst or **not**?"

Massah means "testing" and *Meribah* means "contention." The explanation of the name of a place by the nature of events happening there is common enough in the Old Testament. See, for example, Genesis 32:23–31.

READING I   The gift of water at Massah ("testing") and Meribah ("contention") has gripped the imaginations of more than one biblical writer. This is, one might say, a text with legs.

In Psalm 95, which is a traditional selection at the beginning of morning prayers in the Liturgy of the Hours, the events at Meribah and Massah provide a paradigmatic example of Israel's hard-hearted grumbling.

In the book of Wisdom (11:1–14), the author, writing in the persona of King Solomon, uses the rhetorical device of comparison (*synkrisis* in Greek) to contrast the first of the plagues on Egypt with the water God (through Moses) causes to flow from the rock. The Egyptians were punished by God's turning the Nile to blood (Exodus 7:14–24), while the Israelites were saved by the miraculous provision of water. "For by the things through which their foes were punished they in their need were benefited" (Wisdom 11:5). The Israelites learn, the author says, from God's gentle punishment of themselves in contrast to the harsh punishment of their enemies. Exactly what the Israelites learn is not clear, but the author sees Israel's role in the story in a much more favorable light than does the psalmist.

Note the linkage of faith, peace, grace, and hope. These are not independent aspects of a justified life as Paul sees it, but intimately related and interdependent aspects.

READING II Romans 5:1–2, 5–8

A reading from the Letter of Saint Paul to the Romans

Brothers and **sisters**:

Since we have been **justified** by faith,
  we have **peace** with **God** through our **Lord** Jesus Christ,
  through whom we have gained access by **faith**
  to this **grace** in which we stand,
  and we boast in **hope** of the **glory** of God.

And **hope** does not **disappoint**,
  because the **love** of **God** has been **poured** out into our **hearts**
  through the **Holy Spirit** who has been **given** to us.
For **Christ**, while we were **still helpless**,
  died at the appointed time for the **ungodly**.
Indeed, only with **difficulty** does one **die** for a **just** person,
  though **perhaps** for a **good** person one might **even**
    find **courage** to **die**.
But **God** proves his **love** for us
  in that while we were **still sinners** Christ **died** for us.

Paul, in 1 Corinthians 10, interprets the story of Massah and Meribah allegorically. "The rock," he says, "was the Christ." Paul intends this and other interpretations of Israel's sacred history in 1 Corinthians to support an ethical argument that spans chapters 8 through 10, which in turn supports his letter's primary aim of urging the divided Church at Corinth to reunify. In Paul's opinion, the events in the wilderness, including Massah and Meribah, happened "as an example" (Greek, *tupikōs*) to the Church.

A similar story is found in Numbers 20:1–13. It may be helpful to compare today's reading with it.

READING II There is a very ancient Greek manuscript tradition (many biblical scholars would maintain that it is the best and most reliable of the available Greek manuscript traditions) containing a slightly different reading of Romans 5:1

than the one preserved in the Greek texts used by the translators who prepared the RNAB. This different reading may be translated as follows: "Since we have been justified by faith, *let us* have peace with God through our Lord Jesus Christ." A single letter changes a statement of fact into an exhortation. What a difference that one letter makes!

What is at stake is how people come to live in peace with God. Does God put an end

GOSPEL   John 4:5–42

A reading from the holy Gospel according to John

Jesus came to a town of **Samaria** called **Sychar**,
    near the plot of land that **Jacob** had given to his son **Joseph**.
Jacob's **well** was there.
Jesus, tired from his journey, sat down there at the well.
It was about **noon**.

A **woman** of **Samaria** came to **draw** water.
Jesus said to her,
    "**Give** me a **drink**."
His disciples had gone into the town to buy food.
The **Samaritan** woman said to him,
    "**How** can **you**, a **Jew**, ask **me**, a **Samaritan woman**,
        for a **drink**?"
—For **Jews** use **nothing** in common with **Samaritans**.—
Jesus answered and said to her,
    "If **you** knew the **gift** of God
    and **who** is saying to you, '**Give** me a **drink**,'
    you would have **asked** him
    and he would have **given** you **living water**."
The woman said to him,
    "**Sir**, you do not even have a **bucket** and the **cistern** is **deep**;
    where then can you get this **living water**?
Are you **greater** than our father **Jacob**,
    who gave us this **cistern** and **drank** from it himself
    with his **children** and his **flocks**?"

See Genesis 33:18–19; 48:22 and Joshua 24:32.

Vary your delivery for each speaker. This is a conversation and ought to sound like one.

to a person's hostility by justifying that person? Or is the person, once justified, the one to declare the truce? If the human role in justification seems unimportant, keep in mind that Catholics and Protestants have vigorously debated the issue for centuries.

The Roman Catholic Church teaches that justification is God's free gift of cleansing from sin, which occurs through the believer's faith in Jesus Christ (Catechism, #1987). Justification, which is preceded by

forgiveness, "reconciles man with God" (Catechism, #1990). But the Roman Catholic Church also teaches that "justification establishes *cooperation between God's grace and man's freedom*" (Catechism, #1993).

The human responsibility to cooperate with God is a distinctive feature of Roman Catholicism. We are free to refuse God's overtures and advances. But the witness of scripture, the guidance of the rule of faith, and the help and examples provided by our brothers and sisters in Christ all aim toward

the formation of men and women willing to enter into peaceful relationship with God.

GOSPEL   Samaria sat between Judea in the south and Galilee in the north. Our Bible states what is also clear from the Greek text, that Jesus "had to pass through Samaria" on his way north to Galilee (4:4). There were other ways to get to Galilee from Judea, but Samaria provided a fairly direct route.

Jesus answered and said to her,
"**Everyone** who **drinks** this **water** will be **thirsty** again;
but **whoever drinks** the **water** I shall give will **never** thirst;
the water I shall **give** will become in him
a **spring** of water **welling up** to eternal **life**."
The woman said to him,
"Sir, **give** me this water, so that I may **not** be **thirsty**
or have to keep coming here to **draw** water."

Jesus said to her,
"**Go** call your **husband** and come **back**."
The woman answered and said to him,
"I do **not** have a **husband**."
Jesus answered her,
"You are **right** in saying, 'I do **not** have a **husband**.'
For you have had **five** husbands,
and the **one** you have now is **not** your husband.
What you have said is **true**."
The woman said to him,
"**Sir**, I can **see** that you are a **prophet**.
Our ancestors worshiped on **this mountain**;
but you people say that the place to worship is in **Jerusalem**."
Jesus said to her,
"**Believe** me, woman, the hour is coming
when you will **worship** the Father
neither on this mountain **nor** in Jerusalem.
You people **worship** what you do **not** understand;
we **worship** what we **understand**,
because **salvation** is from the **Jews**.

Here the conversation partners refer to religious differences that account in part for the difficulty of Jewish and Samaritan relationships.

The Samaritan woman's surprise that a Jewish man has asked her for a drink of water (4:9) and her mention of specific religious differences between Jews and Samaritans (4:20) testifies to the strained relationship Samaritans and Jews shared in Jesus' day. In Luke's parable of the Good Samaritan, Jesus relies upon this difficult relationship to redefine what it means to be a neighbor to someone (Luke 10:25–37).

The response of faith by the Samaritans to Jesus in John 4:39–42 presents them in a favorable light. Perhaps the evangelist included this detail in order to show Jesus' appeal among a people marginalized and despised by "the Jews," who are Jesus' main opponents in John's Gospel. Then there are also the fascinating verses of John 8:48–49. In them some Jews suggest that Jesus is both a Samaritan and possessed by a demon. Jesus answers the charge that he is a demon, but lets pass the charge that he is a Samaritan.

One way to sustain your listeners' interest throughout this long reading is to deliver the part of each speaker in a distinct emotional register and tone appropriate to each. It may help to ask oneself a few questions about the Samaritan woman. How surprised or shocked is she by Jesus' initial request for a drink of water? How should your reading reflect her specific questions, replies, and requests? One may ask similar questions about Jesus, who does not dispel the Samaritan woman's confusion about "living water." Is he having his own fun in this conversation full of double entendres? Is he, perhaps, even teasing her a little?

But the **hour** is **coming**, and is now **here**,
    when true worshipers will **worship** the Father
        in **Spirit** and **truth**;
    and indeed the Father **seeks** such people to worship him.
God is **Spirit**, and those who worship him
    must worship in **Spirit** and truth."
The woman said to him,
    "I **know** that the Messiah is coming, the one called the Christ;
    when he **comes**, he will **tell** us **everything**."
Jesus said to her,
    "I am **he**, the one **speaking** with you."

At that moment his disciples returned,
    and were **amazed** that he was talking with a woman,
    but still no one said, "What are you looking for?"
    or "**Why** are you talking with **her**?"
The woman left her water jar
    and went into the town and said to the people,
    "**Come** see a man who told me **everything** I have done.
Could he **possibly** be the **Christ**?"
They went out of the town and came to him.
Meanwhile, the disciples urged him, "Rabbi, **eat**."
But he said to them,
    "I have **food** to **eat** of which you do **not** know."
So the disciples said to one another,
    "Could someone have **brought** him something to **eat**?"
Jesus said to them,
    "My **food** is to **do** the will of the **one** who **sent** me
    and to **finish** his work.
Do you not say, 'In four months the harvest will be here'?
I tell you, look up and see the fields ripe for the harvest.

At several points in John's Gospel, Jesus uses "I am" to reveal that his own identity and that of God (see Exodus 3:13–14). While the phrase can simply mean "I am he," as in answer to woman's question, Jesus' disclosure of his unity with God is likely at issue (see also 18:5–8). For clear examples of Jesus' use of "I am" in identification with the name of God, see John 8:24, 28, 58, 13:19.

The **reaper** is already receiving payment
   and gathering crops for **eternal life**,
   so that the **sower** and **reaper** can rejoice **together**.
For here the saying is verified that 'One **sows** and another **reaps**.'
I sent you to **rea**p what you have **not** worked for;
   others have done the work,
   and you are **sharing** the fruits of **their** work."

Many of the **Samaritans** of that town began to **believe** in him
   because of the **word** of the woman who **testified**,
   "He told me **everything** I have **done**."
When the Samaritans came to him,
   they **invited** him to **stay** with them;
   and he **stayed** there two days.
Many more began to **believe** in him because of his **word**,
   and they said to the woman,
   "We no longer **believe** because of **your** word;
   for we have **heard** for **ourselves**,
   and **we** know that this is **truly** the savior of the **world**."

[Shorter: John 4:5–15, 19b–26, 39a, 40–42]

4TH SUNDAY OF LENT

Lectionary #33

READING I   Joshua 5:9a, 10–12

A reading from the Book of Joshua

The LORD said to Joshua,
    "Today I have **removed** the **reproach** of Egypt from you."

While the **Israelites** were encamped at **Gilgal** on the plains
        of **Jericho**,
    they celebrated the **Passover**
    on the evening of the fourteenth of the month.
On the day after the **Passover**,
    they **ate** of the produce of the land
    in the form of unleavened **cakes** and parched **grain**.
On that same day after the **Passover**,
    on which they ate of the produce of the land, the **manna** ceased.
No longer was there **manna** for the **Israelites**,
    who that year ate of the yield of the land of **Canaan**.

Gilgal = Gil-GAL

See Exodus 16:4–36.

READING II   2 Corinthians 5:17–21

A reading from the second Letter of Saint Paul to the Corinthians

Brothers and **sisters**:
Whoever is in **Christ** is a **new** creation:
    the **old** things have **passed** away;
    behold, **new** things have **come**.

On the Third, Fourth, and Fifth Sundays of Lent in Years B and C, there are two sets of readings assigned by the Church and therefore two sets in the *Workbook*. If the parish has catechumens and people elected for initiation or full communion at the Easter Vigil, it's likely that you will use the readings from Year A. Check with the person who coordinates the schedule of readers to find out which readings to prepare.

READING I   The book of Joshua is the first of a series of books biblical scholars typically call the deuteronomistic history (see commentary, February 18). Today's reading places us at the beginning of this history. The Israelites are camped east of Jericho, having just crossed the Jordan River (see Joshua 3:14—4:18). They have barely entered the land scripture records God promised their ancestors. Israel has no king, nor is there any kingdom of Israel. The people are ruled by Moses' successor, Joshua. And Canaan still belongs to

the different nations, tribes, and peoples with whom Israel will live in peace and in war for centuries to come. Israel, poised at the border of the land, stands on the edge of a decisive moment.

The first verse quotes God directly. For this reason, you should consider how to deliver these words in a manner that calls due attention to them.

The "reproach" that God has removed is the Israelites' enslavement by Egypt. In the immediately preceding verses, the men

Paul's vocabulary of reconciliation in this section is composed of a verb *(katallassō)* and its related noun *(katallassē)*. Pay careful attention, in your study and when you read, to the strong emphasis Paul gives to the theme of reconciliation in this portion of the letter.

And **all** this is from **God**,
    who has **reconciled** us to himself through Christ
    and given us the ministry of **reconciliation**,
    namely, God was **reconciling** the world to himself in Christ,
    not counting their trespasses against them
    and entrusting to us the message of **reconciliation**.
So **we** are ambassadors for **Christ**,
    as if God were **appealing** through **us**.
We **implore** you on behalf of **Christ**,
    be **reconciled** to God.
For our sake he made him to be **sin** who did **not** know sin,
    so that **we** might become the **righteousness** of God in **him**.

GOSPEL   Luke 15:1–3, 11–32

A reading from the holy Gospel according to Luke

This is the sneering complaint Jesus answers with the story of the prodigal son.

Tax collectors and **sinners** were all drawing near to **listen** to Jesus,
    but the **Pharisees** and **scribes** began to **complain**, saying,
    "This man **welcomes** sinners and **eats** with them."
So to them Jesus addressed this parable:

A good reading of this parable will take note of the emotional register of the characters in it.

"A man had **two** sons, and the **younger** son said to his father,
    '**Father** give me the share of your estate that should come
        to me.'
So the father **divided** the property between them.
After a few days, the younger son **collected** all his belongings
    and **set off** to a distant country
    where he **squandered** his inheritance on a life of **dissipation**.

are circumcised and through this rite newly consecrated to God. Now they celebrate the Passover. Passover, the feast of unleavened bread, is the most important of the annual festivals in the Old Testament, and it remains so for modern Jews. The reading also informs us that on the day after the Israelites' celebrated this Passover, manna ceased feeding the people. Manna was bread provided by God to Israel in the course of its wanderings in the wilderness (see Exodus 16). The end of the manna means that Israel's total dependence on God for physical sustenance is

also at an end. The land Israel is about to take is fertile and good.

Those who observe Lent may be feeling, by the season's Fourth Sunday, that they are more than ready to leave behind the wilderness of their discipline and privations for the festive season of Easter. By the Fourth Sunday the Church is poised to enter into the season of Easter. But the time is not yet.

READING II Paul's second letter to the Church of Corinth is probably a collection of fragments of several let-

ters (perhaps as many as five) Paul wrote to that community. This section of 2 Corinthians likely comes from the earliest of these fragments, which spans 2:14—6:13; 7:2–4. The letter is a response to the Corinthians who have questioned and criticized Paul's ministry in part because he, unlike certain Christian missionaries lately arrived in Corinth, never showed them any letters of recommendation (see especially 2 Corinthians 3:1–3).

Paul's relationship with this community was difficult, partly because the cosmopolitan Corinthians kept him busy with hard

When he had freely spent **everything**,
  a severe **famine** struck that country,
  and he found himself in dire **need**.
So he **hired** himself out to one of the local citizens
  who **sent** him to his farm to **tend** the **swine**.
And he **longed** to eat his fill of the pods on which the swine fed,
  but **nobody** gave him any.
Coming to his **senses** he thought,
  'How many of my father's hired workers
  have **more** than enough food to eat,
  but here am **I**, **dying** from hunger.
I shall **get up** and **go** to my father and I shall **say** to him,
  "**Father**, I have **sinned** against **heaven** and against **you**.
I no longer **deserve** to be called your **son**;
  treat me as **you** would **treat** one of your **hired** workers."'
So he **got** up and **went** back to his **father**.
While he was still a long way off,
  his **father** caught **sight** of him, and was filled with **compassion**.
He ran to his son, **embraced** him and **kissed** him.
His **son** said to **him**,
  '**Father**, I have **sinned** against **heaven** and against **you**;
  I no longer **deserve** to be called your **son**.'
But his **father** ordered his servants,
  '**Quickly** bring the **finest** robe and put it on him;
  put a **ring** on his finger and **sandals** on his feet.
Take the **fattened** calf and **slaughter** it.
Then let us **celebrate** with a feast,
  because this **son** of mine was **dead**, and has come to life again;
  he was **lost**, and has been **found**.'
Then the **celebration** began.

Is the son genuinely repentant or shrewdly calculating? More importantly, does it matter?

questions. A principle subject of this section of 2 Corinthians, as we read today, is reconciliation. It is not merely the reconciliation of believers with God, but the reconciliation of the Corinthians with their once-beloved leader and friend. Paul's authority has been questioned, relations are strained, and Paul is seeking to improve the situation on his own terms.

Catholics celebrate the sacrament of Reconciliation when (not if!) we have chosen to remove ourselves from God's care, come to regret our decision, repented of what we've done, and want to reconcile with God. This sacrament is a cornerstone of our Lenten journey. Lent anticipates Easter, but it is also a time to call to mind the ways in which our decisions to sin have set us against God and one another. Notice how many times Paul repeats the word "reconciliation" in this passage. Take care to emphasize this word so that listeners' attentions are drawn to it. At the very least, don't let it become a drone. Paul wanted to be clear that the Corinthians' reconciliation with God, with himself, and with each other was very important. His Church is divided.

It is up to you to make Paul's point to your own people.

GOSPEL Rembrandt's famous painting of the return of the prodigal son shows the young man on his knees, eyes closed, while his father hugs him close. Few images in Western art convey so perfectly the emotional dimension of reconciliation. Perhaps you can find this popular image online or in a book and meditate on it before proclaiming this text.

Now the **older** son had been out in the field
and, on his way back, as he neared the house,
he heard the sound of **music** and **dancing**.
He **called** one of the servants and **asked** what this might mean.
The servant said to him,
'Your **brother** has returned
and your **father** has **slaughtered** the **fattened** calf
because he has him back **safe** and **sound**.'
He became **angry**,
and when he **refused** to enter the house,
his father came out and **pleaded** with him.
He said to his father in reply,
'Look, all these years I **serve**d you
and not once did I **disobey** your orders;
yet you **never** gave me even a young goat
to feast on with my **friends**.
But when your **son** returns
who **swallowed** up your **property** with **prostitutes**,
for him you **slaughter** the **fattened** calf.'
He said to him,
'My **son**, you are here with me **always**;
everything I have is **yours**.
But now we must **celebrate** and **rejoice**,
because your brother was **dead** and has come to **life** again;
he was **lost** and has been **found**.'"

The story Jesus tells has three main characters: two sons and a father. Give each character their due. Will the younger son sound the same when he first asks his father for his inheritance and later when, far down on his luck, he plans to present himself to his father as a slave? Will the father sound the same when he excitedly prepares for his lost son's return and when he lovingly responds to his angry older son?

The older brother makes a good case for himself. He *has* worked hard (and perhaps didn't always want to). He has *never* disobeyed an order (and maybe now wishes he had). Who wouldn't be furious? Take care to emphasize his angry objection when you proclaim this reading. It's the kind of objection many regular churchgoers can probably identify with. It is also important to emphasize the older brother's words because the Father's answer to his objection is also Jesus' answer to the Pharisees, to the scribes, and to everyone who thinks and acts as if God's love and favor should be a matter of self-justification—in a word, to all of us. This Gospel reading tells us that reconciliation with God is not anyone's to deny—but tax collectors? These people were hated collaborators with Rome, men who took what little their neighbors had, kicked some up to their bosses, and kept a hefty cut for themselves. Jesus is telling us that there is love and mercy for one of his society's most despicable and hated classes of people. Reconciliation with God must lie beyond all earthly notions of just reward and punishment if even tax collectors can know it.

There is apparently no human constraint upon the mercy and love of God.

4TH SUNDAY OF LENT, YEAR A

Lectionary #31

READING I   1 Samuel 16:1b, 6–7, 10–13a

A reading from the first Book of Samuel

The LORD said to **Samuel**:
  "Fill your horn with **oil**, and be on your way.
I am sending you to **Jesse** of **Bethlehem**,
  for I have chosen my **king** from among his **sons**."

As **Jesse** and his **sons** came to the **sacrifice**,
  Samuel looked at **Eliab** and thought,
  "**Surely** the LORD's **anointed** is here before him."
But the LORD said to **Samuel**:
  "Do not **judge** from his **appearance** or from his **lofty stature**,
  because I have **rejected** him.
Not as **man** sees does **God** see,
  because **man** sees the **appearance**
  but the LORD looks into the **heart**."
In the same way **Jesse** presented seven sons before **Samuel**,
  but **Samuel** said to **Jesse**,
  "The LORD has not chosen **any** one of these."
Then **Samuel** asked **Jesse**,
  "Are these **all** the sons you have?"
Jesse replied,
  "There is still the **youngest**, who is tending the sheep."
Samuel said to **Jesse**,
  "**Send** for him;
  we will **not** begin the **sacrificial banquet** until he **arrives** here."

Eliab = El-ee-ab

Compare Romans 8:26–27.

READING I   The historical circumstances of the rise of monarchy in Israel likely had much to do with the growing military threat posed by the Philistines. Prior to Saul, dynastic monarchy was apparently foreign to Israel. One can detect several different views on monarchy in 1 Samuel. When the Israelites first demand a king, Samuel, who has exercised religious and political rule in the land for some time, grows upset. But God says, "Grant the people's every request. It is not you they reject, it is me they are rejecting as their king" (1 Samuel 8:7). One also encounters a positive perspective on the monarchy's rise (see, for example, 1 Samuel 9:15–16). This ambivalence is perhaps the result of several different accounts having been combined into the book we know today as 1 Samuel.

David, despite a "splendid appearance," apparently did not seem much like king material to his father. There must be at least one candidate, Samuel thinks, among the strapping sons Jesse lines up for inspection. "Not as man sees does God see," the Lord informs him, "because man sees the appearance, but the Lord looks into the heart." People appreciate exteriors, while God searches the inner person.

Jesse **sent** and **had** the young man **brought** to them.
He was **ruddy**, a youth **handsome** to **behold**
      and making a splendid **appearance**.
The LORD said,
      "There—**anoint** him, for this is the **one**!"
Then **Samuel**, with the horn of **oil** in hand,
      anointed David in the presence of his **brothers**;
      and from that day on, the **spirit** of the LORD
            rushed upon **David**.

READING II   Ephesians 5:8–14

A reading from the Letter of Saint Paul to the Ephesians

Brothers and **sisters**:
You were once **darkness**,
      but now you are **light** in the Lord.
Live as **children** of **light**,
      for **light** produces every kind of **goodness**
      and **righteousness** and **truth**.
Try to **learn** what is **pleasing** to the **Lord**.
Take no part in the **fruitless** works of **darkness**;
      rather **expose** them, for it is **shameful** even to mention
      the things done by them in **secret**;
      but everything **exposed** by the **light** becomes **visible**,
      for **everything** that becomes **visible** is **light**.
Therefore, it says:
      "**Awake**, O **sleeper**,
      and **arise** from the **dead**,
      and **Christ** will give you **light**."

This is early Christian hymnic material, perhaps from a baptismal context.

It is clichéd to say that God knows us better than we know ourselves. But this fact makes the statement no less true. And it is not necessarily comforting. Who among us has not tried to lock away some secret portion of ourselves? Our reception of the sacrament of Reconciliation, which is part of the journey of Lent, provides God with no new information. But there is relief in scuttling the charade that certain regions of us remain hidden from God's attention.

READING II "You were once darkness, but now you are light in the Lord." The author is writing to Gentiles who, as was typical in the first century, were baptized in adulthood. There is no middle ground for this author between what the Ephesians were before and after their incorporation into Christ. Back then they did not just live in darkness; they *were* darkness.

This author has a very low view of Gentile life and culture in his day. "You must no longer live as the Gentiles do," he urges, "in the futility of their minds; darkened in understanding, alienated from the life of God because of their ignorance, because of their hardness of heart" (4:17–18). The author does not mean that non-Christian Gentiles are stupid or incapable of reason, but that their minds are not properly oriented. Certain

GOSPEL   John 9:1–41

A reading from the holy Gospel according to John

As **Jesus** passed by he saw a man **blind** from **birth**.
His **disciples** asked him,
  "**Rabbi**, who **sinned**, this **man** or his **parents**,
  that he was born **blind**?"
Jesus answered,
  "**Neither he nor** his **parents** sinned;
  it is so that the **works** of **God** might be made **visible**
    through him.
We have to do the **works** of the one who **sent** me while it is **day**.
Night is coming when **no** one can **work**.
While I am **in** the **world**, I am the **light** of the **world**."
When he had said this, he **spat** on the ground
  and made **clay** with the **saliva**,
  and **smeared** the **clay** on his **eyes**, and said to him,

  "Go **wash** in the **Pool** of **Siloam**"—which means **Sent**—.
So he **went** and **washed**, and came back able to **see**.

His **neighbors** and those who had **seen** him earlier
    as a **beggar said**,
  "Isn't this the **one** who **used** to **sit** and **beg**?"
Some said, "**It is**,"
  but others said, "**No**, he just looks like him."
He said, "**I am**."
So they said to him, "**How** were your eyes **opened**?"
He replied,
  "The **man** called **Jesus** made **clay** and **anointed** my eyes
  and told me, '**Go** to **Siloam** and **wash**.'
So I **went** there and **washed** and was able to **see**."

It is significant that night falls immediately after Judas leaves to betray Jesus (13:30). Night also likely symbolizes the ignorance of Nicodemus, well meaning though he is (3:2; 19:39).

Compare Mark 8:22–26.

Notice how the neighbors have trouble "seeing" the man. Although he is familiar to them, they cannot agree on whether or not he is the blind beggar they remember from the pool precincts.

terms in ensuing verses suggest that our author is thinking mainly of sexual behavior. Both "licentiousness" (in Greek, *aselgeia*) and "uncleanness" (in Greek, *akatharsia*) in 4:19 have primarily this connotation.

Can non-Christian Gentiles have been as awful as this? This world and time produced some outstanding non-Christian moral philosophers. Epictetus and Seneca are but two of many more. And can Christians have been so good? For all his talk of Christians and light, our author still must encourage his readers to stay away from all kinds of vice in 5:3–5. While it is not unusual for people who have adopted new ways of thought and behavior to imagine the new self in stark contrast to the rest of the world, and to describe life in dramatic terms of before and after, the truth is usually a good bit blurrier.

GOSPEL   The skeleton of this Gospel selection is a story of a healing miracle found also in Mark 8:22–26. Like John, Mark writes that Jesus spits and uses his saliva to restore a person's sight (in Greek, *ptuō*). In Mark, the purpose of the healing is to restore a man to sight. In John, it is to demonstrate God's power (John 9:3). The healing becomes a controversy between

And they said to him, "**Where** is he?"
He said, "I don't **know**."

They brought the one who was once **blind** to the **Pharisees**.
Now **Jesus** had made **clay** and opened his **eyes** on a **sabbath**.
So then the **Pharisees** also asked him how he was able to **see**.
He said to them,
   "He put **clay** on my **eyes**, and I **washed**, and now I can **see**."
So some of the **Pharisees** said,
   "This man is **not** from God,
   because he does not **keep** the **sabbath**."
But others said,
   "How can a **sinful** man do such **signs**?"
And there was a **division** among them.
So they said to the **blind** man **again**,
   "What do you have to **say** about him,
   since he **opened** your eyes?"
He said, "He is a **prophet**."

Now the **Jews** did not **believe**
   that he had been **blind** and **gained** his sight
   until they summoned the **parents** of the one
      who had **gained** his sight.
They asked them,
   "Is this your **son**, who you say was born **blind**?
How does he now **see**?"
His **parents** answered and said,
   "We **know** that this is our **son** and that he was born **blind**.
We do **not** know how he **sees** now,
   nor do we **know** who **opened** his eyes.
Ask him, he is of **age**;
   he can **speak** for himself."

the man born blind and his community, with sight and blindness, light and darkness, serving as metaphors for belief and disbelief in Jesus.

The man's testimony ends in his rejection by neighbors, family, and religious leaders, leaving him, at last, utterly alone. Some biblical scholars have contended that John's story is a symbolic retelling of the history of his Church. They hypothesize that John reworked a traditional story to reflect his community's traumatic experience in response to its testimony about Jesus.

Biblical scholar Father Raymond Brown notes the modesty and humility of the man born blind in contrast to his interrogators. The interrogators make several strident claims about Jesus, but do so in ignorance (9:16, 24, 29). The man admits his ignorance, yet holds fast to the truth of what Jesus did for him (9:12, 25, 36).

As of this writing, archaeologists in Jerusalem claim to have found the first-century remains of the pool of Siloam. The Gihon spring, which still flows from the base of

the ridge on which the most ancient part of Jerusalem was built, fills a different pool today. It is a source of drinking water, though of poor quality, for impoverished Arabs who live nearby. Foreign tourists in Israel often miss the residents' poverty in their zeal to view the site.

Blindness comes in many forms.

His **parents** said this because they were **afraid**
    of the Jews, for the **Jews** had already **agreed**
    that if anyone acknowledged him as the **Christ**,
    he would be **expelled** from the **synagogue**.
For this reason his **parents** said,
    "He is of **age**; **question** him."

So a second time they called the man who had been **blind**
    and said to him, "**Give** God the **praise**!
We **know** that this man is a **sinner**."
He replied,
    "If he is a **sinner**, I do not **know**.
One thing I **do** know is that I was **blind** and now I **see**."
So they said to him,
    "What did he **do** to you?
    How did he **open** your eyes?"
He answered them,
    "I **told** you already and you did **not** listen.
Why do you want to **hear it again**?
Do you **want** to become his disciples, too?"
They ridiculed him and said,
    "**You** are that **man's** disciple;
    we are disciples of **Moses**!
We **know** that **God** spoke to **Moses**,
    but **we** do not know **where** this one is **from**."
The man **answered** and said to them,
    "This is what is so **amazing**,
    that you do not **know** where he is from,
        yet he **opened** my eyes.
We **know** that God does not **listen** to **sinners**,
    but if one is **devout** and does his **will**, he listens to him.

It is **unheard** of that **anyone** ever **opened** the eyes
    of a person born **blind**.
If this man were **not** from **God**,
  he would **not** be **able** to do **anything**."
They **answered** and said to him,
  "You were **born** totally in **sin**,
  and are you trying to teach us?"
Then they **threw** him out.

When **Jesus** heard that they had **thrown** him out,
  he **found** him and **said**, "Do you **believe** in the **Son** of **Man**?"
He **answered** and said,
  "**Who** is he, sir, that I may **believe** in him?"
Jesus said to him,
  "You have **seen** him,
  the one **speaking** with you is **he**."
He said,
  "I do **believe**, Lord," and he **worshiped** him.
Then **Jesus** said,
  "I came into this **world** for **judgment**,
  so that those who do **not** see might **see**,
  and those who do **see** might become **blind**."

Some of the **Pharisees** who were with him heard this
  and said to him, "**Surely** we are **not** also **blind**, are we?"
Jesus said to them,
  "**If** you were **blind**, you would have no **sin**;
  but **now** you are **saying**, 'We **see**,' so your **sin** remains."

[Shorter: John 9:1, 6–9, 13–17, 34–38]

In this exchange between Jesus and the man born blind it is especially clear that sight and belief are the same thing. Note also how Jesus goes unseen by everyone except the man born blind until this point.

See how the Pharisees themselves are aware of the meaning of sight and belief, blindness and disbelief.

5TH SUNDAY OF LENT

Lectionary #36

READING I   Isaiah 43:16–21

A reading from the Book of the Prophet Isaiah

Here is God's self-description as the victorious warrior of the Exodus.

Thus says the LORD,
    who opens a **way** in the **sea**
    and a **path** in the mighty **waters**,
who **leads** out **chariots** and **horsemen**,
    a **powerful** army,
till they lie **prostrate** together, **never** to rise,
    snuffed out and **quenched** like a wick.
Remember **not** the events of the **past**,
    the things of **long ago** consider **not**;
see, I am doing something **new**!
    Now it springs forth, do you not **perceive** it?
In the **desert** I make a **way**;
    in the **wasteland**, **rivers**.
Wild beasts **honor** me,
    jackals and **ostriches**,
for I put **water** in the **desert**
    and **rivers** in the **wasteland**
    for my **chosen** people to **drink**,
the people whom I **formed** for **myself**,
    that they might **announce** my **praise**.

The end of the exile and the people's return to their home is here conceived as a new Exodus.

On the Third, Fourth, and Fifth Sundays of Lent in Years B and C, there are two sets of readings assigned by the Church and therefore two sets in the *Workbook.* If the parish has catechumens and people elected for initiation or full communion at the Easter Vigil, it's likely that you will use the readings from Year A. Check with the person who coordinates the schedule of readers to find out which readings to prepare.

READING I   In 586 BC, armies of the Babylonian Empire overran the kingdom of Judah. Jerusalem and its Temple were looted and destroyed. Thousands of Jews were deported from Judah to Babylon in the so-called "Babylonian Exile" (see Jeremiah 39 and 52; 2 Kings 25). This passage from Isaiah comes from a portion of the book (chapters 40 to 55) many biblical scholars believe was composed in joyful response to the opposition and overthrow of Babylon by Cyrus of Persia later in the sixth century before Christ.

The reading opens with the typical prophetic formula, "Thus says the Lord," which authenticates the divine origin of the message to follow. Verses 16 and 17 introduce God as the victor of the Exodus, the one who destroyed the Egyptian army as it pursued Israel (Exodus 14:10—15:10). But even as God introduces himself as the victorious divine warrior of earlier days, "events of the past" and "the things of long ago" are not on the agenda (Isaiah 43:18–19).

The word translated here as "rubbish" *(skubala)* typically means "excrement."

This is athletic terminology of Greek civic games. For other examples of athletic language and images in Paul's letters, see Philippians 2:16; 1 Corinthians 9:24–27; and 2 Corinthians 4:8–9.

READING II   Philippians 3:8–14

A reading from the Letter of Saint Paul to the Philippians

Brothers and **sisters**:
I consider **everything** as a **loss**
    because of the supreme good of knowing **Christ Jesus** my Lord.
For his sake I have **accepted** the loss of all things
    and I **consider** them so much **rubbish**,
    that I may **gain** Christ and be **found** in him,
    not having any **righteousness** of my own based on the **law**
    but that which comes through **faith** in **Christ**,
    the **righteousness** from **God**,
    depending on **faith** to **know** him and the **power**
        of his **resurrection**
    and the sharing of his **sufferings** by being **conformed**
        to his **death**,
    if somehow I may **attain** the **resurrection** from the **dead**.

It is **not** that I have already taken **hold** of it
    or have already attained **perfect** maturity,
    but I **continue** my pursuit in **hope** that I may **possess** it,
    since I have indeed **been** taken **possession of** by **Christ Jesus**.
Brothers and **sisters**, I for my part
    do not consider myself to have taken **possession**.
Just one thing: **forgetting** what lies **behind**
    but **straining** forward to what lies **ahead**,
    I **continue** my pursuit toward the **goal**,
    the **prize** of God's upward calling, in **Christ Jesus**.

God's new deed, according to the prophet, is a new Exodus. As God once vanquished the Egyptians and led Israel out of captivity, so now does God lead Israel out of Babylonian captivity. And as water was provided in the desert during the former Exodus (Exodus 17:1–7; Numbers 20:1–13), so now is it provided in the new one.

It is a pleasing image, the desert animals honoring God for bringing water to an arid land. But make no mistake: this text is deeply political. God wars against Babylon as God once warred against Egypt. Indeed, the prophet goes so far as to call Cyrus, the king of Persia, God's "anointed" (Isaiah 45:1). Cyrus is the only foreign monarch to bear this designation in the Old Testament. If God's new Exodus celebrates water in the desert, it also celebrates the advent of Israel's new imperial master.

READING II Philippians is a letter written from prison (Philippians 1:7, 13–14). Paul faces the real possibility of death (1:18–24). Roman prisons were not penal institutions in which convicts served sentences. They were holding pens pending punishment, which was often torture, execution, or both. For early Christians in the Roman Empire, the credible threat of violence was never too far away.

The Philippian Church had recently endured strain, perhaps due to the quarrel between Euodia and Syntyche (4:2–3), although perhaps more directly related to the presence in Philippi of people Paul perceives as opponents (1:15–17, 27–28; 3:2, 18–19). The letter is on balance a warm one,

GOSPEL   John 8:1–11

A reading from the holy Gospel according to John

Jesus went to the **Mount** of **Olives**.
But early in the morning he arrived again in the **temple** area,
    and all the people started coming to him,
    and he **sat** down and **taught** them.
Then the **scribes** and the **Pharisees** brought a **woman**
    who had been **caught** in **adultery**
    and made her **stand** in the middle.
They said to him,
    "**Teacher**, this **woman** was **caught**
    in the very act of committing **adultery**.
Now in the **law**, **Moses** commanded us to **stone** such women.
So what do you say?"
They said this to **test** him,
    so that they could have some **charge** to bring against him.
Jesus bent down and began to **write** on the ground with his **finger**.
But when they continued asking him,
    he **straightened** up and said to them,
    "Let the one among you who is **without** sin
    be the **first** to throw a **stone** at her."
Again he **bent** down and **wrote** on the ground.
And in response, they went away **one** by **one**,
    beginning with the **elders**.
So he was left **alone** with the **woman** before him.

See Leviticus 20:10 and Deuteronomy 22:22–29. This is probably the legal material to which the Pharisees refer.

---

however, perhaps Paul's warmest. He was close to this community (1:8–11; 4:14–20).

What are we to make of Paul's words in 3:10 about conformity to the death of Christ? The main moral admonition of this letter may be summed up by the following words: "complete my joy by being of the same mind, with the same love, united in heart, thinking one thing" (2:2). The next verse gives the practical step to take in order to accomplish this unity: placing the needs of others ahead of one's own (2:3). The

examples of Paul (imprisoned for the sake of others' salvation), Epaphroditus (who almost died working for the same end, 2:25–30), and Jesus (who humbled himself for others to the point of death; see 2:6–8) all testify to the importance of self-sacrifice. In this context, conformity to Christ's death means a life, cut however short, of unremitting service to others.

What might conformity to Christ's death mean today?

GOSPEL The most ancient Greek copies of the Gospel of John do not contain 7:53—8:11. Other copies of John have the story elsewhere, after 7:36 or at the Gospel's tail end, while some copies of the New Testament have the story right after Luke 21:38.

Pharisees are often made to stand for soulless legalism and grandiose, hypocritical displays of religiosity. We owe this portrait in large part to their roles in the Gospels as Jesus' dogged opponents and as hostile

According to Roman Catholic teaching, Jesus was fully human in every way except with respect to sin. In the light of this teaching, his refusal to condemn the woman cannot be for the same reason that the Pharisees refuse. Their refusal is based on Jesus' exposure of their hypocrisy. Jesus' refusal to condemn is an act of mercy.

Then **Jesus** straightened up and said to her,
    "**Woman**, **where** are they?
Has **no** one **condemned** you?"
She replied, "**No** one, sir."
Then Jesus said, "**Neither** do I **condemn** you.
Go, and from now on do not **sin** any more."

conspirators in his arrest. While the Gospels' cumulative portrait of them is undeniably negative, the earnest Nicodemus of John 3 is a Pharisee (see also 7:50–52; 19:39) and Jesus dines at the home of a Pharisee in Luke 7:36–50. The first-century Jewish historian Josephus describes the Pharisees as members of a tight-knit movement enjoying broad popular support among Jews in Palestine. Pharisees were particularly distinguished by their observance of Jewish law and scripture scholarship. More than the other Jewish religious parties known to us, the Pharisees contributed to the development of Rabbinic Judaism following Rome's destruction of Jerusalem and the Temple (70 AD), and its suppression of the Bar Kochba revolt (132–135 AD).

In today's Gospel selection, the Pharisees and Jesus debate the application of scriptural law. According to what we know of the Pharisees, this kind of debate was distinctively theirs. In other words, the Pharisees engage Jesus as they would one of their own. Jesus, accepting the challenge, responds in kind. Jesus convicts these religious experts of their hypocrisy, but fluently argues as if he were one of them.

5TH SUNDAY OF LENT, YEAR A

Lectionary #34

READING I   Ezekiel 37:12–14

This reading is a solemn proclamation. Proclaim it with great conviction.

A reading from the Book of the Prophet Ezekiel

Thus says the **Lord G**OD:
O my **people**, I will **open** your **graves**
 and have you **rise** from them,
 and **bring** you back to the **land** of Israel.
Then you shall know that **I** am the **L**ORD,
 when I **open** your **graves** and have you **rise** from them,
 O my **people**!
I will **put** my **spirit** in you that you may **live**,
 and I will **settle** you upon your **land**;
 thus you shall **know** that **I** am the **L**ORD.
I have **promised**, and I will **do** it, says the **L**ORD.

READING I Imagine the destruction of Rome and the deportation of its people. Everyone—the Roman people, the leadership of the Church—and everything—the unparalleled treasures of classical and Christian art and architecture, the tombs of saints and martyrs, the physical environment of close to 3,000 years of human history—gone. Imagine this and you can begin, but only begin, to understand what the destruction of Jerusalem and the Babylonian exile meant to the Jews who went through it.

By the time the prophet Ezekiel set down the words of today's reading, he had been in exile for some time. His fellow deportees had begun to die off, while others likely despaired of ever seeing their homes again. In this context the word of the Lord comes to him. Ezekiel sees a vision of a valley of dry bones, which, at God's word, grow sinew and flesh, reassembling themselves into living bodies (Ezekiel 37:1–10). God tells Ezekiel, in the verse immediately before the first verse of our reading: "these bones are the whole house of Israel. They have been

This reading presumes that the reader has followed Paul's argument over the course of the letter, giving special attention to the section of the letter beginning in 6:1. The gift of the Spirit is conferred in Baptism, which is Paul's topic beginning in 6:1. There is a sacramental dimension to these words.

READING II   Romans 8:8–11

A reading from the Letter of Saint Paul to the Romans

Brothers and **sisters**:
Those who are in the **flesh** cannot please **God**.
But you are **not** in the **flesh**;
　　on the contrary, you are in the **spirit**,
　　if only the **Spirit** of **God dwells** in **you**.
Whoever does **not have** the **Spirit** of **Christ**
　　does **not belong** to him.
But if **Christ** is in you,
　　although the **body** is **dead** because of **sin**,
　　the **spirit** is **alive** because of **righteousness**.
If the **Spirit** of the **one** who raised **Jesus** from the **dead**
　　dwells in you,
　　the one who raised **Christ** from the **dead**
　　will give **life** to your **mortal** bodies also,
　　through his **Spirit dwelling** in you.

GOSPEL   John 11:1–45

A reading from the holy Gospel according to John

Now a **man** was **ill**, **Lazarus** from **Bethany**,
　　the village of **Mary** and her sister **Martha**.
Mary was the one who had **anointed** the **Lord** with perfumed **oil**
　　and **dried** his **feet** with her **hair**;
　　it was her brother **Lazarus** who was **ill**.

This is a reference to an episode that has not yet happened in the Gospel (see 12:1–8; Matthew 26:6–13; Mark 14:3–9; and Luke 7:36–50). It is perhaps the insertion of a later editor.

saying, 'Our bones are dried up, our hope is lost' " (Ezekiel 37:11).

　　Ezekiel's Hebrew word for "hope" (tiq-vah) in 37:11 is elpis in the Septuagint, the Greek translation of the Old Testament. Among early Christians, the word elpis functioned as shorthand for the general Resurrection and salvation of believers. It is in the context of the general Resurrection, of our hope of settlement in God's own land,

that the Roman Catholic Church proclaims this text as scripture. It is a prayer of Christian hope, which "does not disappoint" (Romans 5:5), that the opened grave of Christ may precede billions more.

| READING II | "Those who are in the flesh cannot please God." Tug at the skin of your forearm, or give your thigh a nice slap, and perhaps a question or two will arise about this passage from Paul's letter to the Christians of Rome. |

　　The Greek word Paul uses in Romans 8:8, which has been translated in our Bible as "flesh," is sarx. Sometimes Paul uses this word as we usually do in English. In 2 Corinthians 12:7, Paul talks about a thorn in his flesh, which perhaps refers to a physical problem or illness of some kind (see also Galatians 4:12–15). Sometimes Paul uses sarx to refer to the entire human person, as in 1 Corinthians 7:28 when he speaks of the trials

In John, the episodes of Jesus' most
divisive controversies occur in Judea.

Compare John 9:4 and the metaphors of
sight and blindness, light and darkness, in
the account of the man born blind in 9:1–41.

So the **sisters** sent **word** to **Jesus** saying,
    "**Master**, the one you **love** is ill."
When **Jesus** heard this he said,
    "This **illness** is not to end in **death**,
    but is for the **glory** of **God**,
    that the **Son** of **God** may be **glorified** through it."
Now **Jesus** loved **Martha** and her **sister** and **Lazarus**.
So when he **heard** that he was **ill**,
    he **remained** for two days in the **place** where he was.
Then after this he said to his disciples,
    "Let us go back to **Judea**."
The **disciples** said to him,
    "**Rabbi**, the **Jews** were just trying to stone you,
    and you want to go back there?"
Jesus answered,
    "Are there not **twelve** hours in a **day**?
If one walks during the **day**, he does not **stumble**,
    because he sees the **light** of this **world**.
But if one walks at **night**, he **stumbles**,
    because the **light** is not in him."
He said this, and then told them,
    "Our friend **Lazarus** is **asleep**,
    but I am **going** to **awaken** him."
So the disciples said to him,
    "**Master**, if he is **asleep**, he will be **saved**."
But **Jesus** was talking about his **death**,
    while they thought that he meant **ordinary sleep**.
So then **Jesus** said to them **clearly**,
    "**Lazarus** has **died**.
And I am **glad** for you that I was **not** there,
    that you may **believe**.
Let us **go** to him."

of married life. But Paul's use of the word in today's reading is a special usage. When Paul contrasts flesh and spirit in Romans, he means, as Father Joseph Fitzmyer, SJ, has observed, "a human being subject to earth-bound tendencies and a human being open to the influence of God's spirit."

The rhetorical technique Paul uses in this passage to contrast flesh and spirit is *antithesis,* which means "opposition." An antithesis emphasizes the difference between two things. Here Paul emphasizes

a contrast between two sets of ideas or, better, forces: flesh, death, and sin oppose spirit, life, and righteousness. The result of incorporation into the body of Christ through Baptism is freedom from the effects of the former group and participation in the latter.

It is not the possession, use, and enjoyment of one's physical body that displeases God. The text shows that the body is neutral; it is the arena, if you will, of the contest between the two sets of opposing forces (see 8:10–11). God's displeasure arises not from human bodies, but from flesh in the special sense Paul gives it here: the refusal

of the free gift of grace that only a person who is open to God can accept. It is up to all of us, nurtured by and helping to sustain Christ's continued presence on earth, the Church, to open ourselves to God's Spirit so that we can be changed into the workers God intends us to be.

| GOSPEL | The first half of the Gospel of John is organized around a series of seven signs. The first six are the changing of the water into wine (2:1–11), the

So **Thomas**, called **Didymus**, said to his fellow disciples,
"Let us also go to **die** with him."

When **Jesus** arrived, he found that **Lazarus**
had already been in the **tomb** for **four** days.
Now **Bethany** was near **Jerusalem**, only about two miles away.
And many of the **Jews** had come to **Martha** and **Mary**
to **comfort** them about their brother.
When **Martha** heard that **Jesus** was coming,
she went to **meet** him;
but **Mary** sat at **home**.
Martha said to **Jesus**,
"**Lord**, if you had been **here**,
my **brother** would not have **died**.
But even **now** I **know** that whatever you ask of **God**,
God will give you."
Jesus said to her,
"Your **brother** will rise."
Martha said to him,
"I **know** he will rise,
in the **resurrection** on the last day."
Jesus told her,
"**I** am the **resurrection** and the **life**;
whoever **believes** in me, even if he **dies**, will **live**,
and **everyone** who **lives** and **believes** in me will **never** die.
Do you **believe** this?"
She said to him, "**Yes**, Lord.
I have come to **believe** that **you** are the **Christ**, the **Son** of **God**,
the **one** who is coming into the **world**."

Consider how you want to deliver Martha's lines. Is she angry? Sad? Resigned? Believing? Is she feeling some combination of these? Is she feeling something else entirely?

healing of an official's son (4:46–54), the healing of a paralyzed man (5:1–9), the multiplication of loaves (6:1–15), the walking on the water (6:16–21), and the healing of a man born blind (9:1–7). The raising of Lazarus is the seventh.

Why does Jesus perform signs in John? In 20:31, the evangelist gives his reason for having selected these seven from among the many signs Jesus did: "these are written that you may come to believe that Jesus is the Messiah, the Son of God, and that through this belief you may have life in his name." The signs' purpose of leading people to belief is the reason Jesus does not travel to heal Lazarus immediately upon hearing of his illness (11:4–6). Having already healed three people of illness and infirmity, Jesus now prepares to perform a greater sign. He will bring a dead man back to life.

John has already prepared us for the raising of Lazarus back in 5:25: "Amen, amen, I say to you, the hour is coming and is now here when the dead will hear the voice of the Son of God, and those who hear will live."

Lectors and Gospel readers give voice to scripture, supplying vocal chords, tongues, and lips to the word of God. This is a very long passage. When you proclaim this scripture, let Jesus' words of John 11:43 wallop every ear: "Lazarus, come out!"

When she had **said** this,
  she **went** and **called** her sister **Mary secretly**, saying,
  "The teacher is **here** and is asking for you."
As soon as she **heard** this,
  she **rose** quickly and **went** to him.
For Jesus had not yet **come** into the village,
  but was still where **Martha** had met him.
So when the Jews who were with her in the house **comforting** her
  saw **Mary** get up quickly and go out,
  they followed her,
  presuming that she was going to the **tomb** to **weep** there.
When **Mary** came to where **Jesus** was and saw him,
  she **fell** at his feet and **said** to him,
  "**Lord**, if you had been **here**,
  my **brother** would not have **died**."
When **Jesus** saw her **weeping** and the Jews who had come
    with her **weeping**,
  he became **perturbed** and deeply **troubled**, and said,
  "**Where** have you **laid** him?"
They said to him, "**Sir**, come and see."
And **Jesus wept**.
So the Jews said, "**See** how he **loved** him."
But some of them said,
  "Could not the **one** who **opened** the eyes of the **blind** man
  have done something so that this **man** would not have **died**?"

So **Jesus**, perturbed again, came to the **tomb**.
It was a **cave**, and a **stone** lay across it.
Jesus said, "Take away the **stone**."
Martha, the **dead** man's **sister**, said to him,
  "**Lord**, by now there will be a **stench**;
  he has been **dead** for four days."

Does Mary respond differently than Martha did? Why do you think she did not come to meet Jesus with her sister?

Jesus said to her,
  "Did I not tell you that if you **believe**
  you will **see** the **glory** of **God**?"
So they took away the **stone**.
And **Jesus** raised his **eyes** and said,
  "**Father**, I thank you for **hearing** me.
I know that you **always** hear me;
  but because of the **crowd** here I have said this,
  that they may **believe** that you sent me."
And when he had said this,
  he cried out in a **loud** voice,
  "**Lazarus**, **come out**!"
The dead man **came out**,
  tied **hand** and **foot** with **burial bands**,
  and his **face** was **wrapped** in a cloth.
So **Jesus** said to them,
  "**Untie** him and **let** him go."

Now many of the Jews who had come to **Mary**
  and **seen** what he had done began to **believe** in him.

[Shorter: John 11:3–7, 17, 20–27, 33b–45]

PALM SUNDAY OF THE LORD'S PASSION

Lectionary #37

GOSPEL AT THE PROCESSION   Luke 19:28–40

A reading from the holy Gospel according to Luke

Jesus proceeded on his **journey** up to **Jerusalem**.
As he drew near to **Bethphage** and **Bethany**
    at the place called the **Mount** of **Olives**,
    he sent two of his disciples.
He said, "**Go** into the village opposite you,
    and as you **enter** it you will **find** a colt tethered
    on which **no** one has **ever** sat.
Untie it and bring it here.
And if anyone should ask you,
    '**Why** are you untying it?'
    you will answer,
    'The **Master** has need of it.'"
So those who had been sent went off
    and found **everything** just as he had told them.
And as they were untying the **colt**, its owners said to them,
    "**Why** are you untying this colt?"
They answered,
    "The **Master** has need of it."
So they brought it to **Jesus**,
    threw their **cloaks** over the colt,
    and helped **Jesus** to **mount**.

Jerusalem lies at a relatively high altitude. "Up to Jerusalem" is the only way for land travelers to go.

The Mount of Olives lies just east of the Temple Mount, beyond the walls of the old city.

PROCESSION GOSPEL | Jesus has been given many titles in the history of the Church. Perhaps the very earliest of these is "Jesus Christ." Some Christians often use this title as Jesus' first and last names; indeed Paul himself, a few decades after the death of Jesus, was already using *Iēsous Christos* (and *Christos*

Iēsous) this way. What we use as Jesus' proper name was likely shorthand for an early Christian creed, a succinct statement of belief: "*Jesus* of Nazareth is the *Christ!*"

The word *xristos* is a Greek adjective meaning "anointed." It translates a Hebrew adjective, *moshiach,* which comes from a Hebrew verb meaning "to smear with oil." In the Old Testament, references to people called "God's anointed" almost always mean

kings of David's line (Isaiah 45:1 is one exception). It is as king, God's *xristos,* who Jesus enters Jerusalem.

Luke, like Matthew, Mark, and John, finds prophecy's fulfillment embedded in Jesus' entry into Jerusalem. The prophet who foresees the restoration of David's royal line is Zechariah: "See, your king shall come to you; a just savior is he, Meek and

See Zechariah 9:9.

As he **rode** along,
>the people were spreading their cloaks on the road;
>and now as he was approaching the **slope** of the **Mount**
>>of **Olives**,
>the whole **multitude** of his disciples
>began to **praise** God aloud with **joy**
>for all the **mighty** deeds they had seen.

They proclaimed:
>"**Blessed** is the **king** who comes
>>in the **name** of the Lord.
>**Peace** in **heaven**
>>and **glory** in the highest."

Some of the **Pharisees** in the crowd said to him,
>"Teacher, **rebuke** your disciples."

He said in reply,
>"I tell you, if they keep **silent**,
>the **stones** will cry out!"

See Psalm 118:26.

Lectionary #38

READING I   Isaiah 50:4–7

A reading from the Book of the Prophet Isaiah

The **Lord GOD** has given me
>a well-trained **tongue**,
>that I might know how to **speak** to the weary
>a word that will **rouse** them.

Morning after **morning**
>he **opens** my ear that I may **hear**;
>and I have **not** rebelled,
>have **not** turned back.

God wants the prophecy to succeed and has outfitted the prophet with the tools to rouse the weary. This is not, however, always the case (see Isaiah 6:9–10).

---

riding on an ass, on a colt, the foal of an ass" (9:9). The people's acclamation of blessedness comes from Psalm 118:26, a psalm probably composed for use in a public liturgy honoring an Israelite or Judahite king's military triumph.

With palms in hand, Roman Catholics walk into this sacred story as we walk into our churches, where in liturgies of word and table we meet and acclaim our anointed king.

READING I "I have set my face like flint, knowing that I shall not be put to shame." Standing to the side of these confident words, and seeking a favorable opportunity to betray them, is the grinning fear that we *will* be put to shame. Some of us need only toy for a moment with the facts that the future is both unknown and largely beyond our control to experience the rapid multiplication of scenarios in which we lose what we have and fail to obtain what we want.

The prophet in this reading faces something different than self-inflicted anxiety. According to a common ancient Israelite understanding of the phenomenon of prophecy, the content of the oracle is God's

I **gave** my **back** to those who **beat** me,
my **cheeks** to those who **plucked** my beard;
my **face** I did not **shield**
from **buffets** and **spitting**.

The Lord **GOD** is my help,
therefore I am **not** disgraced;
I have **set** my **face** like **flint**,
knowing that I shall **not** be put to **shame**.

READING II   Philippians 2:6–11

A reading from the Letter of Saint Paul to the Philippians

Christ Jesus, though he was in the **form** of God,
did not regard **equality** with God
something to be **grasped**.
Rather, he **emptied** himself,
taking the **form** of a **slave**,
coming in **human** likeness;
and found **human** in appearance,
he **humbled** himself,
becoming obedient to the point of **death**,
even **death** on a **cross**.
Because of this, God **greatly exalted** him
and **bestowed** on him the name
which is **above every** name,
that at the **name** of **Jesus**
every knee should **bend**,
of those in **heaven** and on **earth** and **under** the earth,
and **every tongue** confess that
Jesus Christ is **Lord**,
to the **glory** of **God** the **Father**.

Note the pivot point in 2:9. The first three verses concern Jesus' actions while the last three concern God's actions on Jesus' behalf.

to determine. He says as much: "Morning after morning, he [God] opens my ear." What has his steadfastness earned him but abuse? And still he stands by the conviction that because he is in God's hands he will not be put to shame.

On February 12, 2005, Sister Dorothy Mae Stang, 74, of the Sisters of Notre Dame, was murdered in the Amazon region of Brazil. She died performing the ministry to which she was called, which was service to people defending their land against theft and destruction by loggers. She died a martyr in the word's truest sense, as someone whose manner of death bears witness to Christ. Her work may not have succeeded.

Her people may yet be defeated and dispersed, their forests turned into chairs and coffee tables. But fidelity to the gospel, no less than to an oracle of God, carries with it no assurance of success.

READING II Many biblical scholars believe that these verses comprise a hymn to Christ that Paul either learned in his travels or composed himself

PASSION   Luke 22:14—23:56

The Passion of our Lord Jesus Christ according to Luke

(1) When the **hour** came,
   Jesus took his **place** at table with the **apostles**.
He said to them,
   "I have **eagerly** desired to eat this **Passover** with you
     before I suffer,
   for, I tell you, I shall **not** eat it again
   until there is **fulfillment** in the **kingdom** of **God**."
Then he took a **cup**, gave thanks, and said,
   "Take this and **share** it among yourselves;
   for I tell you that from **this time** on
   I shall **not** drink of the fruit of the vine
   until the kingdom of God comes."
Then he took the **bread**, said the **blessing**,
   broke it, and **gave** it to them, saying,
   "**This** is my **body**, which will be **given** for you;
   do this in **memory** of me."
And likewise the cup after they had eaten, saying,
   "**This** cup is the **new covenant** in my **blood**,
   which will be **shed** for you.

(2) "And yet **behold**, the hand of the one who is to **betray** me
   is with me on the table;
   for the **Son** of **Man** indeed goes as it has been **determined**;
   but woe to that man by whom he is **betrayed**."
And they began to **debate** among themselves
   who among them would **do** such a **deed**.

(3) Then an **argument** broke out among them
   about which of them should be **regarded** as the greatest.

on another occasion. But there is no reason to assume Paul could not have written these lyrical lines for the Philippians at the time he composed this letter. The main purpose of this letter is to encourage the community to end its divisions, with each individual placing the interests of others ahead of her own (2:1–4). Christ's obedient example well serves Paul's purpose in writing this letter.

Paul's world was full of both men who were worshipped as gods, and men who aspired to divinity. A man who fit into both categories was the emperor Gaius (37–41 AD), who reigned during Paul's apostolate. Philo, a Jewish writer from Alexandria, records the shameful and ridiculous degree to which Gaius styled himself after Greek gods and demanded that his subjects honor him as one. In contrast, Philo elsewhere

writes that the God of Israel ordered the natural world to obey Moses as a god precisely *because* Moses sought neither wealth nor power, but only to serve. Jesus' self-emptying, obedience, and subsequent exaltation fits Moses' pattern, not that of Gaius, whose grandiose pretensions to divinity ended abruptly when he was assassinated by his own guards.

He said to them,
"The **kings** of the **Gentiles** lord it over them
and those in authority over them are addressed as
'**Benefactors**';
but among you it shall not be so.
Rather, let the **greatest** among you be as the **youngest**,
and the **leader** as the **servant**.
For who is **greater**:
the one **seated** at table or the one who **serves**?
Is it not the **one seated** at table?
I am among you as the one who **serves**.
"It is you who have **stood** by me in my **trials**;
and I **confer** a kingdom on you,
just as my **Father** has conferred **one** on **me**,
that you may **eat** and **drink** at my **table** in my kingdom;
and you will **sit** on thrones
judging the **twelve** tribes of **Israel**.

(4) "**Simon**, **Simon**, behold **Satan** has demanded
to sift all of you like wheat,
but I have **prayed** that your own faith may not **fail**;
and once you have turned back,
you must **strengthen** your brothers."
He said to him,
"**Lord**, I am prepared to go to **prison** and to **die** with you."
But he replied,
"I tell you, **Peter**, before the **cock** crows this day,
you will deny **three times** that you **know** me."

(5) He said to them,
"When I sent you forth without a money bag or a sack
or sandals,
were you in **need** of anything?"

The enthronement of the disciples in the kingdom of God for the purpose of judging Israel is a variation on a traditional apocalyptic motif of the exalted position to be held by the righteous on the day of the Lord.

The first three verses of this reading describe what Jesus Christ did (2:6–8). The last three describe what God the Father did for him (2:9–11). "Because of this" is the point where the passage pivots from the deeds of Jesus to those of the Father, and it may be fitting to account for the transition in your delivery, perhaps by pausing briefly before continuing on with 2:9.

PASSION "This man was innocent beyond doubt." The centurion's words are the first recorded speech after Jesus' death in Matthew, Mark, and Luke. Mark, however, recalls it somewhat differently. According to Mark 15:39, the centurion exclaims, "Truly this man was the Son of God!" Matthew 27:54 contains something nearly identical.

The uniqueness of Luke's depiction of Jesus' execution is his emphasis on the innocence of Jesus. What happened to Jesus, in Luke's eyes, was a monstrous injustice. The so-called good thief, in the course of a conversation we find only in Luke, believes his own punishment fair, but declares that Jesus "has done nothing criminal" (23:41). Three times Pilate declares Jesus innocent of any crime (23:4, 14–15, 22).

"**No**, **nothing**," they replied.
He said to them,
　"But **now** one who has a money bag should take it,
　and likewise a sack,
　and one who does **not** have a **sword**
　should **sell** his cloak and **buy** one.
For I tell you that this **Scripture** must be **fulfilled** in me,
　namely, 'He was counted among the **wicked**';
　and indeed what is **written** about me is coming to **fulfillment**."
Then they said,
　"**Lord**, **look**, there are **two** swords here."

Perhaps Jesus means "Enough!"

But he replied, "It is **enough**!"

(6) Then going out, he went, as was his custom, to the Mount
　　of Olives,
　and the disciples followed him.
When he **arrived** at the place he said to them,
　"**Pray** that you may not **undergo** the test."
After withdrawing about a **stone's** throw from them and **kneeling**,
　he **prayed**, saying, "Father, if you are **willing**,
　take this cup **away** from me;
　still, not **my** will but **yours** be done."
And to strengthen him an **angel** from **heaven** appeared to him.
He was in such **agony** and he prayed so **fervently**
　that his **sweat** became like **drops** of **blood**
　falling on the ground.
When he **rose** from **prayer** and **returned** to his disciples,
　he found them **sleeping** from grief.
He said to them, "**Why** are you **sleeping**?
Get up and **pray** that you may **not** undergo the test."

And Jesus himself begs his Father to forgive his killers for his murder because, out of ignorance, they are executing an innocent man (23:34).

　Let us imagine ourselves at the foot of the cross—not Jesus' cross, but the cross of the Good Thief. Let us be patient and silent as he gives us all an account of himself— how he deserves what he's getting, that he is depraved beyond reckoning, that he didn't just steal but caused unspeakable harm, how maybe his death will do his victims some good. Perhaps we will agree with him on all counts, even as we wonder at such honesty, and even something like generosity of spirit, trembling on the lips of a man at once wicked, perverted, and dying in as cruel a manner as humankind ever devised. And perhaps we will hear in Jesus' promise of paradise what we, who are witnessing the spectacle of three human bodies tortured to death, must now hope and believe: that God, with paradise, will vindicate all, and that we shall not be judged too harshly for just watching it all happen from the foot of the cross.

(7) While he was still speaking, a **crowd** approached
and in front was **one** of the **Twelve**, a man named **Judas**.
He went up to Jesus to **kiss** him.
Jesus said to him,
  "**Judas**, are you **betraying** the **Son** of **Man** with a **kiss**?"
His disciples realized what was about to happen, and they asked,
  "**Lord**, shall we **strike** with a **sword**?"
And one of them struck the high priest's **servant**
  and **cut** off his right ear.
But Jesus said in reply,
  "**Stop**, no more of this!"
Then he **touched** the servant's ear and **healed** him.
And Jesus said to the chief **priests** and **temple** guards
  and elders who had come for him,
    "Have you come out as against a **robber**, with **swords**
      and **clubs**?
Day after day I was **with** you in the **temple** area,
  and you did **not** seize me;
  but this is **your** hour, the time for the **power** of **darkness**."

(8) After **arresting** him they **led** him away
  and took him into the **house** of the **high priest**;
  Peter was following at a **distance**.
They lit a **fire** in the **middle** of the **courtyard** and sat around it,
  and **Peter** sat down with them.
When a maid saw him **seated** in the light,
  she looked **intently** at him and said,
    "This man too was with him."
But he **denied** it saying,
  "Woman, I do not know him."

The nighttime setting for Jesus' arrest suggests that it may have been closer to a kidnapping or abduction.

A short while later someone **else** saw him and said,
"You **too** are one of them";
but **Peter** answered, "My friend, I am **not**."
About an hour later, still **another** insisted,
"**Assuredly**, this man **too** was **with** him,
for he **also** is a **Galilean**."
But **Peter** said,
"My friend, I do **not** know what you are **talking** about."
Just as he was saying this, the **cock crowed**,
and the **Lord turned** and **looked** at **Peter**;
and **Peter remembered** the **word** of the **Lord**,
how he had **said** to him,
"Before the **cock** crows today, you will **deny** me three times."
He **went** out and **began** to **weep bitterly**.

(9) The men who held Jesus in custody were **ridiculing** and
beating him.
They **blindfolded** him and **questioned** him, saying,
"**Prophesy**! Who is it that **struck** you?"
And they **reviled** him in saying many other things against him.

(10) When day came the council of elders of the people met,
both **chief priests** and **scribes**,
and they brought him **before** their **Sanhedrin**.
They said, "If **you** are the **Christ**, **tell us**,"
but he **replied** to them, "If I tell **you**, **you** will **not believe**,
and if I **question**, you will **not respond**.
But from **this** time on the **Son** of **Man** will be **seated**
at the **right** hand of the **power** of **God**."
They all asked, "Are you then the Son of God?"
He replied to them, "**You** say that I am."
Then they said, "What further need have **we** for **testimony**?
We have **heard** it from his **own mouth**."

Presumably the people in the courtyard can tell Peter is a Galilean from his accent. This is explicit in Matthew 26:73. Compare this with Mark 14:70.

"Son of Man" is an important title of Jesus in Luke as in the rest of the Gospels. To begin to find out what it means, see Luke 9:22, 44–45; 18:31–34.

Pontius Pilate, Roman prefect of Judea (26–36 AD).

(11) Then the **whole** assembly of them **arose** and **brought** him
     before **Pilate**.
They brought **charges** against him, saying,
   "We found this man **misleading** our people;
   he **opposes** the payment of taxes to **Caesar**
   and **maintains** that he is the **Christ**, a **king**."
Pilate asked him, "Are **you** the **king** of the **Jews**?"
He said to him in reply, "**You** say so."
Pilate then addressed the chief priests and the crowds,
   "I find this man **not guilty**."
But they were **adamant** and said,
   "He is **inciting** the people with his **teaching**
      throughout **all** Judea,
   from **Galilee** where he began **even** to here."

Herod Antipas, tetrarch of Galilee (4 BC–39 AD).

(12) On hearing this Pilate asked if the **man** was a **Galilean**;
   and upon learning that he was under **Herod's** jurisdiction,
   he sent him to **Herod**, who was in **Jerusalem** at that time.
Herod was very **glad** to see **Jesus**;
   he had been **wanting** to see him for a **long** time,
   for he had **heard** about him
   and had been **hoping** to see him perform some sign.
He **questioned** him at length,
   but he gave him **no** answer.
The **chief priests** and **scribes**, meanwhile,
   stood by **accusing** him harshly.
Herod and his **soldiers** treated him **contemptuously**
      and **mocked** him,
   and after **clothing** him in **resplendent** garb,
   he **sent** him back to Pilate.
Herod and **Pilate** became **friends** that very **day**,
   even though they had been **enemies** formerly.

(13) **Pilate** then summoned the **chief priests**, the **rulers** and
   the **people**
 and said to them, "**You** brought this man to **me**
 and **accused** him of **inciting** the people to **revolt**.
I have **conducted** my investigation in your **presence**
 and have **not** found this man **guilty**
 of the charges you have brought against him,
 nor did **Herod**, for he sent him **back** to us.
So **no** capital crime has been **committed** by him.
Therefore I shall have him **flogged** and then **release** him."

But all together they shouted out,
 "**Away** with this man!
 Release Barabbas to us."
—Now Barabbas had been **imprisoned** for a **rebellion**
 that had taken place in the **city** and for **murder**.—
Again Pilate addressed them, still **wishing** to release Jesus,
 but they **continued** their shouting,
 "**Crucify** him! **Crucify** him!"
Pilate addressed them a third time,
 "What **evil** has this man done?
 I found him **guilty** of **no** capital crime.
Therefore I shall have him **flogged** and then **release** him."
With **loud** shouts, however,
 they **persisted** in calling for his **crucifixion**,
 and their voices **prevailed**.
The **verdict** of **Pilate** was that their **demand** should be granted.
So he **released** the man who had been **imprisoned**
 for **rebellion** and **murder**, for whom they **asked**,
 and he **handed** Jesus **over** to them to **deal** with as they **wished**.

(14) As they **led** him away
　　they took hold of a certain **Simon**, a **Cyrenian**,
　　who was coming in from the country;
　　and after **laying** the **cross** on him,
　　they **made** him **carry** it behind **Jesus**.
A **large** crowd of people followed **Jesus**,
　　including **many women** who **mourned** and **lamented** him.
Jesus **turned** to them and **said**,
　　"**Daughters** of Jerusalem, do **not** weep for me;
　　weep instead for **yourselves** and for your **children**
　　for indeed, the **days** are **coming** when **people** will **say**,
　　'**Blessed** are the **barren**,
　　the **wombs** that never **bore**
　　and the **breasts** that never **nursed**.'
At that time people will say to the **mountains**,
　　'**Fall** upon us!'
　　and to the **hills**, '**Cover** us!'
　　for if these things are done when the **wood** is **green**,
　　what will **happen** when it is **dry**?"
Now **two others**, **both criminals**,
　　were **led** away with him to be **executed**.

(15) When they came to the **place** called the **Skull**,
　　they **crucified** him and the **criminals** there,
　　one on his **right**, the **other** on his **left**.
Then Jesus said,
　　"**Father**, **forgive** them, they **know not** what **they do**."
They **divided** his garments by **casting** lots.

Compare Jesus' cry of desolation in Mark
15:34 and Matthew 27:46.

Victims of crucifixion often had their crimes posted on their crosses.

The people **stood** by and **watched**;
   the rulers, meanwhile, **sneered** at him and said,
   "He **saved** others, let him **save himself**
   if he is the **chosen** one, the **Christ** of **God**."
Even the **soldiers** jeered at him.
As they **approached** to **offer** him **wine** they called out,
   "If **you** are **King** of the **Jews**, save **yourself**."
Above him there was an inscription that read,
   "**This** is the **King** of the **Jews**."

(16) Now **one** of the criminals hanging there **reviled** Jesus, saying,
   "Are you **not** the **Christ**?
   Save yourself and us."
The other, however, **rebuking** him, said in reply,
   "Have **you no fear** of **God**,
   for you are **subject** to the **same** condemnation?
And indeed, we have been **condemned** justly,
   for the **sentence** we **received corresponds** to our **crimes**,
   but **this** man has done **nothing** criminal."
Then he said,
   "**Jesus**, **remember** me when you **come** into your **kingdom**."
He replied to him,
   "**Amen**, I say to **you**,
   today you will be **with** me in **Paradise**."

(17) It was **now** about **noon** and **darkness** came
      over the **whole** land
   until **three** in the **afternoon**
   because of an **eclipse** of the sun.
Then the **veil** of the **temple** was **torn** down the **middle**.
Jesus cried out in a **loud** voice,
   "**Father**, into your hands I **commend** my spirit";
   and when he had **said** this he **breathed** his last.

[Here all kneel and pause for a short time.]

(18) The **centurion** who **witnessed** what had **happened glorified
God** and said,
"This **man** was **innocent** beyond doubt."
When all the people who had **gathered** for this spectacle **saw**
what had **happened**,
they returned **home beating** their **breasts**;
but **all** his acquaintances **stood** at a **distance**,
including the **women** who had **followed** him from **Galilee**
and **saw** these events.

(19) Now there was a **virtuous** and **righteous** man
named **Joseph**, who,
though he was a **member** of the **council**,
had **not** consented to their plan of action.
He came from the **Jewish** town of **Arimathea**
and was **awaiting** the **kingdom** of God.
He went to **Pilate** and **asked** for the body of **Jesus**.
After he had taken the **body** down,
he **wrapped** it in a linen cloth
and **laid** him in a **rock-hewn tomb**
in which **no one** had yet been **buried**.
It was the **day** of **preparation**,
and the **sabbath** was about to **begin**.
The **women** who had come from **Galilee** with him
followed behind,
and when they had **seen** the tomb
and the way in which his body was **laid** in it,
they **returned** and **prepared** spices and perfumed oils.
Then they **rested** on the **sabbath** according to the **commandment**.

[Shorter: Luke 23:1–49]

HOLY THURSDAY: MASS OF THE LORD'S SUPPER

Lectionary #39

Compare Exodus 12:21-27.

READING I   Exodus 12:1–8, 11–14

A reading from the Book of Exodus

The LORD said to **Moses** and **Aaron** in the land of **Egypt**,
"This month shall stand at the **head** of your calendar;
    you shall reckon it the **first** month of the **year**.
Tell the **whole** community of **Israel**:
    On the tenth of this month **every** one of your **families**
    must procure for itself a **lamb**, one apiece for **each** household.
If a family is too small for a **whole** lamb,
    it shall join the nearest household in procuring one
    and shall **share** in the **lamb**
    in proportion to the number of **persons** who **partake** of it.
The **lamb** must be a year-old male and without **blemish**.
You may take it from either the **sheep** or the **goats**.
You shall keep it **until** the fourteenth day of this month,
    and **then**, with the **whole** assembly of Israel present,
    it shall be **slaughtered** during the evening twilight.
They shall take **some** of its **blood**
    and apply it to the two **doorposts** and the **lintel**
    of **every** house in which they **partake** of the **lamb**.
That same **night** they shall **eat** its roasted **flesh**
    with unleavened **bread** and bitter **herbs**.

READING I   All three of today's readings contain accounts of the institutions of religious rituals. In the Gospel we read an account of the foot-washing *mandatum*, which Roman Catholics celebrate today as a rite expressing fundamental truths about Christian discipleship and service. In the second reading, Paul reminds the Corinthians of how Jesus instituted the sacrament of the Lord's Supper. In the first reading, we read of the institution of the Passover.

Many of the religious feasts and festivals of Judaism and Christianity have historical roots extending outside of the religions themselves. One occasionally encounters someone, who, upon learning that one practices one's Christian faith, crows that Easter is "really" the Passover playing Christian dress-up, or that the Passover is "really" a pagan holiday playing Jewish or Christian dress-up. This is tiresome to endure, perhaps, but one must also admit that the information bears a smudge of truth. Christians

from very ancient times have pegged their annual celebration of Easter to that of Passover, remembering that the events of Jesus' Crucifixion and Resurrection happened in the course of a Passover celebration in Jerusalem. At different times and locations Christians have called Easter *Pascha*, which comes from the festival's Hebrew name, *Pesach*. And the Jewish Passover itself likely has its roots in the New Year religious festivals of nomadic

"**This** is how you are to **eat** it:
    with your **loins girt**, **sandals** on your **feet** and your **staff**
      in **hand**,
    you shall **eat** like those who are in **flight**.
It is the **Passover** of the LORD.
For on this **same** night I will go through **Egypt**,
    striking down every firstborn of the **land**, both **man** and **beast**,
    and executing **judgment** on all the **gods** of Egypt—**I**, the LORD!
But the **blood** will mark the **houses** where you **are**.
Seeing the **blood**, I will pass **over** you;
    thus, when I **strike** the land of **Egypt**,
    no destructive **blow** will come upon **you**.

"This day shall be a **memorial feast** for you,
    which **all** your generations shall celebrate
    with pilgrimage to the LORD, as a perpetual institution."

READING II   1 Corinthians 11:23–26

A reading from the first Letter of Saint Paul to the Corinthians

Brothers and **sisters**:
I **received** from the **Lord** what I also **handed on** to you,
    that the **Lord Jesus**, on the night he was **handed over**,
    took bread, and, **after** he had **given thanks**,
    broke it and said, "**This** is my **body** that is for **you**.
Do **this** in **remembrance** of **me**."
In the **same** way also the **cup**, after **supper**, saying,
    "This **cup** is the **new** covenant in my **blood**.

herdsmen, who sacrificed an animal to a god or gods in order to assure a good year.

What makes the Passover "really" Jewish and Easter "really" Christian is that the testimony of our sacred texts and traditions ordain that we celebrate them in memory of God's great acts of salvation on behalf of our two peoples. As our religions are fraternally linked by the shared roots their festivals, so also are they in fraternity with all religions formed in response to the fundamental human impulse to seek and know God.

READING II The New Testament contains four accounts of the institution of the Eucharist at the final meal Jesus shared with his disciples. The locations of these passages are Matthew 26:26–30; Mark 14:22–26; Luke 22:14–20; and today's reading from 1 Corinthians. Note that Paul and Luke specify that the bread was broken at the beginning of the meal and a cup shared after dinner. Luke, in fact, mentions a cup before dinner as well. These details might seem unimportant, but they likely reflect these authors' awareness of the structure of the Passover liturgy, or *seder*,

which Jesus and his disciples, as pious Jews, probably celebrated. And it may also reflect their Eucharistic practice as well.

Why does Paul provide the Corinthians with this information? Wouldn't they have already known it? To answer these questions, we need to start reading back in verse 17 and continue on until verse 34. It turns out that Paul believed the Corinthians needed a refresher course in how to celebrate the sacrament.

Do **this**, as **often** as you **drink** it, in **remembrance** of me."
For as **often** as you **eat** this **bread** and **drink** the **cup**,
   you **proclaim** the **death** of the **Lord** until he **comes**.

GOSPEL   John 13:1–15

A reading from the holy Gospel according to John

Before the **feast** of **Passover**,
   Jesus knew that his **hour** had come
   to pass from this **world** to the **Father**.
He **loved** his own in the **world** and he **loved** them to the **end**.
The **devil** had already induced **Judas**, son of **Simon** the **Iscariot**,
      to **hand him over**.
So, **during supper**,
   fully **aware** that the Father had put **everything** into his power
   and that he had **come** from **God** and was **returning** to **God**,
   he **rose** from **supper** and **took off** his outer **garments**.
He took a **towel** and tied it around his **waist**.
Then he **poured water** into a **basin**
   and began to **wash** the disciples' **feet**
   and **dry** them with the **towel** around his waist.
He came to **Simon Peter**, who said to him,
   "**Master**, are you going to **wash** my feet?"
Jesus answered and **said** to him,
   "**What** I am **doing**, you do **not** understand **now**,
   but you **will** understand **later**."
Peter said to him, "You will **never** wash my feet."

It seems that wealthy members of the Corinthian Church have been bringing lavish meals to the Eucharist and have not shared of their abundance. Some of these have even gotten drunk while their less well-off brothers and sisters in Christ have gone hungry and felt ashamed of their lack. Imagine a summer picnic where some families bring loaded baskets, swigging good wine or beer and feasting on sandwiches piled high with meats and cheese, while others sharing the table or reclining on adjacent blankets nibble on peanuts.

This situation upsets Paul a good deal. "What can I say to you? Shall I praise you? In this matter I do not praise you." The divisions that separate people in the world outside the Church must not intrude on the sanctified community.

GOSPEL Christian leadership involves service. Today's text makes that clear. "I have given you a model to follow," Jesus says when he has finished washing his disciples' feet, "so that as I have done for you, you should also do." There are Protestants in the American South, sometimes called either "foot-washing" or "primitive" Baptists, who acknowledge and practice the washing of the feet as a sacrament. They base their practice on this passage from John. And it is not hard to see their reason, since Jesus here instructs his disciples to imitate his example in much the same way that he instructs them to commemorate him by celebrating the Lord's Supper.

But the Catholic Church has traditionally interpreted this text differently. While

Jesus answered him,
  "Unless I wash you, you will have no inheritance with me."
Simon Peter said to him,
  "Master, then not only my feet, but my hands
    and head as well."
Jesus said to him,
  "Whoever has bathed has no need
    except to have his feet washed,
  for he is clean all over;
  so you are clean, but not all."
For he knew who would betray him;
  for this reason, he said, "Not all of you are clean."

So when he had washed their feet
  and put his garments back on and reclined at table again,
  he said to them, "Do you realize what I have done for you?
You call me 'teacher' and 'master,' and rightly so, for indeed I am.
If I, therefore, the master and teacher, have washed your feet,
  you ought to wash one another's feet.
I have given you a model to follow,
  so that as I have done for you, you should also do.

our parishes typically perform a foot-washing rite on Holy Thursday in accordance with Jesus' command, the Catholic understanding of Jesus' instruction is much broader. We are to lead by serving.

This concept of leadership is expressed in a variety of ways in the New Testament. In Luke's Gospel, an argument breaks out at the Last Supper among the disciples about who is the greatest among them. This is how Gentile kings behave, Jesus says. "Rather, let the greatest among you be as the youngest, and the leader as the servant" (Luke 22:24–27). The account of the argument is also found in Matthew and Mark, although they do not place it at the Last Supper (Matthew 18:1–5; Mark 9:33–37).

Jesus' instruction to us, his disciples, to follow his example is, according to the teaching of the Roman Catholic Church, a *mandatum* ("command" in Latin). And while we duly celebrate it as a rite on Holy Thursday, its application extends well beyond the walls of our churches.

GOOD FRIDAY OF THE LORD'S PASSION

Lectionary #40

READING I   Isaiah 52:13—53:12

This text is often called the "Song of the Suffering Servant." It is one of four so-called "servant songs" in Isaiah 40—55. In its original historical context, the servant mentioned in this reading may have been Israel, or perhaps one of the prophets. Early Christians interpreted it christologically (1 Peter 2:22).

Compare this text with Philippians 2:6–11, particularly Isaiah 53:12 with Philippians 2:9–11.

A reading from the Book of the Prophet Isaiah

See, my **servant** shall **prosper**,
    he shall be raised **high** and greatly **exalted**.
Even as many were **amazed** at him—
    so **marred** was his **look** beyond human semblance
    and his **appearance** beyond that of the **sons** of **man**—
so shall he **startle** many nations,
    because of him **kings** shall stand **speechless**;
for those who have **not** been **told** shall **see**,
    those who have **not heard** shall **ponder** it.

Who would **believe** what we have **heard**?
    To **whom** has the **arm** of the LORD been **revealed**?
He grew up like a **sapling** before him,
    like a **shoot** from the **parched earth**;
there was in him **no stately bearing** to make us **look** at him,
    nor appearance that would **attract** us to him.
He was **spurned** and **avoided** by people,
    a man of **suffering**, accustomed to **infirmity**,
one of those from whom people **hide** their faces,
    spurned, and we held him in **no esteem**.

Yet it was **our** infirmities that he bore,
    our sufferings that he endured,
while we thought of him as **stricken**,
    as one **smitten** by **God** and **afflicted**.

READING I   Who is the servant of this passage? As a question of history, determining the servant's identity is at best educated guesswork. Perhaps, some biblical scholars have said, the figure mentioned by the author was Jeremiah, who suffered at the hands of his countrymen. Or perhaps it was Israel itself, who was led like a sheep to slaughter into exile in Babylon. Considered not as a question of theological truth, but of history and the cultural context of the author alone, the identity of the servant is elusive.

As the Vatican II document *Dei verbum* insists, the original cultural contexts of the human authors of the Bible matter greatly to our understanding of what the Bible means. But the Church also acknowledges the Holy Spirit as an author of scripture. Within the Church, the interpretation of the texts of biblical texts can never be a matter of history exclusively.

In Acts 8:1, readers learn of a general persecution in Jerusalem that drives the disciples into Judea and Samaria. In Acts 8:26–39, the apostle Philip, who was sheltering

But he was **pierced** for **our** offenses,
 crushed for **our** sins;
upon him was the **chastisement** that makes **us** whole,
 by his stripes **we were healed**.

We had **all** gone astray like sheep,
 each following his **own** way;
but the LORD laid upon him
 the **guilt** of us all.

Though he was **harshly** treated, he **submitted**
 and opened **not** his mouth;
like a **lamb** led to the **slaughter**
 or a **sheep** before the **shearers**,
 he was **silent** and opened **not** his mouth.
Oppressed and **condemned**, he was taken away,
 and who would have **thought** any **more** of his **destiny**?
When he was **cut off** from the **land** of the **living**,
 and **smitten** for the **sin** of his **people**,
a **grave** was assigned him among the **wicked**
 and a **burial place** with **evildoers**,
though he had done **no wrong**
 nor spoken any **falsehood**.
But the LORD was **pleased**
 to **crush** him in **infirmity**.

If he gives his **life** as an **offering** for sin,
 he shall **see** his **descendants** in a long life,
 and the **will** of the LORD shall be **accomplished** through him.

Because of his **affliction**
 he shall **see** the **light** in **fullness** of **days**;

in Samaria, is directed by the angel of the Lord to travel on the road from Jerusalem to Gaza. He obeys and meets an Ethiopian eunuch, a court official of the queen of Ethiopia. Directed by the Holy Spirit to join up with his chariot, the two fall into conversation about Isaiah 53:7–8: "I beg you," the eunuch asks Philip, "about whom is the prophet saying this? About himself, or about someone else?" (8:34). Philip's reply is to proclaim Jesus.

The Ethiopian's question is the same one asked by many modern scholars: who is the servant of this passage? For Philip, for the Ethiopian, and for the Church, the answer is Jesus.

READING II "Let us hold fast to our confession." The author's choice of the word here translated by "confession" (homologia) might give some people pause. This refers not to confession of sin and wrongdoing as in the sacrament of Reconciliation. In this context, the word's meaning is probably closer to "creed."

through his **suffering**, my **servant** shall **justify** many,
    and their **guilt** he shall bear.
Therefore I will **give** him his **portion** among the **great**,
    and he shall **divide** the **spoils** with the **mighty**,
because he **surrendered** himself to **death**
    and was **counted** among the **wicked**;
and he shall take away the **sins** of many,
    and win **pardon** for their **offenses**.

READING II   Hebrews 4:14–16; 5:7–9

A reading from the Letter to the Hebrews

Brothers and **sisters**:
Since we have a **great high priest** who has **passed**
    through the **heavens**,
    Jesus, the **Son** of **God**,
    let us hold **fast** to our **confession**.
For we do **not** have a **high priest**
    who is **unable** to **sympathize** with our **weaknesses**,
    but **one** who has **similarly** been **tested** in **every** way,
    yet without **sin**.
So let us **confidently** approach the **throne** of **grace**
    to receive **mercy** and to find **grace** for timely help.

In the days when **Christ** was in the **flesh**,
    he offered **prayers** and **supplications** with loud **cries** and **tears**
    to the one who was **able** to **save** him from **death**,
    and he was **heard** because of his **reverence**.

**Pause briefly before proclaiming the
second stanza.**

The phrase recalls Hebrews 3:1, where Jesus is called "the apostle and high priest of our confession." In Hebrews, Jesus' high priesthood is tied to his humanity coexisting with his divinity, a fact of his person that makes him accessible and available to humankind. Because Jesus came to help human beings, "he had to become like his brothers in every way," and "because he himself was tested through what he suffered, he is able to help those who are being tested" (Hebrews 2:17–18).

"Our confession," therefore, concerns someone who is able to help us because he is like us in every way (except in sin). This is a high priest who understands, based on his own experience, what it is like to live as a body of flesh and to think with a human mind. This is a fundamentally different situation, the author claims, than that of angels. Angels are indeed divine and close to God, but their lack of experience of human life

Son though he **was**, he learned **obedience** from what he **suffered**;
and when he was made **perfect**,
he became the **source** of **eternal** salvation for **all** who
obey him.

PASSION John 18:1—19:42

The Passion of our Lord Jesus Christ according to John

(1) **Jesus** went out with his **disciples** across the **Kidron** valley
to where there was a **garden**,
into which he and his **disciples** entered.
Judas his **betrayer also** knew the place,
because **Jesus** had often met there with his **disciples**.
So **Judas** got a band of **soldiers** and **guards**
from the **chief priests** and the **Pharisees**
and went there with **lanterns**, **torches**, and **weapons**.
Jesus, knowing **everything** that was going to **happen** to him,
went out and said to them, "**Whom** are you **looking** for?"
They answered him, "**Jesus** the **Nazorean**."
He said to them, "**I AM**."
Judas his **betrayer** was also with them.
When he said to them, "**I AM**,"
they **turned away** and **fell** to the ground.
So he again asked them,
  "**Whom** are you **looking** for?"
They said, "**Jesus** the **Nazorean**."
Jesus answered,
  "**I told** you that **I AM**.
So if you are **looking** for me, let **these men** go."

Some of Jesus' "I AM" statements are intended to link Jesus' identity with the divine name introduced in Exodus 3:13–14; 6:3. This is a probable example. For unambiguous examples, see 8:24, 28, 58; 13:9.

means they are incapable of interceding on our behalf as our high priest can.

Jesus prayed, wept, and cried out from the cross to God. His broken body did not only seem to suffer, and thus he can intercede for us as angels cannot. Yet he lived without sin, and so may approach God as we cannot. This is, according to our author, "our confession."

PASSION The veneration of the cross is a devotion that entered the Good Friday liturgy during the Middle Ages. Other parts of today's liturgy are far older, such as the full prostration of the celebrant. People joining in the veneration are invited forward to perform an act of reverence, bowing, kneeling, or kissing the cross.

It is worth pausing for a moment to reflect on the object of our veneration.

The cross was an instrument of death, the common end of slaves, the poor, common criminals, revolutionaries, and seditionists. Crucifixion was a death intended to humiliate its victims, shame their families, and terrorize everyone else. The crosses were often set up along public thoroughfares. The Roman writer Appian records that

This was to **fulfill** what he had **said**,
   "I have not lost **any** of those you **gave** me."
(2) Then **Simon Peter**, who had a **sword**, **drew** it,
   struck the high priest's **slave**, and **cut off** his right ear.
The slave's name was **Malchus**.
Jesus said to **Peter**,
   "Put your **sword** into its **scabbard**.
Shall I not **drink** the **cup** that the **Father** gave me?"

So the **band** of **soldiers**, the **tribune**, and the **Jewish** guards
      seized Jesus,
   bound him, and **brought** him to **Annas** first.
He was the **father-in-law** of **Caiaphas**,
   who was **high priest** that year.
It was **Caiaphas** who had **counseled** the Jews
   that it was **better** that **one** man should **die**
      rather than the **people**.

(3) **Simon Peter** and **another** disciple followed **Jesus**.
Now the **other** disciple was known to the **high priest**,
   and he **entered** the courtyard of the high priest with **Jesus**.
But **Peter** stood at the gate outside.
So the **other** disciple, the **acquaintance** of the **high priest**,
   went out and **spoke** to the **gatekeeper** and brought **Peter** in.
Then the **maid** who was the **gatekeeper** said to **Peter**,
   "You are **not one** of this man's disciples, are you?"
He said, "I am **not**."
Now the **slaves** and the **guards** were **standing**
      around a **charcoal fire**
   that they had made, because it was **cold**,
   and were **warming** themselves.
Peter was **also** standing there keeping **warm**.

in the second century before Christ, 6,000
followers of the slave revolutionary Spartacus
were crucified at once along the Via Appia.
The Romans believed the cross was an
effective means of social control and used it
unsparingly during their occupation of Judea
and Palestine. The execution of Jesus was
a day in the life of empire.

(4) The **high priest** questioned **Jesus**
   about his disciples and about his **doctrine**.
Jesus **answered** him,
   "I have spoken **publicly** to the world.
I have always taught in a **synagogue**
   or in the temple area where **all** the Jews gather,
   and in **secret** I have said **nothing**. **Why** ask **me**?
Ask those who **heard** me what I said to them.
They know what I said."
When he had said this,
   one of the temple guards standing there struck Jesus and said,
   "Is **this** the way you **answer** the **high priest**?"
Jesus answered him,
   "If I have spoken **wrongly**, **testify** to the wrong;
   but if I have spoken **rightly**, **why** do you **strike** me?"
Then Annas sent him **bound** to **Caiaphas** the **high priest**.

Now **Simon Peter** was standing there keeping **warm**.
And they **said** to him,
   "You are **not** one of his **disciples**, are you?"
He denied it and said,
   "**I am not**."
One of the slaves of the high priest,
   a relative of the one whose ear Peter had cut off, said,
   "Didn't I **see** you in the **garden** with him?"
Again Peter denied it.
And **immediately** the **cock crowed**.

The Praetorium was the seat of Roman authority in Jerusalem.

(5) Then they brought **Jesus** from **Caiaphas** to the **praetorium**.
It was **morning**.
And they themselves did **not enter** the praetorium,
   in order **not** to be **defiled** so that they could **eat** the **Passover**.

Pontius Pilate, prefect of Judea (26–36 ad).

So **Pilate** came out to them and said,
    "What **charge** do you **bring** against this **man**?"
They answered and said to him,
    "If he were **not** a criminal,
    we would not have **handed** him **over** to you."
At this, Pilate **said** to them,
    "Take him **yourselves**, and **judge** him according to **your** law."
The **Jews** answered him,
    "We do not have the **right** to **execute anyone**, "
    in order that the **word** of **Jesus** might be **fulfilled**
    that he **said** indicating the **kind** of death he would **die**.
So **Pilate** went back into the **praetorium**
    and summoned **Jesus** and said to him,
    "Are **you** the **King** of the **Jews**?"
Jesus answered,

Pilate and Jesus are sparring verbally. Consider what kind of delivery will bring out this feature of the text.

    "Do **you** say this on your **own**
    or have **others** told you about me?"
Pilate answered,
    "**I** am not a **Jew**, **am** I?
Your **own nation** and the **chief priests** handed **you** over to **me**.
What have you **done**?"
Jesus answered,
    "My kingdom does not belong to **this** world.
If my kingdom **did** belong to this world,
    my attendants would be **fighting**
    to keep me from being **handed over** to the Jews.
But as it is, my kingdom is not **here**."
So Pilate said to him,
    "**Then** you are a **king**?"
Jesus answered,
    "**You** say I am a **king**.

For **this** I was **born** and for **this** I came into the **world**,
    to **testify** to the **truth**.
Everyone who belongs to the truth **listens** to my voice."
Pilate said to him, "What is **truth**?"

(6) When he had said this,
    he **again** went out to the **Jews** and **said** to them,
    "I find **no** guilt in him.
But you have a **custom** that I **release** one prisoner
        to you at Passover.
Do you want me to release to you the **King** of the **Jews**?"
They cried out **again**,
    "Not **this** one but **Barabbas**!"
Now **Barabbas** was a revolutionary.

(7) Then **Pilate** took **Jesus** and had him **scourged**.
And the soldiers wove a **crown** out of **thorns**
        and **placed** it on his **head**,
    and **clothed** him in a **purple** cloak,
    and they **came** to him and **said**,
    "**Hail**, **King** of the **Jews**!"
And they struck him repeatedly.
Once more **Pilate** went out and **said** to them,
    "**Look**, I am bringing him out to **you**,
    so that **you** may **know** that I find **no** guilt in him."
So **Jesus** came out,
    wearing the **crown** of **thorns** and the **purple cloak**.
And he said to them, "**Behold**, the **man**!"
When the **chief priests** and the **guards** saw him they cried out,
    "**Crucify** him, **crucify** him!"
Pilate said to them,
    "Take him **yourselves** and **crucify** him.

No such custom is known from any source not dependent on the Gospels.

Note the irony: Jesus' antagonists have dressed him as a king to mock him, but have unwittingly testified to his true identity. The entire Crucifixion scene in John is laden with irony. Jesus' ironic royalty is also quite clear in verses 19:19–22.

I find **no** guilt in him."
The Jews answered,
    "We have a **law**, and **according** to that law he **ought** to **die**,
    because he **made** himself the **Son** of **God**."
Now when **Pilate** heard **this** statement,
    he became **even more afraid**,
    and went **back** into the praetorium and **said** to **Jesus**,
    "**Where** are you **from**?"
Jesus did not answer him.
So **Pilate** said to him,
    "Do you **not speak** to me?
Do you **not know** that I have **power** to **release** you
    and I have **power** to **crucify** you?"
Jesus answered him,
    "You would have **no** power over **me**
    if it had **not** been **given** to you from **above**.
For this **reason** the one who **handed** me over to you
    has the **greater** sin."
Consequently, **Pilate** tried to **release** him; but the **Jews** cried out,
    "If you **release** him, you are **not** a Friend of Caesar.
Everyone who makes himself a **king** opposes **Caesar**."

When **Pilate** heard these words he **brought Jesus** out
    and **seated** him on the judge's bench
    in the place called **Stone Pavement**, in Hebrew, **Gabbatha**.
It was preparation day for **Passover**, and it was about noon.
And he said to the Jews,
    "**Behold**, your **king**!"
They cried out,
    "**Take** him away, **take** him away! **Crucify** him!"

Stone pavement, probably the same as that mentioned here, has been uncovered by archaeologists working in Jerusalem.

Pilate said to them,
    "Shall I **crucify** your king?"
The chief priests answered,
    "We have **no** king but **Caesar**."
Then he **handed** him over to them to be **crucified**.

(8) So they took **Jesus**, and, carrying the cross **himself**,
    he went out to what is called the **Place** of the **Skull**,
    in Hebrew, **Golgotha**.
There they **crucified** him, and with him two others,
    one on **either side**, with **Jesus** in the **middle**.
Pilate also had an inscription **written** and **put** on the **cross**.
It read,
    "**Jesus** the **Nazorean**, the **King** of the **Jews**."
Now many of the Jews read this inscription,
    because the place where **Jesus** was **crucified** was near the city;
    and it was written in **Hebrew**, **Latin**, and **Greek**.

So the **chief priests** of the **Jews** said to **Pilate**,
    "Do not write 'The **King** of the **Jews**,'
    but that he **said**, 'I am the **King** of the **Jews**'."
Pilate answered,
    "What I have **written**, I have **written**."

When the soldiers had **crucified** Jesus,
    they **took** his clothes and **divided** them into four shares,
    a share for **each** soldier.
They **also** took his **tunic**, but the **tunic** was **seamless**,
    woven in **one** piece from the **top** down.
So they said to one another,
    "Let's **not tear** it, but cast **lots** for it to **see** whose it will be,"

Greek and Hebrew were by far the dominant languages in Jerusalem. Even a good number of the Roman soldiers would have had Greek as their mother tongue. In Jerusalem, Latin was principally the language of imperial administration and the officer corps.

in order that the passage of **Scripture** might be **fulfilled**
   that says:
      *They **divided** my **garments** among them,*
         *and for my **vesture** they cast **lots**.*
This is what the soldiers did.
Standing by the **cross** of **Jesus** were his **mother**
   and his mother's sister, **Mary** the wife of **Clopas**,
   and **Mary** of **Magdala**.
When Jesus saw his **mother** and the **disciple** there whom he **loved**
   he said to his **mother**, "**Woman**, behold, your **son**."
Then he said to the disciple,
   "**Behold**, your **mother**."
And from that hour the **disciple** took her into his home.

After this, aware that **everything** was now **finished**,
   in order that the **Scripture** might be **fulfilled**,
   Jesus said, "**I thirst**."
There was a vessel **filled** with common wine.
So they put a sponge **soaked** in **wine** on a **sprig** of **hyssop**
   and **put** it up to his **mouth**.
When **Jesus** had taken the **wine**, he said,
   "It is **finished**."
And bowing his **head**, he handed over the **spirit**.

[Here all kneel and pause for a short time.]

Now since it was preparation day,
   in order that the **bodies** might not **remain** on the **cross**
      on the **sabbath**,
   for the **sabbath** day of that week was a solemn one,
   the **Jews** asked **Pilate** that their **legs** be **broken**
   and that they be **taken** down.

The beloved disciple (see also 13:23; 20:2; 21:7; and 21:20) never receives a proper name in the text. He was obviously of great importance to the author of the Gospel of John. Many biblical scholars believe that the Gospel of John was written in a community founded by this disciple.

In the Gospel of John, Jesus dies on the day before Passover. The other three Gospels place Jesus' death on Passover itself. On the day of preparation, the Passover lamb was slain in the Temple precincts.

So the soldiers **came** and **broke** the legs of the first
 and then of the other one who was **crucified** with Jesus.
But when they came to **Jesus** and saw that he was already **dead**,
 they did not **break** his legs,
 but **one** soldier thrust his **lance** into his side,
 and **immediately blood** and **water** flowed out.
An **eyewitness** has **testified**, and his **testimony** is **true**;
 he **knows** that he is speaking the **truth**,
 so that **you also** may **come** to **believe**.
For this happened so that the **Scripture** passage might be **fulfilled**:
 *Not a **bone** of it will be **broken**.*
And again another passage says:
 *They will look upon **him** whom they have **pierced**.*

After this, **Joseph** of **Arimathea**,
 secretly a disciple of Jesus for **fear** of the **Jews**,
 asked **Pilate** if he could remove the body of Jesus.
And **Pilate** permitted it.
So he **came** and **took** his body.
Nicodemus, the one who had **first** come to him at **night**,
 also came bringing a mixture of **myrrh** and **aloes**
 weighing about one **hundred** pounds.
They took the **body** of **Jesus**
 and bound it with **burial** cloths along with the **spices**,
 according to the **Jewish** burial custom.
Now in the **place** where he had been **crucified** there was a **garden**,
 and in the **garden** a new **tomb**, in which **no one**
  had **yet** been **buried**.
So they **laid** Jesus there because of the **Jewish** preparation day;
 for the **tomb** was close by.

This eyewitness was probably the beloved disciple.

Lectionary #41

READING I   Genesis 1:1—2:2

A reading from the Book of Genesis

In the **beginning**, when **God** created the **heavens** and the **earth**,
    the **earth** was a **formless wasteland**, and **darkness**
        covered the **abyss**,
    while a **mighty wind swept** over the **waters**.

Then God said,
    "**Let** there be **light**," and there was **light**.
God saw how **good** the light **was**.
God then **separated** the **light** from the **darkness**.
God called the light "**day**" and the darkness he called "**night**."
Thus **evening** came, and **morning** followed—the **first day**.

Then God said,
    "**Let** there be a **dome** in the middle of the **waters**,
    to separate **one** body of water from the **other**."
And so it **happened**:
    God made the **dome**,
    and it **separated** the water above the dome
        from the water below it.
God called the **dome** "**the sky**."
Evening came, and **morning** followed—the **second day**.

Then God said,
    "**Let** the **water** under the **sky** be **gathered** into a **single** basin,
    so that the **dry land** may **appear**."

Emphasize and enunciate this phrase. It's the first time God speaks in the Bible.

Notice that the dome of the sky separates waters above from waters below. The waters above the sky are the rains, restrained by gates under God's control (see Genesis 7:11, 8:2).

READING I   "In the beginning was the Word" (John 1:1). The setting of the first verse of the Gospel of John is eternity. In Genesis, God speaks heaven and earth into existence. In John, God's creative act of speaking is personified in the Word, which, as we soon learn, participates in creating before taking shape in human history as Jesus Christ. If Christians adhere to a historical religion—a religion arising in

response to events that happened in human history, it is also true that some Christians soon came to believe that the reasons for those events lay much further in the past than Jesus' Baptism and his birth; than the prophets who were believed to have testified about him; than the Exodus and Israel; than Abraham, Noah, and Adam; than the world; than even time itself. For the author

of the Gospel of John, Jesus Christ is present and at work in Genesis 1:1: "Let there be light."

John's placement of the Word (Christ) with God in eternity is the result of the christological lens through which he views scripture. In other words, John 1:1 is a result of the interpretation of Genesis 1:1 in the light of Christian belief. For John, all scripture, when it is properly interpreted, testifies

The sea that ancient Israelites knew was the Mediterranean.

And so it **happened**:
  the water **under** the sky was gathered into its basin,
  and the **dry land** appeared.
God called the **dry land** "the **earth**,"
  and the basin of the **water** he called "**the sea**."
God **saw** how **good** it was.
Then God said,
  "Let the **earth** bring forth **vegetation**:
  every kind of **plant** that bears **seed**
  and **every** kind of **fruit tree** on earth
  that bears **fruit** with its **seed** in it."
And so it **happened**:
  the earth brought forth **every** kind of **plant** that bears **seed**
  and **every** kind of **fruit** tree on **earth**
  that bears **fruit** with its **seed** in it.
God **saw** how **good** it was.
Evening came, and **morning followed**—the **third day**.

Then God said:
  "Let there be **lights** in the **dome** of the **sky**,
  to separate **day** from **night**.
Let them **mark** the fixed times, the **days** and the **years**,
  and serve as **luminaries** in the **dome** of the **sky**,
  to shed **light** upon the **earth**."
And so it **happened**:
  God made the **two** great **lights**,
  the **greater** one to govern the **day**,
  and the **lesser** one to govern the **night**;
  and he made the **stars**.
God **set** them in the **dome** of the sky,
  to shed **light** upon the **earth**,
  to govern the **day** and the **night**,
  and to separate the **light** from the **darkness**.

The planets are not mentioned, although ancient people, particularly the Babylonians, kept record of their movements.

to Jesus (John 5:39). Some 300 years after John wrote, Saint Augustine, in book 13 of the *Confessions,* saw in Genesis a symbolic account of the creation of the Church. This also was an act of interpretation by which Augustine, through an ecclesiastical lens, observed the foundations of the Church amid the foundations of the world.

Faith and reason are twin pillars of Roman Catholicism's interpretive traditions. If we do not find, as some of our fellow Christians demand of us, a "literal" or "inerrant" account of how the world and its creatures came to be in this reading, we nevertheless remain in the company of Saint Augustine who didn't either. By the standards of his own time, Augustine's speculation about the spiritual meaning of scripture was reasonable. In our own time we may read differently. Even when it is read in different ways, the story retains sufficient power to refer us to the One it ultimately concerns.

God **saw** how **good** it was.
Evening came, and **morning** followed—the **fourth day**.

Then God said,
    "Let the water **teem** with an **abundance** of living creatures,
    and on the **earth** let birds fly **beneath** the **dome** of the **sky**."
And so it **happened**:
    God created the **great** sea **monsters**
    and **all kinds** of **swimming creatures** with which
        the water **teems**,
    and **all kinds** of winged **birds**.
God **saw** how **good** it was, and God blessed them, saying,
    "Be **fertile**, **multiply**, and **fill** the water of the **seas**;
    and let the **birds** multiply on the **earth**."
Evening came, and **morning** followed—the **fifth day**.

Then God said,
    "Let the earth bring **forth all kinds** of **living** creatures:
    cattle, **creeping** things, and **wild** animals of all kinds."
And so it **happened**:
    God made **all kinds** of wild animals, **all kinds** of cattle,
    and all **kinds** of **creeping** things of the **earth**.
God **saw** how **good** it was.

Then God said:
    "Let us make **man** in our **image**, after our **likeness**.
Let them have **dominion** over the **fish** of the **sea**,
    the **birds** of the **air**, and the **cattle**,
    and over **all** the wild **animals**
    and **all** the creatures that **crawl** on the ground."
God created **man** in his **image**;
    in the **image** of **God** he **created** him;
    male and **female** he **created** them.

Note the shift from the singular to the plural.

READING II This text has been of great interest to Jews, Christians, and Muslims for centuries. "Take your son Isaac, your only one, whom you love, and go to the land of Moriah. There you shall offer him up as a holocaust." This reading would be dreadful enough if God simply said, "Kill your son for me." It is worse than this, for the son God tells Abraham to offer up is "your son Isaac, your only one, whom you love." God knows what this child means to his father. And why doesn't Abraham speak up for his son? When God was planning to destroy Sodom and Gomorrah, Abraham interceded on behalf of complete strangers! (See Genesis 18:22–33.)

Even though Abraham passes God's test and Isaac is spared, relief cannot mask the horror of the earlier verses. What sense are we to make of this reading? One might find, as did an anonymous author near the turn of the second century, that Abraham's obedience in the matter of his son's sacrifice is a positive example of obedience to religious

God **blessed** them, saying:
   "Be **fertile** and **multiply**;
   fill the earth and **subdue** it.
Have **dominion** over the **fish** of the **sea**, the **birds** of the **air**,
   and **all** the **living** things that **move** on the **earth**."
God **also** said:
   "**See**, I give you **every** seed-bearing **plant** all over the **earth**
   and **every** tree that has seed-bearing fruit on it to be **your** food;
   and to **all** the **animals** of the land, **all** the **birds** of the air,
   and **all** the living creatures that **crawl** on the ground,
   I give **all** the green plants for food."
And so it **happened**.
God **looked** at **everything** he had made, and he **found** it
   very good.
Evening came, and **morning** followed—the **sixth day**.

Thus the **heavens** and the **earth** and **all** their array
   were completed.
Since on the **seventh** day God was **finished**
   with the **work** he had been doing,
he rested on the **seventh** day from all the **work**
   he had **undertaken**.

[Shorter: Genesis 1:1, 26–31a]

This account of the creation of the world takes six days of work and culminates in God's own Sabbath day of rest.

READING II   Genesis 22:1–18

A reading from the Book of Genesis

God put **Abraham** to the **test**.
He called to him, "**Abraham**!"
"**Here** I am," he replied.

---

authority (*1 Clement* 10). Or perhaps one might focus upon Isaac as did Bishop Irenaeus of Lyons, who in the 180s compared Isaac's acceptance of his burden of wood to Christians shouldering their crosses to follow Jesus (*Against Heresies,* 4.5.3). Irenaeus alludes to Jesus' words that the cost of discipleship is self-denial and the cross (Matthew 16:24; Mark 8:34; Luke 9:23). For these authors,

and perhaps for us, the story contains patterns and examples on which Christian behavior should be modeled. These examples cannot obscure the horror of this story. But in them we may discern our ancestors grappling with a hard text and trying to make sense of it. Theirs is a worthy example.

READING III   In Exodus 3, Moses meets God for the first time and discovers, much to his shock, that he has been commissioned to lead Israel out of Egypt. According to God, the purpose of Moses' mission is clear: "Come now! I will send you to Pharaoh to lead my people, the Israelites, out of Egypt" (Exodus 3:10). But

Some Jewish and Christian traditions identify Mount Moriah with the Temple Mount.

The Hebrew word for "holocaust" comes from a verb meaning "to ascend" or "to go up." It refers to the smoke of the burning sacrifice.

Then God said:
"Take your son **Isaac**, your **only** one, whom you **love**,
and **go** to the **land** of **Moriah**.
There you shall offer him up as a **holocaust**
on a **height** that I will point **out** to you."
Early the next morning **Abraham** saddled his **donkey**,
took with him his son **Isaac** and **two** of his servants as **well**,
and with the **wood** that he had cut for the **holocaust**,
set out for the **place** of which **God** had **told** him.

On the **third** day **Abraham** got sight of the place from **afar**.
Then he said to his servants:
"**Both** of you **stay here** with the **donkey**,
while the **boy** and **I** go on over **yonder**.
We will **worship** and then **come back** to you."
Thereupon **Abraham** took the **wood** for the **holocaust**
and **laid** it on his son **Isaac's** shoulders,
while **he** himself carried the **fire** and the **knife**.
As the two walked on together, **Isaac** spoke
to his **father Abraham**:
"**Father**!" Isaac said.
"Yes, **son**," he replied.
Isaac continued, "**Here** are the **fire** and the **wood**,
but **where** is the **sheep** for the **holocaust**?"
"**Son**," Abraham answered,
"**God** himself will **provide** the **sheep** for the **holocaust**."
Then the two continued going forward.

When they **came** to the **place** of which **God** had **told** him,
Abraham built an **altar** there and arranged the **wood** on it.
Next he tied up his son **Isaac**,
and **put** him on **top** of the **wood** on the **altar**.

Consider your delivery here. This is not just any father-son conversation. It is between an unwitting child and the parent ordered to kill him.

Moses shortly learns that God has decided to use elaborate means to achieve this mission, repeatedly making Pharaoh obstinate so that he will refuse to let Israel go. In this reading it is not only Pharaoh who is made obstinate, but also all the Egyptians pursuing the Israelites (Exodus 14:17).

It is one thing for God to save Israel from slavery. It is another for God to save Israel from slavery by first manipulating its captors into even worse behavior. Origen of Alexandria (185 AD–early 250s), a scholar of the early Church, knew God's behavior toward Pharaoh required explanation. If God was both just and good as Origen believed, then how could God manipulate Pharaoh so badly? With help from Hebrews 6:7–8, Origen builds a case. From some land rain produces fruit, from some land thorns. God gives the rain, but the quality of the land, Origen contends, determines its produce. Like thorns raised by rain from inferior land, Pharaoh's already

Then he **reached** out and **took** the knife to **slaughter** his son.
But the LORD's messenger **called** to him from heaven,
    "**Abraham**, **Abraham**!"
"**Here** I am," he answered.
"Do **not** lay your hand on the boy," said the messenger.
"Do **not** do the **least** thing to him.
I know **now** how **devoted** you are to **God**,
    since you did **not** withhold from me your own **beloved** son."
As **Abraham** looked about,
    he spied a **ram** caught by its **horns** in the **thicket**.
So he **went** and **took** the ram
    and **offered** it up as a **holocaust** in **place** of his son.
Abraham named the site **Yahweh-yireh**;
    hence people now say, "On the mountain the LORD will **see**."

Again the LORD's messenger called to **Abraham** from **heaven**
    and said:
    "I **swear** by **myself**, declares the LORD,
    that because you **acted** as you did
    in not **withholding** from me your **beloved** son,
    I will **bless** you **abundantly**
    and make your **descendants** as **countless**
    as the **stars** of the **sky** and the **sands** of the **seashore**;
    your **descendants** shall take **possession**
    of the **gates** of their **enemies**,
    and in your **descendants all** the nations of the earth
        shall find **blessing**—
    all this because you **obeyed** my command."

[Shorter: Genesis 22:1–2, 9a, 10–13, 15–18]

Yahweh is God's personal name; *yireh* means "he will see."

God has already blessed and made promises to Abraham in similar terms. See 12:2–3; 13:14–17; 15:1–20; 18:3–14.

nasty disposition (see Exodus 5:1–10, 15–19) was amplified by God's acts on Israel's behalf (*On First Principles*, 3.1.10).

Whatever you may think of Origen's defense of God's actions, take note that he does not accept that Pharaoh was just a puppet on a string.

READING IV Guilty, according to Hosea, of serving other gods, Israel is depicted in the prophetic book bearing the prophet's name as a straying wife begged to return by her faithful husband, God. In today's reading the situation is different. Having at one time grown bored with her and cast her aside, God now promises unfailing love and essentially renews his wedding vows with Israel, his spouse.

The historical situation of these verses is the end of Israel's period of captivity and exile in Babylon. The end of Israel's exile was, in geopolitical terms, a small event, the tiniest sideshow to the Persian overthrow of Babylon by Cyrus the Great. But

Read Exodus 15:1–18, a very early Hebrew poem describing the events of the Exodus. Does the poem describe the destruction of the Egyptians in the same way as this reading?

READING III   Exodus 14:15—15:1

A reading from the Book of Exodus

The LORD said to **Moses**, "**Why** are you **crying** out to me?
Tell the **Israelites** to go **forward**.
And you, **lift** up your **staff** and, with **hand outstretched**
    over the sea,
    split the sea in **two**,
    that the **Israelites** may pass through it on dry land.
But I will make the **Egyptians** so obstinate
    that they will go in **after** them.
Then I will receive **glory** through **Pharaoh** and all his **army**,
    his **chariots** and **charioteers**.
The **Egyptians** shall **know** that I am the LORD,
    when I receive **glory** through **Pharaoh**
    and his **chariots** and **charioteers**."

The **angel** of **God**, who had been leading **Israel's** camp,
    now **moved** and went **around behind** them.
The **column** of **cloud** also, leaving the **front**,
    took up its place **behind** them,
    so that it **came** between the **camp** of the **Egyptians**
    and that of **Israel**.
But the **cloud** now became **dark**, and thus the **night** passed
    without the rival camps coming any closer together
        all night **long**.
Then **Moses** stretched out his **hand** over the **sea**,
    and the LORD swept the **sea**
    with a **strong east wind** throughout the **night**
    and so **turned** it into **dry land**.

---

that is not how things are viewed here, where the only event to which the end of the exile is compared is the epic event of the flood (Genesis 6—9). And as at the end of the flood (Genesis 9:8–17), God makes both a promise and a covenant: "my love shall never leave you, nor my covenant of peace be shaken" (Isaiah 54:10).

It is one thing to say, "God loves." Many gods, not just the God of the Old and New Testaments, have been believed to love people, towns, cities, regions, nations, and empires serving them. It is another thing entirely to say, in the words of 1 John 4:8, "God is love." It is characteristically Christian to cultivate the *activity* of love because we believe that this is how human beings share in God's life.

READING V   The previous reading talked of an enduring covenant of "steadfast peace" (Isaiah 54:10) while looking back toward an earlier covenant established between God and the earth at the end of the flood (Genesis 9:8–17). This reading refers to the renewal of yet another covenant, this time with David, king of Israel. At this point it is probably appropriate to ask, "What is a covenant?"

When the **water** was thus **divided**,
    the **Israelites** marched into the **midst** of the **sea** on dry **land**,
    with the **water** like a **wall** to their **right** and to their **left**.

The **Egyptians** followed in **pursuit**;
    all Pharaoh's **horses** and **chariots** and **charioteers**
        went **after** them
    right into the **midst** of the **sea**.
In the **night** watch just before **dawn**
    the LORD cast through the **column** of the **fiery** cloud
    upon the **Egyptian** force a **glance** that **threw** it into a **panic**;
    and he so **clogged** their **chariot wheels**
    that they could **hardly** drive.
With that the **Egyptians** sounded the **retreat** before **Israel**,
    because the LORD was **fighting** for them against the **Egyptians**.

Then the LORD told **Moses**, "Stretch out your **hand** over the **sea**,
    that the **water** may **flow** back upon the **Egyptians**,
    upon their **chariots** and their **charioteers**."
So **Moses** stretched out his **hand** over the **sea**,
    and at **dawn** the **sea** flowed **back** to its normal **depth**.
The **Egyptians** were **fleeing** head on toward the **sea**,
    when the LORD hurled them into its **midst**.
As the water flowed **back**,
    it covered the **chariots** and the **charioteers**
        of Pharaoh's **whole army**
    which had **followed** the Israelites into the **sea**.
Not a **single one** of them **escaped**.
But the **Israelites** had marched on dry **land**
    through the **midst** of the sea,
    with the **water** like a **wall** to their **right** and to their **left**.
Thus the LORD saved **Israel** on that **day**
    from the **power** of the **Egyptians**.

A covenant is an agreement between two or more parties to do or not to do certain things. In the Hebrew of the Old Testament, the typical way to describe the establishment of a covenant *(berit)* is to say the parties "cut" *(barat)* a covenant. If you pronounce the words, listening especially to the consonants *b*, *r*, and *t*, you will see that the Hebrew words for "covenant" and "cut" are closely related.

There are several covenants cut between God and humans in the Old Testament. The first covenant between God and the world at the end of the flood has already been mentioned (Genesis 9:8–17). The second one God cut with Abram concerning the promise of land, descendants, and circumcision (Genesis 15; 18). The third is the covenant of the law given at Sinai (Exodus 24). Today's reading refers to a fourth, monarchical covenant established between God and David (2 Samuel 7).

In its historical context, this reading was addressed to Israel. But Roman Catholics have typically interpreted the "everlasting covenant" as one cut between God and all humanity through the life, work, death, and Resurrection of David's descendant, Jesus of Nazareth.

When **Israel** saw the **Egyptians** lying **dead** on the **seashore**
 and **beheld** the great **power** that the LORD
 had **shown** against the **Egyptians**,
 they **feared** the LORD and **believed** in him
 and in his **servant Moses**.

Then **Moses** and the **Israelites** sang this **song** to the LORD:
 I will **sing** to the LORD, for he is **gloriously triumphant**;
 horse and **chariot** he has **cast** into the **sea**.

READING IV   Isaiah 54:5–14

A reading from the Book of the Prophet Isaiah

The **One** who has **become** your **husband** is your **Maker**;
 his **name** is the LORD of **hosts**;
your **redeemer** is the **Holy One** of Israel,
 called **God** of all the **earth**.
The LORD calls you **back**,
 like a **wife forsaken** and **grieved** in spirit,
 a wife **married** in **youth** and **then** cast off,
 says your **God**.
For a **brief moment** I **abandoned** you,
 but with **great tenderness** I will **take** you **back**.
In an **outburst** of **wrath**, for a **moment**
 I hid my **face** from you;
but with **enduring love** I take **pity** on you,
 says the LORD, your **redeemer**.

The "brief moment" of abandonment is the exile in Babylon.

READING VI It is unfortunate that the compilers of our Lectionary have left out Baruch 3:16–31. Try reading the full text from 3:9—4:4 in your Bible.

It is unlikely that Jeremiah's scribe, Baruch son of Neriah (see Baruch 1:1–2 and Jeremiah 36:4–36) actually wrote this book. Nor is it likely that the book dates from the time of the Babylonian exile. A person or per

sons to whom Baruch's legacy was important probably wrote it much later. The book survives in Greek, although it was probably composed, in whole or in part, in Hebrew.

With this reading we enter into a literary realm biblical scholars commonly call "wisdom literature." The book of Wisdom, Ecclesiastes, Sirach, and Proverbs 8 are

some examples of wisdom literature in the Bible. As the name suggests, a principal theme of wisdom literature is wisdom, often depicted as an animate female being behaving similarly to an angel. While there is considerable ambiguity in the Greek text, the "she" of this poetic passage is probably the Greek noun *sophia* (wisdom, see Baruch 3:23).

This is for me like the **days** of **Noah**,
    when I **swore** that the **waters** of **Noah**
    should **never again deluge** the **earth**;
so I have **sworn** not to be **angry** with you,
    or to **rebuke** you.
Though the **mountains** leave their **place**
    and the **hills** be **shaken**,
my **love** shall **never** leave you
    nor my **covenant** of **peace** be **shaken**,
    says the LORD, who has **mercy** on you.
O **afflicted** one, **storm-battered** and **unconsoled**,
    I lay your **pavements** in **carnelians**,
    and your **foundations** in **sapphires**;
I will make your **battlements** of **rubies**,
    your **gates** of **carbuncles**,
    and **all** your **walls** of **precious stones**.
All your **children** shall be taught by the LORD,
    and **great** shall be the **peace** of your **children**.
In **justice** shall you be **established**,
    far from the **fear** of **oppression**,
    where **destruction** cannot come **near** you.

READING V   Isaiah 55:1–11

A reading from the Book of the Prophet Isaiah

Thus says the LORD:
All you who are **thirsty**,
    come to the **water**!
You who have **no money**,
    come, receive **grain** and **eat**;

It is helpful to know that the word translated "prudence" in 3:9 is a Greek word called *phronēsis*. It can be translated as "wisdom," but in philosophical literature often signifies the kind of practical wisdom people use when trying to make enlightened choices given their current circumstances. What *sophia* means is different. *Sophia*

functions not unlike New Testament descriptions of the Holy Spirit, particularly in the Gospel of Luke, the Acts of the Apostles, and in the Gospel of John. She is active, creative (God's "master worker" in Proverbs 8:30), and divine, at work and at play in the world, present not only in the law of Israel but coursing through the very structure of the cosmos itself.

READING VII To a great many Jews, and probably especially to a priest like Ezekiel, the intact physical structure of the Temple and its location in Jerusalem were necessary conditions for communication with God. To speak in Ezekiel's terms, the Temple was the dwelling place of God's name. Perhaps the greatest theological problem of the book of Ezekiel, which is set during the first half of

come, without **paying** and without **cost**,
  drink **wine** and **milk**!
Why spend your **money** for what is not **bread**,
  your **wages** for what **fails** to **satisfy**?
Heed me, and you shall **eat well**,
  you shall **delight** in rich **fare**.
Come to me **heedfully**,
  listen, that you may have **life**.
I will **renew** with you the **everlasting** covenant,
  the **benefits** assured to **David**.
As I made him a **witness** to the **peoples**,
  a **leader** and **commander** of **nations**,
so shall you **summon** a **nation** you knew **not**,
  and **nations** that **knew** you **not** shall **run** to you,
because of the LORD, your **God**,
  the Holy One of **Israel**, who has **glorified** you.

Seek the LORD while he may be **found**,
  call him while he is **near**.
Let the **scoundrel** forsake his **way**,
  and the **wicked** man his **thoughts**;
let him **turn** to the LORD for **mercy**;
  to our **God**, who is **generous** in **forgiving**.
For my **thoughts** are not **your** thoughts,
  nor are **your** ways **my** ways, says the LORD.
As **high** as the **heavens** are **above** the **earth**,
  so **high** are **my ways** above **your ways**
  and **my thoughts** above **your thoughts**.

For **just** as from the **heavens**
  the **rain** and **snow** come **down**

See 2 Samuel 7.

the Babylonian exile, is how Israel can have a relationship with God with the Temple destroyed and its liturgies suspended. Ezekiel's first recorded vision contains the answer to this problem: God has followed the people into exile (Ezekiel 1).

If one finds the words of this oracle harsh, that is because they are. To Ezekiel,

the Babylonian exile is the result of his people's depraved commission of multiple, repeated, and severe religious crimes. The people bear full responsibility for their captivity. Yet harsh as these words are, it is God who seeks the people in order to restore them, not the other way around.

The language of ritual pollution and purification is very important to Ezekiel. In its

historical context, this language is associated with the Jerusalem Temple's liturgy. In its context as Christian Scripture, the rite of purification by water and the provision of the new heart and spirit are prophetic witness to later Christian understandings of the sacraments of Baptism (see, for example, Hebrews 10:19–25), Confirmation, and Reconciliation.

and do **not** return there
  till they have **watered** the earth,
  making it **fertile** and **fruitful**,
giving **seed** to the **one** who sows
  and **bread** to the **one** who **eats**,
so shall my **word** be
  that goes **forth** from my **mouth**;
my **word** shall not **return** to me **void**,
  but shall **do** my **will**,
  achieving the **end** for which I **sent** it.

READING VI   Baruch 3:9–15, 32—4:4

A reading from the Book of the Prophet Baruch

Hear, O **Israel**, the **commandments** of life:
  listen, and **know** prudence!
How is it, **Israel**,
  that you are in the **land** of your **foes**,
  grown **old** in a foreign **land**,
defiled with the **dead**,
  accounted with those **destined** for the **netherworld**?
You have **forsaken** the **fountain** of **wisdom**!
  Had you **walked** in the **way** of God,
  you would have **dwelt** in enduring **peace**.

Learn where **prudence** is,
  where **strength**, where **understanding**;
that you may know **also**
  where are **length** of **days**, and **life**,
  where **light** of the **eyes**, and **peace**.

This reference is to the exile in Babylon.

In many cultures and religions, contact with dead corpses results in ritual defilement or pollution. This is also the case in Israelite religion (see, for example, Numbers 9:6–13 and 19:11–21). The description here is probably metaphorical, but the metaphor's power is the belief that a defiled Israel is barred from God's presence.

EPISTLE   Paintings adorned the walls of a third-century baptistry in the Syrian town of Dura. Today they are on display at Yale University. One image portrays Jesus healing the paralyzed man (Matthew 9:1–8; Mark 2:1–12; Luke 5:17–26; John 5:1–9). Another, less well preserved, shows Jesus calming the storm (Matthew 8:23–27; Mark 4:35–41; Luke 8:22–25). A third and slightly more cryptic image depicts two women standing next to a closed sarcophagus while a star shines overhead. Putting aside whether or not this third image depicts a scene from scripture (Matthew 28:1 is a possibility), why would anyone paint a tomb on the wall of a baptistry?

This reading provides an answer. The identification of Baptism with death comes from a very early period in the development of the sacrament. Jesus, for example, twice speaks of his own death as a kind of Baptism (see Mark 10:38–39 and Luke 12:50). If Baptism grants new life in Christ, Paul reasons, then it also requires dying to one's old life.

Who has **found** the **place** of **wisdom**,
 who has **entered** into her **treasuries**?

The **One** who **knows** all **things** knows **her**;
 he has **probed** her by his **knowledge**—
the One who **established** the **earth** for all **time**,
 and **filled** it with four-footed **beasts**;
he who **dismisses** the **light**, and it **departs**,
 calls it, and it **obeys** him **trembling**;
before whom the **stars** at their **posts**
 shine and **rejoice**;
when he **calls** them, they **answer**, "**Here** we are!"
 shining with **joy** for their **Maker**.
Such is our **God**;
 no **other** is to be **compared** to him:
He has **traced** out the **whole** way of **understanding**,
 and has **given** her to **Jacob**, his **servant**,
 to **Israel**, his beloved **son**.

Since **then** she has **appeared** on earth,
 and **moved** among **people**.
She is the **book** of the **precepts** of **God**,
 the **law** that **endures** forever;
all who **cling** to her will **live**,
 but those will **die** who **forsake** her.
Turn, O **Jacob**, and **receive** her:
 walk by her **light** toward **splendor**.
Give **not** your **glory** to **another**,
 your **privileges** to an **alien** race.
Blessed are **we**, O **Israel**;
 for what **pleases God** is **known** to us!

The equation of Torah (Genesis, Exodus, Leviticus, Numbers, and Deuteronomy) with wisdom, specifically the association of principles of cosmic order with principles of Israel's law, is a characteristic notion of wisdom literature.

Father Aidan Kavanagh, OSB, a scholar of liturgy, often said that baptismal fonts should contain water deep enough to drown in. Although he enjoyed the raised eyebrows, Kavanagh was quite serious that the sign language of liturgy ought to express the basic sense of Paul's meaning. Death precedes rebirth. There is no Resurrection without the cross.

In the earliest baptismal rite of the Roman Church, the third-century *Apostolic Tradition,* Baptism of adults at the Easter Vigil is the preferred method of initiating people into Catholic Christianity. The structure of this rite is partially preserved in the Rite of Christian Initiation of Adults. If you are fortunate enough to belong to a community in which adults will receive the sacraments of Baptism, Confirmation, and first Eucharist at the Easter Vigil, you have the opportunity to participate in one of the most ancient liturgical structures of the Roman Catholic Church.

READING VII   Ezekiel 36:16–17a, 18–28

A reading from the Book of the Prophet Ezekiel

The **word** of the LORD came to me, **saying**:
  Son of **man**, when the **house** of **Israel lived** in their **land**,
    they **defiled** it by their **conduct** and **deeds**.
Therefore I **poured** out my **fury upon** them
    because of the **blood** that they **poured** out on the **ground**,
    and because they **defiled** it with **idols**.
I **scattered** them among the **nations**,
    dispersing them over **foreign** lands;
    according to their **conduct** and **deeds** I **judged** them.
But when they **came** among the **nations** wherever they **came**,
    they **served** to **profane** my holy name,
    because it was **said** of them: "**These** are the **people** of the LORD,
    yet they had to **leave** their **land**."
So I have **relented** because of my **holy** name
    which the **house** of **Israel profaned**
    among the **nations** where they **came**.
Therefore say to the **house** of **Israel**: **Thus** says the **Lord GOD**:
    Not for **your** sakes do I **act**, house of **Israel**,
    but for the **sake** of my **holy name**,
    which you **profaned** among the **nations** to which you **came**.
I will **prove** the **holiness** of **my great name**,
      profaned among the **nations**,
    in whose **midst** you have **profaned** it.
Thus the **nations** shall **know** that I am the LORD,
      says the **Lord GOD**,
    when in their **sight** I **prove** my **holiness** through **you**.

The phrase "Son of man" in Ezekiel does not have the Messianic overtones of Christian and Jewish apocalypticism. In Ezekiel the phrase calls attention to the mere humanity and mortality of the prophet in comparison with the divinity and immortality of God.

Note God's reason for acting on Israel's behalf.

GOSPEL   In Luke 9:18–21, Jesus asks his disciples, "Who do the crowds say that I am?" According to the disciples, answers vary. Some say that Jesus is John the Baptist, recently killed by Herod Antipas (Luke 9:7–9). Others say that he is Elijah. Still others say that Jesus is a prophet from the past. Then Jesus asks, "But who do you say that I am?" Peter replies, "The Messiah of God." Right after this, Jesus tells his disciples that the Son of Man must suffer rejection and death before being raised on the third day (Luke 9:22).

In today's reading, it is clear that the disciples have not yet grasped either that Jesus is the Son of Man or even what that means (24:5–7). To them Jesus' death is just horror. It casts into doubt everything he ever said or did, and everything they have believed and done since they foolishly left their old lives behind. How could Jesus be the Messiah? He may have entered Jerusalem as the Lord's anointed (Luke 19:28–40). But then, tortured and humiliated, he was killed in front of everyone.

The women at the tomb are the first to begin to understand what Christians have been coming to know ever since: we are people of the Resurrection (24:8–11). Without it we have no good news for anyone—just a tale of terror, agony, murder, and despair. But our story does not end there. We are the people of the empty tomb.

This is a prediction of the end of the exile.

For I will **take** you **away** from among the **nations**,
   gather you from **all** the **foreign** lands,
   and **bring** you **back** to **your** own **land**.
I will **sprinkle** clean **water upon** you
   to **cleanse** you from **all** your **impurities**,
   and from **all** your **idols** I will **cleanse** you.
I will give you a **new heart** and place a **new spirit within** you,
   taking from your **bodies** your **stony** hearts
   and **giving** you **natural** hearts.
I will **put** my **spirit within** you and make you **live** by my **statutes**,
   careful to **observe** my **decrees**.
You shall **live** in the **land** I **gave** your **fathers**;
   you shall be my **people**, and I will be your **God**.

EPISTLE   Romans 6:3–11

A reading from the Letter of Saint Paul to the Romans

Brothers and **sisters**:
Are you **unaware** that **we** who were **baptized** into **Christ Jesus**
   were **baptized** into his **death**?
We were **indeed buried** with him through **baptism** into **death**,
   so **that**, just as **Christ** was **raised** from the **dead**
   by the **glory** of the **Father**,
   we **too** might **live** in **newness** of **life**.

Pause briefly between stanzas.

For **if** we have **grown** into **union** with him
   through a **death** like **his**,
   we shall **also** be **united** with him in the **resurrection**.

We **know** that our **old** self was **crucified** with him,
  so that our **sinful** body might be **done** away with,
  that we might **no longer** be in **slavery** to sin.
For a **dead** person has been **absolved** from sin.
If, then, we have **died** with **Christ,**
  we **believe** that we shall **also live** with him.
We **know** that **Christ, raised** from the **dead, dies** no more;
  death no **longer** has **power** over him.
As to his **death,** he **died** to **sin once** and for **all;**
  as to his **life,** he **lives** for **God.**
Consequently, you **too** must think of yourselves
    as being **dead** to **sin**
  and **living** for **God** in **Christ Jesus.**

GOSPEL   Luke 24:1–12

A reading from the holy Gospel according to Luke

At daybreak on the **first day** of the week
  the **women** who had come from **Galilee** with **Jesus**
  took the **spices** they had **prepared**
  and **went** to the **tomb.**
They found the **stone** rolled **away** from the **tomb;**
  but when they **entered,**
  they did **not** find the **body** of the **Lord Jesus.**
While they were **puzzling** over this, **behold,**
  two men in **dazzling** garments **appeared** to them.
They were **terrified** and **bowed** their faces to the **ground.**

Fear and gestures of obeisance are normal responses of humans to divinity in much ancient literature and in the Gospel of Luke and Acts in particular. See, for example, the responses of Zechariah (Luke 1:12–13), Mary (1:29–30), and Peter (5:8). Also note the response of Cornelius to Peter and Peter's reply in Acts 10:25–26.

See Jesus' predictions of his Passion in Luke 9:22, 44–45; 18:31–34.

They **said** to them,
  "**Why** do you **seek** the **living** one among the **dead**?
He is **not here**, but he has been **raised**.
Remember what he **said** to you while he was **still** in **Galilee**,
  that the **Son** of **Man** must be **handed over** to **sinners**
  and be **crucified**, and **rise** on the **third day**."
And they **remembered** his words.
Then they **returned** from the **tomb**
  and **announced** all these things to the **eleven**
  and to **all** the others.
The women were **Mary Magdalene**, **Joanna**,
    and **Mary** the mother of **James**;
  the **others** who **accompanied** them **also** told this
    to the apostles,
  but their **story** seemed like **nonsense**
  and they did **not believe** them.
But **Peter** got up and **ran** to the tomb,
  bent **down**, and **saw** the burial cloths **alone**;
  then he went **home amazed** at what had **happened**.

EASTER SUNDAY

Lectionary #42

READING I   Acts 10:34a, 37–43

A reading from the Acts of the Apostles

Peter proceeded to **speak** and **said**:
"You **know** what has **happened** all over **Judea**,
    beginning in **Galilee** after the **baptism**
    that **John** preached,
    how **God** anointed **Jesus** of **Nazareth**
    with the **Holy Spirit** and **power**.
He went about doing **good**
    and **healing** all those **oppressed** by the **devil**,
    for **God** was with **him**.
We are **witnesses** of **all** that he **did**
    both in the **country** of the **Jews** and in **Jerusalem**.
They **put** him to **death** by hanging him on a **tree**.
This man **God raised** on the **third day** and **granted**
        that **he be visible**,
    not to **all** the people, but to **us**,
    the **witnesses** chosen by **God** in advance,
    who **ate** and **drank** with him after he **rose** from the **dead**.
He **commissioned** us to **preach** to the **people**
    and **testify** that he is the **one** appointed by **God**
    as **judge** of the **living** and the **dead**.
To him **all** the **prophets** bear **witness**,
    that **everyone** who **believes** in him
    will **receive forgiveness** of **sins** through his **name**."

Calling the cross a tree suggests Deuteronomy 21:23, which states that a corpse hung on a tree is cursed (see also Acts 5:30). Also compare Paul in Galatians 3 (especially 3:13). Paul reinterprets the significance of this curse in the course of an argument about law and faith.

See Luke 24:36–49 and Acts 1:1–12.

READING I   Peter delivers this speech at a critical turning point in the account of the growth of the Church in Acts. After the execution of Stephen (7:60), Acts reports that members of the Church fled Jerusalem due to persecution (8:1). The missionary activity previously confined to Jerusalem relocates, in the next two chapters, to points north, west, and northeast of Jerusalem. In 6:7 we read that "the number of the disciples in Jerusalem increased greatly." In 9:31 we find the Church present and growing in "all Judea, Samaria, and Galilee." The geographical expansion of the Church is taking place as Jesus predicted it would in 1:8.

As the geographical range of the Church expands, so does the diversity of its membership. Cornelius, a Roman centurion, and Peter, a Jewish disciple of a crucified Jewish seditionist, are an especially unlikely pair. Peter gives this speech before Cornelius and his entire household in 10:34b–35: "In truth, I see that God shows no partiality. Rather in every nation whoever fears him and acts uprightly is acceptable to him."

The Greek of 10:39 is ambiguous, but the Jews are most likely "they" whom Peter charges with Jesus' murder. Compare, for example, Acts 2:23, where Peter singles out "Israelites" and charges them with killing Jesus without a word about Roman responsibility. In 4:8–12, Peter directly accuses Jewish leaders of killing Jesus, again saying nothing about Rome (see Luke 23:24–25).

In royal seating arrangements in Greco-Roman antiquity, the right side is the favored spot.

Note the tension between the "already" of the believers' hidden life with Christ, and the "not yet" of a shared appearance in glory. The appearance of Christ in 3:4 almost certainly refers to his return.

READING II   Colossians 3:1–4

A reading from the Letter of Saint Paul to the Colossians

Brothers and **sisters**:
If then you were **raised** with **Christ**, **seek** what is **above**,
    where **Christ** is **seated** at the **right** hand of **God**.
Think of **what** is **above**, not of what is on **earth**.
For you have **died**, and your **life** is **hidden** with **Christ** in **God**.
When **Christ** your **life** appears,
    then **you too** will **appear with** him in **glory**.

Or:

Look at the assembly as you read the first line.

READING II   1 Corinthians 5:6b–8

A reading from the first Letter of Saint Paul to the Corinthians

Brothers and **sisters**:
Do you **not know** that a **little yeast leavens** all the **dough**?
Clear out the old yeast,
    so that you may become a **fresh** batch of **dough**,
    inasmuch as you are **unleavened**.
For our paschal **lamb**, **Christ**, has been **sacrificed**.
Therefore, let us **celebrate** the **feast**,
    not with the old **yeast**, the **yeast** of **malice** and **wickedness**,
    but with the **unleavened bread** of **sincerity** and truth.

There is a choice of second readings today. Speak with the liturgy coordinator or homilist to find out which reading will be used.

READING II   **COLOSSIANS.** What does it mean that the Colossians "were raised with Christ"? This is a question that requires a wider look at the letter than the snippet from the Lectionary allows us. The first four verses of the third chapter begin a new section of the letter while recapitulating themes and ideas developed earlier. There's more here than meets the eye.

In 2:8 the Colossians get a warning: "See to it that no one captivates you with an empty, seductive philosophy according to human tradition, according to the elemental powers of the world and not according to Christ." It is hard to describe in brief what may have comprised this philosophy. More obvious, however, is that things "according to Christ" are opposed to things "according to human tradition." In our reading, this antithesis is expressed in terms of earthly and heavenly things.

In 2:12 we also find the term "raised with." But here it is explained in detail: "You were buried with him in baptism, in which you were also *raised with* him through faith in the power of God, who raised him from the dead." To be "raised with Christ" means to participate in Christ's death and Resurrection through the sacrament of Baptism. The author's sacramental theology is both "according to Christ" and part of "what is

GOSPEL John 20:1–9

A reading from the holy Gospel according to John

On the first day of the week,
   Mary of **Magdala** came to the **tomb** early in the **morning**,
   while it was still **dark**,
   and saw the **stone removed** from the **tomb**.
So she **ran** and **went** to Simon Peter
   and to the **other** disciple whom **Jesus loved**, and **told** them,
   "They have **taken** the **Lord** from the **tomb**,
   and we don't know **where** they put him."
So **Peter** and the **other** disciple went out and **came** to the **tomb**.
They both **ran**, but the **other** disciple ran **faster** than Peter
   and **arrived** at the tomb **first**;
   he bent **down** and saw the **burial** cloths there, but did
      not go in.
When **Simon Peter** arrived **after** him,
   he **went into** the **tomb** and **saw** the **burial cloths** there,
   and the **cloth** that had **covered** his head,
   not with the **burial** cloths but **rolled** up in a **separate** place.
Then the **other** disciple **also** went in,
   the one who had **arrived** at the **tomb first**,
   and he **saw** and **believed**.
For they did **not yet** understand the **Scripture**
   that he had to **rise** from the **dead**.

The footrace seems intended to elevate the stature of the beloved disciple. The Gospel of John encourages and demands *belief* in Jesus above all else.

above," not "according to human tradition" and part of "what is on earth."

Despite the letter's dismissive characterization of philosophy as in league with deceit, Christian thinkers have made extensive use of philosophy (and other forms of learning) in their attempts to craft good theology. Augustine and Origen are inconceivable absent Plato. One cannot imagine Thomas Aquinas without "the philosopher," a reverential moniker for his beloved Aristotle. Christianity is the richer for much of its philosophy.

1 CORINTHIANS. The apostle Paul wrote "occasional" letters. This does not mean that he wrote letters from time to time, but rather that he wrote letters on particular occasions to address particular communities. His letters are not theological treatises aimed at a generalized, anonymous audience. The theology of Paul's letters is situational, and largely determined by the circumstances of his addressees.

A Corinthian man, we learn back in 5:1, is in a sexual relationship with his father's wife. One can only hope that the woman is his stepmother and widowed. In any case, to Paul this behavior qualifies as "sexual sin" (in Greek, *porneia*). Reproaching the Corinthians for being puffed up when they ought to be ashamed (5:2), Paul, using a particularly vivid turn of phrase ("you are to deliver this man to Satan for the destruction of his flesh"), urges them to kick the man out of the Church (5:4–5).

In today's reading Paul imagines the body of the Corinthian Church as an unleavened lump of Passover dough. Recall that Passover is the feast of unleavened bread

The location of Emmaus has not been satisfactorily established.

Compare John 20:11–18, in which Mary does not immediately recognize the post-Resurrection Jesus.

Lectionary #46

AFTERNOON GOSPEL Luke 24:13–35

A reading from the holy Gospel according to Luke

That very day, the first day of the week,
   two of **Jesus'** disciples were going
   to a village seven miles from **Jerusalem** called **Emmaus**,
   and they were conversing about **all** the things
      that had **occurred**.
And it **happened** that while they were **conversing** and **debating**,
   Jesus himself drew **near** and **walked** with them,
   but their **eyes** were **prevented** from recognizing him.
He **asked** them,
   "**What** are you **discussing** as you **walk** along?"
They **stopped**, looking **downcast**.
One of them, named **Cleopas**, said to him in **reply**,
   "Are **you** the **only** visitor to **Jerusalem**
   who does **not** know of the **things**
   that have **taken** place there in these **days**?"
And he **replied** to them, "What **sort** of things?"
They **said** to him,
   "The **things** that **happened** to Jesus the **Nazarene**,
   who was a **prophet** mighty in **deed** and **word**
   before **God** and all the **people**,
   how our **chief priests** and **rulers** both **handed** him **over**
   to a **sentence** of **death** and **crucified** him.
But we were **hoping** that he would be the **one** to **redeem** Israel;
   and **besides** all this,
   it is **now** the third day since this took **place**.

(see Exodus 12:1–28, 43–49; Deuteronomy 16:1–8). As yeast leavens dough, so also does the offending man pollute the Church. With the Passover lamb, Christ, already sacrificed on the community's behalf, the community must "un-leaven" itself by removing the source of its pollution and return to spiritual health.

There is a choice of Gospels today; the Gospel proclaimed at the Easter Vigil is also an option. Speak with the liturgy coordinator or homilist to find out which one will be used.

GOSPEL   What "Scripture" is meant in 20:9? Is it a general statement like 1 Corinthians 15:4? Does John have a particular book and verse from the Old Testament in mind (perhaps Hosea 6:2)? Or is the scripture in question words of Jesus, perhaps another Christian text (the

Gospel of Mark?) or even Jesus' own words *in John's Gospel itself* (see John 2:21–22)? "Scripture" in the New Testament means the Old Testament. But in John 18:32 Jesus' words are fulfilled much as scripture is repeatedly fulfilled in Gospel. Do we see in John 20:9 and 18:32 the beginnings of a Christian understanding of scripture that includes Christian writings in addition to the Old Testament?

All four Gospels place Mary Magdalene first among the women who arrived at the tomb early on the morning after Jesus rose.

The two men in white garments (Luke 24:4).

For the prophets as important witnesses to Jesus' Passion, see Jesus' third prediction of his Passion (Luke 18:31–34; also see 24:44).

In the first of his predictions of his Passion, Jesus stresses the Passion's necessity (see Luke 9:22; 24:7, 44).

Some **women** from our **group**, however, have **astounded** us:
  they were at the **tomb** early in the **morning**
  and did **not** find his body;
  they came **back** and **reported**
  that they had **indeed** seen a **vision** of **angels**
  who **announced** that he was **alive**.
Then **some** of those **with** us went to the **tomb**
  and found things **just** as the **women** had **described**,
  but **him** they did not **see**."
And he **said** to them, "Oh, how **foolish** you are!
How **slow** of **heart** to **believe** all that the **prophets** spoke!
Was it not **necessary** that the **Christ** should **suffer** these things
  and **enter** into his **glory**?"
Then **beginning** with **Moses** and **all** the **prophets**,
  he **interpreted** to them what **referred** to him
  in all the **Scriptures**.
As they **approached** the **village** to which they were **going**,
  he gave the **impression** that he was going on **farther**.
But they **urged** him, "**Stay** with us,
  for it is nearly **evening** and the **day** is almost **over**."
So he went in to **stay** with them.
And it **happened** that, while he was **with** them at **table**,
  he took **bread**, said the **blessing**,
  broke it, and **gave** it to them.
With that their **eyes** were **opened** and they **recognized** him,
  but he **vanished** from their **sight**.

Matthew reports that she came to see the tomb with another woman named Mary (Matthew 28:1). Mark writes that three women came to the tomb bearing spices, Mary Magdalene, Mary the wife (or perhaps the sister) of James, and Salome (Mark 16:1). Luke records that the women who came to the tomb were Mary Magdalene, Joanna, Mary the wife or sister of James, and female "others who accompanied them" (see Luke 24:10; in 8:2–3, Luke lists a number of women who followed Jesus in Galilee). John records that Mary Magdalene journeyed alone. And not only is Mary the one who finds Jesus' tomb empty in John, but she is also the first person to whom Jesus appears after he has been raised (John 20:11–18).

The tomb's second and third visitors come because they have heard a fantastic story about it. John does not tell us why the first one came. From the other three Gospels we can glean the women's likely purpose, even if it is only, as in Matthew, "to see" the tomb. It is not possible to discern even this in John. All we know is that before sunrise, before Peter and the beloved disciple held their footrace, before Jesus appeared to anyone at all, before the shock, anguish, fear, and horror of the cross were slain together and reborn as joy, this woman walked alone to Jesus' tomb and returned (to understate matters) with some very important news.

AFTERNOON GOSPEL The Gospel of Luke, like the other three canonical Gospels, was written decades after the events it describes. Today's reading gives us an interesting look at what

Then they **said** to each other,
  "Were not our **hearts burning** within **us**
  while he **spoke** to us on the **way** and **opened** the **Scriptures**
    to us?"
So they set out at **once** and **returned** to **Jerusalem**
  where they found **gathered** together
  the **eleven** and those **with** them who were **saying**,
  "The **Lord** has truly been **raised** and has **appeared** to **Simon**!"
Then the **two recounted**
  what had taken **place** on the **way**
  and how he was made **known** to them in the **breaking** of **bread**.

the author of this Gospel, who wrote either toward the end of the first century or the beginning of the second, believed was the mindset of Jesus' earliest followers in the days immediately following the Crucifixion.

For one thing, our author believes the disciples' expectations had not been met. To a stranger who has joined them on the road, two disciples recount how Jesus, whom they call "a prophet," was executed, adding, "But we were hoping that he would be the one to redeem Israel." A dead redeemer is clearly no redeemer at all. The hopes raised

when Jesus' entered Jerusalem, acclaimed as king with words of a royal psalm, have been dashed against the hard reality of the cross (Luke 19:29–40).

For another thing, our author believes that the christological interpretation of the Old Testament was among the earliest and most exciting projects of the early Church. The act of biblical interpretation, initiated by Jesus himself, sets slow hearts ablaze.

For yet another, our author believes that Jesus was perceived with clarity in the sacrament of Eucharist. The revelation of Jesus' identity in the breaking of bread shows that

our author believes that the Eucharist is a means to an encounter with God.

Lastly, our author believes that piecing together the facts about Jesus' resurrection was the collective task of the community. No one person provided all the information. The experience of the disciples on the road to Emmaus enables partial understanding, but it remains partial until all are gathered together.

Lectionary #45

READING I   Acts 5:12–16

A reading from the Acts of the Apostles

Many **signs** and **wonders** were **done** among the **people**
   at the **hands** of the **apostles**.
They were **all** together in Solomon's **portico**.
None of the others **dared** to join them, but the **people**
   esteemed them.
Yet **more** than **ever**, **believers** in the **Lord**,
   great **numbers** of **men** and **women**, were **added** to them.
Thus they **even carried** the **sick** out into the **streets**
   and **laid** them on **cots** and **mats**
   so that when **Peter** came by,
   at least his **shadow** might **fall** on **one** or **another** of them.
A **large** number of **people** from the **towns**
   in the **vicinity** of **Jerusalem also** gathered,
   bringing the **sick** and those **disturbed** by **unclean spirits**,
   and they were **all** cured.

Emphasize this paragraph. "Yet more than ever," "Thus they even," and "at least his shadow" are verbal cues that the section contains extraordinary information.

". . . and they were *all* cured." Not some, or even most. All.

READING I In our Bible, the original Greek phrase used in 5:12 *(homothumadon)* is translated as "all together." The translation permits the interpretation that the apostles were simply occupying the same physical space. It is possible that this is what the author intends here. But the word also means "unanimously" or "with one accord." The roots of the word, *homo-* and *thum-,* communicate "similarity" on the one hand, and "accord" (also "mind," "heart," "spirit," "will") on the other.

At several points in the early chapters of Acts, the author provides readers with summaries of the activities of Jesus' followers and then, starting with the events of Pentecost, the early Church. In 1:14, we find *homothumadon* describing the ongoing activities of prayer among the apostles and those with them. In 2:46, another summary, the word characterizes the early Church in the Temple. In 4:24, the word describes the united voice of praise the Church raises upon its successful defense before a council of Jewish religious leaders. In 15:25, the word characterizes the harmonious agreement of a council of the Church.

The history of the early Church Luke offers is highly idealized. We find no mention in Acts, for example, of the disagreement Paul recalls between himself and Peter at Antioch on questions of table fellowship between Jews and Gentiles (Galatians 2:11–14). In Acts, the question of Gentile

READING II   Revelation 1:9–11a, 12–13, 17–19

Read this paragraph slowly, pausing between clauses. There's a lot of information here about John and his perspective on his situation. If it's hastily run together, it will be lost.

Patmos = PAT-mos

This is the point in Revelation when John's visions begin. First he hears, and then he sees. Let your delivery distinguish not only between John's introduction to his vision and the vision itself, but between the aural and the visual dimensions to the vision.

These are words of Jesus. Proclaim them boldly.

A reading from the Book of Revelation

I, **John**, your **brother**, who **share** with you
    the **distress**, the **kingdom**, and the **endurance** we have
        in Jesus,
    found myself on the **island** called **Patmos**
    because I proclaimed God's **word** and gave **testimony** to Jesus.
I was caught up in **spirit** on the **Lord's** day
    and **heard behind** me a **voice** as **loud** as a **trumpet**, which said,
    "**Write** on a **scroll** what you **see**."
Then I **turned** to **see** whose **voice** it was that **spoke** to me,
    and when I **turned**, I saw **seven** gold **lampstands**
    and in the **midst** of the **lampstands** one **like** a **son** of **man**,
    wearing an **ankle-length robe**, with a **gold sash**
        around his chest.

When I caught **sight** of him, I **fell down** at his **feet** as though **dead**.
He **touched** me with his **right hand** and said, "Do **not** be afraid.
I am **the first** and **the last**, the **one** who **lives**.
Once I was **dead**, but **now** I am **alive forever** and **ever**.
I hold the **keys** to **death** and the **netherworld**.
Write **down**, therefore, what you have **seen**,
    and what is **happening**, and what will **happen** afterwards."

incorporation into the church happens by revelation and without rancor (10:9–16; 11:1–18; 15:1–35). The Church of Acts is a Church that thinks and acts "with one accord."

READING II The name of the book of Revelation comes from the first word of its first verse. The word is *apokalupsis* in Greek, which means "revelation" or "disclosure," and is the origin of

the English word "apocalypse." As a particular kind of writing, an apocalypse discloses information, often in a cryptic, mysterious, and symbolic manner, concerning both the configuration of heaven and the course of future events.

Ancient and medieval portraits of John of Patmos sometimes depict him sleeping with the subjects of his vision occupying the space above his slumbering form. Is John's vision a dream? Is he "awake"? What kind of visionary consciousness permits John's

experience? These questions are probably unanswerable on the basis of the text.

As lectors, we can seek answers to different sorts of questions. While "Son of Man" is a familiar messianic title of Jesus in the Gospels, what is the significance of John's description of the speaker among the lampstands as "one like a son of man"?

This description depends upon the book of Daniel. Like Revelation, Daniel 7—12 is an apocalypse. Like John, Daniel contains a

GOSPEL   John 20:19–31

A reading from the holy Gospel according to John

There are four voices in this reading: the narrator, Jesus, the disciples, and Thomas.

On the **evening** of that **first day** of the **week**,
    when the **doors** were **locked**, where the **disciples** were,
    for **fear** of the **Jews**,
    Jesus came and **stood** in their **midst**
    and said to them, "**Peace** be with **you**."
When he had **said** this, he **showed** them his **hands** and his **side**.
The **disciples rejoiced** when they **saw** the **Lord**.
Jesus said to them again, "**Peace** be with **you**.
As the **Father** has **sent** me, so **I** send **you**."
And when he had **said** this, he **breathed** on them and **said**
    to them,
    "**Receive** the **Holy Spirit**.
Whose **sins** you **forgive** are **forgiven** them,
    and whose **sins** you **retain** are **retained**."

Didymus (DIH-dih-mus) means "twin."

Thomas, called **Didymus**, one of the **Twelve**,
    was not with them when **Jesus** came.
So the **other** disciples said to him, "We have **seen** the **Lord**."
But **he** said to them,
    "**Unless** I **see** the **mark** of the **nails** in his **hands**
    and **put** my **finger** into the **nailmarks**
    and **put** my **hand** into his **side**, I will **not believe**."

Gospel readers should avoid the temptation to proclaim Thomas' words as though he might be a little prissy. Give him his due when you proclaim this passage.

Now a **week** later his **disciples** were **again** inside
    and **Thomas** was **with** them.
Jesus came, although the **doors** were **locked**,
    and **stood** in their **midst** and said, "**Peace** be with **you**."

---

report of visions about the course of future events. In Daniel 7:13–14, "One like a son of man" receives power from an enthroned figure called "the Ancient of Days." In the original historical context of the book of Daniel, the "one like a son of man" was perhaps the archangel Michael, while the Ancient of Days was certainly God. Not surprisingly, Christians have often interpreted the scene to depict God the Son receiving authority from God the Father. In Revelation, the "one like a son of man" is clearly Christ.

And what about the lampstands? Revelation 1—3 includes instructions from the "one like a son of man" to John to write seven letters to seven angels, each one associated with a different Church in Asia Minor (modern-day Turkey). The seven lampstands represent the seven Churches.

GOSPEL   Jesus goes by many names and titles in the New Testament. He is called Christ, Lord, Rabbi, Teacher, Son of God, Son of Man, Son of David, High Priest, Advocate, and Lamb of

God, to name a few. Although Roman Catholic doctrine confesses that Jesus is God, the second person of the Trinity, he is rarely called God in the New Testament. But today we encounter one of those places in which Jesus is clearly called God.

In terms of the Gospel's literary structure, Thomas' confession of 20:29 ties back to 1:1 and 1:18, which are the two other places in John where Jesus (or the Word) is called God. It is important to note that although Jesus is prepared to let Thomas

"But these are written that you may come to believe." Read this sentence slowly, with emphasis, giving particular attention to "you may believe." Belief is much of what discipleship is about for John. John 20:30–31 is one of two conclusions to the Gospel (see also 21:24–25), containing the narrator's statement about why a large part of it has been written. It's important pause before you read these verses, setting them apart from what goes before.

Then he said to **Thomas**, "**Put** your finger **here** and **see** my **hands**,
   and **bring** your **hand** and **put** it into my **side**,
   and **do** not be **unbelieving**, but **believe**."
Thomas answered and said to him, "**My Lord and my God**!"
Jesus **said** to him, "Have you **come** to **believe**
   because you have **seen** me?
Blessed are **those** who **have not seen** and have **believed**."

Now **Jesus** did **many other signs** in the **presence** of his **disciples**
   that are **not** written in this book.
But **these** are **written** that you may **come to believe**
   that **Jesus** is the **Christ**, the **Son** of **God**,
   and that **through** this **belief** you may have **life** in his **name**.

satisfy his doubts by placing hands and fingers in his wounds, the text does not say that Thomas actually does so. Based on Jesus' reply to Thomas' confession of "My Lord and my God," the sight of Jesus may bring Thomas to belief. Jesus' word of blessing on those who have not seen but believed recalls both the experience of the man born blind in John 9 and the metaphorical relationship between seeing and believing in that chapter.

In the Gospel of John, the most important requirement for discipleship is belief in Jesus. A primary purpose of recording the signs in a Gospel, according to the author, is to lead its audience to belief (20:30–31). Belief does not simply consist in believing that Jesus is the Christ, or the Son of Man, but believing that Jesus has been sent as the Father's unique envoy and exclusive Mediator (14:27, 30; 17:8; see also 10:1–18, in which the exclusivity of Jesus' role is clear).

3RD SUNDAY OF EASTER

Lectionary #48

READING I   Acts 5:27b–32, 40b–41

A reading from the Acts of the Apostles

When the **captain** and the **court officers** had **brought**
    the **apostles** in
and made them **stand** before the **Sanhedrin**,
the **high priest** questioned them,
    "We gave you **strict** orders, did we **not**,
    to **stop teaching** in that **name**?
Yet you have **filled Jerusalem** with your **teaching**
    and want to **bring** this man's **blood** upon us."
But **Peter** and the **apostles** said in reply,
    "We must **obey God** rather than **men**.
The **God** of our **ancestors** raised **Jesus**,
    though **you** had him **killed** by **hanging** him on a **tree**.
God **exalted** him at his **right hand** as **leader** and **savior**
    to grant **Israel repentance** and **forgiveness** of **sins**.
We are **witnesses** of these things,
    as is the **Holy Spirit** whom **God** has **given** to those who
    obey him."

The **Sanhedrin** ordered the **apostles**
    to **stop speaking** in the **name** of Jesus, and **dismissed** them.
So they **left** the presence of the **Sanhedrin**,
    rejoicing that they had been found **worthy**
    to **suffer dishonor** for the **sake** of the **name**.

This is essentially a courtroom scene. Imagine an irate judge dealing with "repeat offenders." Let your proclamation reflect the high priest's anger at the disciples.

Proclaim the apostles' response with stridency, perhaps reflecting fearlessness, perhaps just simple confidence. But it has to be more than a match for the high priest's anger.

READING I In *Nostra aetate,* the Second Vatican Council held that while "Jewish authorities and those who followed their lead pressed for the death of Christ" (see John 19:6), their guilt does not extend to the entire Jewish people. In *Dei verbum,* the Council urged interpreters of scripture to pay due attention to the human writer's time and culture in the attempt to explain scripture's meaning. A measure of the progress made in the Church's attitude toward both Jews and the task of biblical interpretation is how peculiar both of these findings appear today. Of course, Jews do not bear collective guilt for the death of Jesus. Of course, the cultural contexts of scripture's human writers affect scripture's meaning. Why would anyone think differently?

In today's reading, Peter charges Jewish authorities with killing Jesus by hanging him on a tree. But Peter is silent about some others who followed their lead. He does not mention Roman authority. According to all four Gospels (Matthew 27:26; Mark 15:15; Luke 23:25; John 19:16), as well as the Roman historian Tacitus (*Annals* 15.44) and the Jewish historian Flavius Josephus (*Antiquities,* 18.63–64), the Roman prefect Pontius Pilate bears ultimate responsibility for Jesus' execution. Indeed, the latter two sources implicate no one but Pilate. Doubtless some Jewish leaders colluded in Jesus' arrest and were pleased with his execution. But the cross and the nails were Rome's.

A part of the author's purpose in writing Luke and Acts is apologetic. In other words, he wants to defend Christianity from attack.

READING II   Revelation 5:11–14

A reading from the Book of Revelation

I, **John**, **looked** and **heard** the voices of **many** angels
who **surrounded** the throne
and the **living creatures** and the **elders**.
They were **countless** in **number**, and they **cried out**
in a **loud voice**:
"**Worthy** is the **Lamb** that was **slain**
to receive **power** and **riches**, **wisdom** and **strength**,
honor and **glory** and **blessing**."
Then I heard **every** creature in **heaven** and on **earth**
and **under** the **earth** and in the **sea**,
everything in the **universe**, cry out:
"To the **one** who **sits** on the **throne** and to the **Lamb**
be **blessing** and **honor**, **glory** and **might**,
forever and **ever**."
The **four** living **creatures** answered, "**Amen**,"
and the **elders** fell **down** and **worshiped**.

What John is describing is a liturgy of worship in which all heaven and earth participate. Proclaim these verses with the cadence of a responsorial psalm.

GOSPEL   John 21:1–19

A reading from the holy Gospel according to John

At that time, **Jesus revealed** himself **again** to his disciples
at the **Sea** of **Tiberias**.
He **revealed** himself in this way.
Together were **Simon Peter**, **Thomas** called **Didymus**,
Nathanael from **Cana** in **Galilee**,
Zebedee's sons, and two others of his **disciples**.

Pilate's declarations of Jesus' innocence (Luke 24:4, 14, 22; Acts 3:13), the centurion's confession (Luke 23:47), the depiction of Cornelius the centurion (Acts 10:1–2), and Roman officials' declarations of Paul's innocence (Acts 16:37–39; 18:15–16; 23:29; 25:8, 25), probably underscore the author's desire to show that, although Jesus was executed as an enemy of the Roman Empire, neither Jesus nor his followers constitute a problem for Rome or have any reason to bear a grudge.

The great fact of the author's cultural context was that he lived under Roman power. He knew both its benefits and its dangers. When one assesses the charges of Peter against Jewish leaders, one cannot discount Luke's cultural context and its likely influence upon whom he blames, and whom he exonerates, for killing Jesus.

READING II In Revelation 4:1, John of Patmos sees a door opened onto heaven and hears a voice telling him to go up. The action then moves from the island of Patmos in the Aegean Sea to heaven. The sights John the visionary sees in today's reading are heavenly, not earthly.

In Revelation 4, the author describes a heavenly throne room. In the center is an enthroned figure (4:2–3), surrounded by 24 white-clad elders sitting on thrones and wearing golden crowns (4:4). A rainbow adorns the central throne (4:3). Seven lampstands (probably to be identified with the seven Churches of Revelation 1—3) stand near the throne, which are called the "seven spirits of God." The central throne emits

Be mindful of the multiple speaking parts of the narrator, Peter, Jesus, and the disciples.

Simon Peter said to them, "**I** am going **fishing**."
They said to him, "We **also** will **come** with you."
So they **went out** and got into the **boat**,
  but that **night** they caught **nothing**.
When it was already dawn, **Jesus** was **standing** on the **shore**;
  but the **disciples** did not **realize** that it was **Jesus**.
Jesus said to them, "**Children**, have you **caught anything** to **eat**?"
They answered him, "**No**."
So he said to them, "**Cast** the **net** over the **right side** of the **boat**
  and you will **find** something."
So they **cast** it, and were **not** able to pull it in
  because of the **number** of fish.
So the **disciple** whom **Jesus** loved said to **Peter**, "It is the **Lord**."
When **Simon Peter** heard that it was the **Lord**,
  he **tucked** in his **garment**, for he was **lightly clad**,
  and **jumped** into the sea.
The **other** disciples **came** in the boat,
  for they were not **far** from **shore**, only about a **hundred yards**,
  dragging the net with the **fish**.
When they **climbed** out on shore,
  they **saw** a charcoal **fire** with **fish** on it and **bread**.
Jesus **said** to them, "**Bring** some of the **fish** you just **caught**."
So **Simon Peter** went over and **dragged** the net ashore
  full of one hundred fifty-three large fish.
Even though there were so **many**, the **net** was not **torn**.
Jesus said to them, "**Come**, have **breakfast**."
And **none** of the **disciples** dared to **ask** him, "**Who** are you?"
  because they **realized** it was the **Lord**.
Jesus came over and **took** the **bread** and **gave** it to them,
  and in like manner the **fish**.

---

thunder and lightning (4:5) with something like a calm sea similar to glass stretching out before the throne (4:6a). In close proximity to the throne are four six-winged "living creatures" covered with eyes (4:6b–8).

The depiction of heaven in Revelation 4 draws on apocalyptic and prophetic accounts of God's throne (see Ezekiel 1 and Isaiah 6). It places God's throne at the "command center" of nature, with lightning, thunder, waters, and a rainbow under God's authority. Even the elders are likely to be imaginative representations of "decans,"

sky deities commonly believed to govern the stars. The picture is one of heaven and the elements under the control of the one seated on the throne.

In today's text, earth joins the unending worship of heaven to praise Christ, "the Lamb who was slain." The worship of the Lamb by the entirety of heaven and earth vividly subordinates all creation to Christ in a way that is similar to Philippians 2:6–11 (see especially verses 9–11).

GOSPEL The trial and Crucifixion of Jesus in the Gospel of John is an elaborate set of scenes. Interspersed among the scenes of Jesus with the high priest, Jesus with Pilate, Pilate with the crowds, and so on are two scenes concerning Simon Peter (18:15–18; 18:25–27). Finding his way into the courtyard of the high priest, Peter warms himself over a fire while Jesus, not far away, endures his Passion. In 18:17, Peter denies that he is a disciple of Jesus for the first time. In the second scene, he

This was now the **third** time Jesus was **revealed** to his **disciples**
after being **raised** from the dead.

When they had finished breakfast, Jesus said to Simon Peter,
"**Simon**, son of **John**, do you **love** me more than **these**?"
Simon Peter answered him, "**Yes**, Lord, you **know** that
I love you."
Jesus said to him, "Feed my **lambs**."
He then said to **Simon Peter** a second time,
"Simon, son of John, do you **love** me?"
Simon Peter answered him, "**Yes**, Lord, you **know** that
I love you."
Jesus said to him, "Tend **my** sheep."
Jesus said to him the **third** time,
"**Simon**, son of **John**, do you **love** me?"
Peter was **distressed** that Jesus had said to him a **third** time,
"Do you **love** me?" and he **said** to him,
"**Lord**, you **know everything**; you **know** that I love you."
Jesus said to him, "**Feed** my sheep.
"**Amen**, **amen**, I say to you, when you were **younger**,
you used to **dress yourself** and **go** where you **wanted**;
but when you **grow old**, you will **stretch** out your **hands**,
and **someone** else will **dress** you
and **lead** you where you do **not** want to go."
He said this **signifying** by what **kind** of **death** he would
glorify God.
And when he had **said** this, he said to him, "**Follow** me."

[Shorter: John 21:1–14]

You might try delivering this repeated command with a slightly different emphasis each time. Perhaps you could accent the word "lambs" the first time, "my" the second, and "feed" the third.

denies the same charge once more (18:25) and then, in the same scene (18:27), he denies to an eyewitness that he was present with Jesus in the garden (18:1–11). Peter's three denials fulfill Jesus' prediction in 13:38 that he would behave as he does.

Today's Gospel reading comes from the final chapter of John and features a conversation between Jesus and Peter. In 21:15–17, John attempts to settle lingering questions readers may have about Peter after his denials of Jesus. Peter's three denials are matched by Jesus' threefold command: "Feed my lambs." The words echo Jesus' Good Shepherd discourse (10:1–18) and reflect the leadership role Peter exercised among the apostles and in the early Church.

Part of Peter's authority in the early Church came from the acknowledgement that the risen Christ had appeared to him. Paul places "Cephas" (another name for Peter) alone and at the head of those to whom Jesus appeared after his Resurrection (1 Corinthians 15:5). In Luke we read that "the Lord has truly been raised and appeared to Simon" (Luke 24:34). Today's reading forms part of the body of New Testament texts recalling a post-Resurrection appearance by Jesus to Peter, and artfully linking that tradition to Peter's earlier denial.

When you read this Gospel, pay attention to the dialogue among the various characters, particularly Jesus and Peter.

4TH SUNDAY OF EASTER

Lectionary #51

READING I   Acts 13:14, 43–52

Barnabas = BAR-nuh-bus
Perga = PER-guh
Antioch = AN-tee-ock
Pisidia = Pih-SIH-di-uh

A reading from the Acts of the Apostles

Paul and **Barnabas** continued on from **Perga**
    and reached **Antioch** in **Pisidia**.
On the **sabbath** they **entered** the **synagogue** and took their seats.
Many Jews and worshipers who were **converts** to **Judaism**
    followed **Paul** and **Barnabas**, who **spoke** to them
    and **urged** them to **remain faithful** to the **grace** of **God**.

On the following **sabbath** almost the **whole city** gathered
    to hear the **word** of the **Lord**.
When the **Jews** saw the **crowds**, they were **filled** with **jealousy**
    and with **violent abuse contradicted** what **Paul** said.
Both **Paul** and **Barnabas** spoke out **boldly** and **said**,
    "It was **necessary** that the **word** of **God** be **spoken** to you **first**,
    but since **you reject** it
    and **condemn** yourselves as unworthy of eternal **life**,
    we **now turn** to the **Gentiles**.
For so the **Lord** has **commanded** us,
    *I have **made** you a **light** to the **Gentiles**,*
    *that you may be an **instrument** of **salvation***
    *to the **ends** of the **earth**."*

The **Gentiles** were **delighted** when they **heard** this
    and **glorified** the **word** of the **Lord**.

The speeches by apostles and disciples in Acts are carefully crafted and often beautifully written. Take care to emphasize them, pausing before the spoken portions begin in order to set them apart from the surrounding narration.

READING I   Jesus was a Jew and so were his first followers. His selection of the Twelve evoked Israel's self-understanding as a people descended from 12 patriarchs and originally composed of 12 tribes. But by the turn of the second century, when the movement begun by Jesus was in the process of transformation from a group within Judaism into a separate religion, only a minority of Church members were Jews. One of the most significant historical facts of the cultural and religious character of the early Church by the end of the first century is the Church's demographic shift from Jewish to largely Gentile membership.

How did early Christians account for the Jewish origins of the Church in the face of its increasingly non-Jewish character? How did they interpret their lack of significant missionary success among Jews? They had no single or unified response to these issues. But in today's reading we can see Luke grappling with them. Despite his claim that Jewish rejection compels him to go to the Gentiles, Paul continues his practice of speaking first to Jews in Acts (18:4–6, 9; 19:8). Readers may also remember, however, that from the time of his conversion Paul has had Gentiles in his sights (9:15). In Romans 9–11, we find Paul struggling with the complicated problem of Jewish disinterest and rejection of the Gospel.

The description of Jews as Paul's antagonists in Acts likely emerges from the experience of some early Christians' persecution by some Jews. Paul, before his conversion, engaged in this persecution himself (Galatians 1:13; Philippians 3:6) before finding himself on its receiving end (2 Corinthians 11:24; Galatians 5:11, 6:12).

All who were **destined** for **eternal** life came to **believe**,
and the **word** of the **Lord continued** to **spread**
through the **whole** region.
The **Jews**, however, incited the **women** of **prominence**
who were **worshipers**
and the **leading men** of the **city**,
stirred up a persecution against **Paul** and **Barnabas**,
and **expelled** them from their **territory**.
So they shook the **dust** from their **feet** in **protest against** them,
and went to **Iconium**.
The disciples were **filled** with **joy** and the **Holy Spirit**.

Pause before the delivery of this
concluding line and enunciate it clearly.
It's a telling aspect of the Christian
mission in Acts that the disciples respond
to rejection with joy.

READING II   Revelation 7:9, 14b–17

A reading from the Book of Revelation

I, John, had a **vision** of a great multitude,
which **no one** could **count**,
from every **nation**, **race**, **people** and **tongue**.
They stood before the **throne** and before the **Lamb**,
wearing white **robes** and holding **palm** branches
in their **hands**.

Then **one** of the **elders said** to me,
"**These** are the **ones** who have **survived** the time
of great **distress**;
they have **washed** their **robes**
and made them **white** in the **blood** of the **Lamb**.

"For this reason they **stand** before **God's throne**
and **worship** him **day** and **night** in his **temple**.

This elder is presumably one of the 24
who ring the throne in Revelation 4.
As such, he is some kind of a divine being,
a fact that perhaps ought to influence your
proclamation of his words.

READING II "These are the ones who have survived the time of great distress." The "great distress" to which the elder refers is probably a persecution. Persecution was a constant fear but only an occasional reality for the early Church. In about 112, the Roman governor of Bithynia, Pliny, wrote to Emperor Trajan (98–117) for legal and administrative advice about how to deal with Christians. Pliny considers cursing Christ and offering a sacrifice to the emperor sufficient to dismiss the charge of being a Christian. In the second of the two rounds of persecution Pliny mentions, the accused apparently took him up on his offer.

Martyrdom in Christianity very early comes to mean bearing witness to Christ by suffering the death penalty rather than compromise the faith.

For a socially suspect and occasionally outlaw religion offering up little of its ritual life for public scrutiny, public martyrdom was a prime occasion for Christians to show their towns and cities who they were, what (and in whom) they believed, and what stern stuff many of them were made of. Origen of Alexandria (185–early 250s AD) wrote an exhortation to martyrdom, in which he compared the blood of Christ to the blood of martyrs. Both are redeeming, Origen contends, for the martyrs, like Jesus, glorify God with their deaths. Origen, believed to be the son and nephew of a martyr, knew firsthand how important the martyrs' testimonies were to strengthening conviction within the Church and proclaiming Christ to those outside.

The one who **sits** on the **throne** will **shelter** them.
They will not **hunger** or **thirst** anymore,
     nor will the **sun** or any **heat** strike them.
For the **Lamb** who is in the **center** of the **throne**
     will **shepherd** them
     and lead them to **springs** of life-giving **water**,
     and **God** will wipe away **every tear** from their **eyes**."

GOSPEL   John 10:27–30

A reading from the holy Gospel according to John

Jesus said:
"My **sheep** hear my **voice**;
     I **know** them, and they follow **me**.
I give them eternal **life**, and they shall never **perish**.
No one can take them out of my hand.
My **Father**, who has given them to **me**, is **greater** than **all**,
     and **no** one can take them out of the **Father's hand**.
The **Father** and I are **one**."

The Gospel selection is quite short and also contains some slightly cryptic language. Read it slowly.

Pause before delivering this line and enunciate it slowly and clearly. It is Jesus' statement of unity with his Father.

GOSPEL   The final words of today's Gospel selection ("The Father and I are one") express the relationship between Jesus and his Father as one of united pastoral purpose and function. One finds similar ideas elsewhere in John. John 14:10–11 expresses the unity of Jesus and his Father in terms of Jesus' speech and deeds (also see 14:20; 17:11, 21). This unity, however, does not always imply equality according to Jesus (14:28).

The question of Jesus' being or essence and its likeness to the Father's was taken up at the Council of Nicea (325). There is no evidence this question ever occurred to John.

The Lectionary's selection ends with 10:30. In the very next verse, "the Jews" pick up stones to throw at Jesus. The violent reaction hearkens back to an earlier episode. Having healed a man on the Sabbath, Jesus answers those criticizing him for violating the Sabbath ordinance, saying, "My Father is at work until now, so I am at work." For this deed and this statement "the Jews" seek to kill him all the more, not simply for

violating the Sabbath, but because they connect the fact that he calls God "Father" with making himself "equal to God" (5:17–18).

In ways quite beautiful, even sublime, the Christology of John's Gospel more clearly exalts Jesus' position in relation to the Father than the other three. But that Christology is also the source of great hostility and division in the pages of the Gospel.

Aspects of Christianity so appealing to its adherents may affect others very differently. It is good manners to remain aware of this and to behave accordingly.

5TH SUNDAY OF EASTER

Lectionary #54

READING I   Acts 14:21–27

A reading from the Acts of the Apostles

After **Paul** and **Barnabas** had proclaimed the good **news**
        to that **city**
    and made a **considerable number** of **disciples**,
        they returned to **Lystra** and to **Iconium** and to **Antioch**.
They **strengthened** the **spirits** of the **disciples**
    and **exhorted** them to **persevere** in the **faith**, saying,
        "It is **necessary** for us to undergo many **hardships**
        to **enter** the **kingdom** of **God**."
They appointed **elders** for them in each church and,
    with **prayer** and **fasting**, commended them to the **Lord**
        in whom they had **put** their **faith**.
Then they traveled through **Pisidia** and reached **Pamphylia**.
After proclaiming the word at **Perga** they went down to **Attalia**.
From there they sailed to **Antioch**,
    where they had been **commended** to the **grace** of **God**
        for the work they had now **accomplished**.
And when they **arrived**, they called the **church** together
    and **reported** what **God** had **done** with them
        and how he had **opened** the **door** of **faith** to the Gentiles.

Barnabas = BAR-nuh-bus

Lystra = LIS-truh
Iconium = i-CONE-i-yum
Antioch = AN-tee-ock

The necessity of suffering is an important theme in Acts. Emphasize these words of Paul and Barnabas, particularly their first three.

Pisidia =- Pih-SIH-di-uh
Pamphylia = Pam-FUL-li-yuh
Perga = PER-guh
Attalia = Ah-TAL-i-yuh

READING I   After his conversion in Acts 9, Paul embarks on three missionary journeys. Today's reading begins in the city of Derbe, the farthest point Paul and his partner Barnabas reached on the first journey (14:20). In 14:24–26, Paul and Barnabas retrace their steps back to Antioch, the Syrian city from which they started out following their selection for the task by the Holy Spirit (13:2–3).

The "hardships" to precede entry into the kingdom of God, Paul and Barnabas say,
are necessary hardships (14:22). Some translations do not highlight the *necessity* of what must be endured. But it is obvious in the Greek text. A little verb, *dei*, makes it clear that Paul and Barnabas believe hardships are part of the price of admission to the kingdom of God.

In his portrayal of Paul's final journey to Jerusalem and Rome, Luke picks up the theme of the necessity to undergo difficulty. At the very beginning of Paul's life in Christ, his need to suffer for Jesus' name is made clear (9:16). In 23:11, Jesus comes to Paul
and tells him that it is necessary to bear witness in Rome. Later, Paul reports that an angel told him it is necessary for him to stand before Caesar (27:24). In these cases, the need for things to unfold as they must is expressed, as they are here, by little *dei*.

One may recall that the theme of necessary suffering also arises in Luke's Gospel, but there it concerns the Son of Man (Luke 9:22; 17:25; 24:7, 26; also see Acts 17:3). Our author's depiction of Paul as an innocent sufferer for the Gospel parallels his portrayal of Jesus in similar terms. In this passage, the need to endure tribulation characterizes not

READING II   Revelation 21:1–5a

A reading from the Book of Revelation

Then **I, John**, saw a **new heaven** and a **new earth**.
The **former** heaven and the **former** earth had **passed away**,
    and the **sea** was no **more**.
I also saw the **holy city**, a new **Jerusalem**,
    coming down out of **heaven** from **God**,
    prepared as a **bride adorned** for her **husband**.
I heard a **loud voice** from the **throne** saying,
    "**Behold**, God's **dwelling** is with the **human race**.
He will **dwell** with them and they will be his **people**
    and **God himself** will **always** be with them as their **God**.
He will **wipe** every **tear** from their **eyes**,
    and there shall be no more **death** or **mourning**, **wailing** or **pain**,
    for the **old order** has passed **away**."

The **One** who sat on the **throne** said,
    "**Behold**, I make **all things new**."

As is often true of the book of Revelation, the contents of John's visions are full of vivid and striking images. Proclaim this reading slowly, pausing before "I saw" and "I heard." Consider also that the voice from the throne and the One on the throne are distinct speaking parts.

only the life of a missionary, but also the Christian life itself.

READING II In literary terms, the word "allegory" may be defined as text that means something other than what it says. Allegorical interpretation was a way of understanding scripture that discerned a spiritual meaning in scripture in addition to the plain sense of the words on the page.

Leaders of the ancient Church often sparred over the use of allegory to understand the Bible. In his interpretation of this reading, Irenaeus of Lyons attacked people he considered heretics for allegorizing the prophecy of a new heaven and a new earth. To Irenaeus, these verses contained solid information about what would happen in heaven and on earth after the Resurrection of the righteous (*Against Heresies*, 5.35). In substantial measure this remains the teaching of the Roman Catholic Church according to the Catechism (#1042–1050).

The notion of two Jerusalems, one above and one below, also arises in Paul's letter to the Church of Galatia (Galatians 4:21–26). Paul prefaces his discussion of two covenants by saying, "Now this is an allegory." Paul argues that people who believe justification requires circumcision are in one covenant of slavery, which is associated with Mount Sinai, Hagar, and "the present Jerusalem." People who believe justification is a matter of faith in Jesus, Paul argues, are in a second covenant of freedom, associated with Sarah and "the Jerusalem above." Interestingly enough, this is the only passage of the New Testament in which a form of the Greek word "allegorize" *(allēgoreō)* appears (Galatians 4:24).

GOSPEL John 13:31–33a, 34–35

A reading from the holy Gospel according to John

When **Judas** had **left** them, Jesus said,
  "**Now** is the **Son** of **Man glorified**, and **God** is **glorified** in **him**.
If **God** is **glorified** in him,
  God will **also glorify** him in **himself**,
  and **God** will **glorify** him **at once**.
My **children**, I will be with you only a little while **longer**.
I give you a **new** commandment: **love one another**.
As **I** have loved **you**, so **you** also should **love one another**.
This is how **all** will **know** that **you** are **my disciples**,
  if **you** have **love** for **one another**."

Proclaim Jesus' new commandment slightly more slowly than the preceding section, enunciating it clearly.

GOSPEL In the Gospel of John, Jesus' glorification occurs as an event. It happens at a moment in time (12:23; 17:1, 5). Not only must Jesus' glorification precede the gift of the Spirit to believers (7:39), but it also permits understanding of Jesus' ministry in the light of scripture (12:16). Today's reading comes immediately after Judas' departure to betray Jesus. Once the events culminating in the cross have been set in motion, Jesus announces the accomplishment of his glorification. The paradox of Jesus' glorification is that it is,

like the glory of Sinai, a manifestation of power, but happens through betrayal, arrest, torture, and death.

In the synoptic Gospels, the so-called Great Commandment is to love God and neighbor (Matthew 22:34–40; Mark 12:28–34; Luke 10:25–28). Jesus in Luke goes even further, radically overhauling the definition of "neighbor" with the parable of the Good Samaritan (10:29–37). In contrast, the love commandment in John is an order to share love *within the Church*. The boundary between Church and world in John is a firm one, perceptible from the prologue forward (1:9—1:13).

The Catechism connects the love command in today's reading with John 13:1 ("He loved his own in the world and he loved them to the end"). "By loving one another, the disciples imitate the love of Jesus which they themselves receive" (Catechism, #1823). However one reads the somewhat ambiguous Greek of 13:34, two things are clear. First, Jesus calls the Church into existence with love. Second, the distinctive, identifying feature of the Church in the world is love shared among its members.

6TH SUNDAY OF EASTER

Lectionary #57

A reading from the Acts of the Apostles

Your proclamation needs to accommodate the multiple speakers in this reading.

Some who had come down from **Judea** were instructing
    the brothers,
    "**Unless** you are **circumcised** according to the **Mosaic practice**,
    you **cannot** be saved."
Because there arose no little dissension and debate
    by **Paul** and **Barnabas** with them,
    it was decided that **Paul**, **Barnabas** and **some** of the **others**
    should go up to **Jerusalem** to the **apostles** and **elders**
    about this question.

The **apostles** and **elders**, in agreement with the whole church,
    decided to choose representatives
    and to send them to **Antioch** with **Paul** and **Barnabas**.
The ones chosen were **Judas**, who was called **Barsabbas**,
    and **Silas**, leaders among the brothers.
This is the letter delivered by them:

Proclaim this as you would if you were reading a personal letter out loud to your family.

"The **apostles** and the **elders**, your **brothers**,
    to the brothers in **Antioch**, **Syria** and **Cilicia**
    of Gentile origin: **Greetings**.
Since we have **heard** that **some** of our number
    who went out without **any** mandate from **us**
    have **upset** you with their **teachings**
    and **disturbed** your **peace** of **mind**,
    we have with one **accord** decided to choose representatives

---

READING I Luke reports that the Jerusalem council rendered its decision "with one accord" (15:25). The Greek adverb, *homothumadon*, is a frequent choice of his (see the commentary for Reading I of the Second Sunday of Easter). While we have little reason to suppose that Luke misused his sources according to the canons of ancient historiography, we do well to wonder whether the decision about circumcision was reached so harmoniously.

Paul includes in his letter to the Church of Galatia some highlights of his missionary career. He mentions two trips to Jerusalem

(1:17–19; 2:1–10). Of these, only the second in any way resembles the Council of Jerusalem described in this reading. But whereas Luke describes Peter, James, Paul, and Barnabas to have been in substantial agreement about requirements for Gentile incorporation, Paul mentions no requirements, no letter, and no agreement to send him there in the first place, saying rather that he journeyed to Jerusalem "in accord with a revelation" (2:2). For Paul, the account of his second trip to Jerusalem sets the stage for a third account of a showdown between himself and Peter

at Antioch over issues of circumcision and Gentile-Jewish table fellowship (2:11–14).

It is wrong to characterize the entire early Church as "fractious" or "factionalized." At different times, in different locales, and on particular issues there was indeed considerable conflict. But it obscures matters simply to say that Paul and Luke disagree. Paul was writing to Christian communities that had been convinced, or very nearly convinced, that he was not an apostle approved by God and that circumcision was necessary for justification. There is no evidence that the requirements of the letter in Acts

and to send them to you along with our **beloved Barnabas**
and **Paul**,
who have dedicated their lives to the **name** of our
Lord Jesus Christ.
So we are sending **Judas** and **Silas**
who will also **convey** this same message by **word** of **mouth**:
'It is the **decision** of the **Holy Spirit** and of **us**
not to **place** on you any **burden** beyond these **necessities**,
namely, to **abstain** from **meat sacrificed** to **idols**,
from **blood**, from **meats** of **strangled animals**,
and from **unlawful marriage**.
If you keep **free** of these,
you will be doing what is **right. Farewell.'"**

READING II   Revelation 21:10–14, 22–23

A reading from the Book of Revelation

The angel took me in **spirit** to a **great**, **high mountain**
and **showed** me the holy city **Jerusalem**
coming **down** out of **heaven** from **God**.
It **gleamed** with the **splendor** of **God**.
Its **radiance** was like that of a **precious** stone,
like **jasper**, **clear** as **crystal**.
It had a **massive**, high wall,
with twelve gates where twelve **angels** were stationed
and on which **names** were **inscribed**,
the **names** of the twelve tribes of the **Israelites**.

While the entire reading needs to be read slowly so that its vivid details may be apprehended, be sure to place special emphasis on the final stanza, particularly the clause beginning, "for its temple is the Lord."

have anything to do with justification. It may be that the council's principal aim was to make it possible for Jewish Christians who remained observant Jews after their conversions to eat with Gentile Christians.

READING II It is perhaps impossible to describe adequately how important was the Jerusalem Temple to the religion of Judaism and to Jews. It was to be, in God's words, "a house for my name" (2 Samuel 7:13).

The building and dedication of the First Temple occurred during the reign of Solomon, son of David (1 Kings 5:15—6:37; 7:13—8:66). It was, in most important respects, a typical example of Ancient Near Eastern tripartite temple design: a porch, sanctuary, and an innermost room where the Ark of the Covenant was kept. Destroyed by the Babylonians in 586 BC, the Temple was rebuilt upon the exiles' return and rededicated in 515 BC (Ezra 6:16–18). Among the many building projects of Herod the Great (37–4 BC) was the refurbishment of the Temple and the extensive reconstruction of

its precincts beginning in 20 BC. The result of Herod's work (which was opposed by many pious Jews) was that the Jerusalem Temple, by the time of Jesus' birth, was among the very largest and most admired religious complexes of the Mediterranean world. The Roman General Titus, later emperor (79–81 AD), destroyed the Temple along with Jerusalem in 70 AD. A piece of Herod's renovations, a western retaining wall, is all that remains.

In our reading today, the New Jerusalem is described as a place in which God requires no separate place for his name to dwell, and

There were **three** gates facing **east**,
   three **north**, three **south**, and three **west**.
The wall of the city had twelve courses of **stones**
    as its foundation,
   on which were inscribed the twelve **names**
   of the twelve **apostles** of the **Lamb**.

I saw **no temple** in the **city**
   for its **temple** is the **Lord God almighty** and the **Lamb**.
The **city** had no **need** of **sun** or **moon** to **shine** on it,
   for the **glory** of **God** gave it **light**,
   and its **lamp** was the **Lamb**.

GOSPEL   John 14:23–29

A reading from the holy Gospel according to John

Jesus said to his **disciples**:
   "Whoever **loves** me will keep my **word**,
   and my **Father** will **love** him,
   and we will **come** to him and **make** our dwelling **with** him.
Whoever does **not** love me does **not** keep my words;
   yet the **word** you **hear** is not **mine**
   but **that** of the **Father** who **sent** me.

"I have **told** you this while I am **with** you.
The **Advocate**, the **Holy Spirit**,
   whom the **Father** will **send** in my **name**,
   will teach you **everything**
   and **remind** you of all that I **told** you.

The clauses of these sentences have a certain balance, often pivoting on "and," "but," and "yet." Upon these little words depends the logical structure of the passage. Emphasize them.

humans require no liturgy to make their petitions known.

The Catechism cites Revelation 21:22 when it teaches that the death of Jesus "presaged the destruction of the Temple, which would manifest the dawning of a new age in the history of salvation" (Catechism, #586). Whatever the Catechism may mean here, it does *not* mean that the destruction of the Temple means the end either of Judaism or of God's covenants with the Jewish people.

GOSPEL Today's Gospel selection comes from a section of John's Gospel often called Jesus' farewell discourse (John 14—17), in which Jesus explains a great deal to his disciples that they are incapable of understanding without the Advocate mentioned in today's reading. Today's reading also explains the Trinity in a dynamic way as it affects the day-to-day life of the Church.

The Greek word for "Advocate" is *paraklētos,* which one may also translate as "Intercessor" or even "Comforter." "Advocate," however, is a good translation in

light of the legal tasks of the Spirit in 16:8–11. Additionally, the Advocate will testify to the Church about Jesus (15:26). In the life of the Church, the functional unity of Jesus and his Father (10:30; 14:10–11, 20; 17:11, 21) includes the Advocate as well: "He will not speak on his own, but what he hears" (16:13). Unity with Jesus and the Father permits the description of the Advocate in today's reading as a teacher of the Church (14:26). See also 1 John 2:1 where Jesus himself, as an advocate to the Father on behalf of Church members who sin, is called *paraklētos.*

Emphasize the word "peace."

Peace I **leave** with you; my **peace** I **give** to you.
Not as the **world** gives do **I give** it to **you**.
Do **not** let your **hearts** be **troubled** or **afraid**.
You heard me tell you,
     'I am **going away** and I will come **back** to you.'
If you **loved** me,
     you would **rejoice** that I am going to the **Father**;
     for the **Father** is **greater** than **I**.
And now I have **told** you this before it **happens**,
     so that when it **happens** you may **believe**."

Beginning in the second century, John 14:28 ("the Father is greater than I") figured in debates among Christians about relationships among the members of the Trinity. Christians arguing that the Father was greater than Jesus, whether in terms of knowledge, essence, origin, or some other factor, found support for their various doctrines here. It is fair to say that there is no evidence John anticipated this debate. Underlying Jesus' words is a simple and common-sense understanding that a person sending an envoy is more important than the envoy himself.

ASCENSION OF THE LOR[D]

Give a bold and spirited reading of the[se]
words. Pause before you deliver th[e]
allowing the implication of the
scene to sink in: Jesus is g[one]
ministry concluded.

Lectionary #58

READING I   A[cts]

A reading from th[e]

In the **first** book, T[heophilus,]
I dealt with **all** t[he]
until the **day** he [was]
after giving **instru**[ctions]
to the **apostles** wh[om]
He presented himsel[f]
by many **proofs** aft[er he had] **suffered**,
appearing to them during forty days
and **speaking** about the kingdom of God.
While **meeting** with them,
he **enjoined** them not to depart from **Jerusalem**,
but to wait for "the **promise** of the **Father**
about which you have heard me **speak**;
for **John baptized** with **water**,
but in a few days you will be **baptized** with the **Holy Spirit**."

This is what the disciples have long hoped for and expected to happen.

When they had gathered together they asked him,
"**Lord**, are you at this time going to **restore**
the **kingdom** to **Israel**?"

Pause before Jesus' reply.

He answered them, "It is **not** for you to **know** the **times**
or **seasons**
that the **Father** has **established** by his own **authority**.

If the Ascension of the Lord is celebrated next Sunday, today's readings are used in place of those for the Seventh Sunday of Easter.

READING I | Compare this reading to Luke 1:1–4. Right off the bat, you may notice some similarities, some of which are probably shared by the many biblical scholars who think the same author wrote both Luke and Acts. The opening address to a certain "Theophilus," for example, is common to both texts. Who was this person? Was he someone Luke wished to convert to Christianity, or to convert from one form of Christianity to another? Did this Theophilus, perhaps a leader within the Church, commission Luke to write the Gospel? Is Theophilus, which means "God-lover," Luke's generic term for his readers? There are plenty of potential clues but no firm answers.

Luke 1:2 stresses the importance of eyewitnesses to Luke's account. Acts 1:3 emphasizes that Jesus "presented himself alive" to the apostles "by many proofs after he had suffered, appearing to them during forty days." Here, Luke informs his readers that his eyewitness testimony comes from the apostles themselves (also see Luke 24:48). Luke also specifies that Jesus ascends to heaven while the apostles were "looking on" and that they continued "looking intently" once he was gone from their sight (Acts 1:9–10; see Luke 24:51). Not only is Luke claiming that his evidence comes from Jesus' inner circle, but that the inner circle came by it reliably.

It is clear from Acts 1:6 that Christ's Passion and Resurrection have not answered all of the apostles' questions about him.

But you will receive **power** when the **Holy Spirit** comes upon you,
and you will be my **witnesses** in Jerusalem,
throughout **Judea** and **Samaria**,
and to the **ends** of the **earth**."
When he had said this, as they were looking on,
he was **lifted** up, and a cloud **took** him from their **sight**.
While they were looking **intently** at the **sky** as he was **going**,
suddenly two men **dressed** in white garments
stood beside **them**.
They said, "**Men** of **Galilee**,
why are you standing there looking at the **sky**?
This **Jesus** who has been **taken up** from you into **heaven**
will **return** in the same way as you have **seen** him
going into **heaven**."

READING II Ephesians 1:17–23

A reading from the Letter of Saint Paul to the Ephesians

Brothers and **sisters**:
May the **God** of our **Lord Jesus Christ**, the **Father** of **glory**,
give you a **Spirit** of **wisdom** and **revelation**
resulting in **knowledge** of him.
May the **eyes** of your **hearts** be **enlightened**,
that you may know what is the **hope** that belongs to his **call**,
what are the **riches** of **glory**
in his **inheritance** among the **holy ones**,
and what is the **surpassing greatness** of his **power**
for us who **believe**,
in accord with the **exercise** of his great **might**,

"Lord," they ask, "are you at this time going to restore the kingdom to Israel?" The question echoes a conversation reported in Luke's Gospel, in which two of Jesus' disciples express their frustrated hope that Jesus would redeem Israel (Luke 24:21). The disciples on the road to Emmaus and the apostles during the 40 days still imagine that the work of the Christ is the political restoration of the Israelite monarchy. Jesus answers by foreshadowing the birth of the Church at Pentecost, not the restoration of the monarchy. He instructs that they shall be "witnesses" *(martyres)*—beyond Jerusalem, Judea, and Samaria—"to the ends of the earth" (Acts 1:8).

There is a choice of second readings today. Speak with the liturgy coordinator or the homilist to find out which reading will be used.

READING II **EPHESIANS.** The word "catholic" is an adjective, Greek in origin *(katholikos)*, and means "general" or "universal." It does not occur in the New Testament. One of the earliest uses of the word is in the *Martyrdom of Polycarp*, a gripping account of the persecution, arrest, and death of Bishop Polycarp of Smyrna in the mid-second century. The 80-year-old Polycarp, about to be taken into custody, prays for everyone he has ever met, and "the whole catholic church around the world" (*Martyrdom of Polycarp*, 8.1). By "world," the authors mean the world as it was known to them, a world composed of the lands ringing the Mediterranean basin in which the Church was a small and diffuse institution. While the known world is much larger today, what

which he **worked** in **Christ**,
raising him from the **dead**
and **seating** him at his **right hand** in the **heavens**,
far above **every principality**, **authority**, **power**, and **dominion**,
and **every name** that is **named**
not only in this **age** but also in the one to **come**.
And he put **all** things beneath his **feet**
and gave him as **head** over **all** things to the **church**,
which is his **body**,
the **fullness** of the **one** who **fills all** things in **every** way.

Or:

A reading from the Letter to the Hebrews

Christ did not enter into a **sanctuary** made by **hands**,
a **copy** of the **true** one, but **heaven itself**,
that he might now **appear** before **God** on **our** behalf.
Not that he might offer himself **repeatedly**,
as the **high priest** enters **each year** into the **sanctuary**
with **blood** that is **not** his own;
if that were **so**, he would have had to **suffer repeatedly**
from the **foundation** of the **world**.
But **now once for all he** has **appeared** at the **end** of the **ages**
to take away **sin** by his **sacrifice**.

Just as it is **appointed** that **men** and **women die once**,
and after this the **judgment**,
so also **Christ**, offered **once** to take away the sins of **many**,

These are long sentences. Read them slowly, not only so your tongue doesn't trip over the multiple clauses and commas, but also so that your hearers can sort out the logical progression of the sentences you are proclaiming.

This passage is a comparison of the high priest of the Temple with Jesus, of then with now. Slow down and enunciate the sentence beginning with "But now."

made the Church catholic then is what makes it so now—its "mission to the whole of the human race" (Catechism, #830–831).

Universal scope of mission is only part of what makes the Church catholic. "The Church is catholic because Christ is present in her" (Catechism, #830). In this reading, Christ is described as "a head over all things" given to the Church, "which is his body." As Paul observes in 1 Corinthians 12:12–13, the body of the Church is composed of Jews and Greeks, slaves and freemen. But, through Baptism, all have been incorporated into a single body. Today within this same body are diverse and varied traditions, ideas, practices, and beliefs. Unifying us into one body is Christ, our head, and the mission to proclaim his death "to the end of the earth" (Acts 1:8).

HEBREWS. The basic imagery of this passage comes from the Day of Atonement liturgy of the Jerusalem Temple. On this day, the high priest entered the most sacred part of the Temple to make sacrificial expiation for the sins of the Jewish people. The anonymous author of Hebrews compares Christ's entry into heaven, having sacrificed himself once on the cross, with the annual sacrificial rite of the high priest.

The comparison of heaven with the Jerusalem sanctuary works in part because of the theology of architecture underlying the structure of the Jerusalem Temple. Temples throughout the ancient near east were built to resemble the heavens so that the god would choose to remain there. We see this theology of architecture at work in the instructions to Moses to build a wilderness sanctuary according to a pattern (in Hebrew, *tabnit*) he received on the mountain where God dwelled (Exodus 24:10; 25:9, 40;

will appear a **second** time, **not** to take away sin
but to bring **salvation** to those who **eagerly** await him.

Therefore, **brothers** and **sisters**, since through the **blood** of **Jesus**
we have **confidence** of **entrance** into the **sanctuary**
by the **new** and **living** way he opened for us through the **veil**,
that is, his **flesh**,
and since we have "a great **priest** over the **house** of **God**,"
let us **approach** with a sincere **heart** and in **absolute trust**,
with our hearts **sprinkled clean** from an **evil conscience**
and our **bodies washed** in pure **water**.
Let us hold **unwaveringly** to our **confession** that gives us **hope**,
for he who made the **promise** is **trustworthy**.

Pause before the final stanza, beginning with "Therefore."

GOSPEL   Luke 24:46–53

A reading from the holy Gospel according to Luke

Jesus said to his disciples:
"**Thus** it is **written** that the **Christ** would **suffer**
and **rise** from the **dead** on the third day
and that **repentance**, for the **forgiveness** of **sins**,
would be **preached** in his **name**
to all the **nations**, beginning from **Jerusalem**.
You are **witnesses** of these things.
And **behold** I am sending the **promise** of my **Father** upon you;
but **stay** in the **city**
until you are **clothed** with **power** from on **high**."

Emphasize the word "You" and look about the assembly as you say it. Pause for a moment after you've read it. It may draw people into the story.

Numbers 8:4). As in any good rhetorical comparison, the Temple and heaven are sufficiently similar for our author to compare them.

Our author's philosophical perspective maps nicely onto this theology. It is hard to come with an accurate label for his philosophy, although biblical scholars typically identify it as a form of middle Platonism in which perishable, transient, earthly things are replicas of imperishable, eternal, and heavenly reality.

Having sought to establish the superiority of Christ's sacrifice on the cross to the annual rite of the high priest, the author ends this section of Hebrews with a rousing peroration. He concludes by saying, "Let us hold unwaveringly to our confession that gives us hope, for he who made the promise is trustworthy." Hope, for our author, is shorthand for salvation. If one accepts that God is trustworthy, our author argues, then one must accept that heaven is the destiny of those holding tightly to their faith.

GOSPEL There is no Old Testament text that clearly says the Messiah must suffer, die, rise from the dead on the third day, and have repentance for the forgiveness of sins proclaimed in his name to all nations (Luke 24:46–47). There is no Old Testament text that says Jesus of Nazareth is the Messiah. But before any of the documents of the New Testament had been composed, followers of Jesus were already busy interpreting scripture in the light of their extraordinary experience of the ministry, Passion, and death of Jesus Christ. In which specific texts did Luke find Christ's Passion, death, Resurrection, and the mission of the Church written down? Luke does not tell us here.

Then he led them out as far as **Bethany**,
　　raised his **hands**, and **blessed** them.
As he **blessed** them he **parted** from them
　　and was **taken** up to **heaven**.
They did him **homage**
　　and then returned to **Jerusalem** with great **joy**,
　　and they were **continually** in the **temple** praising God.

Justin Martyr, who lived during the first half of the second century, wrote that Jesus spoke to Moses from the burning bush (Exodus 3:4–22), manifested himself as the pillar of fire that guarded Israel during the Exodus (Exodus 13:21–22) and appeared to prophets (*Apology* I.63). How was he able to make this case?

Early Christians justified their christological interpretations of the Old Testament in various ways. The memory that Jesus himself began and encouraged the activity was one such way. John records a speech by Jesus in which Jesus names various witnesses supporting the claims he has made about himself. "The Jews" search the scriptures in vain, says Jesus, for "even they testify on my behalf" (John 5:39; also see 5:45–47). In today's Gospel selection, Jesus says that his Passion, death, and Resurrection, as well as the coming mission of the Church, are "written." By the phrase "It is written," Jesus means these things are the fulfillment of Old Testament writings. Furthermore, it is Jesus' own exegesis of scripture that reveals their christological significance (Luke 24:27, 45).

7TH SUNDAY OF EASTER

Lectionary #61

READING I Acts 7:55–60

A reading from the Acts of the Apostles

Stephen, **filled** with the **Holy Spirit**,
    looked up **intently** to **heaven** and **saw** the **glory** of **God**
    and **Jesus** standing at the **right hand** of **God**,
    and **Stephen** said, "**Behold**, I see the **heavens** opened
    and the **Son** of **Man** standing at the **right hand** of **God**."
But they cried out in a loud voice,
    covered their **ears**, and rushed upon him **together**.
They **threw** him out of the **city**, and began to **stone** him.
The **witnesses** laid down their **cloaks**
    at the **feet** of a young man named **Saul**.
As they were stoning **Stephen**, he called out,
    "**Lord Jesus**, **receive my spirit**."
Then he **fell** to his **knees** and **cried out** in a loud voice,
    "**Lord**, do not hold this **sin** against them";
    and when he **said** this, he fell **asleep**.

This is our introduction to Saul, later the apostle Paul. Read it slowly, emphasizing "Saul."

If the Ascension of the Lord is celebrated today, please see pages 185–189 for the appropriate readings.

READING I Having upset a synagogue seemingly made up of various groups of foreign Jews residing in Jerusalem, Stephen is dragged before the Sanhedrin by a mob of "the people, the elders, and the scribes" (Acts 6:12). He is charged with blaspheming Moses and God (6:11), repeatedly speaking out against "this holy place" (the Temple) and the law (6:13), and that Jesus the Nazarene will destroy the Temple and change Mosaic tradition (6:14). The high priest asks him if the charges are true (7:1). Stephen never answers the question. Instead, he offers a polemical recitation of Israel's history of a sort one finds at several points in the Old Testament (Joshua 24:2–28; Ezekiel 20:5–44; Psalm 78; 105).

Although he delivers his speech in defense of himself, Stephen's words are far more provocative than apologetic. Impelling the crowd to fury is his assertion (backed up by exegesis of Isaiah 66:1) that God does not inhabit the Temple (7:48).

One may notice similarities between Luke's description of Stephen's martyrdom and Jesus' trial and death. The collusion of "the people" and "the scribes" is familiar from Luke's account of Jesus' passion. The Temple figures prominently in both texts as a basis for popular incitement. Jesus' statement in Luke 23:69 about the Son of Man sitting at God's right hand turns out to have been prophecy, for this is precisely what Stephen sees and bears witness to in Acts

READING II   Revelation 22:12–14, 16–17, 20

There are a great many different voices in this reading. Pause in your delivery before each new voice.

A reading from the Book of Revelation

I, **John**, heard a voice saying to me:
 "**Behold**, I am coming **soon**.
I bring with me the **recompense** I will give to **each**
 according to his **deeds**.
I am the **Alpha** and the **Omega**, the **first** and the **last**,
 the **beginning** and the **end**."

Blessed are they who **wash** their **robes**
 so as to have the **right** to the **tree** of **life**
 and enter the **city** through its **gates**.

"**I, Jesus**, sent my angel to give you this **testimony**
 for the **churches**.
I am the **root** and **offspring** of **David**,
 the **bright morning star**."

Pause before and emphasize each time the word "Come" is used.

The **Spirit** and the **bride** say, "**Come**."
Let the **hearer** say, "**Come**."
Let the **one** who **thirsts** come **forward**,
 and the **one** who **wants it** receive the gift of life-giving **water**.

Read these sentences as they are punctuated. They are exclamations!

The **one** who gives this **testimony** says, "**Yes**, I am coming **soon**."
Amen! **Come, Lord Jesus**!

7:55–56. With his last breath Stephen forgives his killers as Jesus forgives his own (Luke 23:34; Acts 7:60).

READING II   "Come, Lord Jesus!" Is this short statement in the second-to-last verse of the New Testament a request, a command, or a wish? How can we tell?

 Biblical scholars have long seen this prayerful exclamation as the Greek translation of an Aramaic expression, *Marana tha* ("Lord, come!"), which we find in 1

Corinthians 16:22. In another early Christian text called *the Didache* ("Teaching"), *Marana tha* concludes the Eucharistic liturgy (*Didache* 10.6). But why do we find an Aramaic exclamation in these Greek documents? What use for Aramaic would the Greek-speaking Corinthians have had? The most likely explanation is that this prayerful exclamation was already traditional by the 50s AD when Paul wrote 1 Corinthians. The exclamation probably originated with the Aramaic-speaking communities of Jesus' earliest followers in Palestine. In other

words, "Come, Lord Jesus" is a prayer of the Church in its infancy.

 Today's reading forms part of the epilogue to Revelation (22:6–21). Biblical scholar David E. Aune has argued that these verses' "central function is to emphasize the divine origin and authority of the entire book of Revelation." In today's reading, a chorus of voices (John, Jesus, Spirit, bride) warn readers (22:12), praise faithful believers (22:14), and invite new people to the waters of Baptism (22:17).

GOSPEL   John 17:20–26

A reading from the holy Gospel according to John

Lifting up his **eyes** to **heaven**, Jesus **prayed** saying:
"**Holy Father**, I pray **not only** for them,
    but also for those who will **believe** in me through their word,
    so that they may **all** be **one**,
    as **you**, **Father**, are in **me** and **I** in **you**,
    that **they** also may be in **us**,
    that the **world** may **believe** that **you** sent me.
And **I** have given **them** the glory **you** gave **me**,
    so that **they** may be **one**, as **we** are **one**,
    I in **them** and **you** in **me**,
    that they may be brought to **perfection** as **one**,
    that the **world** may **know** that **you** sent **me**,
    and that **you** loved **them** even as **you** loved **me**.
Father, **they** are your **gift** to **me**.
I **wish** that where **I** am they **also** may be with **me**,
    that they may **see** my **glory** that you **gave** me,
    because **you** loved **me** before the foundation of the **world**.
Righteous Father, the world also does **not know you**,
    but **I know you**, and **they know** that **you** sent **me**.
I made **known** to them your **name** and **I** will make it **known**,
    that the **love** with which **you** loved **me**
    may be in **them** and **I** in **them**."

GOSPEL   The importance of belief in the Gospel of John begins in the prologue (1:7, 12). Belief is the proper response to Jesus' signs (2:11, 23; 4:53; 6:69; 9:38), the reason why Jesus performs the signs (4:48; 10:38; 11:42; 14:11), and the reason the signs have been recorded in the Gospel (20:30–31).

And so it is worth asking: what does belief in Jesus mean? In 5:38, Jesus tells his audience they do not believe in God because "you do not believe in the one he has sent."

In 6:29, Jesus says, "This is the work of God, that you believe in the one he sent." In 11:42, before the last and greatest of his recorded signs, the raising of Lazarus, Jesus prays to his Father—out loud for the sake of the crowd—"that they may believe that you sent me." And in today's Gospel we read something quite similar. In his final moments in the company of his friends (15:14–15), Jesus prays "that the world may know that you sent me" (17:23).

Why does John place such emphasis on believing that the Father sent Jesus? The likely reason is that some Jews repeatedly

challenged members of John's community on precisely this point. John wants his readers to be perfectly clear that Jesus came not on his own authority, nor was in any way less than Old Testament figures sent by God, such as Moses (chapter 5 and 6) or Abraham (chapter 8), but that he—and he alone—came down from heaven on orders from his Father for the sake of the world.

PENTECOST: VIGIL

Lectionary #62

READING I   Genesis 11:1–9

A reading from the Book of Genesis

The **whole world** spoke the **same language**, using the
    same words.
While the people were migrating in the **east**,
    they came upon a **valley** in the land of **Shinar** and settled there.
They said to one another,
    "**Come**, let us mold **bricks** and **harden** them with **fire**."
They used **bricks** for **stone**, and **bitumen** for **mortar**.
Then they said, "**Come**, let us build ourselves a **city**
    and a **tower** with its top in the **sky**,
    and so make a **name** for **ourselves**;
    otherwise we shall be **scattered** all over the **earth**."

The **LORD** came down to see the **city** and the **tower**
    that the **people** had **built**.
Then the **LORD** said: "**If now**, while they are **one** people,
    all speaking the **same** language,
    they have **started** to do this,
    nothing will **later** stop them from **doing**
        whatever they presume to do.
Let us then go down there and **confuse** their language,
    so that **one** will **not understand** what **another** says."
Thus the **LORD** scattered them from there **all** over the **earth**,
    and they **stopped** building the **city**.

Pause briefly after the first sentence
and also before the last sentence.
These are transitions between the
account between them.

Shinar = Shih-NAR

There is a choice of first readings today.
Speak with the liturgy coordinator or the
homilist to find out which reading will
be used.

READING I   GENESIS. The so-called prehistory of Israel spans chap-
ters 1 through 11 of Genesis. It comprises
twin accounts of Creation (1:1–2:4a; 2:4b–
25); the fall (3:1–24); Cain, Abel, and descendants of Cain and Seth (4:1–26); the Nephilim
(6:1–4); Noah, the flood, and Noah's sons
(6:5—9:28); and today's reading, the Tower

of Babel (11:1–9). Interspersed among these
historical works are a male-line genealogy
from Adam to Noah (5:1–32), a genealogy of
the nations of the earth (10:1–32), and a
male-line genealogy from Noah's son Shem
to Abraham (11:10–32).

The theme of the building of the Tower
of Babel is as modern as it is ancient: pride
goes before a fall. Also quite modern is the
place of technology in the attempts of the
human race to realize its ambitions. It is only
because humans have discovered and
taught one another the building crafts that

they gain possession of the means to "make
a name" for themselves (Genesis 11:4).

There is some similarity between the
accounts of the Tower of Babel and the fall.
Both feature the misuse of human ingenuity
and freedom. But this similarity does not
extend to God's behavior. In the account
of the fall, Adam and Eve receive explicit
instructions not to do what they later do. The
human race in Genesis 11:1–9, however,
receives no instructions. Indeed, it betrays
no awareness of God at all. God, observing
his creatures' display of talent and ambition,

That is why it was called **Babel**,
    because there the LORD confused the **speech** of all the **world**.
It was from that **place** that he **scattered** them all over the **earth**.

Or:

READING I   Exodus 19:3–8a, 16–20b

A reading from the Book of Exodus

Moses went up the **mountain** to **God**.
Then the LORD called to him and said,
"Thus shall you say to the house of **Jacob**;
    tell the **Israelites**:
        You have seen for yourselves how I treated the **Egyptians**
        and how I **bore** you **up** on **eagle wings**
        and brought you **here** to **myself**.
Therefore, if you hearken to my **voice** and keep my **covenant**,
    you shall be my special possession,
        dearer to me than **all other people**,
        though all the earth is **mine**.
You shall be to me a **kingdom** of **priests**, a **holy nation**.
That is what you must tell the **Israelites**."
So **Moses** went and summoned the **elders** of the **people**.
When he set before them
    all that the LORD had **ordered** him to tell them,
    the **people** all answered **together**,
        "**Everything** the LORD has **said**, we will **do**."

Proclaim God's words in a strong and
resolute manner.

Emphasize the word "Everything."
The Israelites are promising a lot here.

reacts with alarm to their seemingly limitless possibility: "If now, while they are one people, they have started to do this, nothing will later stop them from doing whatever they presume to do" (Genesis 11:6). Once given to strolling about paradise (Genesis 3:8), God has by now withdrawn from the intelligent, willful, and dangerous creatures crafted in his image (Genesis 1:26–27).

By this point in Genesis, having cursed, expelled, and then destroyed all but a handful of humanity, God seems almost out of ideas for dealing with them. Only with the confusion of tongues and the covenant with Abraham, starting in Genesis 12:1, do matters begin to improve.

EXODUS. God precedes the establishment of covenant with a recitation of Israel's recent history with himself (Exodus 19:3–4). Israel has been rescued from Egypt's clutches in dramatic fashion while its enemies have suffered humiliation and defeat. God is reminding Moses, and through Moses the elders and the people, that Israel's own experience testifies that God is trustworthy. God is not asking for faith, but for Israel to reflect on how events have unfolded in its favor.

Mystics of the ancient Church were fascinated by Moses' journey up Mount Sinai (Exodus 19:20; 20:21). Both Gregory of Nyssa (fourth century AD) and Dionysius the Areopagite (fifth century AD) found in Moses' physical ascent up the mountain an example of a Christian's ascent to God in prayer. Gregory and Dionysius built on the ideas of the Jewish philosopher, Philo of Alexandria (first century AD), who understood the true meaning of Moses' ascent in very similar terms.

On the **morning** of the **third day**
    there were **peals** of **thunder** and **lightning**,
    and a **heavy cloud** over the **mountain**,
    and a very loud **trumpet** blast,
    so that **all** the people in the camp **trembled**.
But **Moses** led the **people** out of the **camp** to meet **God**,
    and they **stationed** themselves at the **foot** of the **mountain**.
Mount Sinai was all **wrapped** in **smoke**,
    for the LORD came down upon it in **fire**.
The smoke **rose** from it as though from a **furnace**,
    and the **whole mountain** trembled **violently**.
The trumpet blast grew **louder** and **louder**,
      while **Moses** was speaking,
    and **God** answering him with **thunder**.

When the LORD came down to the top of Mount **Sinai**,
    he summoned **Moses** to the top of the **mountain**.

Or:

READING I   Ezekiel 37:1–14

A reading from the Book of the Prophet Ezekiel

The hand of the LORD came **upon** me,
    and he **led** me out in the **spirit** of the LORD
    and set me in the **center** of the **plain**,
    which was now **filled** with **bones**.
He made me **walk** among the **bones** in every **direction**
    so that I saw how **many** they were on the **surface** of the **plain**.
How dry they **were**!

Pause briefly before "But Moses." It will direct attention to the contrast between the descriptions of the people's fear and Moses' courage.

Pause before this sentence and deliver it slowly.

Look up at this point and view the assembly as you say these words. Emphasize both "How" and "dry."

For Philo, Moses was the ideal philosopher. Philo interpreted Moses' ascent and his entry into the cloud concealing God's presence to mean that Moses apprehended truth beyond sight and sense (*Life of Moses,* 1.155–159). Gregory interpreted Moses' entry into the cloud similarly. The darkness of the cloud Gregory called "brilliant darkness," which was his way of saying that Moses' vision of God was sight beyond seeing and knowledge beyond knowing (*Life of Moses,* 2.162–169). Dionysius interpreted Moses' ascent into the darkness of the cloud as Moses' union with God. For Dionysius, God

is so far beyond human understanding and the descriptive powers of language that he can only be understood and described negatively, in terms of what he is not, rather than in terms of what or who he is (*Mystical Theology,* 1.3).

The mystical interpretation of scripture in the early Church was above all an exercise in prayer. Our own meditations on Moses' journey up Sinai may lead us down different paths than Philo, Gregory, and Dionysius. But the search for God their writings exemplify is open to any Christian willing to sit quietly with scripture and wait for God to speak.

EZEKIEL. In the third, ninth, and eleventh verses, God calls the prophet Ezekiel "Son of man." The Hebrew phrase is *ben-adam,* which at its most literal means "son of a human being." In the Septuagint, the Greek translation of the Old Testament, *adam* is translated by *anthrōpos.* Both words mean "human being" without reference to gender. This title, which is what God usually calls the prophet in Ezekiel, draws attention to the mortality of the prophet in comparison with the divinity of God. This is a very different

Keep in mind you have two speaking parts in addition to the prophet's narration. Consider the voice and tone you will use for both the prophet and God.

Stress the word "prophesy," particularly the second instance of the word.

Slow down and deliver this sentence clearly, slowly, and with emphasis.

He asked me:

Son of man, can these bones come to life?

I answered, "Lord GOD, you alone know that."

Then he said to me:

Prophesy over these bones, and say to them:

Dry bones, hear the word of the LORD!

Thus says the Lord GOD to these bones:

See! I will bring spirit into you, that you may come to life.

I will put sinews upon you, make flesh grow over you,

cover you with skin, and put spirit in you

so that you may come to life and know that I am the LORD.

I, Ezekiel, prophesied as I had been told,

and even as I was prophesying I heard a noise;

it was a rattling as the bones came together, bone joining bone.

I saw the sinews and the flesh come upon them,

and the skin cover them, but there was no spirit in them.

Then the LORD said to me:

Prophesy to the spirit, prophesy, son of man,

and say to the spirit: Thus says the Lord GOD:

From the four winds come, O spirit,

and breathe into these slain that they may come to life.

I prophesied as he told me, and the spirit came into them;

they came alive and stood upright, a vast army.

Then he said to me:

Son of man, these bones are the whole house of Israel.

They have been saying,

"Our bones are dried up,

our hope is lost, and we are cut off."

meaning than we find in the Gospels, where the evangelists apply the title to Jesus and use it to communicate essential information about his messianic identity and destiny.

In Ezekiel 37:9, God says, "Prophesy to the spirit, prophesy, son of man, and say to the spirit: Thus says the Lord God: From the four winds come, O spirit, and breathe into these slain that they may come to life." God appoints the prophet to mediate the resurrection of these dry bones, which are likely (in the book's original context) meant to represent the bones of those Jews who died in

exile. The destiny of the exiles is not despair and death.

In the Gospel of John, greeting his gathered disciples for the first time after his Resurrection, Jesus says, "Peace be with you. As the Father has sent me, so I send you." Then he breathes on them, saying, "Receive the holy Spirit" (John 20:21–22). In the context of Pentecost, when Roman Catholics celebrate the birth of the Church and the gift of the Holy Spirit, these verses from John help to interpret the passage from Ezekiel. The Church is an institution that exists to end human exile from God. As the

continued presence of the risen Christ on earth, the Church proclaims that we need not endure the despair of exile from God, nor accept that death is inevitable human destiny.

JOEL. In Joel 3:4, the prophet refers to "the day of the Lord, the great and terrible day." The day of the Lord is the main subject of this short book. But what is it?

The day of the Lord is a very ancient idea in Israelite religion. Some roots of the idea lie in the belief that when Israel went to war, God marched and fought with it. Other roots lie in liturgical calendar of the monarchies of Israel and Judah, when a

Therefore, **prophesy** and say to them: Thus says the **Lord God**:
   O my **people**, I will **open** your **graves**
   and have you **rise** from them,
   and bring you **back** to the **land** of **Israel**.
Then you shall know that **I** am the **Lord**,
   when I **open** your **graves** and have you **rise** from them,
   O my **people**!
I will put my **spirit** in you that you may **live**,
   and I will **settle** you upon your **land**;
   thus you shall **know** that **I** am the **Lord**.
I have **promised**, and I will **do** it, says the **Lord**.

Or:

READING I Joel 3:1–5

A reading from the Book of the Prophet Joel

Thus says the **Lord**:
I will **pour** out my **spirit** upon all **flesh**.
Your **sons** and **daughters** shall **prophesy**,
   your **old men** shall dream **dreams**,
   your **young men** shall see **visions**;
even upon the **servants** and the **handmaids**,
   in those days, I will **pour out** my **spirit**.
And I will work **wonders** in the **heavens** and on the **earth**,
   blood, **fire**, and **columns** of **smoke**;
the **sun** will be **turned** to **darkness**,
   and the **moon** to **blood**,

Read this passage slowly and deliberately.

particular day was designated for a festival commemorating the conquest of Canaan. In later prophetic texts, like Joel, and in apocalyptic literature, the day of the Lord came to mean a day when God would intervene directly into human history to judge Israel and in some cases the whole world. In early Christianity, the day of the Lord became associated with the return of the Son of Man and the arrival of the kingdom of God.

Many early Christians expected that the day of the Lord would not be long in coming. So soon did some expect its arrival that members of the Church in Thessalonica were anxious that some church members had died before the day came. Paul reassures them that these dead will be saved along with the living members of the Church (1 Thessalonians 4:13–18). Immediately afterward, Paul reminds the Thessalonians "that the day of the Lord" will come suddenly and without warning "like a thief at night" (1 Thessalonians 5:2). Matthew (24:43–44) and Luke (12:39–40) record these words as having been spoken by Jesus himself.

For Paul, the day of the Lord will be a day of salvation for believers. In support of this conviction, Paul quotes Joel 3:5 in Romans 10:13: "For 'everyone who calls on the name of the Lord will be saved.'"

READING II "For in hope we were saved." This is not Paul's typical way of writing about salvation. Usually salvation is something in the future. This is clear at a number of points in his letter to the Romans. In 5:9–10, justification and peace with God lie in the past, but salvation

Pause before the final stanza. This will
heighten the contrast between the vision's
startling images and the proclamation
of salvation.

at the **coming** of the **day** of the LORD,
     the **great** and **terrible** day.
Then **everyone** shall be **rescued**
     who calls on the **name** of the LORD;
for on **Mount Zion** there shall be a **remnant**,
     as the LORD **has said**,
and in **Jerusalem survivors**
     whom the LORD shall **call**.

The word hope is repeated four times in
this stanza. Pay attention to your delivery
so that it does not become a drone.

READING II   Romans 8:22–27

A reading from the Letter of Saint Paul to the Romans

Brothers and **sisters**:
We know that **all creation** is **groaning** in labor pains
     even until **now**;
     and not only that, but **we ourselves**,
     who have the **firstfruits** of the **Spirit**,
     we also **groan** within **ourselves**
     as we **wait** for **adoption**, the **redemption** of our **bodies**.
For in **hope** we were **saved**.
Now **hope** that sees is not **hope**.
For who **hopes** for what one **sees**?
But if we **hope** for what we do **not** see, we **wait** with **endurance**.

In the **same way**, the **Spirit** too comes to the **aid** of our **weakness**;
     for we do **not know** how to **pray** as we **ought**,
     but the **Spirit himself intercedes** with inexpressible **groanings**.

---

still lies ahead. In 10:9, Paul writes that a believer's future salvation depends solely upon confessing that Jesus is Lord and believing in his Resurrection. In 11:14, it is Paul's wish that by the Gentiles' example of faith he will make his fellow Jews jealous "and thus save some of them" (also see 1 Corinthians 3:15; 5:5; 7:16; 9:22; 11:33; Philippians 2:12; 1 Thessalonians 2:16; 5:9). Why does Paul write about the Romans' salvation in 8:24 as though it has already happened?

Consider the relation of hope to salvation in this passage. Believers' hope of life with Christ is not, for Paul, just a strong possibility. In Romans, Paul boasts of a hope that "does not disappoint" (Romans 5:2, 5). For Paul, hope is the reasonable perspective of people who have faith that they shall be raised as Christ was raised.

Paul argues in 8:24–25 that the object of hope is "what we do not see." A thing in sight, either present or within reach, he reasons, is a thing one possesses already and is therefore no longer an object of hope. "In hope we were saved" does not mean that

salvation has already been accomplished, but that it is *all but* accomplished for those with the "hope that does not disappoint."

| GOSPEL | One of the curious features of the Gospel of John is of how much division Jesus is the cause. The hostility to him slowly increases as the Gospel progresses. In Jerusalem, the scene of the fiercest opposition, John reports a response by Passover pilgrims that is at first largely positive (2:23). Later, after the miracle of the loaves and fishes and the discourse

And the one who searches **hearts**
>   knows what is the **intention** of the **Spirit**,
>   because he **intercedes** for the **holy ones**
>   according to God's **will**.

GOSPEL   John 7:37–39

A reading from the holy Gospel according to John

On the last and greatest day of the **feast**,
>   Jesus stood up and **exclaimed**,
>   "Let **anyone** who thirsts come to **me** and **drink**.
As **Scripture** says:
>   *Rivers of living water will **flow** from **within** him*
>   who **believes** in me."

He said this in reference to the **Spirit**
>   that those who came to **believe** in him were to **receive**.
There was, of course, **no Spirit** yet,
>   because **Jesus** had **not yet** been **glorified**.

Pause briefly before Jesus' citation of scripture.

Emphasize the explanation for the Holy Spirit's absence.

about the bread of life in the sixth chapter, many of Jesus' disciples desert him, leaving him alone with the Twelve (6:67–68). The words of the brothers of Jesus at the beginning of the seventh chapter are disturbing, even sinister. Although they joined him in Capernaum after his first sign at the wedding at Cana, Jesus' brothers now encourage him attend the feast of Tabernacles (Succoth) in Jerusalem (7:3–4). The trip requires him to pass through Judea where, as we have just learned in 7:1, "the Jews" are trying to kill him. According to John, the reason Jesus' brothers have suggested that he risk his life

to travel to Jerusalem is because they do not believe in him (7:5). Hostile opposition has penetrated even the family.

In today's Gospel selection, Jesus presents himself publicly in Jerusalem at the feast of Tabernacles. He has gone up in secret, perhaps to protect himself from his brothers' ill will (7:10). As Jesus did not make himself clear to the Samaritan woman about the meaning of "living water" (4:4–26), preferring double entendre and riddles to plain speech, neither does Jesus now explain the term. The information readers get about the spirit comes in a narrator's

aside (7:39), much as readers learn what Jesus *really* means when he predicts the Temple's destruction (2:21).

There is no indication in John that Jesus ever preached openly about the Holy Spirit (14:26). Information about the Spirit is private teaching Jesus provides his circle of disciples. Indeed, it is striking how Jesus' cryptic speech to outsiders actually frustrates attempts, such as that of the earnest Pharisee Nicodemus (3:1–13), at understanding him at all. In more ways than one, John's Jesus is an enigma.

PENTECOST: DAY

Lectionary #63

READING I   Acts 2:1–11

A reading from the Acts of the Apostles

When the time for Pentecost was **fulfilled**,
   they were **all in one place together**.
And **suddenly** there came from the sky
   a **noise** like a strong driving **wind**,
   and it **filled** the entire house in which they **were**.
Then there appeared to them **tongues** as of **fire**,
   which **parted** and came to **rest** on **each** one of them.
And they were **all filled** with the **Holy Spirit**
   and began to **speak** in different **tongues**,
   as the **Spirit** enabled them to **proclaim**.

Now there were devout **Jews** from every **nation** under **heaven**
   staying in **Jerusalem**.
At this sound, they gathered in a large crowd,
   but they were **confused**
   because each one heard them **speaking** in his own **language**.
They were **astounded**, and in **amazement** they asked,
   "Are not all these people who are speaking **Galileans**?
Then how does **each** of us **hear** them in his **native language**?
We are **Parthians**, **Medes**, and **Elamites**,
   inhabitants of **Mesopotamia**, **Judea** and **Cappadocia**,

Pause briefly before "And suddenly." Read the rest of the stanza with an eye and ear to communicating the miraculous quality of the scene.

Pause briefly after each ethnic, linguistic, and geographical designation you read. Let the international scope of what the Spirit is getting ready to do sink in.

READING I   The Gospel of Luke and its companion text, the Acts of the Apostles, are, on one level, historical works. Part one (Luke) relates the birth, youth, ministry, Passion, and Resurrection of Jesus Christ. Part two (Acts) relates the history of the spread of the Church from Jerusalem to Judea, Samaria, Syria, Asia Minor, Greece, and finally Rome. There is much that is historical about them.

But it is perhaps more accurate to call Luke and Acts a two-volume story of the Holy Spirit. The Holy Spirit is present at Jesus' conception (Luke 1:35). The Holy Spirit is upon Simeon, a prophet given an oracle by the Holy Spirit that he would not die before seeing the Messiah (Luke 2:25–27). When Jesus is brought to the Temple, the prophecy is fulfilled. The Holy Spirit descends on Jesus at his Baptism (Luke 3:22) and leads him out into the wilderness (Luke 4:1). The Spirit is upon Jesus as he begins his ministry (Luke 4:18) and is present in his joy at the missionaries' return (Luke 10:21). The Holy Spirit is the source of testimony for believers (12:12). The Holy Spirit Jesus received at his Baptism he returns to his Father's hands with his last words from the cross (Luke 23:46).

The story of the Holy Spirit continues in the prologue to Acts (Acts 1:1–2; compare Luke 1:1–4). The disciples have yet to receive their Baptism in the Holy Spirit, as Jesus says prior to his Ascension (Acts 1:5, 8; compare Luke 3:16). In today's reading, the Holy Spirit descends on the disciples and the Church is born. The story of the Holy Spirit is not finished, but continues through the rest of Acts as it leads the Church out from Jerusalem and into the world.

Pontus and Asia, Phrygia and Pamphylia,
Egypt and the districts of Libya near Cyrene,
as well as travelers from Rome,
both Jews and converts to Judaism, Cretans and Arabs,
yet we hear them speaking in our own tongues
of the mighty acts of God."

READING II   1 Corinthians 12:3b–7, 12–13

A reading from the first Letter of Saint Paul to the Corinthians

Brothers and sisters:
No one can say, "Jesus is Lord," except by the Holy Spirit.
There are different kinds of spiritual gifts but the same Spirit;
    there are different forms of service but the same Lord;
    there are different workings but the same God
    who produces all of them in everyone.
To each individual the manifestation of the Spirit
    is given for some benefit.

As a body is one though it has many parts,
    and all the parts of the body, though many, are one body,
    so also Christ.
For in one Spirit we were all baptized into one body,
    whether Jews or Greeks, slaves or free persons,
    and we were all given to drink of one Spirit.

Or:

Look at the assembly when you address them as brothers and sisters.

This reading is full of balanced clauses and contrasts. Pause before any words or phrases emphasizing contrast or reversal (but, on the contrary, and so forth). Your delivery needs to respect and communicate Paul's comparisons.

There is a choice of second readings today. Please check with the liturgy coordinator or the homilist to find out which reading will be used.

READING II | 1 CORINTHIANS. Catholic liturgy has changed over the centuries as the needs and concerns of our assemblies have changed. Usually subtle, though sometimes sudden and radical, these alterations have typically been aimed at improving the Church's worship. Baptism, for example, has been performed in different ways at different times and in different places. What has remained constant is a cleansing with water in the name of the triune God by which the baptized person is joined to Christ and enters the Church. The setting in the life of the early Church, from which come these words of Paul's is baptismal liturgy. The ritual underlying this text probably looked very different from a typical Sunday Baptism in a North American parish. What has remained constant between then and now is the water bath, the triune God invoked in the baptismal formula, the gift of the Spirit, and a new member joined to the body of Christ.

In 12:13, having described the diverse unity of the Church, like both Christ and the Spirit, as a single body, Paul cites from what was probably the baptismal liturgy with which he was familiar. "For in one Spirit we were all baptized into one body, whether Jews or Greeks, slaves or free persons, and we were all given to drink of one spirit." The words are quite close to Galatians 3:28, which adds the erasure of the distinction between male and female to those of Jew and Greek, slave and free. Also related is

READING II   Romans 8:8–17

A reading from the Letter of Saint Paul to the Romans

Brothers and **sisters**:
Those who are in the **flesh cannot** please **God**.
But you are **not** in the **flesh**;
    on the **contrary**, you are in the **spirit**,
    if only the **Spirit** of **God dwells** in you.
Whoever does **not** have the **Spirit** of **Christ** does **not** belong
        to him.
But if **Christ** is in you,
    although the **body** is **dead** because of **sin**,
    the **spirit** is **alive** because of **righteousness**.
If the **Spirit** of the **one** who raised **Jesus** from the **dead** dwells
        in **you**,
    the **one** who raised **Christ** from the **dead**
    will give **life** to your **mortal bodies** also,
    through his **Spirit** that **dwells** in you.
Consequently, **brothers** and **sisters**,
    we are **not** debtors to the flesh,
    to live **according** to the flesh.
For if you live according to the **flesh**, you will **die**,
    but if by the **Spirit** you put to **death** the **deeds** of the **body**,
    you will **live**.

For those who are **led** by the **Spirit** of **God** are **sons** of **God**.
For you did not receive a **spirit** of **slavery** to fall back into **fear**,
    but you received a **spirit** of **adoption**,
    through whom we cry, "**Abba, Father!**"

Colossians 3:11, which adds "circumcision and uncircumcision," as well as the cultural and ethnic designations of "barbarian" and "Scythian," to those distinctions eliminated in Christ.

The Church is not the world. And if we live in the world, we cannot help but bring its distinctions to worship with us. Yet through Baptism we stand on an equal footing before God and each other.

ROMANS. This passage from Romans is rich in key terms from Paul's theological vocabulary as he contrasts the situations of those "in the flesh" and those "in the spirit."

The rhetorical figure that Paul uses to create this contrast is called *antithesis*. It is not simply that flesh, death, sin, and slavery—individually and collectively—are different from spirit, life, righteousness, and adoption. It is rather that each group of words is the complete opposite of the other. The body is their battlefield.

Paul considers many questions and argues many different points in Romans. But the main and recurring subject of the letter is that Jews and Gentiles have equal standing before God. All suffer the same problems of estrangement from God through sin and of

the power of death, but all have been offered the same solution through faith in Christ. As Paul observes in 11:32, "God delivered all to disobedience, that he might have mercy upon all" (also see Romans 2:9–11; 3:9; 3:22–29; 5:16; 9:23; 10:12).

Note that there is a choice of Gospel readings today.

GOSPEL   JOHN 20. One still hears from time to time the old charge that Roman Catholics don't know

The **Spirit** himself bears **witness** with our **spirit**
    that we are **children** of **God**,
    and if **children**, then **heirs**,
    heirs of **God** and joint **heirs** with **Christ**,
    if only we **suffer** with him
    so that we may also be **glorified** with him.

GOSPEL   John 20:19–23

A reading from the holy Gospel according to John

On the evening of that first day of the week,
    when the **doors** were **locked**, where the disciples were,
    for **fear** of the Jews,
    Jesus came and stood in their **midst**
    and said to them, "**Peace** be with you."
When he had said this, he showed them his **hands** and his **side**.
The disciples **rejoiced** when they saw the Lord.
Jesus said to them again, "**Peace** be with you.
As the Father has **sent** me, so I **send you**."
And when he had said this, he **breathed** on them
      and said to them,
    "**Receive** the **Holy Spirit**.
Whose sins you **forgive** are **forgiven** them,
      and whose **sins** you **retain** are **retained**."

Or:

Stress both instances of "Peace be with you."

Give special stress to the second occurrence of the word "peace."

Stress the sentence beginning with the word "Receive."

(or care) much about scripture. Typically leveled more in ignorance than in malice, the history of the accusation in North America is enmeshed in attempts by a largely Protestant citizenry to come to terms with Roman Catholic immigrants. To many Protestants, for whom the cry of *sola scriptura* ("scripture alone") was an inspiring credo of Christian freedom, Roman Catholics' embrace of tradition as a source of belief, worship, and Church governance seemed odd at best, and at worst a rejection of the Gospel of Jesus Christ.

In point of fact, the responses and prayers of the Roman Catholic Eucharistic liturgy are laden with scripture. Indeed, scripture is the principal source of the language of the Mass. In today's reading we have one such example in "Peace be with you," which is a reiteration of 14:27. Of the five verses in which the word peace occurs in John, three of them occur in John 20 and in precisely this form: "Peace be with you" (20:19; 21; 26). We encounter two of them in our reading today.

A clue to the significance of this greeting of Jesus lies in 16:33, in which Jesus, having at last been understood by his disciples, contrasts the peace "in me" with the trouble the disciples can expect in the world. This scene from today's reading is itself a liturgical demonstration of what being "in Christ" means. Presented with evidence of the cross (the wounds to which Jesus points) and the empty tomb (Jesus' presentation of himself as alive), the disciples read the sign language of sight, speech, breath, and gesture as the fact of their peace is disclosed by Jesus, their celebrant, and the Holy Spirit comes to them.

Pause between each stanza and before
the sentence beginning with the words
"Those who do not."

GOSPEL   John 14:15–16, 23b–26

A reading from the holy Gospel according to John

Jesus said to his disciples:
"If you **love** me, you will keep my **commandments**.
And I will ask the **Father**,
    and he will give you another **Advocate** to be with you **always**.

"Whoever **loves me** will keep my **word**,
    and my **Father** will **love** him,
    and we will **come** to him and **make** our dwelling **with** him.
Those who do **not** love me do **not** keep my words;
    yet the word you **hear** is not **mine**
    but that of the **Father** who **sent** me.

"I have **told** you this while I am **with** you.
The **Advocate**, the **Holy Spirit** whom the **Father**
        will **send** in my **name**,
    will teach you **everything**
    and remind you of **all** that I told you."

JOHN 14. In John 14:16, Jesus tells his disciples that he will send them "another Advocate." So that there is no confusion, in John 14:17 (also see 15:26; 16:13; 1 John 4:6) the Advocate is called the "Spirit of truth" and "the Holy Spirit" (also see 14:26; 20:22).

As one sees in 1 John 2:1, a letter that certainly comes from the same orbit as the Gospel of John, "Advocate" is a title of Jesus. Thus the significance of the disciples' reception of "*another* Advocate" is that it will take over when Jesus leaves to return to the Father.

The news that someone else will occupy Jesus' place in the Church is important. Indeed, by this point in the Gospel it is shocking to learn that anyone else *can*. For this reason, Jesus stresses that the Holy Spirit is "*another* Advocate." Like Jesus and his Father (see 10:30; 14:10–11, 20; 17:11, 21), the functions of Jesus and the Advocate are a practical unity. The Advocate's twin functions in 14:26 are to teach the Church and to remind it of what Jesus said. Jesus is the content of the Advocate's testimony (15:26). The Advocate convicts the world because of disbelief in Jesus (16:9).

The expression of Trinitarian doctrine fell to ecclesiastical councils of subsequent centuries. The doctrinal questions and controversies concerning these councils were often of a highly theoretical nature. In contrast, Jesus' discussion of the Trinity in John is quite practical: how does the interaction among Father, Son, and Holy Spirit affect the Church? John is more interested in what the Trinity *does* than in what it *is*.

MOST HOLY TRINITY

Lectionary #166

READING I   Proverbs 8:22–31

Proclaim this reading with attention to its rhythm, paying due attention to the balance of the clauses and the repeated words (when, before) and refrains.

There is no need to adopt an especially solemn tone with this reason. Wisdom, we learn, is playful and a delight to God.

A reading from the Book of Proverbs

Thus says the **wisdom** of **God**:
"The LORD **possessed** me, the beginning of his **ways**,
    the **forerunner** of his **prodigies** of long ago;
from of old I was poured **forth**,
    at the first, before the **earth**.
When there were no **depths** I was brought **forth**,
    when there were no **fountains** or **springs** of **water**;
before the mountains were **settled** into place,
    before the hills, I was **brought forth**;
while as yet the **earth** and **fields** were not made,
    nor the first **clods** of the world.

"When the LORD established the **heavens** I was there,
    when he marked out the **vault** over the **face** of the **deep**;
when he made **firm** the skies **above**,
    when he fixed fast the **foundations** of the **earth**;
when he set for the **sea** its **limit**,
    so that the **waters** should not **transgress** his **command**;
then was I **beside** him as his **craftsman**,
    and I was his **delight** day by day,
playing before him all the while,
    playing on the surface of his earth;
    and I found **delight** in the human race."

READING I   In the fourth book of *Against Heresies,* Irenaeus of Lyons points out a fundamental difference between God and humanity: God creates, while humanity is created (*Against Heresies* 4.11). One of Irenaeus' tasks in this section of his work is to show that all three members of the Trinity—Father, Son, and Holy Spirit—worked together to fashion the cosmos. In support of his position that the Spirit assisted both the Father and the Son, Irenaeus cites both Proverbs 3 and today's reading, Proverbs 8. As the Word is the same as the Son, Irenaeus claims that, in the same way, wisdom is identical to the Holy Spirit (*Against Heresies,* 4.20). The Catechism refers to this passage from Irenaeus' work when it teaches that the creative work of the Son and Holy Spirit is "inseparably one with the Father" (Catechism, #292).

The Hebrew word translated as "wisdom" in Proverbs 8 is *hochma*. Perhaps more familiar is the Greek translation of this Hebrew word *sophia*. Both are feminine nouns. The importance of *sophia* to the early Church as a force guiding the development of its theology and doctrine is expressed in the name of one of antiquity's most beautiful Christian churches: Hagia Sophia (Holy Wisdom).

In today's reading we meet wisdom as a "craftsman," who does not toil so much as play in the cosmic playground she helped bring into being. This reading reminds us that the world's seas, rivers, forests, plains, and creatures are not only good, as God saw at Creation (Genesis 1), but also have stamped on them the impress of their Creator's joy.

Read this passage slowly so that the logical relationship of the clauses is not lost. Emphasize words such as "therefore," "since," "not only" and "but even."

Pause between each virtue and its repetition.

READING II   Romans 5:1–5

A reading from the Letter of Saint Paul to the Romans

Brothers and sisters:
Therefore, **since** we have been **justified** by **faith**,
    we have **peace** with God through our Lord Jesus Christ,
    through whom we have gained access by **faith**
    to this **grace** in which we stand,
    and we boast in **hope** of the **glory** of God.
Not only that, but we even boast of our **afflictions**,
    knowing that **affliction** produces **endurance**,
    and **endurance**, proven **character**,
    and proven **character**, **hope**,
    and **hope** does **not** disappoint,
    because the **love** of God has been poured out into our **hearts**
    through the **Holy Spirit** that has been **given** to **us**.

READING II Paul often writes about boasting. Boasting can be evidence, in some cases, of hypocrisy. "Your boasting is not appropriate," writes Paul to the Church at Corinth, accusing the Corinthians of pretensions to wisdom and spiritual living while tolerating a member's misbehavior (1 Corinthians 5:6). In a subsequent letter to the Church at Corinth, Paul defends himself against the charge of being boastful and even attempts to tar his opponents with the same charge (2 Corinthians 10—13). But sometimes boasting is fitting

and acceptable. Paul boasts in Christ (Philippians 3:3) and claims that his ministry is one in which others may boast because of its authenticity (2 Corinthians 5:12). While Paul tells the Corinthians not to boast "about human things" (1 Corinthians 3:21), God is an acceptable boast, indeed the only acceptable boast (1 Corinthians 1:31).

If there is a principle underlying Paul's writing on boasting, it is that a person can boast only about God or what God has done. "In Christ Jesus, then," he writes, "I have reason to boast in what pertains to God. For I will not dare to speak of anything except

what Christ has accomplished through me," he writes, "I have a reason to boast of my work for God. For I will not venture to speak of anything except what Christ has accomplished through me" (Romans 15:17–18). It is in general accord with this principle that Paul, in today's reading, can "boast in hope of the glory of God" (Romans 5:2). Paul boasts not because he has somehow earned this glory, but because he believes God's justification of him gives him the hope of it.

GOSPEL   John 16:12–15

A reading from the holy Gospel according to John

Jesus said to his disciples:
"I have **much more** to tell you, but you **cannot** bear it now.
But when he comes, the **Spirit** of **truth**,
    he will guide you to **all truth**.
He will **not** speak on his own,
    but he will **speak** what he **hears**,
    and will **declare** to you the things that are **coming**.
He will **glorify** me,
    because he will take from what is mine and declare it to you.
Everything that the Father has is **mine**;
    for this reason I told you that he will take from what is **mine**
    and **declare** it to **you**."

Read this passage slowly, emphasizing the proper nouns and personal pronouns so that the relationship among them is clear.

Paul's "afflictions" are also apparently God-given, and therefore something to boast about, since they lead to a hope whose cause is God's love and the outpouring of the Holy Spirit (Romans 5:3).

GOSPEL | Today's Gospel selection comes from John's farewell discourse (John 14—17), which is an account of Jesus' final evening with his disciples. In a few verses the disciples will claim to at last understand and believe in Jesus. But Jesus will cast doubt on these claims. "Do you believe now? Behold, the hour is coming and has arrived when each of you will be scattered to his own home and you will leave me alone" (16:31–32). The disciples cannot stand to hear that Jesus will be taken from them; that he will be tried, executed, and raised from the dead; and that they will all flee, leaving him to face his fate alone.

Christ's Passion, which in John is associated with his glorification, must take place before the disciples, under the guidance of the spirit, can fully understand Jesus. Attentive readers already know that Jesus' glorification precedes the arrival of the Spirit (7:39). After Jesus' glorification and his return to the Father, the Spirit is promised to help the disciples interpret the events of which they cannot now bear to hear. "But when he comes, the Spirit of Truth, he will guide you to all truth" (John 16:13).

The unity among the members of the Trinity in this passage is quite striking, while its purpose is quite practical from the standpoint of the Church. Jesus and the Father share all, just as Jesus and the Spirit share all.

MOST HOLY BODY AND BLOOD OF CHRIST

Lectionary #169

READING I   Genesis 14:18–20

A reading from the Book of Genesis

Melchizedek = Mel-kih-ZEH-dek

Salem = SAY-lem

Abram = AY-bram

Emphasize Melchizedek's blessing
on Abram by proclaiming it more slowly
and with a bit more volume than the
preceding text.

In those days, **Melchizedek**, king of **Salem**,
    brought out **bread** and **wine**,
    and being a priest of **God Most High**,
    he blessed **Abram** with these words:
    "**Blessed** be **Abram** by **God Most High**,
        the creator of **heaven** and **earth**;
    and blessed be **God Most High**,
        who **delivered** your foes into your **hand**."
Then **Abram** gave him a tenth of **everything**.

READING II   1 Corinthians 11:23–26

A reading from the first Letter of Saint Paul to the Corinthians

Emphasize Jesus' words of institution.

Pause after "remembrance of me." This is
the point at which Jesus' words end and
Paul's begin again.

Brothers and **sisters**:
I **received** from the Lord what I **also** handed on to you,
    that the Lord Jesus, on the night he was **handed over**,
    took **bread**, and, after he had given **thanks**,
    broke it and said, "**This** is my **body** that is for **you**.
Do this in **remembrance** of me."

READING I Apart from this reading, Melchizedek appears nowhere else in the Old Testament except at Psalm 110:4. His name (in Hebrew *melech* = king, *zedeq* = righteousness) is translated in Hebrews 7:2 to mean "king of righteousness." He and his name were the subjects of considerable speculation by Jews and Christians. There was a text found among the Dead Sea Scrolls mentioning an angelic being called Melchizedek (11Q13). The anonymous author of Hebrews devotes a fair chunk to a comparison of Abram with Melchizedek, attempting to demonstrate the inferior quality of the earthly priesthood of the Jerusalem Temple in comparison with the heavenly high priesthood of Christ. The first-century Jewish philosopher Philo of Alexandria, translating Melchizedek's name as "just king," sees in the priest-ruler of Salem an allegory for reason, whose proffered wine offers a kind of "divine drunkenness" (*Allegorical Interpretation*, III.80–82).

Melchizedek remains the subject of speculation, both mystical and allegorical, in the Roman Catholic Church. In Melchizedek, the Catechism teaches, the Church sees a "figure of Christ" (Catechism, #58). This figurative reading of Melchizedek extends to his offering of food and blessing upon Abram in which the Eucharistic sacrifice of the Mass is seen: "The Church sees in the gesture of the king-priest Melchizedek, who 'brought bread and wine,' a prefiguring of her own offering" (Catechism, #1333).

READING II Paul, though called an apostle, was not one of the Twelve. He did not attend the Last Supper. By his own admission (1 Corinthians 15:9; Galatians 1:13, 23; Philippians 3:6), he persecuted the Church in the several years

In the **same** way also the **cup**, after **supper**, saying,
"This cup is the **new covenant** in my **blood**.
Do this, as **often** as you drink it, in **remembrance** of me."
For as **often** as you **eat** this **bread** and **drink** the **cup**,
you **proclaim** the **death** of the **Lord** until he **comes**.

GOSPEL   Luke 9:11b–17

A reading from the holy Gospel according to Luke

Jesus spoke to the crowds about the **kingdom of God**,
and he **healed** those who **needed** to be cured.
As the day was drawing to a close,
the Twelve approached him and said,
"**Dismiss** the **crowd**
so that they can go to the surrounding villages and farms
and find **lodging** and **provisions**;
for we are in a **deserted** place here."
He said to them, "**Give** them some **food yourselves**."
They replied, "Five loaves and two fish are **all** we have,
unless we **ourselves** go and buy food for all these people."
Now the men there numbered about **five thousand**.
Then he said to his disciples,
"Have them **sit down** in groups of about **fifty**."
They **did** so and made them **all** sit down.

Be aware of the exchange of dialogue here. Pause briefly before each speaker.

between Jesus' death and his conversion (Galatians 1:15–17; Acts 9). There is no evidence Paul knew about Jesus during Jesus' lifetime.

So what does it mean in today's reading that Paul received his Eucharistic tradition "from the Lord"? A similar case presents itself earlier in this letter, when Paul says that "the Lord," not Paul, forbids divorce. Paul probably knew this word of Jesus from the body of teachings preserved and handed on by the earliest disciples (1 Corinthians 7:10; see Matthew 5:27–32; Mark 9:43–48; Luke 16:18). Along with what Jesus said, the

disciples also preserved and handed on what he did, as in this tradition about Jesus' final meal (Matthew 26:26–29; Mark 14:22–25; Luke 22:15–20). The tradition is "from the Lord" in the sense that Paul inherited it from people to whom it was passed down in a human chain from those who were at the Last Supper and were witnesses to what Jesus said and did there.

Commemorations by family, friends, and associates of the dead were common events in antiquity (and today in many cultures). Such commemorations were probably most often held in the context of a memorial

meal. The command to "Do this in remembrance of me" suggests that the basic structure of Eucharistic tradition was contributed by commemorative meal customs of the Greco-Roman world into which Christianity was born.

Whenever we participate in the Mass with our brothers and sisters in Christ, we participate in an ancient tradition handed down to us from our ancestors in faith, commemorating Jesus in obedience to his command to eat and remember.

Then **taking** the five **loaves** and the two **fish**,
   and looking up to **heaven**,
   he said the **blessing** over them, **broke** them,
   and gave them to the **disciples** to set before the **crowd**.
They all **ate** and were **satisfied**.
And when the leftover fragments were picked up,
   they filled twelve wicker baskets.

GOSPEL In the Gospel of Luke the miraculous feeding of the 5,000 takes place at "a town called Bethsaida" (Luke 9:10). This Galilean fishing village, located on the northeastern shore of the Sea of Galilee, is one of the most frequently mentioned towns in the Gospels. John reports that it was the hometown of the apostles Philip, Andrew, and Peter (John 1:44). Mark records that Jesus performed a healing miracle here, curing a man of blindness (Mark 8:22–26). In both Matthew and Luke, Jesus criticizes Bethsaida and the neighboring village of Chorazin for not repenting in response to Jesus' acts of power (Matthew 11:21; Luke 10:13). The site of the miracle in today's Gospel selection lies at the center of Jesus' Galilean ministry in country he and his disciples knew well.

Luke's account of Jesus' miracle foreshadows his description of the Last Supper. This is especially apparent when one compares the Greek of Luke 9:16 with that of 22:19. The only significant difference between the verbs of the two verses is that Jesus looks up to heaven in 9:16. Otherwise, the verbs describing Jesus' taking, blessing, breaking, and giving of the bread are identical and occur in the same order.

Eucharist lies at the heart of what it means to be a Roman Catholic Christian. Sacrifice, commemoration, family meal, and wedding feast are all ways of describing the mystery by which Catholics are nourished and sustained as members of Christ's body. Today's reading underscores an aspect of Eucharistic theology infrequently commented on. In addition to all of these things, the Eucharist is mercy shown to people hungry for God.

11TH SUNDAY IN ORDINARY TIME

Lectionary #93

READING I   2 Samuel 12:7–10, 13

A reading from the second Book of Samuel

Nathan said to **David**:
"**Thus** says the **Lord God** of Israel:
    'I **anointed** you king of **Israel**.
I **rescued** you from the hand of **Saul**.
I **gave** you your lord's **house** and your lord's **wives** for your **own**.
I **gave** you the **house** of Israel and of **Judah**.
And if **this** were not enough, I could count up for you **still more**.
Why have you **spurned** the Lord and done **evil** in his sight?
You have **cut down Uriah** the **Hittite** with the **sword;**
    you **took** his **wife** as your **own**,
    and **him** you **killed** with the **sword** of the **Ammonites**.
Now, **therefore**, the sword shall **never** depart from your house,
    because **you** have **despised** me
    and have **taken** the **wife** of **Uriah** to be your **wife**.'"
Then **David** said to **Nathan**,
    "I have **sinned** against the Lord."
Nathan answered **David**:
    "The Lord on his part has **forgiven** your sin:
    you shall **not** die."

Proclaim these words firmly. This is God's judgment on David for conspiring to kill a man in order to take his wife.

Saul = Sawl

Judah = JU-dah

Uriah = U-RI-yah
Hittite = HIH-tite

Ammonites = AM-mon-nites

Pause between the end of Nathan's oracle and David's reply. Bring out David's contrition, shock, and horror at what he has done.

READING I The story of David, Bathsheba, and Uriah the Hittite begins in 2 Samuel 11. It is the first part of a longer story, as gripping as any first-rate novella, often designated by Old Testament scholars as the "succession narrative." The full story spans 2 Samuel 11—1 Kings 2. A sign of the trouble to come is in the very first verse of chapter 11: in the season when kings "go out on campaign," David remains behind in Jerusalem. Why, in the season when kings take the field, does Israel's king stay at home? In any case, while his troops battle the Ammonites, David lingers in the capital. Following an afternoon nap in the palace, he spies a beautiful woman bathing. David sees her, wants her, and decides to take her.

Learning that the woman, Bathsheba, is the wife of Uriah (2 Samuel 11:3), a soldier of unimpeachable loyalty (11:6–13), David quickly exchanges voyeurism for betrayal and treachery. He writes a letter to Joab, Israel's field commander against Ammon, in which he orders that Uriah be placed in the front line, but that Joab suddenly draw the rest of the line back leaving Uriah to be killed. The cruelest irony is that David uses loyal Uriah to deliver the letter to Joab containing the instructions for his own murder (11:14–15). The dutiful Joab shortly engineers Uriah's death (11:16–17).

READING II   Galatians 2:16, 19–21

A reading from the Letter of Saint Paul to the Galatians

Brothers and **sisters:**
We who know that a person is **not** justified by works of the **law**
   but through **faith** in **Jesus Christ**,
   even **we** have **believed** in Christ Jesus
   that **we** may be **justified** by **faith** in Christ
   and **not** by works of the **law**,
   because by **works** of the **law no one** will be **justified**.
For **through** the law **I died** to the **law**,
   that I might **live** for **God**.
I have been **crucified** with **Christ**;
   yet **I live**, no longer **I**, but **Christ lives** in **me**;
   insofar as **I** now **live** in the **flesh**,
   I live by **faith** in the **Son** of **God**
   who has **loved me** and **given himself** up for **me**.
I do not **nullify** the **grace** of **God**;
   for if **justification** comes through the **law**,
   then Christ died for **nothing**.

This passage must be read slowly. The logic is complicated.

Emphasize the words "I," "we," and "Christ."

The prophet Nathan carefully sets David up so that the king convicts himself of his own sin. Nathan tells David of a poor man received as a visitor by a rich man. The rich man, who has flocks and flocks of sheep, slaughters a ewe, the only piece of livestock the poor man owns. David flies into a rage, demanding that justice be done. Then Nathan springs his trap in 2 Samuel 12:7: "You are the man!"

Nathan understood how much easier it is to condemn someone else than to take a good look in the mirror. Jesus' word for this is hypocrisy. "How can you say to your brother, 'Brother, let me remove that splinter in your eye,' when you do not even notice the wooden beam in your own eye?" (Luke 6:41–2; also see Matthew 7:3–5). And while forgiveness awaits a repentant David, his sin does not go unpunished (12:7–25).

READING II Paul writes this letter to Christian communities he founded in the Roman province of Galatia. The situation Paul addresses must be redrawn from the letter itself since the Galatians left us no record. It seems that after Paul had moved on, missionaries came to Galatia claiming that if the Galatians wanted a full relationship with God and other Christian assemblies, then the men would have to get circumcised in accord with Jewish law. These missionaries also claimed that Paul was not a real apostle.

Paul responded with a forceful but carefully written letter. As to the claim that he is not a real apostle, Paul comes out swinging. In the first verse of the letter he calls himself "Paul, an apostle not from human beings nor through a human being but through Jesus Christ and God the Father."

GOSPEL   Luke 7:36—8:3

A reading from the holy Gospel according to Luke

A **Pharisee** invited **Jesus** to dine with him,
    and he entered the **Pharisee's** house and reclined at table.
Now there was a **sinful** woman in the city
    who learned that he was at table in the house of the **Pharisee**.
Bringing an alabaster flask of **ointment**,
    she stood behind him at his feet **weeping**
    and began to **bathe** his feet with her **tears**.
Then she **wiped** them with her **hair**,
    kissed them, and **anointed** them with the ointment.
When the Pharisee who had invited him saw this he said to
        himself,
    "If **this man** were a **prophet**,
    he would **know who** and **what sort** of **woman** this is who is
        touching him,
    that she is a **sinner**."
Jesus said to him in reply,
    "**Simon**, I have something to say to **you**."
"**Tell me**, teacher," he said.
"Two people were in **debt** to a certain **creditor**;
    one **owed** five hundred days' wages and the other **owed** fifty.
Since they were **unable** to **repay** the **debt**, he **forgave** it for both.
Which of them will **love** him more?"
Simon said in reply,
    "The one, I suppose, whose larger debt was forgiven."
He said to him, "You have judged **rightly**."

Slow down as you proclaim Luke's description of what the woman does to Jesus.

Simon the Pharisee is skeptical. Let your delivery of his interior monologue reflect his skepticism.

In Jesus' words to Simon you can emphasize the contrast between their treatments of Jesus by stressing occurrences of "you" and "she" and pausing between description of what Simon did and what the woman did.

In the first two chapters of this letter, Paul emphasizes that his commission is divine, not human. Time after time he emphasizes the divine source of his apostolate. We do not know if the Galatians were persuaded.

In this reading Paul deals mainly with the question of how the observance of Jewish law relates to faith in Christ. For Paul, trouble arises not with observance of Jewish religious law alone, but with what the Galatians think observance will accomplish. If a Galatian man decides to get circumcised because he thinks it is the only

way to have a full relationship with God, then, Paul would argue, the man has rejected God's justification of him in the vain attempt to justify himself. By placing his trust in the law, the man cancels his trust in Christ. It is God, not anything human, who accomplishes justification and puts right the relationship between people and himself (Catechism, #1987–2005).

GOSPEL Luke takes a special interest in women in his Gospel. Much of the first two chapters are taken up

with Elizabeth and Mary. In addition to these, there are many other sections of Luke concerning women not found in the other Gospels. Anna (2:36–38), the widow of Nain and her son (7:11–17), women traveling with Jesus (8:1–3), Mary and Martha (10:38–42), the crippled woman (13:10–17), the widow and the judge (18:1–8), and the crying daughters of Jerusalem (23:27–31) are all unique to the Gospel of Luke. It is not clear why Luke records so much more material about

Then he turned to the woman and said to **Simon,**
   "Do you **see** this woman?
When I entered your house, you did **not** give me **water** for my **feet,**
   but she has **bathed** them with her **tears**
   and **wiped** them with her **hair.**
You did **not** give me a **kiss,**
   but she has **not ceased kissing** my **feet** since the time I entered.
You did **not** anoint my head with oil,
   but she **anointed** my **feet** with ointment.
So I tell you, **her many** sins have been **forgiven**
   because **she** has shown **great love.**
But the one to whom **little** is forgiven, **loves little.**"
He said to **her,** "**Your** sins are **forgiven.**"
The **others** at table said to themselves,
   "**Who** is **this** who even forgives **sins?**"
But he said to the woman,
   "Your **faith** has **saved** you; go in **peace.**"

Afterward he journeyed from one **town** and **village** to another,
   preaching and **proclaiming** the good news of the **kingdom**
      of **God.**
Accompanying him were the **Twelve**
   and some **women** who had been **cured** of evil spirits
      and infirmities,
   Mary, called **Magdalene,** from whom seven demons had
      gone out,
   Joanna, the wife of **Herod's** steward **Chuza,**
   Susanna, and many others who provided for them out
      of their resources.

Stress the name of each woman in 8:2–3.

women than the other evangelists. Some biblical scholars have interpreted this emphasis as a reflection of Luke's characteristic concern for the marginalized and outcast.

All four evangelists record an event very much like this one (Matthew 26:6–13; Mark 14:3–9; John 12:1–8). Unique to Luke is the story's setting in the house of Simon the Pharisee. Simon has not come to any firm conclusions about Jesus and sees in the sinful woman's anointing of him an opportunity to question whether Jesus is really a prophet. But we might also turn the story around on Simon and ask what this sinful woman is doing in the house of a pious Pharisee.

NATIVITY OF SAINT JOHN THE BAPTIST: VIGIL

Lectionary #586

READING I   Jeremiah 1:4–10

A reading from the book of the prophet Jeremiah

Slow down and emphasize the extra-ordinary claim "Before I formed you . . . before you were born." This is no ordinary prophetic call, but a call received *in utero!*

Let the prophet respond somewhat uncertainly, even nervously.

In the days of King **Josiah**, the word of the LORD
        came to me, saying:

Before I formed you in the **womb** I **knew** you,
        before you were **born** I **dedicated** you,
        a **prophet** to the **nations** I **appointed** you.

"Ah, Lord GOD!" I said,
        "I know **not** how to **speak**; I am too **young**."
But the LORD answered me,
        Say not, "I am too **young**."
        To whomever I **send** you, you shall **go**;
        whatever I **command** you, you shall **speak**.
Have no **fear** before them,
        because I am with you to **deliver** you, says the LORD.

Stress the sentence beginning with "See, I place my words."

Then the LORD **extended** his **hand** and **touched**
        my **mouth**, saying,
See, I place my **words** in your **mouth**!
        This day I set you
        over **nations** and over **kingdoms**,
    to **root up** and to **tear down**,
        to **destroy** and to **demolish**,
        to **build** and to **plant**.

READING I   When Paul had to answer charges that God never made him an apostle, he replied by saying that not only had God made him one, but that he was set apart for precisely this task before he was born (Galatians 2:13–16). In so doing he alluded to Jeremiah's account of his own prenatal prophetic call. Paul understood the power of the passage from today's reading: challenge the one whom God has set apart, and you really challenge God.

There were many more prophets at work in Israel and Judah than the Bible's so-called major and minor prophets. There were, for example, the 400 court prophets who prophesied victory for King Ahab of Israel and King Jehoshaphat of Judah in their campaign against Aram. The kings were defeated (1 Kings 22). There were also the prophets Jeremiah excoriated in an oracle: "Yes, I am against the prophets who prophesy lying dreams, says the Lord, and who lead my people astray by recounting

their lies and by their empty boasting. From me they have no mission or command and they do the people no good at all, says the Lord" (Jeremiah 24:32). The situation must have been very confusing for people seeking to know and to do God's will.

Jeremiah's account of his call, like Paul's, is hard to challenge when placed beside the sum of his career. For much of it Jeremiah was reviled and abused for prophesying what the rich and the powerful found

READING II 1 Peter 1:8–12

A reading from the first letter of Saint Peter

Read the first stanza slowly and deliberately, slowing down to give special emphasis to "you love him."

Beloved:

Although you have not **seen** Jesus Christ you **love** him;
    even though you do not **see** him now yet **believe** in him,
    you **rejoice** with an indescribable and glorious **joy**,
    as you attain the **goal** of your **faith**, the **salvation**
      of your **souls**.

Concerning this **salvation**,
    prophets who **prophesied** about the **grace** that was to be yours
    searched and **investigated** it,
    investigating the time and **circumstances**
    that the Spirit of Christ within them indicated
    when he **testified** in advance
    to the **sufferings** destined for **Christ**
    and the **glories** to follow them.

Pause between "themselves" and "but you," pausing again before "with regard."

It was **revealed** to them that they were **serving**
    not **themselves** but **you**
    with regard to the things that have now been announced
      to you
    by those who preached the **good news** to you
    through the **Holy Spirit** sent from heaven,
    things into which **angels** longed to look.

---

uncomfortable and inconvenient. But the final destruction of Jerusalem in 586 BC happened much as Jeremiah predicted. It is no mistake that subsequent generations preserved Jeremiah's oracles and not those of the prophets who offered soothing words.

READING II First Peter is addressed to Christians who live in northern Asia Minor, territory that is part of the modern state of Turkey (1 Peter 1:1). The letter contains information suggesting that the

Christians of this region have suffered some kind repression (1:6; 2:20; 3:14; 4:1, 12–13; 5:9). Persecution was a constant worry for the Church during its first three centuries, breaking out from time to time in different regions and cities of the Roman Empire. Usually, persecution amounted to little more than harassment. But sometimes it involved the legal machinery of the imperial administration, confiscations of property, torture, and public executions. Whatever the recipients of this letter have experienced, its

author now seeks to bolster spirits that may have flagged by comparing the superiority of the recipients' new lives in Christ to what they used to do and who they used to be.

In this reading the author roots the recipients' Christian belief in much deeper and richer soil than their accusers' attacks permitted them. Not only did Old Testament prophets testify according to "the Spirit of Christ within them," he says, but the prophets were also well aware that they spoke their oracles for the benefit of the Church in its current period of tribulation. Such words

GOSPEL   Luke 1:5–17

A reading from the holy Gospel according to Luke

Herod = HAIR-ud
Zechariah = Zek-ah-RI-yah
Abijah = Ah-BI-jah

In the days of **Herod**, King of **Judea**,
   there was a priest named **Zechariah**
   of the priestly division of **Abijah**;
   his wife was from the daughters of **Aaron**,
   and her name was **Elizabeth**.
Both were **righteous** in the eyes of God,
   observing **all** the **commandments**
   and **ordinances** of the **Lord** blamelessly.
But they had no child, because **Elizabeth** was barren
   and both were **advanced** in years.
Once when he was serving
   as priest in his division's turn before God,
   according to the practice of the priestly service,
   he was **chosen** by **lot**
   to enter the **sanctuary** of the **Lord** to burn **incense**.
Then, when the whole assembly of the people
     was **praying** outside
   at the hour of the incense offering,
   the angel of the Lord **appeared** to him,
   standing at the **right** of the **altar** of **incense**.
Zechariah was troubled by what he **saw**, and **fear** came
     upon him.
But the **angel** said to him, "Do not be **afraid**, **Zechariah**,
   because your **prayer** has been heard.
Your wife Elizabeth will bear you a **son**,
   and you shall name him **John**.

Proclaim the angel Gabriel's words
clearly, strongly, and slowly.

were aimed, at least in part, to calm Christian anxieties, since a typical charge leveled against Christians was that their religion was brand new. In a culture that prized antiquity like little else, this was a damning charge. The author of today's reading does not let this charge stand. The traditions of the Church are nothing novel, he contends, but ancient indeed.

GOSPEL John the Baptist was killed by Herod Antipas (4 BC–39 AD), who was the Tetrarch of Galilee and Perea. Two of four Gospels clearly attest to Jesus' Baptism by John before he began his own mission (Matthew 3:13–17; Mark 1:9–11). Luke gives John no clear role in Jesus' Baptism, but suggests Jesus was among those who came to John for Baptism in 3:7. In any case, Luke relates Jesus' Baptism in 3:21–22 immediately after writing of John's imprisonment (3:19–20). The account of the Jewish historian Flavius Josephus about Jewish anger at John's execution illustrates quite vividly how popular John was in his lifetime (*Antiquities* VIII, 116–119). Herod Antipas' fear of John makes good sense in light of the prophet's popularity (Mark 6:20). The period of John's ministry is of enormous significance to the formation of the nucleus of Jesus' movement (Acts 1:22).

Elijah = El-LI-jah

And you will have **joy** and **gladness**,
     and many will **rejoice** at his birth,
     for he will be **great** in the **sight** of the **Lord**.
John will drink neither **wine** nor strong **drink**.
He will be filled with the **Holy Spirit**
     even from his mother's **womb**,
     and he will turn many of the **children** of **Israel**
     to the **Lord** their **God**.
He will go before him in the **spirit** and **power** of **Elijah**
     to turn their **hearts** toward their **children**
     and the **disobedient** to the **understanding** of the **righteous**,
     to prepare a people **fit** for the **Lord**."

In today's Gospel selection, John's father, Zechariah, celebrates the liturgy of the Jerusalem Temple. As he does so, the angel Gabriel comes to him to tell him about the son his wife Elizabeth will bear. Like Abram and Sarah in Genesis, Zechariah and Elizabeth are old and well past the typical age of childbearing. Elizabeth, Luke tells us, cannot have children (1:7; see Genesis 18:11). Therefore, we can perhaps understand Zechariah's skepticism at the angel's words (1:18—1:20).

Like Jeremiah in today's first reading, John is set apart for his mission "even from his mother's womb" (Luke 1:15). The detail that John is filled with the Holy Spirit distinguishes John's commission from Jeremiah's. It is Luke's opinion that the Holy Spirit is not only the divine agent of Jesus' ministry and the Church, but also speaks through the prophets (Acts 28:25). Indeed, the Holy Spirit is what unifies the prophetic traditions of Israel, the ministry of John the Baptist, the ministry of Jesus, and the Church, establishing continuity between Israel and the Church.

NATIVITY OF SAINT JOHN THE BAPTIST: DAY

Lectionary #587

READING I   Isaiah 49:1–6

A reading from the book of the prophet Isaiah

Hear me, O **coastlands**,
  listen, O distant **peoples**.
The LORD called me from **birth**,
  from my mother's **womb** he gave me my **name**.
He made of me a sharp-edged **sword**
  and concealed me in the **shadow** of his **arm**.
He made me a polished **arrow**,
  in his **quiver** he hid me.
You are my **servant**, he said to me,
  Israel, through whom I show my **glory**.

Though I thought I had **toiled** in **vain**,
  and for **nothing**, **uselessly**, spent my **strength**,
yet my **reward** is with the LORD,
  my **recompense** is with my **God**.
For now the LORD has **spoken**
  who formed me as his **servant** from the **womb**,
that **Jacob** may be brought back to him
  and **Israel** gathered to him;
and I am made **glorious** in the **sight** of the LORD,
  and my God is now my **strength**!

Pause briefly before beginning the second stanza.

READING I Today's reading has many features of a typical prophetic call (see Jeremiah 1:5–10), except that the prophet addressed is Israel itself. In reply to prophetic Israel's complaint, God says, "I will make you a light to the nations." As Jeremiah was commissioned to be "a prophet to the nations" (Jeremiah 1:5), now Israel receives a commission that God's "salvation may reach to the ends of the earth" (Isaiah 49:6).

Isaiah 49:6 is an important text in the Christology and ecclesiology of Luke. Luke reports that a man called Simeon greeted the mother and father of Jesus when they came to present their son in the Jerusalem Temple. The Holy Spirit rests upon him, reveals information to him, and even leads him to the Temple on the day of Jesus' presentation. Simeon is a man Luke describes as "righteous and devout, awaiting the consolation of Israel" (Luke 2:25–27). Taking Jesus into his arms, Simeon says that he has at last seen God's "salvation," "a light for revelation to the Gentiles and glory for your people Israel" (Luke 2:30, 32). Simeon has quite literally seen "salvation"—the translation of Jesus' Hebrew name, *Yeshua*— when he held the infant in his arms. The worldwide scope of the "light for revelation" strongly evokes Isaiah 49:6 and the universal salvation Jesus provides.

In Acts 1:6, it is clear that the disciples are, like Simeon, still awaiting the consolation of Israel (also see Luke 24:21). But the risen Jesus, echoing God's words to prophetic Israel in Isaiah 49:5–6, informs the disciples that they are thinking too small: "you will be my witnesses in Jerusalem, throughout Judea and Samaria, and to the ends of the earth" (Acts 1:8).

It is too **little**, he says, for you to be my **servant**,
   to raise up the tribes of **Jacob**,
   and restore the survivors of **Israel**;
I will make you a **light** to the **nations**,
   that my **salvation** may reach to the **ends** of the **earth**.

Read the final couplet more slowly than the preceding text, emphasizing especially the words "light" and "salvation."

READING II   Acts 13:22–26

A reading from the Acts of the Apostles

In those days, Paul said:
"**God** raised up **David** as their **king**;
   of him he testified,
   *I have found **David**, son of **Jesse**, a man after my own **heart**;
   he will carry out my **every wish**.*
From this man's descendants **God**, according to his promise,
   has brought to **Israel** a **savior**, **Jesus**.
John heralded his coming by proclaiming a **baptism**
      of repentance
   to **all** the people of **Israel**;
   and as **John** was completing his course, he would say,
   '**What** do you suppose that I am? I am **not** he.
Behold, one is coming **after** me;
   I am not **worthy** to unfasten the **sandals** of his **feet**.'

"My **brothers**, **children** of the family of **Abraham**,
   and those others among you who are **God-fearing**,
   to **us** this word of **salvation** has been sent."

Pause before Paul's quotations of scripture and John's words.

Stress the word "us" and read the line containing it slowly and strongly.

READING II   Today's reading is a portion of a speech by Paul in the city of Antioch in the region of Pisidia, located in the southern part of Asia Minor. Acts records that the martyrdom of Stephen and the subsequent persecution of the Church had first brought the disciples to Antioch, where they were, for the first time, called Christians (Acts 11:19–26; also see 8:1).

Paul's speech in Pisidian Antioch takes place in a synagogue and is addressed to "Fellow Israelites and you others who are God-fearing" (13:16). Paul's synagogue audience perhaps explains his concentration

upon Israel's monarchy. David all Jews will know from scripture. But John the Baptist? Why would anyone in Asia Minor know or care?

The disciples of John the Baptist continued to follow him after Jesus began his own ministry (Matthew 9:14–17; Mark 2:18–22; Luke 5:33–39). There is even the suggestion in the Gospel of John of rivalry between disciples of Jesus and John (4:1). John remained popular in Judea after his death (Matthew 21:23–27; Mark 11:27–33; Luke 20:1–8). John's reputation, and perhaps groups of his disciples, traveled well beyond

Judea, Samaria, and Galilee. When Paul arrives in Ephesus of Asia Minor he meets Apollos, a solid teacher who knew "only the baptism of John" (Acts 18:25; see 1 Corinthians 1—4). In Ephesus Paul also finds other people who know the Baptism of John, but have never heard of the Holy Spirit (19:1–7).

John was a respected and famous man. It is likely for this reason that Paul speaks of him without much introduction. But Paul wants Jesus to enjoy the even greater reputation that he and the Church believe he deserves.

GOSPEL Luke 1:57–66, 80

A reading from the holy Gospel according to Luke

When the **time** arrived for **Elizabeth** to have her child
    she gave **birth** to a **son**.
Her **neighbors** and **relatives** heard
    that the **Lord** had shown his great **mercy** toward her,
    and they **rejoiced** with her.
When they **came** on the eighth day to **circumcise** the child,
    they were going to call him **Zechariah** after his **father**,
    but his **mother** said in reply,
    "**No**. He will be called **John**."
But they answered her,
    "There is **no** one among your **relatives** who has this name."
So they made **signs**, asking his father what he **wished** him
        to be called.
He asked for a tablet and wrote, "**John** is his **name**,"
    and **all** were amazed.
Immediately his mouth was **opened**, his tongue **freed**,
    and he **spoke blessing God**.
Then **fear** came upon all their neighbors,
    and all these matters were discussed
    throughout the hill country of **Judea**.
All who heard these things took them to heart, saying,
    "**What**, then, will this **child** be?"
For surely the **hand** of the **Lord** was with him.

The child **grew** and became **strong** in **spirit**,
    and he was in the **desert** until the **day**
    of his manifestation to **Israel**.

Zechariah = Zech-a-RI-ah

Imagine the pressure Elizabeth was under!
Read her refusal firmly.

Read the sentence beginning with "What
then" slowly and as a question. Try to
convey some of the speakers' amazement.

GOSPEL One day, celebrating the liturgy of the Jerusalem Temple alone, Zechariah, a priest, meets the angel Gabriel. Among other things, Gabriel tells Zechariah that his wife, Elizabeth, will have a child and that he will call him John (Acts 1:13). The name John in the Greek text of Luke is *Iōannēs,* which is a phonetic rendering of his Hebrew name, *Yōhanan.* The literal meaning of this name is "Yahweh has shown favor." The child's name describes the source and character of the gift he is.

But before the angel has introduced himself as one of God's own attendants, while he is still a frightening and chatty interloper in the Temple (1:13–17), Zechariah responds to his strange predictions and promises with a simple and quite reasonable query: "How shall I know this? For I am an old man, and my wife is advanced in years" (1:18). Presuming Zechariah's question means unbelief, Gabriel at last discloses his identity and strikes Zechariah dumb "until the day these things take place" (1:18–20). It is not until John's circumcision eight days after his birth that Zechariah,

upon writing John's name, is made able to speak.

The onlookers respond with fear (1:65), which is a typical human response in ancient literature to appearances of divinities and gods and a common response in Luke and Acts to miracles and supernatural occurrences. The onlookers respond, therefore, as people who have witnessed the manifestation of supernatural power.

13TH SUNDAY IN ORDINARY TIME

Lectionary #99

READING I   1 Kings 19:16b, 19–21

Shaphat = Sha-FAT
Abelmeholah = Ah-bel-MEH-ho-lah

A reading from the first Book of Kings

The LORD said to **Elijah**:
  "You shall anoint **Elisha**, son of **Shaphat** of **Abelmeholah**,
  as **prophet** to succeed you."

Elijah set out and came upon **Elisha**, son of **Shaphat**,
  as he was plowing with twelve yoke of oxen;
  he was following the twelfth.
Elijah went over to him and threw his cloak over him.
Elisha left the oxen, ran after **Elijah**, and said,
  "Please, let me **kiss** my **father** and **mother** goodbye,
  and I will **follow** you."
Elijah answered, "**Go back**!
Have I done anything to you?"
Elisha left him, and taking the yoke of oxen, **slaughtered** them;
  he used the plowing equipment for **fuel** to **boil** their **flesh**,
  and gave it to his people to **eat**.
Then **Elisha** left and followed **Elijah** as his attendant.

READING I It is not always true that religious leaders of genuine conviction refuse the embrace of powerful people and institutions. One thinks, for example, of the prophet Isaiah, who was a champion of King Hezekiah of Judah and perhaps a member of the Temple's elite establishment. The social location of the prophet Elijah, one of the two principals in this reading, contrasts sharply with that of Isaiah. While Isaiah served at the right hand of Judah's political and religious institutions, Elijah spent much of his career on the run from the authorities he challenged in his aggressive and uncompromising manner. The Old Testament offers us few figures as solitary and isolated as Elijah.

Elijah was from Tisbeh, a town in the northern kingdom of Israel. When we encounter him today, he has recently slaughtered 450 prophets of Baal, a cult enjoying royal patronage and support (1 Kings 18:22, 40). King Ahab's humiliated and furious consort, Queen Jezebel, has threatened to kill him in retaliation (1 Kings 19:2). Elijah wisely flees to Judah, where, completely alone, he prays to die, but instead receives orders to journey 40 days to Mount Horeb. There he receives a curious revelation containing within it the essence of what is sometimes considered an exclusively modern theological problem: where is God? For Elijah, we learn, God is present in the inspired speech of prophecy (19:3–18).

But God is also present in another form, that of Elisha. The solitary Elijah finally gets some help. Right off the bat Elisha already seems a chip off the old block, slaughtering valuable work beasts and distributing the meat. Unswerving dedication to God's call, not prudence, characterize the careers of these two men.

READING II   Galatians 5:1, 13–18

A reading from the Letter of Saint Paul to the Galatians

Brothers and **sisters**:
For **freedom** Christ set us free;
    so stand **firm** and do not submit **again** to the yoke of **slavery**.

For you were called for **freedom**, brothers and sisters.
But do not use this **freedom**
    as an opportunity for the **flesh**;
    rather, serve one another through **love**.
For the **whole law** is fulfilled in **one** statement,
    namely, *You shall **love** your **neighbor** as **yourself***.
But if you go on **biting** and **devouring** one another,
    beware that you are not **consumed** by one another.

I say, then: **live** by the **Spirit**
    and you will certainly not **gratify** the **desire** of the **flesh**.
For the **flesh** has **desires** against the **Spirit**,
    and the **Spirit** against the **flesh**;
    these are **opposed** to each other,
    so that you may **not** do what you **want**.
But if you are **guided** by the **Spirit**, you are **not** under the **law**.

Proclaim "stand firm" with resolve.

Pause before and after the word "rather" and stress the word "love."

Read the phrase beginning with "namely, 'You shall love' " slowly and with emphasis.

Stress the words "live" and "Spirit" in the first line of the third stanza.

READING II The situation Paul addresses in his letter to the Christian communities of Galatia can be reconstructed in a general way from the letter itself. The Galatians have welcomed into their assemblies some Christian missionaries who say that a right relationship with God requires the Galatian men to be circumcised. Paul responds vigorously that faith in Jesus, not observance of Jewish law, establishes a right relationship with God.

Christ, Paul argues, offers freedom. In Galatians, Paul is primarily concerned with the Galatians' freedom from the gods and divinities they served before their evangelization (4:8–9) and from Jewish legal observance (5:1–12). In today's reading, although he claims the Galatians "are not under law," he also speaks positively of law, summing it up as "You shall love your neighbor as yourself" (5:14; see Leviticus 19:18). Indeed, he goes on to mention specific vices and virtues in 5:20–23. Why does Paul speak of law favorably and unfavorably in practically the same breath?

The likely answer is related to why the Galatians welcomed the missionaries in the first place. Paul tells them they are free. If so, then what *can't* they do? Or can they behave exactly as they wish? If their people "are not under law," on what grounds can the Church forbid behaviors or punish transgressors? Jewish law, the missionaries probably told them, was given by God to deal with exactly these questions and circumcision was the first step. Seen in this light, one can well imagine the Galatians welcoming with relief the missionaries and their talk of law.

As Paul makes clear in 5:14, the law has value, but service to it does not set up a

Samaritan = Sa-MAR-i-tan

Pause between the words of those speaking to Jesus and Jesus' replies. Emphasize Jesus' responses by slowing down to read them.

GOSPEL   Luke 9:51–62

A reading from the holy Gospel according to Luke

When the days for **Jesus'** being taken up were **fulfilled**,
    he **resolutely** determined to **journey** to **Jerusalem**,
    and he sent messengers ahead of him.
On the way they entered a **Samaritan** village
    to **prepare** for his reception there,
    but they would **not** welcome him
    because the **destination** of his **journey** was **Jerusalem**.
When the disciples **James** and **John** saw this they asked,
    "**Lord**, do you want us to call down **fire** from **heaven**
    to **consume** them?"
Jesus turned and **rebuked** them, and they journeyed
        to another village.

As they were proceeding on their journey someone said to him,
    "I will **follow** you wherever you go."
Jesus answered him,
    "Foxes have **dens** and birds of the sky have **nests**,
    but the **Son** of **Man** has **nowhere** to rest his head."

And to another he said, "**Follow** me."
But he replied, "**Lord**, let me go **first** and bury my father."
But he answered him, "Let the **dead** bury their **dead**.
But you, **go** and **proclaim** the **kingdom** of **God**."
And another said, "I will **follow** you, Lord,
    but **first** let me say farewell to my family at home."
To him Jesus said, "**No one** who sets a **hand** to the **plow**
    and **looks** to what was left **behind** is **fit** for the **kingdom**
        of **God**."

right relationship between a believer and God. Only faith in Jesus can do that, and both the condition and the product of that faith are love and service shared among, and on behalf of, one another in the Church.

| GOSPEL | The first verse of this reading is an important transition in the narrative of Luke's Gospel. Previously, Jesus has worked in Galilee, his hilly home country north of Judea and Samaria around the Sea of Galilee. When a centurion sends Jewish elders to beg healing for a sick servant, Jesus is in Capernaum

on the north shore of the Sea of Galilee (7:1). Jesus is in Nain, far southwest but still in Galilee, when he resuscitates a widow's dead son (7:11), then in Bethsaida, back on the northern coast of the Sea of Galilee, for the feeding of the 5,000 (9:10). Verse 9:51 is the first mention in Luke that Jesus intends to go to Jerusalem. His meandering journey will take the next nine-and-a-half chapters, climaxing in his entry into the city (19:28–44).

Jerusalem is of central importance in the Gospel of Luke. The Gospel's action begins in Jerusalem—in the Temple, no less—when the angel Gabriel visits Zechariah, the

father of John the Baptist (1:8). The Gospel also concludes in Jerusalem following Jesus' Ascension (24:52). Verse 51 foreshadows Jesus' Ascension. The word our Bible translates as "be taken up" is actually a noun *(analēmpsis)* that comes from a verb Luke uses to describe Jesus' Ascension *(analambanō)* (Acts 1:2). With this word, Luke foreshadows the vindication awaiting Jesus.

14TH SUNDAY IN ORDINARY TIME

Lectionary #102

READING I   Isaiah 66:10–14c

A reading from the Book of the Prophet Isaiah

Your delivery of this reading should be joyful.

Thus says the LORD:
Rejoice with **Jerusalem** and be **glad** because of her,
  all you who **love** her;
exult, **exult** with her,
  all you who were **mourning** over her!
Oh, that you may suck **fully**
  of the **milk** of her **comfort**,
that you may **nurse** with **delight**
  at her **abundant** breasts!
For **thus** says the LORD:
Lo, I will spread **prosperity** over **Jerusalem** like a **river**,
  and the **wealth** of the **nations** like an **overflowing torrent**.
As nurslings, you shall be **carried** in her arms,
  and **fondled** in her lap;
as a mother **comforts** her child,
  so will I **comfort** you;
  in **Jerusalem** you shall find your **comfort**.

When you **see** this, your heart shall **rejoice**
  and your bodies **flourish** like the grass;
the LORD's **power** shall be **known** to his **servants**.

READING I   At several places in today's reading, which comes from Isaiah's final chapter, one hears echoes of Isaiah 40. The passage "as a mother comforts her child, so will I comfort you, in Jerusalem you shall find your comfort" (66:13; also see 66:11) hearkens back to the first verses of Isaiah 40, where the prophet reports God's instructions to him: "Comfort, give comfort to my people, says your God. Speak tenderly to Jerusalem, and proclaim to her that her service is at an end" (40:1–2). The Hebrew verb for "comfort" in both

places is the same. The image of bodies flourishing like grass calls to mind Isaiah 40:6–8, in which the prophet compares the transience of human life with the imperishable word of God. In 66:14, it is God who speaks through the prophet, and it is God who, while alluding to these earlier words of human mortality, rejoices at the prospect of a people growing in abundance, spreading like grass on the land.

The Catechism refers to this passage's description of God comforting as a mother comforts when it says, "God's parental tenderness can also be expressed by the image of motherhood, which emphasizes God's immanence, the intimacy between Creator and creature" (Catechism, #239). By "immanence" the Catechism means God's pervasive and sustaining power at work throughout the cosmos. God's immanence is an idea always in tension with God's "transcendence," which is the situation of limitless

READING II   Galatians 6:14–18

A reading from the Letter of Saint Paul to the Galatians

Brothers and **sisters**:
May I **never** boast except in the **cross** of our **Lord Jesus Christ**,
   through which the **world** has been **crucified** to me,
   and **I** to the **world**.
For neither does **circumcision** mean anything,
    nor does **uncircumcision**,
   but only a **new creation**.
Peace and **mercy** be to all who follow this rule
   and to the **Israel** of **God**.

From now on, let **no** one make **troubles** for me;
   for I **bear** the **marks** of **Jesus** on my **body**.

The **grace** of our **Lord Jesus Christ** be with your **spirit**,
   brothers and **sisters**. **Amen**.

Stress the phrase "but only a new creation."

Pause between "on my body" and "The grace."

God with respect to the limited powers of human sense and reason. The end of the exile, which the prophet interprets as God's direct intervention into the common life of Israel's people, is profound testimony to an immanent God intimately involved in the healing and care of a people sundered from its land and home. At the same time, Isaiah 40:6–8 speaks to a God whose transcendent word stands beyond comparison with anything human, able to endure forever, even as human flesh, like grass, must wither.

READING II In Galatians 5:4, Paul says to those Galatian men seeking circumcision: "You are separated from Christ, you who are trying to be justified by law; you have fallen from grace." But in two verses he says, "For in Christ Jesus neither circumcision nor uncircumcision counts for anything, but only faith working through love" (5:6). And in today's reading he seems to make much the same point as in 5:6: "For neither does circumcision mean anything, nor uncircumcision, but only a new creation" (6:15). How can Paul tell men who

have sought circumcision that they have fallen from grace for doing so while at the same time claiming that neither circumcision nor uncircumcision means anything at all?

Paul sometimes speaks of baptized believers in Jesus almost as if they are a new species. In 2 Corinthians 5:17, in the course of a defense of the legitimacy of his apostolate, Paul writes, "So whoever is in Christ is a new creation: the old things have passed away; behold, new things have

GOSPEL   Luke 10:1–12, 17–20

A reading from the holy Gospel according to Luke

At that time the **Lord** appointed seventy-two **others**
    whom he sent **ahead** of him in **pairs**
    to every **town** and **place** he intended to visit.
He said to them,
    "The **harvest** is **abundant** but the **laborers** are **few**;
    so ask the **master** of the **harvest**
    to send out **laborers** for his **harvest**.
Go on your way;
    behold, I am sending you like **lambs** among **wolves**.
Carry no money **bag**, no **sack**, no **sandals**;
    and greet **no** one along the way.
Into whatever house you enter, first say,
    '**Peace** to this **household**.'
If a peaceful person lives there,
    your **peace** will **rest** on him;
    but if **not**, it will **return** to you.
Stay in the **same house** and **eat** and **drink** what is offered to you,
    for the **laborer** deserves his **payment**.
Do **not** move about from **one** house to **another**.

come." This is much the same idea we see in this reading, in which the value of a "new creation" renders that new creation's legal status insignificant. Baptized Christians are removed from the authority of the law— unless they actively seek to place themselves under it in the belief that only by doing so can they have a right relationship with God. In that case, Paul argues, circumcision matters a great deal, since one is exchanging one's identity as a new creation for one's pre-baptismal state.

To Paul, all of this is intimately personal. The "marks of Jesus" are perhaps symptoms of a chronic illness (2 Corinthians 12:7–8; Galatians 4:13–15) or wounds he suffered for proclaiming his Gospel (2 Corinthians 11:23–29). These "marks of Jesus" he associates with Jesus' Crucifixion. In addition to Paul's testimony that God selected him to be an apostle by revealing Jesus to him, these marks demonstrate the legitimacy of his apostolate to the Church of Galatia.

GOSPEL Jesus' commission of 70 wandering preachers in addition to the Twelve is unique to the Gospel of Luke. Ordered to abide by rules and standards similar to the Twelve (9:1–6, 10; see Matthew 10, Mark 6:7–13), the 70 are sent out to proclaim the same message: "The kingdom of God is at hand for you" (see 9:2).

In this reading, as in 9:1–6, Luke opens a window on the early Christian movement and some of the means by which it spread.

Emphasize "The kingdom of God is at hand." This is the content of the Gospel proclamation at this point in Jesus' ministry.

Sodom = SAH-dum

The return of the 72 is a happy reunion between Jesus and people he loves and who love him. Proclaim Jesus' words on the occasion of this joyful meeting in a different tone than the instructions he gives above. The instructions are commands. With the exception of his report of Satan's fall, Jesus' words to the 72 upon their return are promises.

Whatever **town** you **enter** and they **welcome** you,
     eat what is set before you,
     cure the sick in it and **say** to them,
     'The **kingdom** of **God** is **at hand** for **you**.'
Whatever town you **enter** and they do **not** receive you,
     go out into the streets and **say**,
     'The **dust** of your **town** that **clings** to our **feet**,
     even that we **shake off against** you.'
Yet know this: the **kingdom** of **God** is at **hand**.
I **tell** you, it will be **more** tolerable for **Sodom** on that day
     than for **that** town."

The seventy-two returned **rejoicing**, and said,
     "**Lord**, even the **demons** are **subject** to us because
     of your **name**."
Jesus said, "I have observed **Satan** fall like **lightning**
     from the **sky**.
Behold, I have given you the **power** to '**tread** upon **serpents**'
     and **scorpions**
     and upon the full force of the **enemy**
     and **nothing** will harm you.
Nevertheless, do not **rejoice** because the **spirits** are **subject** to you,
     but **rejoice** because your **names** are **written** in **heaven**."

[Shorter: Luke 10:1–9]

The 72 are to rely upon the generosity of households in the towns and villages they visit. This instruction contrasts with Paul's practice of supporting himself. The principle of "the laborer deserves his payment" is in obvious tension with Paul's decision to "offer the gospel free of charge" (1 Corinthians 9:18). Paul claimed the right to support (1 Corinthians 9:1–12), but, typically, he chose to forego it. Although such refusals of remuneration stand in line with Greek tradition as far back as Socrates, who claimed a wise man should not seek or accept payment for his wisdom, Paul occasionally ran into trouble for not taking money for his services. At one point in 2 Corinthians, Paul defends himself and his apostolate to some in Corinth who have decided that a legitimate apostle is someone who accepts remuneration (2 Corinthians 11:7–11).

One of the differences between the mission of the 72 and the Pauline mission has to do with differences between the rural setting in which the former was carried out and the urban setting of the latter. When Paul entered a city, he usually stayed put for some months, likely renting a room or a storefront where he could ply his trade and talk to whomever came by. In contrast, there were scarcely any sizable cities in Palestine for the 72 to enter and far more ground to cover. The possibility of a missionary's self-support on Paul's model was negligible. Thus, Jesus instructs the 72 to travel light, to accept hospitality along the way while burdening as few households as possible, and, above all, to keep moving.

15TH SUNDAY IN ORDINARY TIME

Lectionary #105

READING I   Deuteronomy 30:10–14

A reading from the Book of Deuteronomy

Moses said to the **people**:
"If only you would heed the **voice** of the LORD, your **God**,
    and keep his **commandments** and **statutes**
    that are **written** in this **book** of the **law**,
    when you **return** to the LORD, your **God**,
    with **all** your **heart** and **all** your **soul**.

"For this **command** that I **enjoin** on you today
    is **not** too **mysterious** and **remote** for you.
It is **not** up in the **sky**, that you should say,
    '**Who** will **go up** in the **sky** to **get** it for us
    and **tell** us of it, that we may **carry** it out?'
Nor is it across the **sea**, that you should say,
    '**Who** will **cross** the **sea** to **get** it for us
    and **tell** us of it, that we may **carry** it out?'
No, it is something **very near** to you,
    already in your **mouths** and in your **hearts**;
    you have **only** to **carry** it out."

Emphasize the final stanza in which Moses tells the people where the word *is*, having just told them where it *isn't*.

READING I In recent weeks we have read a number of selections from Paul's letter to the Church of Galatia in which the topics of law and faith came up repeatedly. Often in Galatians Paul sets law in opposition to faith. In the tenth chapter of his letter to the Romans, Paul uses bits of today's reading in an attempt to reconcile law with faith.

As biblical scholar Richard Hays has shown in *Echoes of Scripture in the Letters of Paul,* much of Paul's exegesis of scripture in Romans is aimed at supporting the position that God's justification of the Gentiles does not cancel prior promises and covenants with Israel. According to Paul, Israel's search for God's righteousness is earnest. But Israel has still not arrived at the understanding that "Christ is the end of the law." This does not mean that Christ is the cessation of the law. The Greek word Paul uses for "end" is *telos,* which means something more like "purpose," "ideal," or even "consummation." According to Paul, the righteousness that comes through faith in Jesus Christ is the law's full realization, not its end.

We have already seen Paul sum up the entire law in a single verse (Galatians 5:14; see July 1, commentary for Reading II). Now in Romans 10:8–9 Paul interprets Deuteronomy 30:14 to equate doing the law with salvation, specifically with the confession that Christ is Lord and the belief that God raised him from the dead. Quoting Deuteronomy 30:14 ("The word is near you, in your mouth and in your heart"), Paul explains that the word to which the verse refers is "the word of faith that we preach" (Romans 10:8). In Romans 10:9, the object

This reading has poetic rhythm and balance to its clauses. Read it as you would a poem.

In the second stanza, stress the words "before," "all things hold together," "head," and "beginning." These words describe who and what Christ is for this author.

READING II   Colossians 1:15–20

A reading from the Letter of Saint Paul to the Colossians

Christ Jesus is the **image** of the **invisible God**,
    the **firstborn** of **all creation**.
For in him were **created** all things in **heaven** and on **earth**,
    the **visible** and the **invisible**,
    whether **thrones** or **dominions** or **principalities** or **powers**;
    all things were **created through him** and **for him**.
He is **before** all things,
    and in him all things **hold together**.
He is the **head** of the **body**, the **church**.
He is the **beginning**, the **firstborn** from the **dead**,
    that in **all** things he himself might be **preeminent**.
For in him **all** the **fullness** was pleased to **dwell**,
    and through him to **reconcile** all things for **him**,
    making **peace** by the **blood** of his **cross**
    through him, whether those on earth or those in **heaven**.

of the confession of the mouth and the belief of the heart is Christ, who is the law's ultimate realization.

READING II Some biblical scholars call certain passages of the New Testament "hymns." They usually do not try to prove that these passages were composed specifically for singing. What scholars typically mean by calling a particular passage a hymn is that it displays a certain elevated literary style, distinctive rhythm,

balance in its clauses, or other grammatical and linguistic features that both set it off from the surrounding material and suggest the passage had an independent life in the worship of the early Church. Some so-called hymns of the New Testament are John 1:1–14; Philippians 2:6–11; 1 Timothy 3:16; 1 Peter 3:18–22; and today's second reading, Colossians 1:15–20.

We know that early Christians sang. New Testament passages such as Colossians 3:16, Ephesians 5:19, and James 5:13 attest to it. We also have a letter, written in either 111 or 112, from a Roman administrator called

Pliny to the Emperor Trajan in which Pliny mentions that the Christians in his province of Bithynia, some of whom he has interrogated, are in the habit of meeting on a certain day and singing a "hymn" (carmen) to Christ "as to a god" (quasi deo).

Verses 15 and 16 describe Christ as "the image of the invisible God, the firstborn of all creation, for in him were created all things." The idea that Christ is God's "image" (eikōn) is not simply that Christ is God's reflection. The text states that Christ is God's

Read the dialogue between Jesus and the scholar of the law with due attention to the inquisitive tone of voice a student uses with a teacher and a teacher's authoritative tone in asking answers and follow-up questions.

GOSPEL   Luke 10:25–37

A reading from the holy Gospel according to Luke

There was a scholar of the law who stood up to **test** him and said,
   "**Teacher**, what must I do to inherit **eternal life**?"
Jesus said to him, "What is **written** in the **law**?
How do you **read** it?"
He said in reply,
   *You shall **love** the **Lord**, your **God**,*
   *with all your **heart**,*
   *with all your **being**,*
   *with all your **strength**,*
   *and with all your **mind**,*
   *and your **neighbor** as **yourself**.*
He replied to him, "You have answered **correctly**;
   do this and you will **live**."

But because he wished to **justify** himself, he said to **Jesus**,
   "And **who** is my **neighbor**?"
Jesus replied,
   "A man fell **victim** to **robbers**
   as he went down from **Jerusalem** to **Jericho**.
They **stripped** and **beat** him and went off **leaving** him **half-dead**.
A **priest** happened to be going down that road,
   but when he **saw** him, he **passed by** on the **opposite** side.
Likewise a **Levite** came to the place,
   and when he **saw** him, he **passed by** on the **opposite** side.

image and the firstborn of creation, "for" *(hoti)* all things were created in him. Because of his role in creation, Jesus Christ is God's image. The Jewish philosopher Philo, whose thought was heavily influenced by the Greek philosopher Plato, similarly sees God's image as a pattern with the power to create (*Allegorical Interpretation,* III.96). This is but one of several ideas in this passage its author borrowed from philosophical systems of thought of his time and place. His reason must have been that such sophistication was appropriate for the grandeur of his subject.

GOSPEL In Luke 8:9–10, Jesus offers his reason for speaking in parables after giving the parable of the sower (8:4–8). "Knowledge of the mysteries of the kingdom of God," Jesus says to his disciples, "has been granted to you; but to the rest, they are made known through parables so that 'they may look but not see, and hear but not understand.' " And yet the disciples have apparently not understood the parable, so Jesus explains it to them (8:11–15). The parable, it turns out, is an allegory of God's and the devil's battle for humanity (also see Matthew 13:1–23 and Mark 4:3–20).

In practice, the evangelists do not apply the term as restrictively as Jesus does in his explanation of the parable of the sower. The word may simply mean a saying or proverb, such as "Physician, cure yourself" (Luke 4:23). For the most part, however, parables

Slow down when the Samaritan comes on the scene. This is Jesus' definition of what a neighbor is, which is the answer to the question at hand.

But a **Samaritan** traveler who came upon him
    was moved with **compassion** at the sight.
He **approached** the victim,
    poured oil and **wine** over his **wounds** and **bandaged** them.
Then he **lifted** him up on his own animal,
    took him to an inn, and **cared** for him.
The **next** day he took out **two** silver coins
    and **gave** them to the innkeeper with the instruction,
    'Take **care** of him.
If you **spend** more than what I have **given** you,
    I shall **repay** you on my way back.'
Which of these three, in your opinion,
    was neighbor to the robbers' victim?"
He answered, "The one who **treated** him with **mercy**."
Jesus said to him, "**Go** and **do** likewise."

are teaching stories blending in varying degrees allegory, metaphor, with common sense folk wisdom. In Luke, Jesus tells four stories that are not called parables, but which must be classed with them. One of these is today's Gospel selection (also see Luke 12:16–21; 16:19–31; 18:9–14).

The parable of the Good Samaritan is not an allegory. It requires no esoteric interpretation. The person Luke calls a "scholar of the law" in 10:25 is not confused, but seems to understand Jesus' meaning even though there is no suggestion he is a disciple. Indeed, Jesus tells the story so that the man can answer his own question.

"Who is my neighbor?" Who *isn't* my neighbor is perhaps a better question once Jesus has finished telling this parable. There is also irony that Jesus urges the young specialist in Jewish law to behave like the Samaritan: "Go and do likewise" (10:35). The radical redefinition of "neighbor," delivered in short, simple form, is simply extraordinary.

Lectionary #108

READING I   Genesis 18:1–10a

A reading from the Book of Genesis

Mamre = MAM-reh

The LORD appeared to **Abraham** by the **terebinth** of **Mamre**,
   as he sat in the **entrance** of his tent,
   while the day was growing hot.
Looking up, Abraham saw **three men standing** nearby.
When he saw them, he **ran** from the entrance of the tent
      to **greet** them;
   and **bowing** to the ground, he said:
   "**Sir**, if I may ask you this **favor**,
   please do not go on past your servant.
Let some **water** be brought, that you may **bathe** your feet,
   and then **rest** yourselves under the tree.
Now that you have come this **close** to your servant,
   let me **bring** you a little **food**, that you may **refresh** yourselves;
   and afterward you may go on your way."
The men replied, "**Very well**, **do** as you have **said**."

Abraham **hastened** into the tent and told Sarah,
   "**Quick**, three measures of fine flour! **Knead** it and
      make rolls."
He ran to the herd, picked out a **tender**, **choice** steer,
   and gave it to a **servant**, who quickly **prepared** it.
Then Abraham got some curds and milk,
   as well as the steer that had been prepared,

Imagine how it is when you're preparing for guests. Bring some of that nervous energy and breathlessness to your reading of Abraham's instructions to Sarah and the report of his activity.

READING I   Traditions of hospitality vary around the world. Justly famous among them are those of the Bedouin, nomadic herders of sheep and goats who range about the Middle East and strive to live much as their ancestors have for centuries. The abundance of their generosity is not only gracious, but stands in stark opposition to the desolate terrain in which they live. The Bedouin consider hospitality to be more than social obligation, more than a point of personal and family pride, for they know that it might one day mean the difference between life and death for themselves or their loved ones. The cultural context for Abraham's reception of his mysterious three guests is the sumptuous hospitality of the desert nomad.

In his *Dialogue with Trypho*, Justin, one of the first great apologists of the Church and made a martyr during the 160s, attempts to prove to a Jewish conversation partner that one of the three visitors appearing to Abraham is Christ (Trypho, 56). Justin's case ultimately rests on his Platonic conception of God the Father, according to which it is inconceivable that he can be confined to any particular terrestrial place, neither seen nor experienced by the human senses. If, in fact, "the Lord appeared to Abraham by the terebinth of Mamre," which Justin believes occurred, then the Lord who appeared must be God the Son (Trypho, 127). God the Father did not appear at Mamre; indeed, he does not "appear" at all. Justin's Platonic doctrine of God, which sees God the Father in transcendent terms, permits him to see God the Son as a principal actor in the salvation history of Israel. Trypho must concede, Justin contends, that it is Christ and two angels whom Abraham received.

and set these before the three men;
and he waited on them under the **tree** while they ate.

They asked Abraham, "**Where** is your wife **Sarah**?"
He replied, "**There** in the tent."
One of them said, "I will **surely** return to you
    about this time next year,
and **Sarah** will then have a **son**."

READING II   Colossians 1:24–28

A reading from the Letter of Saint Paul to the Colossians

Brothers and **sisters**:
Now I **rejoice** in my sufferings for **your** sake,
    and in my **flesh** I am filling up
    what is **lacking** in the **afflictions** of Christ
    on behalf of his **body**, which is the **church**,
    of which I am a minister
    in accordance with God's **stewardship** given to me
    to bring to **completion** for you the word of God,
    the **mystery** hidden from ages and from generations **past**.
But **now** it has been **manifested** to his **holy** ones,
    to whom **God** chose to make known the **riches** of the glory
    of this **mystery** among the **Gentiles**;
    it is **Christ** in you, the **hope** for **glory**.
It is **he** whom we **proclaim**,
    admonishing **everyone** and teaching **everyone**
      with **all wisdom**,
    that we may **present everyone perfect** in Christ.

Slow down for the second stanza, pausing after the words "But now."

READING II | "Now I rejoice in my sufferings for your sake, and in my flesh I am filling up what is lacking in the afflictions of Christ" (1:24). While this verse may be translated in several different ways that affect its meaning, let us interpret it as our Bibles present it here. What could Christ's suffering lack? The first point is a logical one, taking into account the writer's incarnational theology of the Church. If the Church is Christ's body into which his individual disciples are incorporated (3:15; also see 1 Corinthians 12:12–27), then the suffering of its members are Christ's suffering. The second point has to do with the interpretation of the phrase "what is lacking." This phrase need not imply that Christ's Passion was defective or somehow fell short, but rather that the suffering of Christians for the Gospel is the necessary continuing work of the Church. In Luke's Gospel, immediately after predicting his Passion for the first time, Jesus explains what following him means: "If anyone wishes to come after me, he must deny himself and take up his cross daily and follow me" (9:23). Both Matthew and Mark record the same saying, but without using the word "daily" (see Matthew 16:24 and Mark 8:34). Whether taken metaphorically or literally, Jesus' point is that the suffering of the cross is the lot of his followers as well.

Early Christians often interpreted the sufferings of martyrs, as they did those of Jesus, in sacrificial terms. While Christ's Passion is the definitive event of human redemption, the sufferings of Christians, ancient and modern, on behalf of the Gospel is a large part of what belonging to Christ's body is about.

GOSPEL Luke 10:38–42

A reading from the holy Gospel according to Luke

Jesus entered a village
  where a **woman** whose name was **Martha** welcomed him.
She had a **sister** named **Mary**
  who sat beside the **Lord** at his feet listening to him speak.
Martha, burdened with much serving, came to him and said,
  "**Lord**, do you not **care**
  that my **sister** has left me by **myself** to do the serving?
Tell her to **help** me."
The Lord said to her in reply,
  "**Martha**, **Martha**, you are **anxious** and **worried**
    about **many** things.
There is need of **only one** thing.
Mary has chosen the **better** part
  and it will **not** be taken from her."

Give expression to Martha's irritation with her sister. Put yourself in her place. She and her sister have a houseful of guests and Mary's acting like one of the guests!

Don't let Jesus' words to Martha sound patronizing. He is teaching her something very important, not telling her simply to relax, calm down, or chill out.

GOSPEL   The verses of this Gospel reading have been very important in the history of Christian mysticism. Origen of Alexandria, and many Christians after him, found in the examples of Martha and Mary paradigms of the active and contemplative lives. Origen inherited this distinction from Plato, who imagined the philosopher's task was less active than contemplative, and Aristotle, Plato's student, who subordinated contemplation to the active life, finding contemplation's chief utility in the help it offered men in politics. Christian contemplatives following Origen found support for their solitary and cloistered lives in a text interpreted both to distinguish prayer from action and to privilege the former.

Only Luke preserves this story, although some relation to traditions about Mary and Martha preserved in John's Gospel is likely (see especially John 11). Note Luke's characteristic interest in women. In Luke 8:2–3, we read of women who traveled with Jesus. Here we see a woman in the role of disciple, sitting at the feet of Jesus and listening to his word. Contained within Jesus' soft rebuke to Martha for her expression of frustration is confirmation of Mary's discipleship. Mary's part "will not be taken from her" (10:42). Not only does Jesus confirm Mary's discipleship; he also gently teases Martha. Worried, anxious, distracted, Martha has a houseful of people to whom she is attempting to show a little hospitality. The phrase "there is need of only one thing," in both Greek and English, reads as though Jesus is going to ask her to bring him something, but the need, it turns out, is not his. The need is Martha's, Mary's, and all of Jesus' disciples.

17TH SUNDAY IN ORDINARY TIME

Lectionary #111

READING I   Genesis 18:20–32

Sodom = SAH-dum
Gomorrah = Go-MOR-rah

A reading from the Book of Genesis

In those days, the LORD said:
"The **outcry** against **Sodom** and **Gomorrah** is so great,
     and their **sin** so **grave**,
   that I must **go down** and **see** whether or not their **actions**
   fully **correspond** to the **cry** against them that **comes** to me.
I mean to find out."

Abraham is interceding for the innocent
with an angry God. Let your delivery
of Abraham's half of the conversation give
expression to the difficulty of this task.

While Abraham's visitors walked on farther toward Sodom,
     the LORD remained **standing** before **Abraham**.
Then **Abraham** drew nearer and said:
   "Will you sweep away the **innocent** with the **guilty**?
Suppose there were **fifty** innocent people in the city;
   would you **wipe out** the place, **rather** than spare it
   for the **sake** of the **fifty innocent people** within it?
Far be it from **you** to do such a thing,
   to make the **innocent** die with the **guilty**
   so that the **innocent** and the **guilty** would be treated **alike**!
Should not the **judge** of all the **world** act with **justice**?"
The LORD replied,
   "If I find **fifty** innocent people in the city of Sodom;
   I will spare the **whole** place for **their** sake."

READING I   "Should he seize me forcibly, who can say him nay? Who can say to him, 'What are you doing?' " (Job 9:12). Job, a righteous man, is subjected to unspeakable misfortune and tragedy as part of a bet wagered between God and Satan. Job's desire to know why God has treated him so badly leads him to acknowledge God's power, but to question God's justice. In a speech from the winds of a storm (Job 38—41), God offers Job no defense of his actions, but, in a litany of his own questions, denies Job's standing to demand any answers at all. In today's reading, Abraham

questions God's justice as well: "Far be it from you," Abraham says to God, "to do such a thing, to make the innocent die with the guilty so that the innocent and the guilty would be treated alike!" But unlike in Job, here God does not dismiss Abraham's standing to inquire about the justice of his proposal. First debating within himself whether to tell Abraham about his intention to destroy Sodom and Gomorrah (18:18–19), God elects to reveal his plans and even seems to welcome Abraham's probing.

In his intercession for the righteous of Sodom and Gomorrah, Abraham acts as a prophet. One of the tasks of prophets in Israel was to intercede on behalf of the people. Jeremiah is instructed multiple times not to intercede on behalf of the people because of their past and current sins (Jeremiah 7:16; 11:14), while representatives of the people ask exactly this of him (Jeremiah 37:3; 42:2–4, 20). Abraham himself is called a "prophet" in Genesis 20:7 in an account where he exercises an intercessory role on behalf of King Abimelech.

Abraham spoke up again:
  "**See** how I am **presuming** to speak to my Lord,
    though I am but **dust** and **ashes**!
What if there are five **less** than **fifty** innocent people?
Will you destroy the **whole city** because of those **five**?"
He answered, "I will **not** destroy it, if I find **forty-five** there."
But Abraham persisted, saying "What if only **forty** are
    found there?"
He replied, "I will **forbear** doing it for the **sake** of the **forty**."
Then Abraham said, "Let **not** my Lord grow **impatient** if I go on.
What if only **thirty** are found there?"
He replied, "I will **forbear** doing it if I can find but **thirty** there."
Still Abraham went on,
  "Since I have thus **dared** to speak to my **Lord**,
    what if there are no more than **twenty**?"
The LORD answered, "I will **not** destroy it, for the **sake**
    of the **twenty**."
But he still persisted:
  "Please, let **not** my Lord grow **angry** if I **speak** up this last time.
What if there are at least **ten** there?"
He replied, "For the **sake** of those **ten**, I will **not** destroy it."

How are we to interpret the conversation between God and Abraham? Has God already fixed on the conditions for his destruction of Sodom and Gomorrah, or does Abraham convince God that the presence of the righteous people should mitigate God's punishment of the cities? The text is not clear. Lest we rule out the second option on the grounds that it is somehow unworthy of God's sovereignty, recall God's regret at having selected Saul to be king over Israel (1 Samuel 15:11). Indeed, what is the use of intercessors if the God they address, cajole, and question cannot be moved?

READING II Ancient Christian structures, while supporting and expressing the religious convictions of the people using them, made extensive use of traditional Greco-Roman patterns of design that were not exclusively Christian. Visitors to ancient Christian baptistries typically encounter a building built on a central plan. It is likely that early Christians selected central design plans for their baptistries because central plans had long been favored by the Roman elite for funerary monuments. While Christian Baptism was understood as a sacrament of initiation and rebirth into Christ and his body the Church, rebirth implied a prior death—death to old associations, practices, beliefs, and ways of life. Traditional Roman funerary design provided an appropriate spatial context for the ritual expression of baptismal death.

In Baptism, the believer did not die and rise to new life alone. He or she participated in Christ's own death as the specific vocabulary of today's reading makes clear. The phrases "buried with," "raised with," and "brought to life along with" translate common verbs *(thaptō, egeirō, zōopoieō)* prefixed

---

READING II Colossians 2:12–14

A reading from the Letter of Saint Paul to the Colossians

Brothers and **sisters:**
You were **buried** with him in **baptism,**
   in which you were also **raised** with him
     through **faith** in the **power** of **God,**
   who **raised** him from the **dead.**
And even when you were **dead**
   in **transgressions** and the **uncircumcision** of your **flesh,**
   he **brought** you to **life** along **with** him,
   having **forgiven** us **all** our **transgressions;**
obliterating the bond **against** us, with its legal claims,
   which was **opposed** to us,
   he also **removed** it from our midst, **nailing** it to the **cross.**

> Stress the word "all." Consider what an extraordinary claim it is that God has forgiven "all our transgressions" by Christ's Resurrection.

GOSPEL Luke 11:1–13

A reading from the holy Gospel according to Luke

Jesus was praying in a certain place, and when he had **finished,**
   one of his disciples said to him,
   "**Lord, teach** us to **pray** just as **John** taught **his** disciples."
He said to them, "When you **pray,** say:
   Father, hallowed be your **name,**
     your kingdom come.
     Give us **each day** our daily bread
     and forgive us **our** sins

> Emphasize the disciple's request that Jesus teach them to pray and read the prayer Jesus offers slowly.

---

with the Greek preposition *sun,* meaning "with." A simple way to look at it is that upon entry into the Church, Christians do nothing alone.

The sequence of baptismal death and rebirth is complicated in this reading by the description of the believers' former lives as a kind of living death from which they have been rescued. Before Baptism, believers "were dead in transgressions." The metaphor describing how Christ rescued them

from this fate is both legal and financial: Christ cancels the "bond." The Greek word for the "bond" against them is *xeirographon,* which means a handwritten document of some kind. Most ancient people understood the desperation of bills, debts, and contracts entered into under pressure of need, including even the sale of oneself into slavery. Themes of new life secured by the cancellation of debt would have resonated strongly.

GOSPEL | A prayer of petition asks something of God. Most religions know some form of petitionary prayer. According to the Catechism, Roman Catholic Christianity classifies prayer into five categories: blessing, petition, thanksgiving, intercession, and praise (#2623–2643). Of these, "petition is centered on the desire and *search for the kingdom to come,* in keeping with the teaching of Christ" (#2632). To petition God for the kingdom is one of the things Jesus teaches his disciples in today's Gospel selection.

for **we ourselves** forgive **everyone** in debt to **us**,
and do **not** subject us to the **final test**."

Pause between each stanza.

And he said to them, "Suppose one of you has a **friend**
to whom he goes at midnight and says,
'**Friend, lend** me three loaves of bread,
for a friend of mine has **arrived** at my house from a **journey**
and I have **nothing** to offer him,'
and he says in reply from within,
'Do **not bother** me; the door has **already** been locked
and my **children** and I are already in **bed**.
I **cannot** get up to give you **anything**.'
I **tell** you,
if he does **not** get up to give the visitor the loaves
because of their friendship,
he **will** get up to give him **whatever** he needs
because of his **persistence**.

"And I **tell** you, **ask** and you will **receive**;
seek and you will **find**;
knock and the door will be **opened** to you.
For **everyone** who **asks**, **receives**;
and the one who **seeks**, **finds**;
and to the one who **knocks**, the **door** will be **opened**.
What **father among** you would hand his **son** a **snake**
when he **asks** for a **fish**?
Or **hand** him a **scorpion** when he **asks** for an **egg**?
If **you** then, who are **wicked**,
know **how** to give good gifts to your **children**,
how much more will the **Father** in **heaven**
give the **Holy Spirit** to those who **ask** him?"

Emphasize the contrast between the good gifts to children and the Holy Spirit to even the wicked. To this end stress the phrase "how much more."

Neither Jesus, nor the evangelist, nor anyone else in Luke's Gospel defines exactly what the kingdom of God is. Biblical scholars can tell us that the kingdom of God as preached was a theological idea current in apocalyptic strains of the Judaism of Jesus' day, in which God would soon and suddenly intervene in human affairs.

The term's first appearance in Luke is in 4:43, in which we learn that Jesus has been sent in order to proclaim the kingdom of God. Verse 9:27 stresses that the kingdom is coming soon: "there are some standing here who will not taste death until they see the kingdom of God." Jesus commissions the Twelve and the 70 to proclaim the kingdom of God (9:2; 10:9–11). The 70 are to say specifically that it is "at hand" (10:9). The nearness of the kingdom is described not only in temporal terms, but also in spatial terms (11:20), as something people enter (18:17, 24–27), and, in an ironic exchange, as somehow present in Jesus himself (17:20–21). The kingdom is something for which one must be "fit" (9:62), but which confers great reward (18:30), which the wealthy have difficulty entering (18:25), but which belongs to children (18:16) and the poor (6:20).

The kingdom is a mystery. What, for example, does Jesus mean by comparing the kingdom of God to a seed that grows into a tree, or as leavening dough (13:18–21)? Does our study of these texts leave us with solid answers or still more questions both for future study and prayer?

18TH SUNDAY IN ORDINARY TIME

Lectionary #114

READING I   Ecclesiastes 1:2; 2:21–23

Qoheleth = Koh-HEL-et

Stress the first phrase especially. Vanity is the subject of this reading.

A reading from the Book of Ecclesiastes

Vanity of **vanities**, says **Qoheleth**,
   vanity of **vanities**! **All** things are **vanity**!

Here is one who has **labored** with **wisdom** and **knowledge**
      and **skill**,
   and **yet** to **another** who has not **labored** over it,
   he must **leave property**.
This **also** is vanity and a **great** misfortune.

Read the rhetorical question of the second stanza as a question to your worshipping community. Pause after you've asked it.

For **what profit** comes to **man** from all the **toil** and **anxiety**
      of **heart**
   with which he has **labored** under the **sun**?
All his days **sorrow** and **grief** are their occupation;
   even at **night** his mind is **not** at rest.

Read the final line slowly, stressing the word "vanity."

This **also** is **vanity**.

READING I   By consideration of "the world's order and beauty," the Catechism reads, "one can come to a knowledge of God as the origin and end of the universe" (#32). Romans 1:19–20 is cited in support of this belief. God's power and divinity, Paul says, are apparent in created things, such that Gentiles cannot claim ignorance of God as an excuse for their sin. Qoheleth, the purported author of Ecclesiastes, would hardly dispute the evidence of divinity and power in the created order that he examines in greater detail than Paul. But, unlike Paul, Qoheleth does not

think this evidence tells people anything useful about God or themselves.

Qoheleth, whose name in Hebrew means something like "gatherer," has long observed his world, assembled much knowledge about it, and concluded that its meaning, like its Creator, cannot be fathomed. In contrast, Paul is a man who had an experience of God, discovered that Jesus Christ was his answer, and then worked backward to find out what were the questions and problems Jesus answered not only for himself, but also for all of humanity. Qoheleth's

experience of God is, perhaps, of a more typical variety. There is nothing of the atheist or even the agnostic about him, but his conviction permits him little more than to raise further questions. And yet his observation, study, and thought have given him sizeable gratitude to God (3:12–13).

Vanity is the only word Qoheleth knows to describe the fevered human drive for wealth and property with all its attendant anxiety, sorrow, grief, and sleeplessness. In light of Christ's word to the rich man that treasure in heaven requires the sale of all he owns and the distribution of the proceeds to

READING II   Colossians 3:1–5, 9–11

A reading from the Letter of Saint Paul to the Colossians

Brothers and sisters:
If you were **raised** with Christ, **seek** what is **above**,
    where **Christ** is seated at the **right hand** of God.
Think of what is **above**, **not** of what is on **earth**.
For **you** have **died**,
    and your **life** is **hidden** with **Christ** in **God**.
When **Christ** your **life** appears,
    then **you too** will **appear** with him in **glory**.

Put to **death**, then, the **parts** of you that are **earthly**:
    immorality, **impurity**, **passion**, **evil desire**,
    and the **greed** that is **idolatry**.
Stop **lying** to one another,
    since you have taken off the **old** self with its practices
    and have put on the **new** self,
    which is being **renewed**, for **knowledge**,
    in the **image** of its **creator**.
Here there is not **Greek** and Jew,
    circumcision and **uncircumcision**,
    barbarian, **Scythian**, **slave**, **free**;
    but **Christ** is **all** and in **all**.

Read the list of vices slowly. These words, when spoken quickly, can sound similar and run together.

Stress each distinction in the final stanza, but with special stress on "Christ" and "all and in all."
Scythian = SITH-i-an

the poor (Matthew 19:21; Mark 10:21; Luke 18:22), the Catholic Christian can see this fevered drive for material things as the human tragedy it truly is. Even if one cannot agree with Qoheleth's provocative verdict on the sum of all possible human thought and effort ("All things are vanity!"), his description of the acquisitive life is on the right track.

READING II In this reading from the letter to the Colossians, the author warns against vices that most philo-

sophical and religious traditions of the Roman Empire also urged people to avoid. A first-century student of Epicurean or Stoic philosophy would agree, for example, that a virtuous life precludes "immorality, impurity, passion, evil desire" (3:5). But this same student would be confused by the use of the statement "For you have died" as a reason to avoid these vices (3:3). And where is this "here" containing so many different kinds of people but also erasing their differences (3:11)? Our philosophy student would go away affirming the basic morality of this

reading, but perplexed about the reasons given for it.

Those of us a bit better informed see that this reading roots Christian morality in Baptism, which is the significance of the language of dying and rising with Christ and the language describing absence of the distinctions of ethnicity, religion, and social status (see 1 Corinthians 12:13; Galatians 3:28). The morality of this reading is therefore grounded in the Gospel, a report about Christ's death and Resurrection, and the lived experience of the people called together to be the Church.

Imagine the different tones of voice Jesus uses in this passage. At one point he's responding to someone's demand, perhaps with a little irritation and humor. Then he's addressing the crowds and telling them a story. Even when the Father's voice enters the story, it is the Son quoting him.

GOSPEL Luke 12:13–21

A reading from the holy Gospel according to Luke

Someone in the crowd said to Jesus,
    "**Teacher**, tell my **brother** to **share** the **inheritance** with me."
He replied to him,
    "**Friend**, **who** appointed me as your **judge** and **arbitrator**?"
Then he said to the crowd,
    "Take **care** to **guard against all** greed,
    for though **one** may be **rich**,
    one's **life** does not consist of possessions."

Then he told them a parable.
"There was a **rich** man whose **land** produced a **bountiful** harvest.
He **asked** himself, '**What** shall I do,
    for I do **not** have **space** to **store** my **harvest**?'
And he said, '**This** is what I shall do:
    I shall **tear down** my **barns** and build **larger** ones.
There I shall store **all** my grain and **other goods**
    and I shall **say** to myself, "**Now** as for **you**,
    you have so **many** good things stored up for **many years**,
    rest, **eat**, **drink**, **be merry**!"'
But **God** said to him,
    '**You fool**, **this** night your life will be **demanded** of you;
    and the things you have **prepared**, to **whom** will they belong?'
Thus will it be for **all** who store up treasure for themselves
    but are **not rich** in **what matters** to God."

GOSPEL The events of today's Gospel happen on Jesus' meandering journey to Jerusalem, which began in 9:51 (see the Thirteenth Sunday in Ordinary Time, Gospel commentary). The setting is the midst of a crowd in which Jesus teaches his disciples (12:1). A man from the crowd, addressing Jesus as "teacher," demands that Jesus settle a family dispute concerning wealth, property, or both (12:13). Jesus replies, essentially, that this is not his job and uses the occasion to speak to the crowd against greed and a life consisting of gathering material possessions (12:14–15). Jesus follows this up with a parable, commonly designated the parable of the rich fool, in order to expose the folly of pursuing earthly riches (12:16–20). It concludes with a statement that the situation of the fictional rich fool shall be the situation of anyone treasuring things up at the expense of being "rich in what matters to God."

These verses occur only in the Gospel of Luke. It is part of a theme of suspicion toward riches and wealthy people that Luke emphasizes more than the other evangelists.

Luke's final verdict is therefore mixed, but his special emphasis on the poor is simply undeniable. "Love for the poor," reads the Catechism, "is incompatible with immoderate love of riches or their selfish use." Citing James 5:1–6, the text continues, quoting Saint John Chrysostom: "Not to enable the poor to share in our goods is to steal from them and deprive them of life. The goods we possess are not ours, but theirs" (#2444–2446).

19TH SUNDAY IN ORDINARY TIME

Lectionary #117

READING I   Wisdom 18:6–9

A reading from the Book of Wisdom

The **night** of the passover was known **beforehand** to our fathers,
    that, with **sure knowledge** of the **oaths** in which they
        put their faith,
    they might have **courage**.
Your people awaited the **salvation** of the **just**
    and the **destruction** of their **foes**.
For when you **punished** our **adversaries**,
    in this you **glorified** us whom you had **summoned**.
For in **secret** the **holy** children of the **good** were offering
        sacrifice
    and putting into **effect** with one accord the **divine institution**.

Slow down to emphasize the phrase beginning "For in secret." Note the contrast between the events apparent to all and the private interpretation of those events by "the holy children."

READING II   Hebrews 11:1–2, 8–19

A reading from the Letter to the Hebrews

Brothers and **sisters**:
Faith is the realization of what is **hoped** for
    and **evidence** of things **not seen**.
Because of it the ancients were well attested.

By **faith** Abraham obeyed when he was **called** to go out to a place
    that he was to **receive** as an inheritance;
    he went **out**, **not knowing** where he was to go.

Give special emphasis to the repeated phrase "By faith." The author is encouraging his recipients to see Old Testament figures as exemplars of perseverance.

READING I The Jewish historian Flavius Josephus knew more than one account of the Exodus. In his apologetic work *Against Apion,* Josephus attacks the Egyptian writer Manetho for distorting the Exodus and mischaracterizing both Moses and the Jewish people. While Josephus on the whole accepts and affirms scripture's account of the Exodus, Manetho apparently claimed that the Jews had to be driven out of Egypt and that Moses was something of a

snake-oil salesman. As Roman Catholic Christians, scripture's story is our story. But we are remiss to forget or ignore that the past looks radically different depending on who you are, when you live, and where you are from.

To Wisdom's author, the events of the Exodus comprised Israel's education by God. It is as though the Exodus was a course of instruction, Israel a class of students, and God the teacher. Beginning in Wisdom 11, the afflictions of the Egyptians are offered as

lessons by which Israel learns virtue and the responsibilities of its election by God. In today's reading, the comparisons continue. The destruction to which the text refers is explained in the verse immediately preceding the verse beginning this selection. It is the destruction of every firstborn creature in Egypt, "from the first-born of Pharaoh on the throne to the first-born of the slave-girl at the handmill, as well as the first-born of the animals" (Exodus 11:5).

By **faith** he sojourned in the **promised** land as
in a foreign country,
dwelling in tents with **Isaac** and **Jacob**,
heirs of the **same promise**;
for he was looking **forward** to the city with foundations,
whose **architect** and **maker** is God.
By **faith** he received **power** to generate,
even though he was **past** the normal age
—and Sarah **herself** was sterile—
for he thought that the one who had made the promise
was trustworthy.
So it was that there came forth from **one** man,
himself as **good** as **dead**,
descendants as **numerous** as the **stars** in the **sky**
and as **countless** as the **sands** on the **seashore**.

All these died in **faith**.
They did **not** receive what had been **promised**
but **saw** it and **greeted** it from afar
and **acknowledged** themselves to be **strangers** and **aliens**
on **earth**,
for those who **speak** thus **show** that they are **seeking**
a homeland.
If they had been **thinking** of the land from which they had **come**,
they would have had **opportunity** to **return**.
But now they desire a **better** homeland, a **heavenly** one.
Therefore, God is **not ashamed** to be called their **God**,
for he has **prepared** a **city** for them.

By **faith** Abraham, when put to the test, offered up **Isaac**,
and he who had received the **promises** was ready
to offer his **only** son,
of whom it was said,

Pause before the word "Therefore."
This is the conclusion to be drawn from
the examples given previously.

READING II Abraham was an important example in early Christian debates about the establishment and maintenance of right relationships between human beings and God. The apostle Paul used Abraham's example of trust in God to support his argument that the Christians of Galatia were justified by faith and not by the observance of the Jewish ordinance of circumcision (see, for example, Galatians 3:6). In his letter to the Romans, Paul revisits the topic of righteousness through faith and

again uses Abraham as an example that justification occurs when a person trusts in God, not because of their submission to the ordinance of circumcision (Romans 4). While Paul does not dispute that justification implies the adoption of some behaviors and the rejection of others, he takes care to argue that one cannot set up a right relationship with God simply by religious observance. Faith is essential.

In the letter of James, which perhaps comes from the orbit of some of those against whom Paul argued, Abraham is again an example used in an argument about justification. But here the author claims Abraham *was* justified by works and cites the binding and offering of Isaac on the altar as an example (James 2:18–26; Genesis 22:1–18). In James, Abraham's faith and works are inseparable. Both are essential.

In this reading, Abraham is again offered as an example of faith. But here the author stresses Abraham's trust in a God

"Through **Isaac** descendants shall bear your name."
He reasoned that **God** was able to raise even from the **dead**,
    and he received **Isaac** back as a symbol.

[Shorter: Hebrews 11:1–2, 8–12]

GOSPEL   Luke 12:32–48

A reading from the holy Gospel according to Luke

Jesus said to his disciples:
    "Do not be afraid any longer, little flock,
    for your **Father** is pleased to give you the **kingdom**.
Sell your belongings and give **alms**.
Provide money bags for yourselves that do **not** wear out,
    an inexhaustible **treasure** in **heaven**
    that no **thief** can reach nor **moth** destroy.
For where your **treasure** is, **there also** will your **heart** be.

"**Gird** your **loins** and **light** your **lamps**
    and be like **servants** who await their master's return
        from a **wedding**,
    ready to open **immediately** when he **comes** and **knocks**.
Blessed are those servants
    whom the master finds **vigilant** on his arrival.
Amen, I say to you, he will **gird** himself,
    have them **recline** at table, and **proceed** to **wait** on them.
And should he **come** in the second or third watch
    and find them **prepared** in this way,
    blessed are those servants.
Be **sure** of this:
    if the **master** of the house had known the hour
    when the **thief** was coming,
    he would **not** have let his house be broken into.

Keep in mind as you proclaim this reading that underpinning all its advice and instruction is the exhortation, "Do not be afraid, little flock, for it is your Father's good pleasure to give you the kingdom." This is good news.

whose promises forecasted a much larger providential plan. Though he can only see the unfolding of that plan from a great distance, Abraham believes nonetheless. If indeed the letter to the Hebrews was written, as many biblical scholars contend, to Jewish Christians increasingly uncertain in their Christian faith, the author's description of Abraham's faith supports his exhortation of the letter's recipients to renewed patience.

GOSPEL   Disowning both father and inheritance and stripping off all of his clothes save a hair shirt, the young Francis of Assisi left his hometown and walked out into the Umbrian countryside in the dead of winter. "He was penniless," wrote G. K. Chesterton, "he was parentless, he was to all appearance without a trade or a plan or a hope in the world; and as he went under the frosty trees, he burst suddenly into song."

Prudence, the Catechism tells us, is a virtue. It is the cardinal virtue "that disposes practical reason to discern our true good in every circumstance and to choose the right means of achieving it" and even "guides the other virtues by setting rule and measure" (Catechism, #1806).

The command to sell belongings and give alms follows a section in which Jesus urges his disciples not to worry about life,

Slow down and emphasize this line.
It is the conclusion that Jesus encourages
his listeners to draw from the example
just given.

You **also** must be prepared, for at an **hour** you do **not** expect,
the **Son** of **Man** will **come**."

Then **Peter** said,
"Lord, is this parable meant for **us** or for **everyone**?"
And the Lord replied,
"**Who**, **then**, is the **faithful** and **prudent steward**
whom the **master** will put in **charge** of his **servants**
to distribute the **food allowance** at the **proper time**?
Blessed is that servant whom his **master** on arrival finds doing so.
Truly, I **say** to you, the **master** will put the servant
in charge of **all** his property.
But if **that servant** says to himself,
'My master is **delayed** in coming,'
and begins to **beat** the menservants and the maidservants,
to **eat** and **drink** and get **drunk**,
then that servant's master will **come**
on an **unexpected** day and at an **unknown** hour
and will **punish** the servant **severely**
and assign him a **place** with the **unfaithful**.
That servant who **knew** his master's will
but did **not** make **preparations nor act** in accord with his **will**
shall be beaten **severely**;
and the **servant** who was **ignorant** of his master's will
but **acted** in a way deserving of a **severe** beating
shall be beaten **only lightly**.
Much will be required of the **person** entrusted with much,
and still **more** will be demanded of the person **entrusted**
with **more**."

[Shorter: Luke 12:35–40]

Once again, emphasize these verses;
they contain the instruction the previous
example illustrates.

food, body, clothing, or work (12:22–31). It hardly seems prudent for children of the kingdom to take their cues in life from ravens and flowers.

If, however, prudence is the guide of the other virtues, love brings them to life. All the virtues, according to the Catechism, are "animated and inspired" by *caritas* (Catechism, #1827), which is a Latin word for "love" often translated by its English cognate "charity." Jesus, who told his disciples that the greatest love is displayed in self-sacrifice (John 15:13) and backed up his word by dying for others, sets the standard for Christian love. Enlivened by such love, Roman Catholic prudence may not look at all like worldly prudence. According to most secular standards of behavior, "Love your enemies" is utterly imprudent, and yet who will dispute that it is prudent for Christians to do it? (See Matthew 5:44 and Luke 6:35.) Francis, traversing the cold Umbrian landscape half-nude and singing, making his way to a life of the fiercest love of God and his fellow creatures, exhibits Roman Catholic prudence at its finest.

ASSUMPTION OF THE BLESSED VIRGIN MARY: VIGIL

Lectionary #621

READING I   1 Chronicles 15:3–4, 15–16; 16:1–2

Proclaim this reading slowly. It is a complex liturgical scene, rich in detail.

Levites = LEE-vites

A reading from the first Book of Chronicles

David assembled all **Israel** in **Jerusalem** to bring the **ark**
    of the **LORD**
    to the place that he had prepared for it.
David also called together the sons of **Aaron** and the **Levites.**

The **Levites** bore the **ark** of **God** on their shoulders with poles,
    as **Moses** had ordained according to the **word** of the **LORD.**

David commanded the **chiefs** of the **Levites**
    to appoint their **kinsmen** as **chanters,**
    to play on **musical instruments, harps, lyres,** and **cymbals,**
    to make a loud **sound** of **rejoicing.**

They brought in the **ark** of **God** and set it within the tent
    which **David** had pitched for it.
Then they offered up **burnt offerings** and **peace offerings** to **God.**
When **David** had finished offering up the burnt offerings
    and peace offerings,
    he **blessed** the people in the **name** of the **LORD.**

READING I David probably had many reasons for making the city of Jerusalem his capital as opposed to setting himself up elsewhere. The Jebusite city sat atop a ridge that was quite narrow at its most slender point. With a gate set on this narrow place, a very small force could defend the city. Indeed, Jerusalem's natural defenses may have encouraged David to attack the city by stealth through the city's water shaft rather than risk a frontal assault (2 Samuel 6:8). Another reason was the presence of the Gihon spring, which flowed from the base of the ridge and provided a reliable source of water. A third reason may have been that the city, while close to the territory claimed by David's tribe of Judah, lay just inside the tribal territory of Benjamin. Saul, under whom scripture records Israel was first united into a single monarchy (1 Samuel 11:15), was a Benjaminite. David may have decided that his strength as king required that he control the territory of his former foe but, at the same time, remain close enough to Judah in order to request and receive prompt aid from his kinsmen.

The decision to bring the Ark of the Covenant south to Jerusalem is closely related to the last of these reasons for David's location of his capital in Jerusalem. The Ark was obviously sacred to many Israelites. David's possession of it in his capital elevated the importance of both the city and its protector. In one stroke, therefore, David made Jerusalem a center of Israel's religious life.

READING II Much of the first letter to the Corinthians addresses a community split by multiple factions and

READING II   1 Corinthians 15:54b–57

A reading from the first Letter of Saint Paul to the Corinthians

Brothers and **sisters**:
When that which is **mortal** clothes itself with **immortality**,
    then the word that is **written** shall come about:

Death *is swallowed up in* **victory**.
Where, *O* **death**, *is your* **victory**?
Where, *O* **death**, *is your* **sting**?

The **sting** of **death** is **sin**,
    and the **power** of **sin** is the **law**.
But thanks be to **God** who gives us the **victory**
    through our **Lord Jesus Christ**.

By this point in 1 Corinthians 15, the answer to these rhetorical questions is a resounding "Nowhere!"

falling well short of the unity Paul encourages. In their disagreements concerning Church leadership, sex, and the Eucharist, to name only a few points of conflict, the people this letter addresses are much like today's Christians, separated by denomination, practice, and belief.

One of the topics on which the Corinthians do not all say the same thing is the Resurrection of the dead. "But if Christ is preached as raised from the dead," Paul writes in 15:12, "how can some of you say there is no resurrection of the dead?" For Paul, the Gospel stands or falls on the

answer to the question of whether or not the Resurrection includes others beside Christ. Paul's description of the subjection of all things to Christ, and Christ's ultimate subjection to God, not only outlines the goal of the Corinthians' hope, but also provides Christ's willing submission to God as an example of the submission demanded of this factionalized Church (15:20–28).

Today's reading is the rhetorical zenith of the chapter in which Paul urges the Corinthians to agree that the dead will be raised. If the Corinthians would share a

common fate at the end time, they must share a common and unified understanding of it in the present.

On some questions of belief Paul is willing to tolerate a variety of opinion. He sees no point in demanding unanimity, for example, on whether eating meat offered to idols is right or wrong as a matter of principle (1 Corinthians 8—10). But on the Resurrection there can be no argument. There is no point to Paul's apostolate, no point to the Church, and no point to his letter if the dead do not share in Christ's Resurrection. The Resurrection was not something that

Pause after the announcement of the reading.

GOSPEL Luke 11:27–28

A reading from the holy Gospel according to Luke

While **Jesus** was **speaking**,
    a **woman** from the crowd **called out** and **said** to him,
    "**Blessed** is the **womb** that **carried** you
    and the **breasts** at which you **nursed**."
He **replied**,
    "**Rather**, **blessed** are those
    who **hear** the **word** of God and **observe** it."

God did for Jesus alone. It would have been spectacular but insignificant if others could not share in it.

GOSPEL The central problem of Christology is the relationship of Jesus' humanity to his divinity. The affirmation of Jesus' full divinity invited an affirmation of Mary as Theotokos, the Mother of God, and therefore unique among humanity. The exaltation of Mary above all humanity, therefore, is in part a consequence of the expression of Christ's divine nature.

But to attribute the place of Mary in the Roman Catholic Church to a secondary effect of particular doctrines ignores her embrace by legions of faithful lay Catholics whose passionate devotion to her over the centuries has had little to do with doctrinal formulations. Even the title Theotokos, speculates historian Jaroslav Pelikan, may have originated in the context of liturgical devotion to Mary before it was used to express christological doctrine.

"Blessed is the womb that carried you and blessed are the breasts at which you nursed," captures well the spirited honor and esteem in which Mary has been held by many Catholics. And yet it is of great significance that Jesus uses the woman's blessing as a springboard for a similarly phrased word of encouragement to hear and do God's word. Pious devotion to Mary (or any saint) is incomplete without prior attention to both the word of scripture and the Word himself, Jesus Christ.

ASSUMPTION OF THE BLESSED VIRGIN MARY: DAY

Lectionary #622

READING I   Revelation 11:19a; 12:1–6a, 10ab

A reading from the Book of Revelation

This reading is laden with the wild and vivid imagery of John's apocalyptic imagination. Proclaim it slowly, pausing frequently, so that its sharp and brilliant hues do not become muddled and run together.

God's temple in heaven was **opened**,
    and the ark of his covenant could be **seen** in the temple.

A great **sign** appeared in the **sky**, a woman **clothed** with the **sun**,
    with the **moon** beneath her **feet**,
    and on her **head** a crown of **twelve stars**.
She was with **child** and **wailed aloud** in **pain** as she **labored**
        to give **birth**.
Then **another sign** appeared in the **sky**;
    it was a **huge red dragon**, with **seven heads** and **ten horns**,
    and on its heads were **seven diadems**.
Its tail **swept away** a **third** of the **stars** in the **sky**
    and **hurled** them down to the **earth**.
Then the **dragon** stood before the **woman** about to give **birth**,
    to **devour** her **child** when she gave **birth**.
She gave **birth** to a **son**, a **male child**,
    destined to rule all the **nations** with an **iron rod**.
Her **child** was caught up to **God** and his **throne**.
The woman **herself** fled into the desert
    where she had a **place prepared** by **God**.

READING I   "Revelation" or "apocalypse" *(apokalupsis)* is the first word of the book of Revelation. The author, who introduces himself as "I, John, your brother," says he received the book's contents on the island of Patmos while "caught up in spirit on the Lord's day" (1:9–10). Before John's testimony to what he saw even begins, we know that we are dealing with a special kind of writing.

One feature commonly found in apocalyptic literature is an author's use of previous literary descriptions of the heavens in his own account (see April 22, 2007, Reading II). As Roman Catholic biblical scholar Adela Yarbro Collins has sensibly observed, Revelation's "imagery did not simply fall out of the sky." Instead, the book's imagery is quite traditional. Revelation's traditional character, Collins shows, extends beyond imagery to the text's basic structure, which echoes a

myth of divine combat found in various forms throughout the ancient Mediterranean and Middle Eastern regions. Revelation 12 is one of the key points in the book where this structure is on display. The "woman clothed with the sun" and later who flees the red dragon has parallels in Greek mythology. More mythical elements from various other cultures underlie chapter 12 of Revelation, leading Collins to conclude that the author

Then I heard a **loud voice** in **heaven** say:
> "**Now** have **salvation** and **power** come,
>   and the **Kingdom** of our **God**
>   and the **authority** of his **Anointed One**."

READING II 1 Corinthians 15:20–27

A reading from the first Letter of Saint Paul to the Corinthians

Brothers and **sisters**:
Christ has been **raised** from the **dead**,
    the **firstfruits** of those who have **fallen asleep**.
For since **death** came through **man**,
    the **resurrection** of the **dead** came **also** through **man**.
For just as in **Adam** all **die**,
    so too in **Christ** shall all be **brought** to **life**,
    but **each one** in **proper** order:
    Christ the **firstfruits**;
    then, at his **coming**, those who **belong** to Christ;
    then comes the **end**,
    when he **hands over** the **Kingdom** to his **God** and **Father**,
    when he has **destroyed every sovereignty**
    and e**very authority** and **power**.
For he must **reign** until he has put **all** his **enemies** under his **feet**.
The last **enemy** to be **destroyed** is **death**,
    for "he subjected **everything** under his feet."

This reading is part of an argument Paul makes in support of the Resurrection of the dead. It should be proclaimed sufficiently slowly so that its logical connections and transitions are stressed.

was "consciously attempting to be international by incorporating and fusing traditional elements from a variety of cultures."

In Roman Catholic tradition, the woman in today's reading has often been identified with Mary. As John's testimony about the woman clothed with the sun draws on the mythical traditions of a number of the cultures of his day, so also has present-day Roman Catholic devotion to the Queen of Heaven taken shape in response to the myriad peoples and cultures who honor her as their mother.

READING II Paul's intent in this section of 1 Corinthians is not merely to inform the Corinthians about correct doctrine concerning the end times, but to explain that doctrine's logic and to use it to encourage the Corinthians to reunify their fractured community.

In 1 Corinthians 15:1, Paul tells the Corinthians that he does not want them to be ignorant of the Gospel. The Corinthians stand within, and are saved by, the Gospel they received from Paul, and which Paul himself in turn received from those in Christ before him (15:1–3). The Gospel, therefore, is not what is in dispute. The content of this Gospel is, first, the report that Christ died, was buried, and raised on the third day (15:3–4). The purpose of his death, Paul says, was on behalf of sins and, like his Resurrection, happened according to the scriptures. Second, the Gospel is the report of eyewitness testimony, including Paul's, to the appearance of the risen Christ (15:5–8).

Bits of this reading have lives in Christian prayer independent of the Gospel text we find here. This reading contains basic elements of the Hail Mary and the Magnificat. Proclaim them as prayer.

Zechariah = Zech-ah-RI-ah

GOSPEL Luke 1:39–56

A reading from the holy Gospel according to Luke

Mary set out
   and traveled to the hill country in **haste**
   to a town of **Judah**,
   where she entered the house of **Zechariah**
   and greeted **Elizabeth**.
When **Elizabeth** heard **Mary's** greeting,
   the infant **leaped** in her womb,
   and **Elizabeth**, filled with the **Holy Spirit**,
   cried out in a loud voice and said,
   "**Blessed** are **you** among **women**,
   and **blessed** is the **fruit** of your **womb**.
And **how** does this happen to me,
   that the **mother** of my **Lord** should **come** to me?
For at the **moment** the **sound** of your **greeting** reached my **ears**,
   the **infant** in my **womb leaped** for **joy**.
Blessed are you who **believed**
   that what was **spoken** to you by the **Lord**
   would be **fulfilled**."

And **Mary** said:
   "My **soul proclaims** the **greatness** of the **Lord**;
     my **spirit rejoices** in **God** my **Savior**
     for he has **looked** upon his **lowly servant**.
   From **this day all** generations will call me **blessed**:
     the **Almighty** has done great **things** for me,
     and **holy** is his **Name**.
   He has **mercy** on those who **fear** him
   in **every** generation.

In 15:12–19, Paul argues that to deny the general Resurrection is nonsensical in light of the Corinthians' acceptance of Christ's Resurrection. In 15:20–28, the section from which today's reading comes, Paul sets out the aim and purpose of the Corinthian community, the reason for which it has been called together: to be raised with Christ at the time of his return.

Paul follows Christ's placement of all things under his feet with Christ's subjection of himself to God (15:28). Just as Paul holds up Christ as an example of self-sacrifice to the Philippians, he also presents Christ as an example to the factionalized Corinthians. How different is the behavior of the feuding community at Corinth from Christ, who willingly subjects himself to God so that "God may be all in all" (15:28).

It is not enough for Paul to state doctrine. He is a pastor with an obligation to understand and explain the doctrine he defends. The inquisitive and skeptical Corinthians appear to have tolerated nothing less.

GOSPEL In a letter purportedly written by Ignatius, bishop of Antioch, in the early years of the second century, Mary's virginity, her giving birth,

"He has shown the **strength** of his **arm**,
 and has scattered the **proud** in their **conceit**.
He has cast down the **mighty** from their **thrones**,
 and has **lifted up** the lowly.
He has filled the **hungry** with **good things**,
 and the **rich** he has sent away **empty**.
He has **come** to the **help** of his **servant Israel**
 for he has **remembered** his **promise** of **mercy**,
 the **promise** he **made** to our **fathers**,
 to **Abraham** and his **children** for **ever**."

Mary remained with her about three months
 and **then** returned to her home.

and Jesus' death "escaped the ruler of this age" and are "three mysteries of a cry, which were accomplished in the silence of God" (*Ignatius to the Ephesians,* 19:1). Ignatius means that these three mysteries occurred with no fanfare, among people so ordinary as to be anonymous, and in the virtual isolation of a rural eastern backwater of the Roman Empire. In the early Church that first

proclaimed him, Jesus' death was not something about which people were silent. But in the early period there is little evidence of the honor shown to Mary in later centuries.

To some Protestants, Catholic devotion to Mary smacks of idolatry, but the Catechism makes clear that the "very special devotion" of the Church to Mary "differs essentially from the adoration which is given to the incarnate Word and equally to the Father and the Holy Spirit" (Catechism, #971). She

is, as the Magnificat in this Gospel selection proclaims, "blessed."

We always do well to pray and work for the establishment of the same unity among all of the Christians of today that Paul encouraged among the factions of the fractured Corinthian community.

20TH SUNDAY IN ORDINARY TIME

Lectionary #120

READING I   Jeremiah 38:4–6, 8–10

A reading from the book of the prophet Jeremiah

In those days, the **princes** said to the **king**:
"**Jeremiah** ought to be put to **death**;
    he is **demoralizing** the **soldiers** who are **left** in this **city**,
    and all the people, by **speaking** such things to them;
    he is **not interested** in the **welfare** of our **people**,
    but in their **ruin**."
King **Zedekiah** answered: "He is in **your** power";
    for the **king** could do **nothing** with them.
And so they **took Jeremiah**
    and **threw** him into the **cistern** of Prince **Malchiah**,
    which was in the **quarters** of the **guard**,
    letting him down with ropes.
There was **no water** in the **cistern**, only **mud**,
    and **Jeremiah** sank into the **mud**.

Ebed-melech, a court official,
    went there from the **palace** and said to him:
    "**My lord king**,
    these **men** have been at **fault**
    in all they have **done** to the **prophet Jeremiah**,
    casting him into the cistern.
He will **die** of **famine** on the **spot**,
    for there is **no more food** in the **city**."

Be aware that this meeting contains multiple speaking parts. There is the quoted oracle of Jeremiah, the angry and accusing speech of the princes, and the resignation of the powerless king.

Zedekiah = Zeh-deh-KI-yah

Jeremiah = Jeh-reh-MI-yah
Malchiah = Mal-KI-yah

READING I   Jeremiah prophesied to the people of Judah, particularly its wealthy and ruling elite, that its corruption, injustice to the poor, and myriad other sins were unacceptable to God and carried serious consequences. To hear Jeremiah tell it, there was no one in Judah less popular than himself, cursed by all, "a man of strife and contention in all the land" (Jeremiah 15:10).

Because Jeremiah prophesied that the consequence of Judah's sins was the kingdom's subjugation to Babylon, he was accused of treason: "Jeremiah ought to be put to death; he is demoralizing the soldiers . . . he is not interested in the welfare of our people, but in their ruin" (Jeremiah 38:4). This was a gross distortion of Jeremiah's message, but his accusers, in no mood to weigh the merit of messenger or message, were certainly not disposed to consider the nuances and fine points of either.

Prophecy, among other things, is a kind of "expert opinion." It was as socially, politically, and religiously potent as it was because its practitioners were widely believed to have a special access to God's counsel that most did not. Prophecy was therefore ripe for abuse. We know, for example, from Jeremiah 23 and from the vivid narrative of 1 Kings 22, to name two examples, that prophets and prophecy were crassly used for brazen ends by the kings of Israel and Judah. Jeremiah was different. That he was cast into the darkness, muck, and mud of a cistern when, had he simply said what he knew the princes wanted to hear, he could have easily enjoyed royal support, is strong testimony to the integrity of Jeremiah's prophetic witness.

Then the **king** ordered **Ebed-melech** the **Cushite**
to take three men along with him,
and **draw** the **prophet Jeremiah** out of the **cistern**
before he should **die**.

A reading from the letter to the Hebrews

Brothers and **sisters**:
Since we are surrounded by so great a **cloud** of **witnesses**,
let us **rid** ourselves of **every burden** and **sin** that **clings** to us
and **persevere** in running the **race** that lies **before** us
while keeping our eyes **fixed** on Jesus,
the **leader** and **perfecter** of **faith**.
For the **sake** of the **joy** that lay **before** him
he **endured** the **cross**, **despising** its **shame**,
and has taken his **seat** at the **right** of the **throne** of **God**.
Consider how he **endured** such **opposition** from **sinners**,
in order that you may not **grow weary** and **lose heart**.
In your **struggle** against **sin**
you have not yet **resisted** to the **point** of **shedding blood**.

Emphasize the word "Since." This clause sets up the reason for the following clauses.

Emphasize the name of Jesus. He and his behavior are the examples the author invites his addressees to consider as additional reasons for persevering in faith.

READING II The earliest known artistic depiction of Jesus' Crucifixion dates from the middle of the fifth century. The scene may be viewed today in an upper panel of the immense wooden doors of Rome's Santa Sabina Basilica. It is not at all easy to see. The near total absence of the Crucifixion from the art of the ancient Church, particularly when compared with the proliferation of its depiction in Byzantine and Western medieval art, calls for an explanation.

This reading offers a clue. Jesus, the anonymous author of Hebrews writes, "endured the cross, despising its shame."

The "shame" *(aischunē)* of the cross was like few other kinds of public humiliation in antiquity. Crucifixion was intended to shame the victim and the victim's family, and to terrorize others contemplating actions similar to those for which the victim had been condemned. It was the punishment of common criminals, slaves, and people judged guilty of sedition against Rome. It is not hard to see why ancient people would shy from representing the Crucifixion in art.

The author of Hebrews writes to encourage his readers to persevere in their Christian faith. In this reading he offers Jesus as an example for them to imitate. Surely the addressees can finish the race they have begun, he contends, since they have suffered so much less than Jesus. Unlike Jesus, the addressees have not shed their blood.

Discipleship implies imitation. On this principle Thomas à Kempis based his *Imitation of Christ*, likely the most widely read book of the Late Middle Ages in the West. The potential trouble with a discipleship founded on imitation is that there are limits to the human capacity to imitate the divine. A theology with a high view of suffering, for example, cannot perversely confuse

The tone of voice is very important in this text. It is not "Jesus meek and mild" who speaks here; rather, a more authoritative tone should be employed here.

GOSPEL   Luke 12:49–53

A reading from the holy Gospel according to Luke

Jesus said to his **disciples**:
  "I have **come** to set the **earth** on **fire**,
    and how I **wish** it were **already blazing**!
There is a **baptism** with which I **must** be **baptized**,
    and how **great** is my **anguish** until it is **accomplished**!
Do you **think** that I have **come** to establish **peace** on the **earth**?
No, I tell you, but rather **division**.
From now on a **household** of **five** will be **divided**,
    three against **two** and **two** against **three**;
    a **father** will be **divided** against his **son**
    and a **son** against his **father**,
    a **mother** against her **daughter**
    and a **daughter** against her **mother**,
    a **mother-in-law** against her **daughter-in-law**
    and a **daughter-in-law** against her **mother-in-law**."

human suffering, which Christians are obliged to try to stop, with the redemptive suffering of Jesus Christ. Nevertheless, the author of Hebrews, as well as Paul, sees no problem with holding up Christ as an example of perseverance in times of trial.

GOSPEL   "If anyone comes to me," Jesus declares to the crowds, "without hating his father and mother, wife and children, brothers and sisters, and even his own life, he cannot be my disciple" (Luke 14:26; also see Matthew 10:37). When his visiting mother and brothers cannot get near him because of the press of the crowds, Jesus is informed that they stand waiting outside. "My mother and my brothers," he replies, "are those who hear the word of God and act on it" (Luke 8:19–21; see Matthew 12:46–50 and Mark 3:31–34). "Rather, blessed are those who hear the word of God and observe it" (Luke 11:27–28). And in today's reading, Jesus declares that allegiance to him divides rather than unites, splitting families right down the middle.

For some early followers the decision to become a disciple of Jesus meant social exile, including family ostracism or disownment. In John's story of the man born blind, the parents of the formerly blind man will not even stand up for their son for fear of being put out of the synagogue (9:21–23). For those so shunned, as well as for those whose family relationships remained intact, the community of the Church offered an intimacy demanding family language. "Brother" and "sister," for example, were ordinary terms of address among members of the Church for which abundant New Testament evidence exists.

21ST SUNDAY IN ORDINARY TIME

Lectionary #123

READING I   Isaiah 66:18–21

A reading from the Book of the Prophet Isaiah

Thus says the LORD:
I know their **works** and their **thoughts**,
and I come to gather **nations** of **every language**;
  they shall **come** and **see** my **glory**.
I will set a **sign** among them;
  from **them** I will send **fugitives** to the **nations**:
  to **Tarshish**, **Put** and **Lud**, **Mosoch**, **Tubal** and **Javan**,
  to the distant **coastlands**
  that have never **heard** of my **fame**, or **seen** my **glory**;
  and they shall **proclaim** my **glory** among the **nations**.
They shall bring all your **brothers** and **sisters** from all the **nations**
  as an **offering** to the LORD,
  on **horses** and in **chariots**, in **carts**, upon **mules**
    and **dromedaries**,
  to **Jerusalem**, my **holy mountain**, says the LORD,
  just as the **Israelites** bring their **offering**
  to the **house** of the LORD in clean **vessels**.
Some of these I will take as **priests** and **Levites**, says the LORD.

Tarshish = Tar-SHEESH
Put = Poot
Lud = Lood
Tubal = Too-BAL
Javan = Ja-VAN

Levites = LEE-vites

READING I   The prehistory of the world as it is related in the first 11 chapters of Genesis is the story, at least in part, of a failed relationship between God and humanity. God's delight in his creations turns to angry shock after the disobedience of Adam and Eve (Genesis 1—3). The shock intensifies with Abel's murder (Genesis 4). As people spread over the earth, God's shock becomes regret, even disgust, as the sins of the original family prove to be more the rule than exceptions to it. The flood improves little, if anything (Genesis 6—9).

With great concern, God observes humankind's attempt to build a tower to heaven (Genesis 11). And so, in Genesis 12, God starts over. He chooses one person and, though his descendents, one people. Abram is the man, Israel the people.

Contained within God's first promise of his election of Abram and his descendents is the information that "All the communities of the earth shall find blessing in you" (Genesis 12:3). The universalism of the prehistory is not concluded, but shall now be mediated through one people. Zion is not merely the destiny of Israel returned from

exile, but the destiny of humanity. Indeed, other peoples are to participate in the cultic life of Israel, a prophecy exceeding the promise of blessing in Genesis 12:3.

The Church's own election by God, the Catechism teaches, does not supersede the election of Israel (see, for example, Catechism, #839). The prophet's vision in today's reading of the corporate worship of God by the earth's peoples is a fitting one for a Church such as ours that has taken steps toward the removal of obstacles and impediments to that vision.

READING II Hebrews 12:5–7, 11–13

A reading from the Letter to the Hebrews

Brothers and sisters,
You have forgotten the exhortation addressed to you as children:
"My son, do not disdain the discipline of the Lord
    or lose heart when reproved by him;
    for whom the Lord loves, he disciplines;
    he scourges every son he acknowledges."
Endure your trials as "discipline";
    God treats you as sons.
For what "son" is there whom his father does not discipline?
At the time,
    all discipline seems a cause not for joy but for pain,
    yet later it brings the peaceful fruit of righteousness
    to those who are trained by it.

So strengthen your drooping hands and your weak knees.
Make straight paths for your feet,
    that what is lame may not be disjointed but healed.

Pause before you recite the proverb. The author is here quoting a piece of traditional wisdom and attention ought to be drawn to it.

Emphasize both "At the time" and "later" in order to highlight the author's contrast between the painful present and the peaceful future.

READING II It says something about ancient schools that the Greek word *paideia* can be translated both as "education" and, as it is in this reading, "discipline." Beatings of pupils by their teachers were practically part of the curriculum. In his *Confessions,* Saint Augustine recalls that he made his earliest attempts at prayer when he prayed not to be beaten at school (*Confessions* 1.9). Unlike the author of Hebrews, for whom the pain of education bears "peaceful fruit of righteousness," Augustine in the *Confessions* judges his teachers and their curricula morally bankrupt and can find little kind to say about them.

"Endure your trials as 'discipline.'" The author of Hebrews likely intends his readers to think of *paideia* in both its senses here. His appeal to readers in 12:5 is an appeal to people who have not merely wavered in faith, but have even forgotten what they learned in kindergarten. What the readers can't recall even little schoolboys know: God disciplines the ones he loves.

Today's reading is not an exhaustive statement on the source of human trials, suffering, and pain. If it were, then we would have to conclude that trials are always God's will. This world contains far too much suffering produced by brazen human deeds in defiance of God to conclude such a thing. Most of the time, there is simply no way to tell, and little profit to be gained, by trying to determine why some of us undergo trials and others do not. In any case, meditating on the "why" of suffering is insignificant in comparison with the call to relieve it.

GOSPEL   Luke 13:22–30

A reading from the holy Gospel according to Luke

Jesus passed through **towns** and **villages**,
    teaching as he went and **making** his **way** to **Jerusalem**.
Someone asked him,
"**Lord**, will **only** a **few people** be **saved**?"

He answered them,
"**Strive** to **enter** through the **narrow** gate,
    for **many**, I tell you, will **attempt** to **enter**
        but will not be **strong** enough.
After the master of the **house** has **arisen** and **locked** the door,
    then will you stand outside **knocking** and **saying**,
        '**Lord**, **open** the **door** for us.'
He will **say** to you in **reply**,
    'I do **not know where** you are **from**.'
And you will **say**,
    'We **ate** and **drank** in your **company** and you **taught**
        in our **streets**.'
Then he will **say** to you,
    'I do **not know where** you are **from**.
Depart from me, **all** you **evildoers**!'
And there will be **wailing** and **grinding** of teeth
    when you see **Abraham**, **Isaac and Jacob**
    and **all** the **prophets** in the **kingdom of God**
    and **you yourselves** cast **out**.
And people will come from the **east** and the **west**
    and from the **north** and the **south**
    and will **recline** at **table** in the **kingdom** of **God**.
For **behold**, some are **last** who will be **first**,
    and some are **first** who will be **last**."

Pause briefly before proclaiming
Jesus' answer.

GOSPEL   "Lord, will only a few people be saved?" Jesus' answer to this question in Luke's Gospel is a little puzzling. He does not answer it directly, replying instead with "Strive to enter through the narrow gate."

Many of us are perhaps aware that there are numerous opinions among Christians about the number of the saved. Some believe few will be saved, others believe all will be, and many fall somewhere in the middle or think the question poorly posed. In the New Testament, we also encounter a variety of opinion. Matthew's parable of the talents, a parable of the end time, concludes with the useless servant cast out into darkness, "where there will be wailing and grinding of teeth" (25:30). In 2 Peter 2:4–10, the author plainly says the Lord will rescue the pious while punishing wrongdoers in the end time. And yet in 1 Timothy 2:4, God is "our savior, who wills everyone to be saved." Finally, in 2 Peter we read that God wishes none of the addressees to perish (2 Peter 3:9).

It is not desirable to explain away these points of genuine difference. They cannot be harmonized. But it is hard to doubt that God desires the salvation of all people while respecting their freedom either to choose or to refuse it.

22ND SUNDAY IN ORDINARY TIME

Lectionary #126

READING I   Sirach 3:17–18, 20, 28–29

Sirach = SEER-ak

A reading from the Book of Sirach

My child, conduct your affairs with **humility**,
    and you will be **loved more** than a **giver** of **gifts**.
Humble yourself the **more**, the **greater** you **are**,
    and you will find **favor** with **God**.
What is **too sublime** for you, **seek not**,
    into **things** beyond your **strength** search **not**.
The **mind** of a **sage** appreciates **proverbs**,
    and an **attentive ear** is the **joy** of the **wise**.
Water quenches a **flaming fire**,
    and **alms atone** for **sins**.

READING II   Hebrews 12:18–19, 22–24a

Stress the word "not." As spectacular as the manifestation of God on Sinai was, it is to something greater that the people come.

A reading from the Letter to the Hebrews

Brothers and **sisters**:
You have **not** approached that which could be **touched**
    and a **blazing fire** and **gloomy darkness**
    and **storm** and a **trumpet** blast
    and a **voice speaking words** such that **those** who **heard**
    begged that no **message** be further **addressed** to them.

READING I The Greek word here translated as "humility" is *prautēs,* which may also be translated as "mildness" or "gentleness." A person with this quality is neither violent nor brash, but calm. "Which do you prefer?" Paul asks the Corinthians, whom he has just accused of spiritual arrogance. "Shall I come to you with a rod, or with love and a gentle spirit?" (See 1 Corinthians 4:21.) Here *prautēs* describes the promised demeanor of Paul's spirit, provided the Corinthians drop what Paul considers their puffed-up charade.

But in today's reading, Sirach is advising the cultivation of a quality much closer to humility than either gentleness or mildness. "What is too sublime for you, seek not, into things beyond your strength search not" (3:20). It takes humility, not a mild or gentle manner, to understand and accept the limits of one's abilities.

At the same time, however, one cannot know with certainty what one's limits are until one has tested them. It is sometimes awfully tempting to justify not striving for something by telling oneself "That's too much for me," or "I could never do that." If one's real reason for not attempting something worthwhile is fear, laziness, and so on, then one simply deceives oneself. This is not humility.

The cultivation of humility means entertaining the real possibility of failure. It means being willing to be proven dead wrong. In the study of scripture, it means accepting that, despite all one's learning, the strange and terrible beauty of God's word is that of a land one may view only at a distance (Deuteronomy 32:52).

No, you have **approached Mount Zion**
 and the **city** of the living **God**, the **heavenly Jerusalem**,
 and countless **angels** in festal **gathering**,
 and the **assembly** of the **firstborn enrolled** in **heaven**,
 and **God** the **judge** of **all**,
 and the **spirits** of the **just** made **perfect**,
 and **Jesus**, the **mediator** of a new **covenant**,
 and the **sprinkled blood** that speaks more **eloquently**
  than that of **Abel**.

GOSPEL   Luke 14:1, 7–14

A reading from the holy Gospel according to Luke

On a **sabbath Jesus** went to **dine**
 at the home of one of the leading **Pharisees**,
 and the **people** there were observing him **carefully**.

He told a **parable** to those who had been **invited**,
 noticing how they were choosing the places of **honor**
  at the **table**.
"When you are **invited** by someone to a **wedding banquet**,
 do not **recline** at table in the **place** of **honor**.
A more **distinguished** guest than you may have been
  invited by him,
 and the **host** who invited **both** of you may **approach** you
  and **say**,
 '**Give** your **place** to this **man**,'
 and then you would **proceed** with **embarrassment**
  to take the **lowest** place.

READING II In this reading, the author of Hebrews compares the blood of Abel with the blood of Christ. Christ's blood, the author writes, "speaks more eloquently than that of Abel" (12:24). The image of Abel's talking blood comes from Genesis. After Cain murdered Abel, Genesis reports that God asked, "Where is your brother Abel?" Compounding the crime of murder with a lie, Cain replies, "I do not know. Am I my brother's keeper?" God retorts, "What have you done! Listen: your brother's blood cries out to me from the soil!" (See Genesis 4:9–10.)

This is not the only point in Hebrews where the author discusses Abel. In 11:4, Abel appears among the Old Testament worthies whose faith made them precursors and forbears of the addressees. "By faith Abel offered to God a sacrifice greater than Cain's. Through this he was attested to be righteous, God bearing witness to his gifts, and through this, though dead, still speaks." There is no mention of Abel's blood, but it is noteworthy that in Genesis 4:2–8 Abel never speaks. Only his blood cries out from the ground.

Why the comparison between Abel's blood and Christ's in today's text? Perhaps Abel's blood cries to God for justice, while Jesus shed his blood on behalf of all, even his killers. Or perhaps, as biblical scholar Harold Attridge suggests, our author understood Abel to be the first martyr whose death helped to atone for the sins of others by the merit of his witness.

GOSPEL Ancient dinner parties sometimes called attention to the social rank of the invited guests and the

Rather, when you are invited,
  go and take the lowest place
  so that when the host comes to you he may say,
  'My friend, move up to a higher position.'
Then you will enjoy the esteem of your companions at the table.
For every one who exalts himself will be humbled,
  but the one who humbles himself will be exalted."
Then he said to the host who invited him,
  "When you hold a lunch or a dinner,
  do not invite your friends or your brothers
  or your relatives or your wealthy neighbors,
  in case they may invite you back and you have repayment.
Rather, when you hold a banquet,
  invite the poor, the crippled, the lame, the blind;
  blessed indeed will you be because of their inability
    to repay you.
For you will be repaid at the resurrection of the righteous."

esteem in which their host held them. In the early second century, Pliny, a Roman of illustrious background, wrote to a friend about his experience at a dinner given by an acquaintance. Depending on social status and the degree of friendship between each and the host, the different guests received food and drink of different quality. Pliny finds the arrangement rude and offers his opinion that one should treat all one's invited guests the same (Pliny the Younger, *Letters* 2.6). As Pliny's host and Jesus' advice make clear, common meals in antiquity were occasions of both honor and humiliation where the social rank of the guests was on display and reinforced.

In 14:12–14, we see Luke's characteristic interest in including the poor (4:18; 6:20; 7:22; 16:20–31; 19:8) and the infirm (5:12–26; 7:21–22; 17:11–19; 18:35–43) among the objects of Jesus' special concern and of the kingdom of God he proclaimed. These verses occur only in Luke.

The units of 14:7–11 and 14:12–14 both end with prophecies of the end time. The phrase "For every one who exalts himself will be humbled, but the one who humbles himself will be exalted" is the true basis of what, at first, reads like little more than well-mannered and sensible dinner party etiquette. Blessing and spiritual repayment await those inviting not their friends, but "the poor, the crippled, the lame, the blind" to table. Prophecies of the end time such as these reveal Luke's view of the great importance of choosing to adopt Jesus' social vision for ourselves and to work as Church to make it a reality.

23RD SUNDAY IN ORDINARY TIME

Lectionary #129

READING I   Wisdom 9:13–18b

A reading from the Book of Wisdom

This reading contains a number of questions. Make sure you go slowly enough to let the various questions sink in.

Who can know God's **counsel**,
    or who can **conceive** what the LORD intends?
For the **deliberations** of **mortals** are **timid**,
    and **unsure** are our **plans**.
For the **corruptible** body **burdens** the **soul**
    and the **earthen** shelter weighs down the **mind**
        that has **many** concerns.
And **scarce** do we **guess** the things on **earth**,
    and what is within our **grasp** we find with **difficulty**;
        but when **things** are in **heaven**, who can **search** them out?
Or **who** ever **knew** your **counsel**, except you had given
        wisdom
    and **sent** your **holy spirit** from on **high**?
And **thus** were the **paths** of those on **earth** made **straight**.

READING I In this selection from the book of Wisdom, the author weighs in on the question of the composition of the human creature, describing physical nature as an impediment to the intellect and spirit contained within: "For the corruptible body burdens the soul and the earthen shelter weighs down the mind that has many concerns."

The understanding of the body as the soul's burden is found in Plato's *Phaedo* (see 81C) and became a major theme of subsequent philosophical thought. Stoic and Middle Platonic thinkers in particular found this idea congenial. Philo of Alexandria, who was solidly in Plato's camp, saw mind and body in similar terms. We scarcely know anything about the author of Wisdom, but the philosophical erudition of this and related passages suggests he wrote from cosmopolitan Alexandria and was familiar with a Judaism similar to Philo's.

Of all Plato's writings, his *Timaeus* probably had the largest impact on the development of early Christian theology. In *Timaeus*, a reader encounters a god who creates out of his sheer goodness. But unlike the account of Genesis 1, the goodness of the creation in *Timaeus* is not highlighted. Indeed, this is the point on which Platonic ideas do not work so well with the biblical witness and with Roman Catholic teaching. Creator and creation are both good. Most Christian denominations affirm that the physical world is good, and this goes for human bodies as well. The body, like the mind and the soul, is the creation of God and, therefore, good.

READING II   Philemon 9b–10, 12–17

A reading from the Letter of Saint Paul to Philemon

This is a warmly personal and friendly letter. Emphasize those signs of Paul's affection for both Philemon and Onesimus, such as the words "beloved" and "brother."

I, **Paul**, an old man,
  and now also a **prisoner** for **Christ Jesus**,
  urge you on behalf of my **child Onesimus**,
  whose **father** I have **become** in my **imprisonment**;
  I am **sending him**, that is, my own **heart**, back to you.
I should have **liked** to **retain** him for **myself**,
  so that he might **serve** me on your **behalf**
  in my **imprisonment** for the **gospel**,
  but I did not want to do **anything** without your consent,
  so that the **good** you **do** might not be **forced** but **voluntary**.
Perhaps **this** is why he was **away** from you for a while,
  that you might have him **back forever**,
  no **longer** as a **slave**
  but **more** than a **slave**, **a brother**,
  beloved especially to **me**, but even **more** so to **you**,
  as a **man** and in the **Lord**.
So if **you** regard **me** as a **partner**, welcome **him** as you would **me**.

READING II   What sort of person was Philemon, the man to whom Paul wrote this letter? In addition to the named recipients (Philemon, Appia, and Achippus), Paul's greeting in verse 2 includes "the church at your house." If Philemon's house was large enough to accommodate a church, then he was probably a man of some means. Philemon also seems to have had space and resources sufficient to entertain an honored guest (see verse 22). And we know that Philemon owned at least one slave, Onesimus, whom Paul met in jail, and whom we meet in this letter (see Colossians 4:9).

Perhaps Philemon owned many other slaves, because Paul makes no suggestion that surrendering Onesimus will be a hardship for his owner.

Onesimus was a runaway. We do not know why he ran away or what circumstances led him to Paul. It is plausible, however, that the young man was in some trouble with Philemon and fled to the protection of someone he knew his owner respected. In verse 18, Paul may touch on the situation that precipitated Onesimus' flight: "And if he has done you any injustice or owes you anything, charge it to me."

Unlike most modern people, who find the ownership of human beings utterly incompatible with Christianity, Paul, like most ancients of all races, probably just accepted slavery as the way of the world. Paul never asks Philemon to free Onesimus, although in verse 8 he claims the authority to do so. Instead, Paul directs Philemon to receive Onesimus back not as property, but as family. Although Paul says that he would have liked to keep Onesimus, he claims that he nevertheless returned him so that the owner might voluntarily do with his property

GOSPEL   Luke 14:25–33

A reading from the holy Gospel according to Luke

Great crowds were traveling with **Jesus**,
   and he **turned** and **addressed** them,
   "If **anyone** comes to me without **hating** his **father** and **mother**,
   wife and **children**, **brothers** and **sisters**,
   and even his **own life**,
   he **cannot** be my disciple.
Whoever does **not** carry his **own cross** and **come after me**
   cannot be my disciple.
Which of you **wishing** to construct a **tower**
   does not first sit down and **calculate** the cost
   to see if there is **enough** for its **completion**?
Otherwise, after laying the **foundation**
   and finding himself **unable** to **finish** the **work**
   the onlookers should **laugh** at him and **say**,
   '**This** one began to **build** but did not have the **resources**
      to **finish**.'
Or what **king marching** into **battle** would not **first** sit **down**
   and **decide** whether with ten thousand troops
   he can **successfully** oppose another **king**
   advancing upon him with twenty thousand troops?
But if not, while he is **still** far away,
   he will **send** a **delegation** to ask for **peace** terms.
In the **same** way,
   anyone of you who **does not renounce all** his **possessions**
   cannot be my disciple."

Pause briefly before the final stanza.

---

as he sees fit (verse 13). Paul's letter leaves the ball, as it were, in Philemon's court.

GOSPEL   The hatred of family and the renunciation of possessions are strict conditions for discipleship to say the least. How are present-day Catholics to understand such a radical teaching: "anyone of you who does not renounce all his possessions cannot be my disciple"?

The conditions of being a follower of Jesus must be seen in the context of a community of people who eagerly expected the quick arrival of the kingdom of God. And yet it is also the case that the Church, the successor to that movement, self-consciously lives with the same expectation of the kingdom, despite its indefinite postponement.

Acts describes the earliest Church in these terms: "All who believed were together and had all things in common; they would sell their property and possessions and divide them among all according to each one's need" (Acts 2:44–45). The difficulty of the teaching has also not stopped men and women over the centuries from giving up homes, land, money, possessions, power, and prestige for lives of prayer, labor, scripture study, and habits of simplicity. Some have joined religious communities, while others have remained in secular society and given up, sometimes gradually, what they had. While it runs counter to the acquisitive economic behavior widely encouraged in contemporary society, there is profound freedom in the removal of the burden of possessions from one's shoulders. Perhaps Jesus, the craftsman who left his home and trade behind, knew this from personal experience.

24TH SUNDAY IN ORDINARY TIME

Lectionary #132

READING I   Exodus 32:7–11, 13–14

A reading from the Book of Exodus

Keep in mind the different emotional register of Moses' and God's words. God speaks to Moses in anger, but Moses reasons with God.

The LORD said to Moses,
"Go **down** at once to your **people**,
    whom you brought out of the **land** of Egypt,
    for they have become **depraved**.
They have soon turned aside from the way I **pointed out** to them,
    making for themselves a **molten calf** and **worshiping** it,
    sacrificing to it and **crying** out,
    '**This** is your **God**, O Israel,
    who brought you out of the **land** of Egypt!'
I **see** how **stiff-necked** this **people** is," continued the LORD
        to Moses.
"Let me **alone**, then,
    that my **wrath** may **blaze up against** them to **consume** them.
Then I will make of you a **great nation**."

But **Moses** implored the LORD, his **God**, saying,
"**Why**, O LORD, should your **wrath blaze up against your**
        own people,
    whom you brought out of the **land** of Egypt
    with such **great power** and with so **strong** a **hand**?
Remember your servants **Abraham**, **Isaac**, and **Israel**,
    and how you **swore** to them by your **own self**, saying,
    'I will make your **descendants** as **numerous** as the **stars**
        in the **sky**;

READING I   The story of the golden calf in Exodus 32 is, among other things, about idolatry. The Israelites, frustrated by Moses' delay in returning from Sinai, demand that Aaron make them a god to worship. The golden calf is what Aaron fashions for the people to worship instead of the God who rescued them from slavery in Egypt. If it seems odd that anyone should worship something so ridiculous as a calf

made of golden earrings and jewelry, consider for a moment the consuming adoration of money, power, celebrity, and sex in contemporary society.

The story of the golden calf also concerns intercession. As Abraham formerly entreated God to spare all the people of Sodom and Gomorrah for the sake of even a few righteous people (see Genesis 18:16–32), Moses now begs God to spare the Israelites despite their creation and worship of a god of their own making.

For Clement of Rome, the purported author of a letter to the Church at Corinth near the turn of the second century AD, the story of the golden calf also told important truths about love. As in Paul's day (roughly 40 years before), the Church at Corinth is experiencing internal division. Clement urges people he does not name, whom he calls "leaders of division and sedition," to aim at "the common goal of hope." "People conducting themselves in fear and love," he

and all this **land** that I **promised**,
    I will **give** your **descendants** as their **perpetual** heritage.'"
So the LORD **relented** in the **punishment**
    he had **threatened** to inflict on his **people**.

READING II   1 Timothy 1:12–17

A reading from the first Letter of Saint Paul to Timothy

Beloved:
I am **grateful** to him who has **strengthened** me, **Christ Jesus**
        our **Lord**,
    because he **considered** me **trustworthy**
    in **appointing** me to the **ministry**.
I was once a **blasphemer** and a **persecutor** and **arrogant**,
    but I have been **mercifully treated**
    because I **acted** out of **ignorance** in my **unbelief**.
Indeed, the **grace** of our **Lord** has been **abundant**,
    along with the **faith** and **love** that are in **Christ Jesus**.
This saying is **trustworthy** and deserves **full acceptance**:
    Christ Jesus came into the **world** to **save sinners**.
Of these **I** am the **foremost**.
But for **that reason** I was **mercifully treated**,
    so that in me, as the **foremost**,
    Christ Jesus might **display** all his **patience** as an **example**
    for those who would come to **believe** in him for **everlasting life**.
To the **king** of **ages**, **incorruptible**, **invisible**, the **only God**,
    honor and **glory forever** and **ever**. **Amen**.

Emphasize the word "Beloved." Look at the assembly when you speak it and pause after it, so that your listeners can consider the intimacy of the address.

Stress "Christ Jesus came into the world to save sinners." This is Roman Catholic creed, one of our central convictions and a basic part of the good news we have to share with the world.

Slow down to give special emphasis to the final sentence of this reading. It is a prayer.

writes, "want themselves to encounter suffering rather than their neighbors" (*1 Clement* 56.1–2). Citing Exodus 32:31–32, in which Moses begs God to destroy him if Israel is not forgiven for making and worshiping the golden calf, Clement exclaims, "O great love! O most unsurpassable perfection! The servant speaks frankly with the Lord, he asks forgiveness for the multitude, or prays

that he be obliterated with them" (*1 Clement* 58.1–5). Moses' intercession on Israel's behalf displays for Clement the conviction that the foundations of Christian love lie in lives lived for the sake of the common good.

READING II   In the biography of Paul in today's reading, "blasphemer," "persecutor," and "arrogant" describe Paul before his conversion. "Blasphemer" is perhaps a little surprising, given Paul's self-portrait as a zealot for Jewish traditions in

Galatians 1:14 and the religious details of his biographical asides in Philippians 3:4–6 and 2 Corinthians 11:22. "Persecutor" squares with Paul's own statements in 1 Corinthians 15:9; Galatians 1:13, 23; and Philippians 3:6, as well as his depiction in Acts. The word *hubristēs* is not adequately translated, as it is in some versions, by "arrogant." The word is not an adjective but a noun and possesses

The speaking parts are 1) the narrator; 2) the Pharisees and scribes; 3) Jesus; and 4) Jesus quoting the shepherd and the woman, and then telling a story in which he quotes the father, the prodigal son, and the elder brother. The Pharisees and scribes are irritated; the woman, the shepherd, and the father are joyful; and the prodigal son is in turn demanding and despairing, while his older brother is very angry. Practice this reading in order to convey the rich characterization that Luke offers us in this reading.

GOSPEL   Luke 15:1–32

A reading from the holy Gospel according to Luke

Tax collectors and **sinners** were all drawing near to **listen** to
    Jesus,
  but the **Pharisees** and **scribes** began to **complain**, saying,
  "This man **welcomes** sinners and **eats** with them."
So to them he addressed this parable.
"**What man** among you having a **hundred** sheep
    and losing **one** of them
  would not leave the **ninety-nine** in the desert
  and go after the **lost one** until he finds it?
And when he does find it,
  he **sets** it on his **shoulders** with **great joy**
  and, upon his arrival home,
  he **calls** together his **friends** and **neighbors** and **says** to them,
  '**Rejoice** with me because I have **found** my **lost sheep**.'
I tell you, in **just** the **same way**
  there will be **more joy** in **heaven** over **one sinner** who **repents**
  than over **ninety-nine righteous people**
  who have **no need** of **repentance**.

"Or **what woman** having **ten coins** and **losing one**
  would not **light** a **lamp** and **sweep** the **house**,
  searching carefully until she **finds** it?
And when she does find it,
  she **calls** together her **friends** and **neighbors**
  and **says** to them,
  '**Rejoice** with me because I have **found** the **coin** that I **lost**.'

the strong implication of violence. "Thug" does the Greek word greater justice. The use of this word takes Paul's career as a persecutor of the Church to a level of sinister specificity beyond what he elsewhere offers. Only the Paul of Acts, who approves of—and perhaps colludes in—Stephen's murder (Acts 7:58; 8:1), who arrests and imprisons members of the Church (Acts 8:3), and who journeys to Damascus "breathing murderous threats" comes close to the *hubristēs* of 1 Timothy 1:13 (Acts 9:1).

Paul was shown mercy, according to today's reading, because he acted "out of ignorance in my unbelief." In other words, God showed Paul clemency due to mitigating circumstances. Paul's conversion and subsequent apostolate, therefore, are based in a verdict of divine justice. Galatians 1:13–16, however, shows that God acted on Paul's behalf *in spite* of Paul, not *because* of him. No personal deficit leads God to favor Paul. Nor, for that matter, do any of his attributes.

Neither in 1 Corinthians 15:9–10 is there any mention of Paul's personal qualities explaining the special favor God showed him. Rather, in 1 Corinthians 15 Paul emphasizes that his apostolate has only to do with God's grace and nothing to do with himself.

GOSPEL   How can Jesus make moral judgments, attaching the label "hypocrites" (Luke 12:56; 13:15) to people whose speech and behavior are inconsistent, and expect to avoid the same charge

"In **just** the **same way**, **I tell you**,
 there will be **rejoicing** among the **angels** of **God**
 over **one sinner** who **repents**."

Then he said,
 "A man had two **sons**, and the **younger** son said to his **father**,
 '**Father give** me the **share** of your **estate** that should **come**
  to me.'
So the **father divided** the **property between** them.
After a few days, the younger son **collected** all his **belongings**
 and set off to a **distant country**
 where he **squandered** his inheritance on a **life** of **dissipation**.
When he had **freely** spent **everything**,
 a **severe famine** struck that **country**,
 and he **found** himself in dire **need**.
So he **hired** himself **out** to one of the local **citizens**
 who sent him to his **farm** to tend the **swine**.
And he **longed** to **eat** his **fill** of the **pods** on which the **swine** fed,
 but **nobody** gave him any.
Coming to his **senses** he **thought**,
 'How **many** of my father's hired workers
 have **more** than **enough** food to eat,
 but here am **I**, **dying** from **hunger**.
I shall **get up** and **go** to my **father** and I shall **say** to him,
 "**Father**, I have **sinned** against **heaven** and **against you**.
I no longer **deserve** to be **called your son**;
 treat me as you would **treat one** of your hired **workers**.'"

when freely choosing the company of sinners? The complaint of the scribes and the Pharisees is not easily dismissed, particularly because Jesus has already accused the Pharisees of hypocrisy without bothering to explain the basis of the charge (Luke 12:1).

Jesus' examples of the lost-and-found sheep and coin make no claim about whether their recovery is right, fair, or just. Similarly, in the story of the prodigal son, we do not know if the younger son either truly repented of the wrong he had done to his father or just

slickly connived to manipulate his old man into taking him back. Perhaps the young man imagines that an emotional show of contrition is just the thing to play on his father's feelings. And perhaps not!

The joy of the shepherd, the woman, and the father of the prodigal apparently have nothing to do with whether it is just and fair that what was lost is found. What matters to Luke is the joy that erupts upon finding what was lost.

The complaint of the Pharisees and scribes is much like that of the elder brother

in the story of the prodigal son. He is understandably angry at his father's double standard. But can a child's diligent fidelity to a parent be so powerful as to deny that parent's love to others? The father's reaction to the return of his wild child makes the answer to this question a resounding "No!" No child can put a limit on a parent's love, and no restriction that the Pharisees and scribes, whether of the ancient or modern variety, can place on God's joyful reception of sinners at his table.

So he **got up** and **went back** to his **father**.
While he was **still** a **long way off**,
   his **father** caught **sight** of him,
   and was **filled** with compassion.
He **ran** to his son, **embraced** him and **kissed** him.
His son **said** to him,
   '**Father**, I have **sinned** against **heaven** and **against you**;
   I no longer **deserve** to be called **your son**.'
But his **father** ordered his **servants**,
   '**Quickly** bring the **finest robe** and put it **on** him;
   put a **ring** on his **finger** and **sandals** on his **feet**.
Take the **fattened calf** and **slaughter** it.
Then let us **celebrate** with a **feast**,
   because this **son** of **mine** was **dead**, and has **come** to **life** again;
   he was **lost**, and has been **found**.'
Then the **celebration** began.
Now the **older** son had been **out** in the **field**
   and, on his way back, as he neared the **house**,
   he heard the **sound** of **music** and **dancing**.
He **called** one of the servants and **asked** what this might mean.
The servant said to him,
   'Your **brother** has **returned**
   and your **father** has **slaughtered** the **fattened calf**
   because he has him back **safe** and **sound**.'
He became **angry**,
   and when he **refused** to enter the house,
   his **father came out** and **pleaded** with him.

He said to his father in reply,
  '**Look**, **all** these **years** I served **you**
  and not **once** did I disobey **your orders**;
  yet you **never** gave me **even** a **young goat** to **feast** on
    with **my friends**.
But when **your** son returns,
  who **swallowed** up **your property** with **prostitutes**,
  for **him** you **slaughter** the fattened calf.'
He said to him,
  '**My son**, **you** are here with me **always**;
  everything I have is **yours**.
But **now** we must **celebrate** and **rejoice**,
  because your **brother** was **dead** and has **come** to **life** again;
  he was **lost** and has been **found**.'"

[Shorter: Luke 15:1–10]

25TH SUNDAY IN ORDINARY TIME

Lectionary #135

READING I   Amos 8:4–7

Keep in mind that there are, in a sense, three speaking parts here. The first is the prophet Amos. The second is that of the people he quotes. The third is God's voice. Be sure to give special attention to the shameless speech of those planning to harm the poor.

A reading from the Book of the Prophet Amos

Hear this, you who **trample** upon the **needy**
    and **destroy** the **poor** of the **land**!
"**When** will the **new moon** be **over**," you ask,
    "that we may **sell** our **grain**,
    and the **sabbath**, that we may **display** the **wheat**?
We will **diminish** the **ephah**,
    add to the **shekel**,
    and **fix** our **scales** for **cheating**!
We will **buy** the **lowly** for **silver**,
    and the **poor** for a **pair** of **sandals**;
    even the **refuse** of the **wheat** we will **sell**!"
The **LORD** has **sworn** by the **pride** of **Jacob**:
    Never will I **forget** a **thing** they have **done**!

Emphasize the word "Never" in the final line.

READING I   Amos hailed from the village of Tekoa, resting among the hills due south of Jerusalem on the edge of the desert. Although Tekoa lay well inside the southern kingdom of Judah, it was on the northern kingdom of Israel that Amos concentrated his energies during his prophetic tenure in the eighth century BC. To Israel Amos delivered the oracle of which today's selection is a portion.

In today's reading, we read the prophet's denunciation of the abuse of the poor and the needy by the rich. This is such a common prophetic theme that there is little need to point out parallels—simply read Amos, Jeremiah, Isaiah, and Micah, and you will shortly come across it. What is striking in today's reading is the intersection of contempt for religious observance with the exploitation of the poor. The wealthy squirm with impatience as they wait for the conclusions to the festival of the new moon to end and the Sabbath so that they can return to their businesses.

And what business people they are! Shamelessly they announce their intention to "diminish the ephah," "add to the shekel," and "fix" their scales. The ephah was a common unit of grain measure in Israel and Judah (we might say something like "bushel"). To diminish it meant that the seller kept more than what was rightfully his, while a buyer went home with less than he agreed to pay for. The shekel was (and in modern Israel is once again) the basic unit of currency. To "add to the shekel" meant to counterfeit the currency, withholding some of the precious ore but giving it the proper weight by the addition of non-precious metals. Scales fixed for cheating with weights is obvious enough.

Stress the word "Beloved" and pause to look at the assembly as you proclaim it.

Many biblical scholars consider 2:5–6 to be a fragment of an early Christian hymn or creed. Slow down to emphasize it.

"I am speaking the truth, I am not lying" is an emphatic statement and deserves due emphasis.

READING II   1 Timothy 2:1–8

A reading from the first Letter of Saint Paul to Timothy

Beloved:
First of all, I ask that supplications, prayers,
    petitions and thanksgivings be offered for everyone,
    for kings and for all in authority,
    that we may lead a quiet and tranquil life
    in all devotion and dignity.
This is good and pleasing to God our savior,
    who wills everyone to be saved
    and to come to knowledge of the truth.
        For there is one God.
        There is also one mediator between God and men,
        the man Christ Jesus,
        who gave himself as ransom for all.
This was the testimony at the proper time.
For this I was appointed preacher and apostle
    —I am speaking the truth, I am not lying,
    teacher of the Gentiles in faith and truth.

It is my wish, then, that in every place the men should pray,
    lifting up holy hands, without anger or argument.

Literally, to "buy the lowly for silver and the poor for a pair of sandals" may have been the work of an afternoon for such people. But as the final line of the reading suggests, consequences await those who cheat their countrymen and treat the poor like commodities to be bought and sold.

READING II It is customary in the Mass for the deacon, a liturgical minister, or, in their absence, the celebrant to offer petitions to God on behalf of authorities both civil and religious. We pray for

Presidents, members of Congress, judges, and for authorities closer to our daily lives in our states, cities, towns, and neighborhoods. We also pray for Pope Benedict XVI, our local bishop, and all clergy and religious. In short, we pray for those entrusted with the authority under which we live.

The "supplications, prayers, petitions, and thanksgivings" for kings and authorities, while similar in form to the petitions for authority in the Mass, would have been offered in a far different context than are the

petitions of a Roman Catholic community today. The first readers of this letter lived under Roman imperial rule, enjoying and suffering the effects of policies and decisions over which they had practically no say. The kings and authorities mentioned were also not Christians, and the fear of persecution was very real. It should not surprise us that the first reason given to pray for kings and authorities is "that we may lead a quiet and tranquil life." This is not a communal prayer with which most of us are familiar. It is, rather, a communal prayer for

Keep in mind the multiple speaking parts in this story that Jesus tells. The master is angry. At first the steward speaks with fear, or at least concern for the future, before gaining confidence as he hatches his scheme.

Note the questions and proclaim them as such.

GOSPEL   Luke 16:1–13

A reading from the holy Gospel according to Luke

Jesus said to his **disciples**,
   "A **rich** man had a **steward**
   who was **reported** to him for **squandering** his **property**.
He **summoned** him and said,
   'What is this I **hear** about you?
Prepare a full **account** of your **stewardship**,
   because you can **no longer** be my **steward**.'
The **steward** said to himself, '**What** shall I **do**,
   now that my master is taking the **position** of steward
      away from me?
I am **not strong** enough to **dig** and I am **ashamed** to **beg**.
I **know** what I shall **do so** that,
   when I am **removed** from the **stewardship**,
   they may **welcome** me into their **homes**.'
He called in his master's **debtors one** by **one**.
To the **first** he said,
   '**How much** do you **owe** my master?'
He replied, '**One hundred measures** of olive oil.'
He said to him, '**Here** is your promissory note.
Sit **down** and quickly **write** one for **fifty**.'
Then to **another** the steward said, 'And you,
   how much do you **owe**?'
He replied, '**One hundred kors** of wheat.'
The steward said to him, '**Here** is your promissory note;
   write one for **eighty**.'

anonymity. To paraphrase *The Fiddler on the Roof,* perhaps included in this order to pray for authorities is the desire that God indeed bless and keep them all—far, far away!

One must not ignore, however, that contained within the order to pray for the aforementioned authorities is an implicit prayer for their conversion. God "wills everyone to be saved and to come to knowledge of the truth."

GOSPEL The rich man's steward was likely a slave. Rural estates at this time were often almost entirely self-sufficient slave communities. The proceeds belonged to an absentee owner, but slaves performed the work. "Steward," which translates the Greek job title *oikonomos,* is sometimes translated as "household manager."

It was a common enough practice, of which this story provides an example, for an owner to trust an *oikonomos* to conduct financial transactions on his behalf and in his name. Unlike the field slave, whose life was rough and short, an *oikonomos* was a skilled and valuable piece of property enjoying a less arduous and better quality of life.

In his commentary on Luke in the Anchor Bible series, Father Joseph Fitzmyer suggests that the economic context of this story is an ordinary and common arrangement between stewards and masters in

And the master **commended** that dishonest steward
    for acting **prudently**.

"For the **children** of this **world**
    are more **prudent** in **dealing** with their **own generation**
    than are the **children** of **light**.
I **tell** you, make **friends** for **yourselves** with **dishonest wealth**,
    so that when it **fails**, you will be **welcomed**
        into **eternal dwellings**.
The **person** who is **trustworthy** in **very small** matters
    is also **trustworthy** in **great ones**;
    and the **person** who is **dishonest** in **very small** matters
    is also **dishonest** in **great ones**.
If, therefore, you are **not trustworthy** with dishonest **wealth**,
    who will **trust** you with **true** wealth?
If you are **not trustworthy** with what **belongs** to another,
    who will **give** you what is **yours**?
No servant can serve **two** masters.
He will **either hate** one and **love** the other,
    or be **devoted** to one and **despise** the other.
You cannot serve both God and mammon."

[Shorter: Luke 16:10–13]

Stress the word "cannot."

---

which a steward was allowed to buy, sell, and lend the proceeds and produce of the country estate on his master's behalf while keeping a percentage of the profits for himself as a commission. We are not told the specific nature of the steward's misbehavior, except that he was "squandering" (in Greek, *diaskorpizō*) his owner's profits. The basic meaning of the Greek verb is "scatter." He was, in other words, losing money.

The steward's solution, observes Father Fitzmyer, may have been to cancel his own commission in order to encourage repayment of the debt. Notice that the debts are not erased or canceled; rather, they are redrawn in the debtor's favor. In other words, the steward may have simply agreed to take the financial loss himself and that this is what led his owner to commend him for his prudence.

26TH SUNDAY IN ORDINARY TIME

Lectionary #138

READING I   Amos 6:1a, 4–7

The description of "the complacent of Zion" portrays them as ridiculous and worthy of contempt. It probably contains some sarcasm. Consider whether you want to try to bring this out in your proclamation.

A reading from the Book of the Prophet Amos

Thus says the LORD the **God** of **hosts**:
Woe to the **complacent** in **Zion**!
Lying upon **beds** of **ivory**,
     stretched **comfortably** on their **couches**,
they eat **lambs** taken from the **flock**,
     and **calves** from the **stall**!
Improvising to the **music** of the **harp**,
     like **David**, they **devise** their own **accompaniment**.
They **drink wine** from **bowls**
     and **anoint** themselves with the **best oils**;
     yet they are **not** made **ill** by the **collapse** of **Joseph**!
Therefore, **now** they shall be the **first** to go into exile,
     and their **wanton revelry** shall be **done away** with.

READING II   1 Timothy 6:11–16

First Timothy 6:11–12 is intended to encourage and to bolster spirits. The subsequent verses are both commission and prayer. Pause between verse 12 and verse 13 and proclaim slowly, but with force, verses 13–16.

A reading from the first Letter of Saint Paul to Timothy

But **you**, **man** of **God**, pursue **righteousness**,
     devotion, **faith**, **love**, **patience** and **gentleness**.
Compete **well** for the **faith**.

READING I   Amos' picture of Judah's elite, languishing in the south during the northern kingdom of Israel's final tumultuous years, is especially vivid. Amos may well have found contemptible, as well as ridiculous, any person happy to lounge the day away, chewing the finest foods, getting drunk, and, covered in the reek of cologne, warbling along to a twanging harp. But what the prophet fiercely denounces in particular is that these "complacent of Zion" insulate themselves from the disintegration of the north. So many lux-

uries they enjoy, "yet they are not made ill by the collapse of Joseph."

Why does the self-indulgence of Judah's elite matter to Amos? He and his family were not from the northern kingdom at all, but rather from the village of Tekoa south of Jerusalem in Judah. The "collapse of Joseph" is not Judah's collapse. But by designating the northern kingdom "Joseph," Amos calls attention to the patriarchal traditions Israel shares with Judah. What kind of brother satisfies expensive tastes while his younger brother suffers? The solidarity one expects of a brother, Amos is saying, cannot be found

among Judah's elite, people who prefer good food and drink to coming to the aid of family.

In Amos 6:2–3, the prophet directs Zion's complacent to cast an eye around at other kingdoms and regions, presumably because these have already suffered at the hands of the Assyrians. Does Judah expect to avoid their fate? In point of fact Judah will suffer badly from Assyrian encroachment and invasion in the latter part of the eighth century BC, although Jerusalem itself will not fall to the Assyrians.

Lay hold of **eternal life**, to which you were **called**
>   when you made the **noble confession** in the presence
>   of **many witnesses**.
I charge you before **God**, who gives **life** to all things,
>   and before **Christ Jesus**,
>   who gave **testimony** under **Pontius Pilate**
>   for the **noble confession**,
>   to **keep** the **commandment** without **stain** or **reproach**
>   until the **appearance** of our **Lord Jesus Christ**
>   that the **blessed** and **only** ruler
>   will make manifest at the proper time,
>   the **King** of **kings** and **Lord** of **lords**,
>   who **alone** has immortality, who dwells
>   in **unapproachable** light,
>   and whom **no** human being has **seen** or **can see**.
To him be **honor** and **eternal power**. **Amen**.

GOSPEL   Luke 16:19–31

A reading from the holy Gospel according to Luke

Jesus said to the **Pharisees**:
"There was a **rich man** who dressed in **purple garments**
>   and **fine linen**
>   and dined **sumptuously** each day.
And lying at his door was a **poor man** named **Lazarus**,
>   **covered** with **sores**,
>   who would **gladly** have eaten his fill of the **scraps**
>   that **fell** from the rich man's **table**.
Dogs even used to **come** and **lick** his **sores**.

Lazarus = LA-zah-rus

READING II The athletic imagery in this reading from 1 Timothy functions as a metaphor for the life of faith in Christ. "Pursue righteousness," Paul coaches, as well as "devotion, faith, love, patience, and gentleness." "Compete well for the faith," we read, and "Lay hold of eternal life." Such language imagines Christian life and access to the world to come as a trophy or a crown of laurels. Paul can also use sporting terms like a disappointed coach giving an earful to a poorly playing team at halftime: "You were running well," he

laments to the Galatians concerning their fumbles. "Who hindered you from following the truth?" (See Galatians 5:7.)

In this reading we twice encounter the phrase "noble confession." In the first instance, the noble confession is something Timothy made "in the presence of many witnesses." In the second instance, Christ is reported to have given "testimony under Pontius Pilate for the noble confession." What is the noble confession?

In texts such as Romans 6 and Colossians 2:11–15, Paul describes the sacrament of Baptism as a sharing in Christ's

death and Resurrection. The "noble confession" that Timothy reportedly made in front of many witnesses probably means a statement of faith that he, along with other adult catechumens, made at his Baptism. The testimony of Christ, provided by his Passion, death, and Resurrection, is likely the substance of Timothy's noble confession. As they have been united in life and death, believer and Lord are also united in confession: the testimony of Christ given through his cross becomes the testimony about Christ that the believer gives upon initiation into the Christian community.

The rich man is in hopeless torment. Proclaim his words so that this comes through.

When the **poor man died**,
  he was carried away by **angels** to the **bosom** of **Abraham**.
The **rich man also died** and was **buried**,
  and from the **netherworld**, where he was in **torment**,
  he **raised** his **eyes** and saw **Abraham** far off
  and **Lazarus** at his side.
And he cried out, '**Father Abraham**, have **pity** on me.
Send Lazarus to **dip** the tip of his finger in **water** and **cool**
    my **tongue**,
  for I am **suffering torment** in these **flames**.'

Abraham replied,
  '**My child**, **remember** that you received
  what was **good** during your **lifetime**
  while **Lazarus** likewise **received** what was **bad**;
  but **now** he is **comforted** here, whereas **you** are **tormented**.
Moreover, between **us** and **you** a **great chasm** is established
  to **prevent anyone** from **crossing** who might **wish** to go
  from **our side** to **yours** or from **your side** to **ours**.'
He said, 'Then I **beg** you, **father**,
  send him to my **father's house**, for I have **five brothers**,
  so that he may **warn** them,
  lest they **too come** to this **place** of **torment**.'
But **Abraham** replied, 'They have **Moses** and the **prophets**.
Let them **listen** to **them**.'
He said, 'Oh **no**, father **Abraham**,
  but if **someone** from the **dead** goes to them, they will **repent**.'
Then **Abraham** said, 'If they will **not** listen to **Moses**
    and the **prophets**,
  neither will they be **persuaded** if someone should **rise**
    from the **dead**.'"

GOSPEL The Catechism cites this story in two places. In the first place, Luke's account of Lazarus and the rich man is used to distinguish mortal from venial sin. Mortal sin is the deliberate and willful decision to oppose God. "Feigned ignorance and hardness of heart," the text reads, "do not diminish, but rather increase, the voluntary character of a sin" (Catechism, #1859). While he lived, the rich man knew full well that Lazarus and others like him could have eaten well from his table scraps.

But he chose, like the brothers he would spare torment, to ignore the prophetic witness against the abuse and neglect of the poor. The rich man knew the good, but he chose the bad.

The second place today's Gospel selection is cited, along with Matthew 25:31–46, is in the Catechism's extended explanation of the significance of the Lord's Prayer. It is worth quoting at length. "The drama of hunger in the world," we read, "calls Christians who pray sincerely to exercise responsibility toward their brethren, both in their personal behavior and in their solidarity with the human family. This petition of the Lord's Prayer cannot be isolated from the parables of the poor man Lazarus and of the Last Judgment" (Catechism, #2831).

Was Lazarus a good man or a bad man? Was he among the so-called deserving or the undeserving poor? Luke does not tell us. There is no evidence that such a distinction mattered much—if at all—to Jesus. Jesus and the prophets have clearly forewarned us of the consequences of turning aside to occupy ourselves with other concerns.

27TH SUNDAY IN ORDINARY TIME

Lectionary #141

READING I   Habakkuk 1:2–3; 2:2–4

Give Habakkuk his due. He is demanding answers of God. Let your proclamation reflect his insistence.

Note that 1:2–3 has a different speaker and far different tone from 2:2–4.

A reading from the Book of the Prophet Habakkuk

How long, O LORD? I cry for **help**
but you do not **listen**!
I cry out to you, "**Violence!**"
but you do **not** intervene.
Why do you let me see **ruin**;
why must I look at **misery**?
Destruction and **violence** are before me;
there is **strife**, and **clamorous discord**.
Then the LORD **answered** me and said:
Write down the **vision** clearly upon the **tablets**,
so that one can **read** it readily.
For the **vision** still has its **time**,
presses **on** to **fulfillment**, and will **not** disappoint;
if it **delays**, **wait** for it,
it will **surely come**, it will **not** be late.
The **rash one** has **no** integrity;
but the **just one**, because of his **faith**, shall **live**.

READING I | The historical period and context of Habakkuk's prophetic tenure are not clear. The superscription of the book simply states, "The oracle which Habakkuk the prophet received in vision" (1:1). Because God says, "For see, I am raising up Chaldea," many biblical scholars have placed the career of Habakkuk near the turn of the sixth century BC when the kingdom of Judah increasingly came under Babylonian power (Habakkuk 1:6). Chaldea is a common name used in the Old Testament for Babylon.

Habakkuk wants some answers. He wants an explanation for why God pays no heed to, or steps in to halt, "destruction and violence." While the prophet perhaps asked this question in relation to the oppressive behavior of Judah's king and ruling elite, who squeezed tribute to Babylon from the people of Judah, the query is a classic question of a more general theological problem called theodicy. If God is good and powerful enough to prevent evil from happening, then why does God permit the evil to occur? The question is perennial, recurring whenever disaster, of human or natural origin, causes

distress and calamity. "God willed it" is not a suitable answer to the problem of theodicy. The one who suffers, like Habakkuk, asks, "Why?" The text provides no clear answer.

Habakkuk 2:4 has had a vigorous life in Christianity apart from the prophetic book in which it is found. It is an important text that demonstrates Paul's belief in the primacy of faith over law. He quotes it in two of his letters (Romans 1:17 and Galatians 3:11). In Galatians, the more openly polemical of the two, Paul uses the phrase to argue for the clarity of his position "that no one is justified before God by law." In Romans, the verse

Stress the word "Beloved" and pause to look at the assembly as you proclaim it.

Emphasize the first line of verse 7, stressing "not" in particular. Slow down to emphasize this trio of virtues.

READING II   2 Timothy 1:6–8, 13–14

A reading from the second Letter of Saint Paul to Timothy

Beloved:
I **remind** you, to **stir** into **flame**
    the **gift** of **God** that you have through the **imposition**
        of my **hands.**
For **God** did not give us a **spirit** of **cowardice**
    but rather of **power** and **love** and **self-control.**
So do **not** be **ashamed** of your **testimony** to our Lord,
    nor of me, a **prisoner** for **his** sake;
    but bear **your** share of **hardship** for the **gospel**
    with the **strength** that comes from **God.**

Take as your **norm** the **sound words** that you **heard** from **me,**
    in the **faith** and **love** that are in **Christ Jesus.**
Guard this **rich trust** with the **help** of the **Holy Spirit**
    that **dwells** within us.

supports Paul's first clear statement of the importance of the Gospel and the gist of the case he will argue in the chapters to come.

READING II In today's second reading, we encounter an example supporting the assignment of 1 Timothy, 2 Timothy, and Titus to a special group within the New Testament known as the "Pastoral Epistles."

In this reading, power, love, and self-control are God's gift to Timothy. They have been provided, it appears, through the imposition of Paul's hands. Perhaps the word that

stands out the most of these three is "self-control." The Greek word is *sōphronismos*, which occurs only here in the New Testament. The word belongs to a family of words having to do with "prudence" and "sobriety" and occurs quite frequently in 1 Timothy, 2 Timothy, and Titus. The closely related virtues of sobriety, prudence, and self-control are standard philosophical virtues of antiquity in addition to being virtues appropriate to a Christian apostle.

Another part of today's reading displaying a distinctive feature of the Pastoral

Epistles is the appearance of "faith" *(pistis)* beside "love" *(agapē)* in 1:13. In 1 Timothy, 2 Timothy, and Titus, love, with the exception of 2 Timothy 1:7, appears either in lists of virtues including faith, or occurs together with faith as a pair (1 Timothy 1:5, 14; 2:15; 4:12; 6:11; 2 Timothy 3:10; Titus 2:2). We admittedly see faith and love together elsewhere (see, for example, 1 Corinthians 13:13), but the nearly exclusive company love keeps with faith in the Pastoral Epistles points to a more explicitly Christian understanding of love, in which love is defined in relation to belief in Jesus Christ.

GOSPEL   Luke 17:5–10

A reading from the holy Gospel according to Luke

The **apostles** said to the **Lord**, "**Increase** our **faith**."
The **Lord** replied,
"If you have **faith** the size of a **mustard seed**,
    you would **say** to this mulberry tree,
    '**Be uprooted** and **planted** in the sea,' and it would **obey** you.

"**Who** among you would **say** to your servant
    who has **just** come in from **plowing** or **tending** sheep
        in the field,
    '**Come here immediately** and **take** your **place** at table'?
Would he **not** rather **say** to him,
    '**Prepare** something for **me** to eat.
Put on your **apron** and **wait** on me while I **eat** and **drink**.
You may **eat** and **drink** when I am **finished**'?
Is he **grateful** to that **servant** because he **did** what
        was **commanded**?
So should it **be** with **you**.
When you have **done all** you have been **commanded**,
    say, 'We are **unprofitable** servants;
    we have **done** what we were **obliged** to do.'"

Keep in mind that Jesus asks several rhetorical questions as he teaches.

GOSPEL Matthew reports the incident of Luke 17:5–6 in the context of a healing story. The disciples' recent inability to heal a child, Jesus implies, has to do with their meager faith. Faith the size of a mustard seed could cast a mountain into the sea, but the disciples do not have even this (Matthew 17:20). In Luke, however, Jesus responds to the disciples' request that he increase their faith with a vivid example of faith's extraordinary power to reorder the world beyond human imagining.

What worldly sense is there, after all, in remaining the disciple of a dead man? But the mystery of the cross is not only suffering death, but also Resurrection. A faith that was formerly radical trust in God's care for men and women as he cares for birds and flowers (Luke 12:22–32) now becomes a belief that God's vindication of the crucified Jesus exposes the world's seeming pointlessness as a lie and presages the release of humankind from the prison of the grave.

The Roman Catholic theologian David Tracy writes in *The Analogical Imagination* that belief in Jesus Christ happens whenever one recognizes the truth "that our deepest yearnings for wholeness in ourselves, in history, in nature, in the whole are grounded in the structure of reality itself. We may now dare," Tracy continues, "to let go of our other, usual 'gods'—success, fame, security, self-justification—by letting go into the final reality with which we all must ultimately deal; the power of that pure, unbounded love who is God, the knowledge that reality itself is finally gracious, that existence—ourselves, history, nature—in spite of all is not absurd."

28TH SUNDAY IN ORDINARY TIME

Lectionary #144

READING I   2 Kings 5:14–17

A reading from the second Book of Kings

Naaman = NAH-a-man

Naaman went down and **plunged** into the **Jordan** seven times
    at the **word** of **Elisha**, the **man** of **God**.
His **flesh** became **again** like the **flesh** of a little **child**,
    and he was **clean** of his **leprosy**.

Naaman returned with his whole retinue to the **man** of **God**.
On his **arrival** he stood before **Elisha** and **said**,
    "**Now I know** that there is **no** God in **all** the earth,
    except in Israel.
Please accept a **gift** from your **servant**."

Express Naaman's gratitude by slowing down and proclaiming his words emphatically.

Stress the word "not" in Elisha's denial.

Elisha replied, "**As** the LORD **lives** whom I **serve**, I will **not**
    take it,"
    and **despite Naaman's** urging, he **still** refused.
Naaman said: "If you will **not** accept,
    please let me, your servant, have **two mule-loads** of **earth**,
    for I will **no longer** offer **holocaust** or **sacrifice**
    to **any** other **god** except to the LORD."

READING I   Naaman was not an Israelite. Second Kings 5:1 reports that he was a successful military commander of the kingdom of Aram, which was, at different times, an ally and an enemy of Israel. Although it is impossible to diagnose Naaman's illness with any precision, he obviously suffered from a humiliating and chronic ailment of the skin or flesh. On the recommendation of an Israelite slave girl, Naaman went to Elijah and was healed.

Having been baptized in the Jordan (Luke 3:21–22) and tested in desert (4:1–13), Jesus returns to his hometown of Nazareth and goes to synagogue. Reading and interpreting the daily Torah portion, Jesus inspires no small wonder among his neighbors. But their initially favorable response turns to hostility when Jesus bluntly states, "Amen, I say to you, no prophet is accepted in his own native place." He supports his claim by pointing out that Elijah healed a Sidonian widow's son (1 Kings 7:9–24) and Naaman, a Syrian. To the people of Israel, in front of whom Jesus now speaks, Jesus claims Elijah was not sent (Luke 4:16–30). The reason for the anger of the synagogue congregation is not hard to guess.

It should be clear that Jesus' interpretation of Naaman's healing can be put to various uses in the proclamation and preaching of 2 Kings 5:4–7. One can highlight, for example, the Jewish reaction to Jesus' interpretation of Naaman's healing by Elijah and relate it to the Christian mission's failure to convert the Jewish people in large numbers. One can point out that God and his emissaries show concern for Gentiles *as well as* Jews long before the ministry of Jesus. One has a number of choices to make.

READING II   2 Timothy 2:8–13

A reading from the second Letter of Saint Paul to Timothy

Beloved:
Remember Jesus Christ, **raised** from the **dead**,
    a **descendant** of **David**:
    such is my **gospel**, for which I am **suffering**,
    even to the point of **chains**, like a **criminal**.
But the **word** of **God** is **not chained**.
Therefore, I bear with **everything** for the **sake** of **those**
    who are **chosen**,
    so that **they too** may **obtain** the **salvation** that is
    in **Christ Jesus**,
    together with **eternal glory**.
This **saying** is **trustworthy**:
    If we have **died** with him
    we shall also **live** with him;
    if we **persevere**
    we shall also **reign** with him.
    But if **we deny him**
    he will deny us.
    If we are **unfaithful**
    he remains **faithful**,
    for he **cannot deny** himself.

Stress and pause after the word "Beloved."

Stress and pause before the word "Therefore."

Pay close attention to rhythm of the final stanza and its series of "if . . . we" and "if . . . he."

READING II In Greek, "Gospel" means "good news." The central piece of the Gospel preached *about* Jesus, according to Paul, has to do with his death and Resurrection. This is "good news" only if one believes that what God did for Jesus is made available to others, us, everyone (1 Corinthian 15:3–19). The Gospel preached *by* Jesus, according to Matthew, Mark, and Luke, concerns his death and Resurrection only obliquely and, in any case, was not the subject of his public teaching. In the Gospel of Luke, for example, Jesus predicts his Passion three times (Luke 9:22, 43–45; 18:31–34). On the second and third occasions it is made clear that Jesus makes his prediction in the hearing his disciples alone. So what is the Gospel preached by Jesus? We read it in Jesus' inaugural sermon at Nazareth when Jesus proclaims Isaiah 61:1–2 and 58:6 and promptly informs the startled synagogue: "Today this scripture passage is fulfilled in your hearing" (4:21). We read it in Jesus' reply to the citizens of Capernaum who beg him to remain with them: "To the other towns also I must proclaim the good news of the kingdom of God" (4:43). And we read it in Jesus' reply to people John the Baptist sent to ask, "Are you the one who is to come, or should we look for another?" "Go and tell John," Jesus answers, "what you have seen and heard: the blind regain their sight, the lame walk, lepers are cleansed, the deaf hear, the poor have good news preached to them" (7:20–22). The Gospel preached by Jesus is a combination of words and deeds on behalf of the poor, the lowly, and the vulnerable.

GOSPEL   Luke 17:11–19

A reading from the holy Gospel according to Luke

As **Jesus** continued his **journey** to **Jerusalem**,
  he traveled through **Samaria** and **Galilee**.
As he was entering a **village**, **ten lepers** met him.
They **stood** at a **distance** from him and **raised** their **voices**, saying,
  "**Jesus**, **Master**! Have **pity** on us!"
And when he saw them, he said,
  "**Go show** yourselves to the **priests**."
As they were **going** they were **cleansed**.
And one of them, **realizing** he had been **healed**,
  returned, **glorifying** God in a loud voice;
  and he **fell** at the **feet** of Jesus and **thanked** him.
He was a **Samaritan**.
Jesus **said** in reply,
  "**Ten** were **cleansed**, were they **not**?
Where are the other **nine**?
Has **none** but this **foreigner** returned to give **thanks** to **God**?"
Then he said to him, "**Stand up** and **go**;
  your **faith** has **saved** you."

Samaria = Sah-MAR-i-ya
Galilee = GAL-li-lee

Samaritan = Sah-MAR-i-tan
Emphasize the words "He was a Samaritan."

Proclaim Jesus' questions as questions.

Stress the word "faith" in the final line.

GOSPEL The only one of the lepers cleansed by Jesus to thank him is a Samaritan. The Samaritans, Father Hans-Josef Klauck writes in *Magic and Paganism in Early Christianity*, "can be considered as half-siblings or hostile brothers of the Jewish people." The Samaritans probably split off from Judaism in the fifth century before Christ. They kept the five books of Moses but rejected the second Temple in Jerusalem in favor of worship in their own territory on Mount Gerizim. Samaria is therefore a religious designation.

The Samaritans' religious differences with Judaism arise in the conversation between Jesus and the woman at the well in John 4. "Our ancestors worshiped on this mountain," the woman says to Jesus, "but you people say the place to worship is in Jerusalem" (John 4:20). Luke's Gospel alludes to this religious disagreement only once, when a Samaritan village denies Jesus welcome "because the destination of his journey was Jerusalem" (9:51–56). Beside this we read only of the so-called "Good Samaritan" of 10:30–35 and the grateful Samaritan of today's reading. Of Samaria we read in the companion work to Luke's Gospel, the Acts of the Apostles, that the 11 apostles are to be Jesus' witnesses "in Jerusalem, throughout Judea and Samaria, and to the ends of the earth" (Acts 1:8).

The ten lepers experience the Gospel preached *by* Jesus on their skins. They can see and feel it. The thankful and faithful response of the Samaritan, while striking, does not eclipse the healing of the other nine, whose immediate obedience to Jesus' command perhaps expresses an equal degree of gratitude.

29TH SUNDAY IN ORDINARY TIME

Lectionary #147

READING I   Exodus 17:8–13

A reading from the Book of Exodus

In those days, **Amalek** came and waged **war** against **Israel**.
Moses, therefore, said to **Joshua**,
   "Pick out certain men,
   and tomorrow go out and engage **Amalek** in battle.
I will be standing on top of the hill
   with the **staff** of **God** in my **hand**."
So **Joshua** did as **Moses** told him:
   he engaged **Amalek** in battle
   after **Moses** had climbed to the top of the hill
      with **Aaron** and **Hur**.
As long as **Moses** kept his **hands** raised up,
   Israel had the **better** of the fight,
   but when he let his **hands** rest,
   Amalek had the **better** of the fight.
Moses' hands, however, grew **tired**;
   so they put a **rock** in **place** for him to **sit** on.
Meanwhile **Aaron** and **Hur** supported his **hands**,
   one on one side and **one** on the other,
   so that his **hands** remained steady till **sunset**.
And **Joshua** mowed down **Amalek** and his **people**
   with the **edge** of the **sword**.

Amalek = AH-mah-lek

Hur = Hoor

Pause between "Amalek had the better of the fight" and "Moses' hands, however, grew tired."

Slow down to emphasize the final sentence.

READING I   On the American frontier in the eighteenth and nineteenth centuries, an average home contained very few books, and often none, beside the Bible. The demand of more recent years for novelty and fresh entertainments was expensive and often impossible to satisfy back then. Thus, many readers contented themselves with the Bible and therefore knew, perhaps better than ourselves, the wealth of its various entertainments. One could read of the romantic and political intrigues of David, Bathsheba, and Absalom in 2 Samuel; the novella of Joseph's betrayal and forgiveness of his brothers in Genesis; the love poetry of the Song of Songs; the philosophical speculations of Ecclesiastes; and Paul's adventures over land and sea in Acts. Whatever its spiritual significance, Israel's fight with Amalek is a ripping vignette of the powers of spirit and sword.

But what is its spiritual significance? Is it enough to say, with today's second reading, that "All Scripture is inspired by God"? (See 2 Timothy 3:16.) How is the Gospel served by text celebrating the day when "Joshua mowed down Amalek and his people with the edge of the sword"?

This was a kind of question early Catholic Christians asked and answered in a variety of ways. They had to, for certain other Christians wanted to jettison the Old Testament from the Church entirely. And so Catholic Christians studied its writings in an effort to flesh out their belief that Christ's death and Resurrection happened, as Paul wrote, "according to the scriptures" (1 Corinthians 15:3–4). To whatever Old Testament passages Paul may have had in mind, later Catholic Christians added their own.

READING II   2 Timothy 3:14—4:2

A reading from the second Letter of Saint Paul to Timothy

Stress the word "Beloved" and pause after it.

Beloved:

Remain **faithful** to what you have **learned** and **believed**,
    because you **know** from **whom** you **learned** it,
      and that from **infancy** you have known the **sacred Scriptures**,
    which are **capable** of giving you **wisdom** for **salvation**
    through **faith** in **Christ Jesus**.

Emphasize the word "All."

All **Scripture** is **inspired** by **God**
    and is **useful** for **teaching**, for **refutation**, for **correction**,
    and for **training** in **righteousness**,
    so that **one** who **belongs** to **God** may be **competent**,
    equipped for **every** good work.

Slow down to emphasize the sentence beginning with "I charge you." This is the language of commission.

I **charge** you in the presence of **God** and of **Christ Jesus**,
    who will **judge** the **living** and the **dead**,
    and by his **appearing** and his kingly **power**:
    proclaim the **word**;
    be **persistent** whether it is **convenient** or **inconvenient**;
    convince, **reprimand**, **encourage** through **all patience**
      and **teaching**.

READING II The previous commentary provides one example of how early Catholic Christians interpreted even seemingly difficult texts in the service of their proclamation of Jesus Christ. In today's reading they would have found useful support in this endeavor. "All Scripture," we read in 2 Timothy 3:16, "is inspired by God." But what can it mean that lines penned by a human author have been "inspired by God"? And how should a belief in the divine inspiration of scripture affect the way we understand it?

In the third century Origen of Alexandria argued in *On First Principles* that interpretations according to the "mere letter" made it impossible to find Christ in the Old Testament. Attention to the "mere letter" also allowed other Christians to claim that the God of the Old Testament was not the same as the God of the New and was, in fact, evil (4.2). Origen also noted that Catholic Christians were inconsistent readers; they freely gave spiritual readings to some hard parts of the Bible but confessed ignorance about other obscure passages. Origen thus attempted to present a consistent rationale for reading scripture

spiritually. If what scripture says makes good and reasonable sense, then its spiritual and its "mere letter" meanings converge. But when scripture says something wrong or impossible, it is a clue woven into the fabric of scripture that a spiritual meaning different from the "mere letter" is present.

Even if Origen's ideas do not square with our own (Origen himself was capable of deciding this issue differently), we may consider them if ever we are told that the Bible is "inerrant" (meaning "without error") and must always be taken literally. Origen

GOSPEL   Luke 18:1–8

A reading from the holy Gospel according to Luke

Jesus told his **disciples** a parable
   about the necessity for them to **pray always**
      without becoming **weary**.
He said, "There was a **judge** in a certain town
   who **neither feared God** nor **respected** any **human being**.
And a **widow** in that town used to **come** to him and **say**,
   '**Render** a just decision for me against my **adversary**.'
For a **long time** the judge was **unwilling**, but eventually
    he thought,
   'While it is **true** that I neither **fear God** nor **respect**
    any **human being**,
   because this **widow** keeps **bothering** me
   I shall **deliver** a just **decision** for her
   lest she finally **come** and **strike** me.'"
The **Lord** said, "**Pay attention** to what the **dishonest judge** says.
Will not **God** then secure the **rights** of his **chosen** ones
   who call **out** to him **day** and **night**?
Will he be **slow** to **answer** them?
I **tell** you, he will **see to it** that **justice** is **done** for them **speedily**.
But when the **Son** of **Man** comes, will he find **faith** on **earth**?"

Keep in mind the multiple speaking parts. The widow is insistent; the judge has had all he can take.

Bear in mind Jesus' rhetorical questions and be sure to proclaim them as such.

---

believed the Bible was inerrant. And he believed he was reading literally. But he also believed that the Holy Spirit was reasonable, did not expect him or the Church to believe what wise and faithful members of the Church would think impossible or wrong, and wished him to know as much as he could of the mysteries hidden in the letters on the pages open before him.

GOSPEL | The figurative stories Jesus tells, only some of which the evangelists call parables, are not all

allegories like the parable of the sower, for example. Why can we not simply read the parable of the judge and the widow as an allegory like the parable of the sower? Well, let us say that the "dishonest judge" equals God; the widow equals the ones who "call out day and night" to God in prayer. Is it reasonable to think that Luke would offer a scene in which Jesus compared God the Father to a dishonest judge?

The way Jesus likely intends his disciples to interpret this passage is as an argument "from the lesser to the greater." This

kind of argument is quite common in rabbinic discourse and in Greek persuasive speech. Compare Luke 12:28. "If God so clothes the grass in the field that grows today and is thrown into the oven tomorrow," Jesus reasons, "will he not much more provide for you?" If a dishonest judge pays attention to a widow's persistent entreaties, how much more will God, who is not dishonest, heed persistence in prayer?

30TH SUNDAY IN ORDINARY TIME

Lectionary #150

READING I   Sirach 35:12–14, 16–18

A reading from the Book of Sirach

The LORD is a **God** of **justice**,
    who knows **no** favorites.
Though not **unduly partial** toward the **weak**,
    yet he **hears** the **cry** of the **oppressed**.
The LORD is **not deaf** to the **wail** of the **orphan**,
    nor to the **widow** when she **pours** out her **complaint**.
The **one** who **serves God willingly** is **heard**;
    his **petition** reaches the **heavens**.
The **prayer** of the **lowly pierces** the **clouds**;
    it does **not rest** till it **reaches** its goal,
nor will it **withdraw** till the **Most High responds**,
    judges justly and **affirms** the **right**,
and the LORD will **not delay**.

Pause between the reading's halves.

READING I   Those of us who have access to decent education, health care, nutrition, and enjoy political, civil, and religious liberties beyond anything in history may find this reading hard. For Sirach writes that God's answer to the persistent "prayer of the lowly" is just judgment and that "he will not be still till he breaks the backs of the merciless and wreaks vengeance upon the proud; Till he destroys the haughty root and branch, and smashes the scepter of the wicked" (Sirach 35:17–22). God is not merely the protector of the lowly but the judge of their exploiters. We do well to recall with this reading the words of Mary in the Magnificat: "The Mighty One," God, "has shown might with his arm, dispersed the arrogant of mind and heart. He has thrown down the rulers from their thrones, but lifted up the lowly" (1:49–52).

Who are the lowly among us? We can and must name first of all the poorest of the world, whose very condition of life includes the looming threat of death. There may be fewer of these in Canada and the United States, but many further south in Central and South America, Africa, Asia, Eastern Europe, and the Middle East. In the Americas, many of these are Roman Catholic brethren.

The Second Vatican Council, in its wide-ranging Pastoral Constitution on the Church in the Modern World *(Gaudium et spes)*, held that social and economic arrangements of inequality oppose the teaching of the Roman Catholic Church about the dignity of the human person *(Gaudium et spes, #29.3)*. The Council here bears witness with elegant simplicity to the substance of today's selection from Sirach. The "God of justice, who knows no favorites," has little tolerance for the abuse of anyone (Sirach, 35:15).

READING II   2 Timothy 4:6–8, 16–18

A reading from the second Letter of Saint Paul to Timothy

Beloved:
I am **already** being **poured out** like a libation,
    and the time of my departure is at hand.
I have **competed well**; I have **finished** the race;
    I have **kept** the faith.
From now on the **crown** of **righteousness** awaits me,
    which the **Lord**, the **just judge**,
    will **award** to me on that day, and **not only** to **me**,
    but to all who have **longed** for his **appearance**.

At my first defense **no one** appeared on my behalf,
    but **everyone** deserted me.
May it **not** be held **against** them!
But the **Lord stood by** me and **gave** me strength,
    so that through me the **proclamation** might be **completed**
    and all the **Gentiles** might hear it.
And I was **rescued** from the **lion's mouth**.
The **Lord** will rescue me from **every evil threat**
    and will bring me **safe** to his **heavenly kingdom**.
To him be **glory forever** and **ever**. **Amen**.

Emphasize and pause after the word "Beloved."
Stress the word "already."

Emphasize "no one" and declare with some conviction the words "May it not be held against them!"

READING II In this reading, as we have previously seen (September 30, Commentary II), the Christian life is depicted through athletic metaphor and imagery. In this case, the life belongs to the apostle Paul, here depicted as a libation poured out.

Although it might not seem so at first, this detail is also part of the passage's athletic theme. Greek games were usually religious affairs. They began and concluded with sacrificial drink offerings, or libations, poured out to the gods to whom the games were dedicated. The Greek verb *spendō*, which refers specifically to the pouring of libations in religious contexts, here depicts what is happening to Paul at the end of his life.

In Philippians 2:17, Paul uses the verb *spendō* in a similar way. In 2:14–15, he urges the Philippians to "do everything without grumbling or questioning, that you may be blameless and innocent, children of God without blemish." Why does he urge them to behave in this way? "So that my boast for the day of Christ may be that I did not run in vain. But, even if I am poured out *[spendō]* as a libation upon the sacrificial service of your faith, I rejoice and share my joy with all of you" (Philippians 2:14–17). Here also Paul's apostolate is a race with its end imagined as a concluding sacrificial rite.

In both 2 Timothy and Philippians, Paul is in jail. This circumstance alone justifies talk of death. Ancient jails were not places where people served sentences of imprisonment. They were rather holding pens where people awaited the adjudication of their cases and the execution of their sentences. Death was often the sentence, even for minor infractions of law or custom. Both letters, therefore, assume a situation of maximum uncertainty for Paul.

GOSPEL   Luke 18:9–14

A reading from the holy Gospel according to Luke

Jesus addressed this **parable**
    to those who were **convinced** of their **own righteousness**
    and **despised everyone else**.
"Two people went up to the temple area to pray;
    one was a **Pharisee** and the other was a **tax collector**.
The **Pharisee** took up his position and spoke this prayer
    to himself,
    'O **God**, **I** thank **you** that I am **not** like the rest of **humanity**—
    greedy, dishonest, adulterous—or even like this **tax collector**.
I fast **twice** a week, and I pay **tithes** on my **whole** income.'
But the **tax collector** stood off at **a distance**
    and would not even **raise** his **eyes** to **heaven**
    but **beat** his **breast** and **prayed**,
    'O **God**, be **merciful** to me a **sinner**.'
I **tell** you, the **latter** went home **justified**, **not** the **former**;
    for whoever **exalts** himself will be **humbled**,
    and the one who **humbles** himself will be **exalted**."

Proclaim the Pharisee's words with all of the irritating sanctimony Luke clearly intends.

Luke intends the tax collector as a humble counterpart to the self-satisfied Pharisee. Slow down and deliver his lines without any particular flourish.

GOSPEL   In today's Gospel selection, two men pray in public (see Matthew 6:5–6). One man is a Pharisee, one a tax collector. These men could not be more different. The tax collector squeezes money out of his fellow Jews on behalf of Rome, helps himself to a slice of the profits, and gives the rest to his bosses. For a poor person to refuse him might mean violence, torture, or even crucifixion. The Pharisee, on the other hand, keeps the traditions of Israel alive even under the boot of Roman occupation. Without Pharisees like him, Judaism might have dwindled and died after the

Romans burned and destroyed the Temple in the year 70 AD. And yet it is the tax collector, not the Pharisee, who goes home justified!

Jesus directs this parable to people who exhibit two symptoms of the same sickness (Luke 8:9). Any of us imagining ourselves morally superior to people we deem inferior suffer from it. Confronted with a God who came to save sinners, not the righteous (Luke 5:32), we are faced with a horrible truth: all our good works, alms, scripture study, prayer, Masses, devotions, penance, and sacraments (see Amos 5:21–24) affect neither how much God loves us, nor how

much God loves others; whether others cultivate brazen sin and act reprehensibly, or simply live and think differently than ourselves, our pious opinions cannot influence God's love for those we suppose stand beneath us. To those of us who too much resemble this Pharisee, there is cause for immense gratitude and relief, and perhaps the beginning of humility, in accepting that God forgives the proud and the smug as surely as anyone.

ALL SAINTS

Lectionary #667

READING I   Revelation 7:2–4, 9–14

A reading from the Book of Revelation

I, **John**, saw **another angel** come up from the **East**,
    holding the **seal** of the living **God**.
He cried out in a loud voice to the four angels
    who were given power to **damage** the **land** and the **sea**,
    "Do **not damage** the **land** or the **sea** or the **trees**
    until we put the seal on the foreheads of the **servants**
        of our **God**."
I heard the **number** of those who had been **marked** with the seal,
    one hundred and forty-four thousand marked
    from **every** tribe of the children of **Israel**.

After this I had a **vision** of a **great multitude**,
    which **no one** could **count**,
    from **every nation**, **race**, **people**, and **tongue**.
They stood before the **throne** and before the **Lamb**,
    wearing **white robes** and holding **palm branches** in their hands.
They cried out in a loud voice:
    "**Salvation** comes from our **God**,
    who is **seated** on the **throne**,
    and from the **Lamb**."

All the **angels** stood around the **throne**
    and around the **elders** and the **four living creatures**.
They **prostrated** themselves before the **throne**,
    worshiped **God**, and exclaimed:

Proclaim the angels' words, as well as the antiphons, strongly, but without shouting. Let them really ring out.

READING I   In today's reading from the book of Revelation, we encounter a traditional feature of the apocalyptic genre of literature. In apocalypses such as Daniel 7—12, the person receiving the vision or, as the case may be, the "tour" of heaven, requires the aid of a heavenly being to interpret and understand the heavenly sights laid out before him. In Daniel, for example, the angel Gabriel explains to Daniel the significance of what he sees. In today's reading, the interpreter's role is performed by one of the 24 elders.

Pay close attention to the liturgical elements of this reading. Notice how in verse 10 the great crowd offers words of praise answered by the angels, elders, and living creatures in verse 12. This is *antiphonal* praise, which means that the praise alternates among different parts of the worshipping assembly. Think of the psalm between the first and second readings of the Mass, which usually alternates between a lector and the assembly.

The scene in today's reading touches on an important component of Roman Catholic religious belief and imagination.

Roman Catholics have often conceived of the Mass in more than merely "terrestrial" terms. When we offer the petitions of the Mass, for example, we offer them not only together with Pope, bishop, and clergy, but also with the angels and saints. The prayers of the Mass join the unending hymn of praise of heaven. The vision of John of Patmos offers an important scriptural witness to this understanding of the Mass.

"**Amen. Blessing** and **glory**, **wisdom** and **thanksgiving**,
  honor, **power**, and **might**
    be to our **God forever** and **ever**. **Amen**."

Pay attention to the conversation between the elder and John. John is a foreigner in this world, perhaps a little scared. The elder is far more self-assured.

Then one of the elders spoke up and said to me,
  "**Who** are these wearing **white robes**, and **where** did they
    come from?"
I said to him, "My lord, **you** are the one who knows."
He said to me,
  "**These** are the **ones** who have **survived** the time
    of **great distress**;
  they have **washed** their **robes**
  and made them **white** in the **Blood** of the **Lamb**."

READING II   1 John 3:1–3

A reading from the first Letter of Saint John

Beloved:

Emphasize the word "Beloved" both times it occurs. Pause after the first instance.

See what **love** the Father has **bestowed** on us
  that we may be called the **children** of **God**.
Yet **so** we **are**.
The reason the world does **not know us**
  is that it did **not know him**.
Beloved, we are **God's children** now;
  what we **shall** be has **not yet** been **revealed**.
We **do** know that when it is **revealed** we shall be **like** him,
  for we shall **see** him as he **is**.

Stress and pause after the word "Everyone."

Everyone who has this **hope** based on him makes **himself pure**,
  as **he** is **pure**.

READING II Having noted the importance of "the image of motherhood" in addition to the language of God's fatherhood, the Catechism states the following: "The language of faith thus draws on the human experience of parents, who are in a way the first representatives of God for man. But this experience also tells us that human parents are fallible and can disfigure the face of fatherhood and motherhood. We ought therefore to recall that God transcends the human distinction between the sexes. He is neither man nor woman: he is God. He also transcends human fatherhood and

motherhood, although he is their origin and standard: no one is father as God is Father" (#239). To say, in this light, that "we are God's children now" (1 John 3:2) requires us to reflect on the incapacity of the language of family to describe the relation of God to ourselves. It is, however, the language we have, and so we use it.

In the Gospel of John, which is closely related to the letter from which this reading comes, we read that although some did not accept "the light," by which John means Jesus, some did accept it. To those who accepted Jesus, he "gave power to become

children of God, to those who believe in his name, who were born not by natural generation nor by human choice nor by a man's decision but of God" (John 1:12–13).

GOSPEL Many Roman Catholics, at one point or another, have been asked the following question by Protestant or non-Christian friends: "What is it with Catholics and saints?" As with much else about Roman Catholicism, different Catholics approach the question differently.

GOSPEL   Matthew 5:1–12a

A reading from the holy Gospel according to Matthew

When **Jesus** saw the crowds, he went up the mountain,
   and after he had sat down, his **disciples** came to him.
He began to **teach** them, saying:
   "**Blessed** are the **poor** in **spirit**,
     for **theirs** is the **Kingdom** of **heaven**.
Blessed are they who **mourn**,
   for **they** will be **comforted**.
Blessed are the **meek**,
   for **they** will **inherit** the land.
Blessed are they who **hunger** and **thirst** for **righteousness**,
   for **they** will be **satisfied**.
Blessed are the **merciful**,
   for **they** will be shown **mercy**.
Blessed are the **clean** of **heart**,
   for **they** will see **God**.
Blessed are the **peacemakers**,
   for **they** will be called **children** of **God**.
Blessed are they who are **persecuted** for the **sake**
    of **righteousness**,
   for **theirs** is the **Kingdom** of **heaven**.
Blessed are you when they **insult** you and **persecute** you
   and utter every kind of **evil** against you **falsely** because of
    me.
Rejoice and be **glad**,
   for your **reward** will be **great** in **heaven**."

Stress the word "Blessed."

Pause between each half of each beatitude.

In the second half of each beatitude, stress the word "they."

Slow down and emphasize the sentence beginning with "Rejoice and be glad."

But the honor shown to the saints by Roman Catholics is undeniable and quite ancient.

Canonization is a procedure by which the heroism and fidelity of certain Christians are recognized as examples of holiness to others (Catechism, #828). The saints, however, comprise a much larger group than the number of the canonized. The biblical lands, for example, are dotted with churches and shrines dedicated to people never recognized by this procedure. We expand the definition even further. The Greek word for saint is *hagios,* which simply means "holy one." Read, for example, Philippians 1:1.

Paul addresses his letter to "all the holy ones who are in Christ Jesus in Philippi." The Greek word for "holy ones" is the same as the word for saint. For Paul, a saint was a believer in Jesus Christ presumed to be in good standing with Paul himself and the Christian assemblies Paul served.

While some Protestants once derided the saints as a remnant of "polytheism" (see Catechism, #2112), the place of saints in the piety of Roman Catholicism is not so easily traded away. One would think that martyr saints especially, men and women "perse-cuted for the sake of righteousness," merit the honor of the faithful.

Whether we see the saints as our patrons, as did many people in the late Roman Empire, or as models of blessed lives well lived, or as friends, confidantes, or confessors, who stand by our sides at work, at home, or one pew over, the saints still crowd the pathways of the Roman Catholic religious mind, as they not only praise God but also make intercession to him on our behalf.

COMMEMORATION OF ALL THE FAITHFUL DEPARTED

Lectionary #668

READING I   Wisdom 3:1–9

A reading from the Book of Wisdom

The **souls** of the **just** are in the **hand** of **God**,
  and no **torment** shall **touch** them.
They **seemed**, in the **view** of the **foolish**, to be **dead**;
  and their **passing away** was thought an **affliction**
  and their **going forth** from us, utter **destruction**.
But they are in **peace**.
For if in the **sight** of **others**, indeed they be **punished**,
  yet is their **hope** full of immortality;
chastised a **little**, they shall be **greatly blessed**,
  because **God** tried them
  and found them **worthy** of himself.
As **gold** in the **furnace**, he **proved** them,
  and as **sacrificial offerings** he **took** them to himself.
In the **time** of their **visitation** they shall **shine**,
  and shall **dart** about as **sparks** through **stubble**;
they shall **judge nations** and **rule** over **peoples**,
  and the LORD shall be their **King forever**.
Those who **trust** in him shall **understand truth**,
  and the **faithful** shall **abide** with him in **love**:
because **grace** and **mercy** are with his **holy ones**,
  and his **care** is with his **elect**.

Deliver this line slowly and with great care.

The readings given here are suggestions. Any readings from the Lectionary for the Commemoration of All the Faithful Departed (#668) or the Masses for the Dead (#1011–1016) may be used.

READING I   The book of Wisdom was originally composed in Greek around the time of Jesus' birth. Its author was a Jew well acquainted with a philosophical understanding of Judaism similar to that of the great Jewish philosopher and Bible interpreter, Philo of Alexandria. Alexandria, Egypt is the most likely site of Wisdom's composition.

Christianity inherited the doctrine of the soul's immortality from both Judaism of the second temple period and Greek philosophy, most notably from Platonism and Stoicism. The image of righteous souls as sparks running through a field of dry stubble squares rather well with what we know of Stoic conceptions of the soul as a fiery substance. Judaism before the Greek period had *Sheol*, a bleak abode of the dead inhabited by good and bad alike. Hades in traditional Greek religious thought was a similarly dreary place. In Judaism, however, the idea of the blessed fate of righteous souls gained currency, as far as we can tell, around the time of the Maccabean revolt in the second century BC.

This reading from Wisdom follows a section in which certain people, who at first seem like harmless pleasure seekers (2:1–9), shortly declare their intention to lie in wait for a righteous man in order to abuse, torture, and kill him (2:10–20). Because he is pious, the righteous man's tormentors hold him in utter contempt and plot to kill him.

READING II   Romans 5:5–11

A reading from the Letter of Saint Paul to the Romans

Brothers and **sisters:**
Hope does **not** disappoint,
  because the **love** of **God** has been **poured out** into our **hearts**
  through the **Holy Spirit** that has been **given** to us.
For **Christ**, while we were **still helpless**,
  died at the appointed time for the **ungodly**.
Indeed, only with **difficulty** does one **die** for a **just person**,
  though **perhaps** for a **good person**
  one might **even** find **courage** to **die**.
But **God** proves his **love** for us
  in that while we were still **sinners** Christ **died** for us.
How much more then, since we are **now justified** by his **blood**,
  will we be **saved** through him from the **wrath**.
Indeed, if, while we were **enemies**,
  we were **reconciled** to God through the **death** of his **Son**,
  how much more, once **reconciled**,
  will we be **saved** by his **life**.
Not only **that**,
  but we **also** boast of **God** through our **Lord Jesus Christ**,
  through whom we have now received **reconciliation**.

Or:

Pause briefly before proclaiming the final two verses.

But in words of consolation to those of us who have ever suffered, or even now still suffer the death of a faithful loved one, the author of Wisdom offers us the collected wisdom of his religious and philosophical traditions: though it may seem so, the faithful departed are *not* dead; they live on in the hands of God.

READING II   **ROMANS 5.** Paul and his earliest known biographer, the author of Acts, maintain that an experience of the risen Jesus began Paul's new

life in the service of the church (Acts 9:1–19; 1 Corinthians 9:1, 15:8; Galatians 1:13–16). Whatever happened to Paul, it was clearly in the way of an immense personal upheaval and convinced him that he had to proclaim Jesus Christ as the only answer for the world. But what was humanity's problem? And how did the cross and Resurrection of Jesus provide a solution?

Paul's letter to the Romans is an answer to this and many other questions. We see part of the problem outlined in this reading. Human beings are "ungodly," even "enemies" of God. If this seems a little extreme,

consider that Paul has spent much of the first three chapters of Romans building toward the conclusion that "all have sinned and are deprived of the glory of God" (3:22).

Paul sees this sin and deprivation in a different way for Gentiles and Jews. Gentiles, although they received no law as did the Jews, were provided with a world containing evidence of its maker. But they ignored this evidence, preferring to worship the creation instead. The Jews, Paul contends, broke the law they were given. Although God initially treated these two groups of

READING II   Romans 6:3–9

A reading from the Letter of Saint Paul to the Romans

Brothers and **sisters**:

Are you **unaware** that **we** who were **baptized** into **Christ Jesus**
  were **baptized** into his **death**?
We were indeed **buried** with him through **baptism** into **death**,
  so that, just as **Christ** was **raised** from the **dead**
  by the **glory** of the **Father**,
  we too might **live** in **newness of life**.

Pause before beginning the second stanza.

For if we have **grown** into **union** with him through a **death**
    like his,
  we shall also be **united** with him in the **resurrection**.
We know that our **old** self was **crucified** with him,
  so that our **sinful body** might be **done away** with,
  that we might **no longer** be in **slavery** to **sin**.
For a **dead** person has been **absolved** from sin.
If, then, we have **died** with **Christ**,
  we believe that we shall also **live** with him.
We know that **Christ**, raised from the **dead**, **dies** no more;
  death no longer has **power** over him.

people differently, sharing the law with one and not the other, they are at last united in a common plight: *all* are ungodly.

The love of God for all humanity, according to Paul, is clear from Jesus' death on humanity's behalf. It would have been something indeed, Paul observes, had the world's people deserved Christ's act. Far more wondrous is the fact that Jesus died for people who did *not* deserve it all. For Paul, the proof of God's reconciling love is revealed in a deed on behalf of people who do not deserve it. The universal human problem is sin. The universal divine solution, proclaimed by the cross, is reconciling love.

ROMANS 6. The direct ancestor of Christian Baptism is the baptism of John the Baptist. As Luke's Gospel says, John "went throughout the whole region of the Jordan proclaiming a baptism for the forgiveness of sins" (Luke 3:3). There is no mention in this verse of baptism into death, nor any description of baptism as burial. On the other hand, we read nothing about baptism as newness of life, old selves and new selves, the slavery of sin, union through death, union in Resurrection, and so on. All of these concepts are present in Romans 6:3–9. The only aspect of today's reading that resonates at all with Luke's description of John's baptism is the reference in Romans 6:7 to the absolution of sin. But even there the meaning of Romans seems very different than Luke's. Christian Baptism has clearly developed somewhat in the 30 years separating the ministry of John the Baptist (ca. 29 AD) and Paul's letter to the Romans (ca. 60 AD).

GOSPEL   John 6:37–40

A reading from the holy Gospel according to John

Jesus said to the **crowds**:
"**Everything** that the **Father** gives me will **come** to me,
　　and I will **not** reject **anyone** who **comes** to me,
　　　　because I **came** down from **heaven** not to do my **own will**
　　　　but the **will** of the one who **sent** me.
And **this** is the **will** of the **one** who **sent** me,
　　that I should not **lose anything** of what he **gave** me,
　　but that I should **raise** it on the **last day**.
For **this** is the **will** of my **Father**,
　　that **everyone** who sees the **Son** and **believes** in him
　　may have **eternal life**,
　　and I shall **raise** him on the **last day**."

Pause briefly before proclaiming these words of Jesus.

John's baptism was a ritual washing by which the baptized expressed public repentance for wrongs done and promised to adhere to a better standard in the future. It may have also served as a rite of initiation into John's religious community. Many of the first disciples, including Jesus, were likely members of this community. In Acts, the apostles recall the baptism of John as the beginning of their association with Jesus (Acts 1:21–22).

Christian Baptism in this reading is about conformity to Jesus and participation in his life. For Paul, Jesus Christ is "the first fruits of those who have fallen asleep" (1 Corinthians 15:20), the first evidence of the general Resurrection. Forgiveness of sins is an undeniable part of this conformity and participation.

GOSPEL Jesus' statement in this passage about his Father's will should reassure us: "I should not lose anything of what he gave me, but . . . raise it on the last day" (6:39). These words allude to the prayer of Jesus on the eve of his Passion: "When I was with them I protected them in your name that you gave me, and I guarded them, and none of them was lost except the son of destruction, in order that the scripture might be fulfilled" (17:12). Not only this but also Jesus words in 6:39 and 17:12 are fulfilled by Jesus' entreaty that his disciples might go free and not suffer the fate in store for him (18:8–9).

...ury #153

...DING I   Wisdom 11:22—12:2

...ding from the Book of Wisdom

...fore the LORD the whole **universe** is as a **grain** from
    a **balance**
  or a **drop** of morning **dew** come down upon the **earth**.
...ut you have **mercy** on **all**, because you can **do all things**;
    and you overlook people's sins that they may **repent**.
For you **love all** things that **are**
    and **loathe nothing** that you have **made**;
    for what you **hated**, you would not have **fashioned**.
And how could a thing **remain**, unless you **willed** it;
    or be **preserved**, had it not been **called forth** by you?
But you **spare** all things, because they are **yours**,
    O LORD and **lover** of **souls**,
    for your **imperishable spirit** is in **all** things!
Therefore you **rebuke** offenders **little** by **little**,
    warn them and **remind** them of the **sins** they are
        committing,
    that they may **abandon** their **wickedness** and **believe** in
        you, **O LORD**!

The final stanza contains two phrases beginning with "O Lord." Slow down and emphasize both of them.

READING I   On its own, this selection from the book of Wisdom is a magisterial walk of the theological tightrope, with images of God's *transcendence* (distance and difference from creation) balancing images of divine *immanence* (closeness and involvement with creation). For the context in which the author offers these words, read back to 11:15. Here the author writes of people in possession of "senseless wicked thoughts, which misled them into worshipping dumb serpents and worthless insects" (Wisdom 11:15). The author describes

Egyptians, who were frequently attacked in antiquity by Jews and Greeks for their veneration of animals and worship of animal deities. The author's reflection on God's mercy, which seems quite general in outlook based on the selection provided by the Lectionary, comes on the heels of a very negative description of native Egyptian religion.

In Romans 1:18–32, Paul identifies idolatry, which is the honor of creature in place of the Creator, as the root sin of the Gentiles. He does so in language demonstrating his familiarity with the perspective of the author of Wisdom concerning Egyptian religion

(see Romans 1:21–23). Both Paul and the author of Wisdom were both Greek-speaking Jews of the urban Diaspora. Their points of agreement can be explained, in part, by their use of a traditional polemical assessment of Gentile religion in comparison with Judaism. We see older examples in such texts as Isaiah 44:9–20, in which idol makers are mocked.

The conception of God as a merciful but all-powerful disciplinarian is part of this author's larger interpretation of the Exodus,

READING II   2 Thessalonians 1:11—2:2

**A reading from the second Letter of Saint Paul
to the Thessalonians**

Brothers and **sisters**:
We **always pray** for you,
that our **God** may make you **worthy** of his **calling**
and powerfully bring to fulfillment **every** good purpose
and **every** effort of faith,
that the **name** of our Lord Jesus may be **glorified** in **you**,
and **you** in **him**,
in accord with the **grace** of our **God** and **Lord Jesus Christ**.

We **ask** you, **brothers** and **sisters**,
with regard to the **coming** of our **Lord Jesus Christ**
and our **assembling** with him,
not to be **shaken** out of your minds suddenly, or to be **alarmed**
either by a "**spirit**," or by an **oral statement**,
or by a **letter allegedly** from **us**
to the effect that the **day** of the **Lord** is at **hand**.

Pause after the first "brothers and sisters."
Look at the assembly when you proclaim
both occurrences of the phrase.

which was, in a symbolic sense, a classroom where Israel learned of its special election and was instructed in virtue. The idea is close to the Roman Catholic understanding of Old Testament narrative as "salvation history," in which God's providential plan for humanity unfolds over time, coming to decisive fruition in the cross of Jesus Christ, his Resurrection, and the birth and spread of the Church.

READING II We actually know very little about the mechanics of Paul's missionary network. Whatever the circumstances of 2 Thessalonians' composition, the Roman Catholic Church unequivocally affirms it as divinely inspired scripture, both according to tradition and the relevant canons and decrees of the Council of Trent. (Please see November 11, Commentary II for further discussion of this question).

GOSPEL An encounter with a rich official in Luke 18:18–23 provides Jesus with a teaching opportunity. "How hard it is," Jesus says in response to the official's sorrow upon being told to renounce his wealth, "for those who have wealth to enter the kingdom of God. For it is easier for a camel to pass through the eye of a needle than for a rich person to enter the kingdom of God." Those within earshot grow concerned at this and ask, "Then who can

Jericho = JER-ih-koh

Zachaeus = Zah-KAI-yus

Proclaim Zacchaeus' promises of money
and emphasize both figures ("half" and
"four times over").

GOSPEL Luke 19:1–10

A reading from the holy Gospel according to Luke

At that time, **Jesus** came to **Jericho** and intended
   to pass through the town.
Now a man there named **Zacchaeus**,
   who was a chief tax collector and also a **wealthy** man,
   was seeking to see **who Jesus was**;
   but he could not **see** him because of the **crowd**,
   for he was **short** in **stature**.
So he **ran** ahead and **climbed** a sycamore tree in order to **see Jesus**,
   who was about to **pass** that way.
When he **reached** the place, **Jesus** looked up and said,
   "**Zacchaeus**, come down quickly,
   for today I must **stay** at your **house**."
And he came down **quickly** and received him with **joy**.
When they **all saw** this, they began to **grumble**, saying,
   "He has **gone** to **stay** at the **house** of a **sinner**."
But **Zacchaeus** stood there and said to the **Lord**,
   "**Behold**, **half** of my **possessions**, **Lord**, I shall **give** to the **poor**,
   and if I have **extorted anything** from **anyone**
   I shall **repay** it **four times over**."
And **Jesus** said to him,
   "Today **salvation** has come to this **house**
   because **this** man too is a **descendant** of **Abraham**.
For the **Son** of **Man** has come to **seek**
   and to **save** what was **lost**."

be saved?" "What is impossible for human beings," answers Jesus, "is not impossible for God" (Luke 18:24–27).

Among deeds possible only for God, one must surely include the arrival of salvation at the house of Zacchaeus. There is a reason why "tax collectors" are frequently paired with "sinners" in the Gospels (Matthew 9:10; 11:19; Mark 2:15–16; Luke 5:30; 7:34; 15:1). The legal collection of taxes in Roman-occupied Judea, to say nothing of illegal collection, amounted to little more than an extortion racket backed by the credible threat of violence, perhaps even crucifixion. We can only imagine how the citizens of Jericho must have loathed this little man.

And yet not only does salvation come to his house, but it comes on terms far easier than those Jesus offered the official in Luke 18:18–23. As far as we can tell, Jesus does not tell Zacchaeus to sell anything. Instead, Zacchaeus is permitted to *volunteer* to give only half his wealth to the poor and to repay fourfold those from whom he has extorted money. Did Zacchaeus have any money left when he was through making amends? Luke does not say. But the salvation of such a man can only mean there is hope for the worst among us!

32ND SUNDAY IN ORDINARY TIME

Lectionary #156

READING I — 2 Maccabees 7:1–2, 9–14

A reading from the second Book of Maccabees

The brothers speak boldly. Proclaim their words with strength.

It happened that **seven brothers** with their **mother** were arrested
 and **tortured** with **whips** and **scourges** by the king,
 to **force** them to eat **pork** in violation of **God's law**.
One of the brothers, **speaking** for the **others**, said:
 "**What** do you **expect** to **achieve** by **questioning** us?
We are **ready** to **die** rather than **transgress** the **laws**
 of our **ancestors**."

The second time the first brother speaks he is undergoing torture. This fact must affect your delivery.

At the point of death he said:
 "You **accursed fiend**, you are **depriving** us of this **present life**,
 but the **King** of the **world** will raise us up to **live** again **forever**.
It is for **his** laws that we are **dying**."

After him the third suffered their cruel sport.
He put out his tongue **at once** when told to do so,
 and **bravely** held out his hands, as he spoke these noble words:
 "It was from **Heaven** that I received these;
 for the **sake** of his **laws** I **disdain** them;
 from **him** I **hope** to **receive** them again."
Even the **king** and his **attendants marveled**
 at the young man's **courage**,
 because he regarded his **sufferings** as **nothing**.

After he had **died**,
 they **tortured** and **maltreated** the fourth brother
 in the same way.

READING I | The compilers of the book of 2 Maccabees offer a condensed version of a longer preceding text about the Jewish rebellion against the Seleucid Empire in the second century BC (2 Maccabees 2:23). The road to the martyrdoms of this reading begins with intrigues among members of Jerusalem's elite priestly families as they vied for the office of high priest by bribing and sucking up to the Seleucid king, Antiochus Epiphanes (reigned 175–164 BC). One aspirant named Jason paid Antiochus an extravagant bribe and sought permission to establish a gymnasium as well other Greek cultural institutions in Jerusalem (2 Maccabees 4:9–12). Although Jason was later beat out by a rival, lines had been drawn among supporters of the various candidates for office, and between supporters and opponents of the establishment of Greek cultural institutions in Jerusalem. In 168 BC, Antiochus attempted to bring the city to order. On his way back from a disappointing military campaign in Egypt, the king swung south to Jerusalem and punished the city with great brutality. He also raided the Temple treasury (1 Maccabees 1:20–23; 2 Maccabees 5:11—6:2). The national uprising, which was eventually successful, began shortly afterward.

The account of the martyrdom of these young Jewish men and their mother was a model for early Christian writers composing their own accounts of Christian martyrdom.

When he was **near death**, he said,
"It is my **choice** to **die** at the **hands** of **men**
with the **hope** God gives of being **raised up** by him;
but for **you**, there will be **no** resurrection to **life**."

READING II   2 Thessalonians 2:16—3:5

**A reading from the second Letter of Saint Paul
to the Thessalonians**

Brothers and **sisters**:
May our **Lord Jesus Christ** himself and **God** our **Father**,
who has **loved** us and **given** us everlasting encouragement
and **good hope** through his **grace**,
encourage your **hearts** and **strengthen** them
in every **good deed** and **word**.

Finally, **brothers** and **sisters**, **pray** for us,
so that the **word** of the **Lord** may speed **forward** and be **glorified**,
as it did among **you**,
and that we may be delivered from **perverse** and **wicked** people,
for **not all** have **faith**.
But the **Lord** is **faithful**;
he will **strengthen** you and **guard** you from the **evil one**.
We are **confident** of **you** in the **Lord** that what **we instruct you**,
you are **doing** and will **continue** to do.
May the **Lord** direct **your hearts** to the **love** of **God**
and to the **endurance** of **Christ**.

Margin notes:

Emphasize both instances of "brothers and sisters."

Slow down to emphasize and pause after "But the Lord is faithful."

The account of the martyrdom of Bishop Polycarp of Smyrna is one such early example. This text was also an important resource for Christians trying to convert the trauma of torture and public death into a good for the strengthening of the Church. In the early third century, Origen of Alexandria, who was the son and nephew of martyrs, held up the example of this family in order to present the kind of behavior Christians facing pain and death for Jesus' sake ought to cultivate (*Exhortation to Martyrdom*, 23–28).

READING II Questions about the authenticity of certain New Testament texts are not new to the Church. No less an authority than Eusebius of Caesarea, whose Catholic credentials include his participation in the council of Nicea in 325 AD, categorized books according whether they were recognized, disputed, or not recognized by the Church (*Ecclesiastical History*, 3.25).

Eusebius offers a few straightforward criteria for his judgments. In writings that are not genuine, Eusebius says, one notices that "the style of diction is contrary to the apostolic character," and that "both the opinion and the plan of the contents within them is quite out of tune with true orthodoxy." Modern biblical scholars seeking answers to questions concerning the authenticity of certain New Testament texts use versions of these criteria, as well as additional ones, in trying to form their own judgments.

GOSPEL   Luke 20:27–38

A reading from the holy Gospel according to Luke

Some **Sadducees**, those who **deny** that there is a **resurrection**,
    came forward and put this question to Jesus, saying,
    "**Teacher**, **Moses** wrote for us,
    *If someone's brother **dies** leaving a **wife** but no **child**,*
    *his **brother** must take the **wife***
    *and raise up **descendants** for his **brother**.*
Now there were **seven** brothers;
    the **first** married a **woman** but **died** childless.
Then the **second** and the **third** married her,
    and likewise all the **seven died childless**.
Finally the woman **also** died.
Now at the **resurrection** whose **wife** will **that woman be**?
For **all seven** had been **married** to her.
Jesus said to them,
    "The **children** of this **age marry** and **remarry**;
    but those who are **deemed worthy** to **attain** to the **coming age**
    and to the **resurrection** of the **dead**
    neither marry nor are **given** in **marriage**.
They can no longer **die**,
    for they are **like angels**;
    and they are the **children** of **God**
    because they are the **ones** who will **rise**.

The Sadducees address Jesus with a term of respect, but they are almost certainly mocking him as an out-of-town yokel.

One of several reasons why many scholars do not think 2 Thessalonians is authentic has to do with its structure, which so closely resembles the already unusual structure of 1 Thessalonians that many suspect 1 Thessalonians served as its template. Second Thessalonians 2:16, for example, mirrors 1 Thessalonians 3:11–13. Both texts have prayers containing identical Greek verbal moods and similar vocabulary. Second Thessalonians 2:16 is preceded by an appeal to shared traditions and followed by an instructional section. 1 Thessalonians 3:11–13 is preceded by an appeal to a shared past and followed by an instructional section. Taken together with other linguistic and structural similarities, today's reading, when examined next to 1 Thessalonians 3:11–13, suggests that an author, writing in Paul's name, used 1 Thessalonians as a model for 2 Thessalonians.

GOSPEL Unlike the Pharisees, who were primarily laymen, the aristocratic Sadducees were largely priestly in outlook and occupation. They rejected the Pharisees' belief in the binding authority of oral commentary on Jewish law and contended that the authentic source of Jewish thought and practice was to be found exclusively within the pages of the Mosaic law. The Resurrection of the dead, a belief held by many Pharisees, was not a doctrine the Sadducees found in the law and they, therefore, denied it. The center of the Sadducees' power was the Temple and its precincts, which is where Jesus encounters them in today's reading (20:1).

That the **dead** will **rise**
 even **Moses** made known in the **passage** about the **bush**,
 when he called out '**Lord**,'
 the **God** of **Abraham**, the **God** of **Isaac**, and the **God** of **Jacob**;
 and he is not **God** of the **dead**, but of the **living**,
 for to him all are **alive**."

[Shorter: Luke 20:27, 34–38]

Imagine the Sadducees' bemused curiosity as they observed the attention paid to an unschooled nobody from, of all places, Galilee. The question they ask Jesus reads as if its aim was to stump and publicly embarrass him.

Jesus' reply accomplishes two things. First, he demonstrates that the Sadducees' question does not make sense as they have posed it. Presuming to describe and define on their own terms a doctrine they do not believe in, the Sadducees have assumed that present-day institutions and conditions will be present in the age to come. Undermining this assumption, Jesus shows the Sadducees' question is built on sand. The "children of God" are "like angels" and "neither marry nor are given in marriage." The question about marriage is moot, for it has no meaning in the Resurrection.

Second, Jesus shows the Sadducees that he knows and can apply the law as well as themselves. As Deuteronomy 25 provides Jesus with a question about marriage (Luke 20:28), Exodus 3 provides the Sadducees with answers about the Resurrection (Luke 20:37). Even accepting the Sadducees' restriction of debate to the text of the law, Jesus prevails. And how do we know he prevails? Keep reading. "Some of the scribes said in reply, 'Teacher, you have answered well.' And they no longer dared to ask him anything" (Luke 20:39–40).

33RD SUNDAY IN ORDINARY TIME

Lectionary #159

READING I   Malachi 3:19–20a

A reading from the Book of the Prophet Malachi

Slow down to emphasize "the day is coming" and "the day that is coming."

> **Lo**, the day is coming, **blazing** like an **oven**,
>   when all the **proud** and all **evildoers** will be **stubble**,
> and the day that is **coming** will set them on **fire**,
>   leaving them **neither root nor branch**,
>   says the LORD of **hosts**.
> But for **you** who **fear** my **name**, there will **arise**
>   the **sun** of **justice** with its **healing rays**.

Stress the words "you," "justice," and "healing."

READING II   2 Thessalonians 3:7–12

**A reading from the second Letter of Saint Paul
to the Thessalonians**

Brothers and **sisters**:

Pause and emphasize the words "Brothers and sisters," looking out at the assembly when you deliver them.

You know how one must **imitate** us.
For we did not **act** in a **disorderly** way **among** you,
   nor did we eat **food** received **free** from **anyone**.
On the **contrary**, in **toil** and **drudgery**, **night** and **day**
   we **worked**, so as not to **burden any** of you.

READING I Malachi likely dates from the fifth century BC, in the period between the return of many of the Jewish exiles and their descendants from Babylon. The prophet's name, which means "my messenger" or "my angel," is perhaps a pen or "professional" name (Malachi 1:1; 3:1). His oracles excoriate priests and Levites, whose teachings "caused many to falter" and who "show partiality" in their judgments (2:8–9). Malachi also denounces the people of Judah, who "break faith with each other,

violating the covenant of our fathers" (2:10). The situation that Malachi describes is complicated, but it appears to have been a combination of corruption among the priestly elite and the disregard of traditional religious duty by the people in the confusion after the exiles' return. The books of Ezra and Nehemiah fill out the portrait of the period that Malachi allows us to glimpse here, but only briefly.

Today's reading concerns a coming day of judgment. Some people, like the stubble of a field burning after the harvest, will perish. For others, "there will arise the sun of

justice with its healing rays." This coming day is a "day of the Lord," which was understood in Jewish thought to be a day of God's judgment of Israel. In Jewish and Christian apocalyptic thought, *the* day of the Lord came to be seen in cosmic terms, involving the judgment of the wicked, the salvation of the righteous, and even the fundamental reordering of all earthly reality. Paul wrote that this day would come unexpectedly "like a thief in the night" (1 Thessalonians 5:2), that it would be "the day of wrath and

Not that we do not **have** the right.
Rather, we wanted to **present** ourselves as a **model** for you,
    so that you might **imitate** us.
In fact, when we were **with** you,
    we **instructed** you that if **anyone** was **unwilling** to work,
    neither should that one eat.
We hear that some are **conducting** themselves among you
        in a **disorderly** way,
    by not keeping **busy** but **minding** the **business** of **others**.
Such people we **instruct** and **urge** in the **Lord Jesus Christ**
        to **work quietly**
    and to **eat** their **own food**.

GOSPEL   Luke 21:5–19

A reading from the holy Gospel according to Luke

While some people were speaking about
    how the **temple** was adorned with **costly stones**
        and **votive offerings**,
    Jesus said, "**All** that you see here—
    the days will come when there will **not** be **left**
    a **stone** upon **another stone** that will not be **thrown down**."

Pause briefly before beginning this stanza.

Then they **asked** him,
"**Teacher**, when will this **happen**?
And what **sign** will there be when **all** these things
        are about to **happen**?"

---

revelation of the last judgment of God"
(Romans 2:5), and that he labored as an
apostle in order to bring together and nur-
ture a people able to survive that day (1
Corinthians 3:10–15).

READING II — In today's reading, the
author reminds his reader-
ship, much as Paul does in 1 Corinthians
4:12, how Paul worked to pay his own way
and tried not to burden anyone. From Paul's
example, the author lays down the principle

that anyone unwilling to work also "should
not eat." Some interpreters have tied this
rule to 2 Thessalonians 2:2 and assumed that
the letter's addressees have been informed
that "the day of the Lord" has either arrived
or drawn so close that they need not work
to support themselves. One interpretation of
this reading is that manipulating religion to
excuse lethargy and abuses of the generosity of the Church are wrong. This is a message well worth proclaiming.

GOSPEL — The Gospels, including
today's reading, relate that
Jesus predicted the destruction of the
Temple (Matthew 24:1–2; Mark 13:1–2; Luke
21:5–6). The Temple was, in fact, destroyed
roughly 40 years later in the year 70 AD when
the Roman general Titus, son of the Emperor
Vespasian (reigned 69–79 AD) and a future
emperor himself (reigned 79–81 AD), took
Jerusalem. That Jesus also threatened the
Temple was a charge arising at his trial
(Matthew 26:61; Mark 14:58). John, unlike

Read Jesus' words slowly, emphasizing their gravity.

He answered,
"**See** that you not be **deceived**,
    for many will come in my name, saying,
    '**I am he**,' and 'The time has come.'
Do **not** follow them!
When you hear of **wars** and **insurrections**,
    do **not** be terrified; for such things must happen first,
    but it will not **immediately** be the end."
Then he said to them,
"**Nation** will rise against **nation**, and **kingdom** against **kingdom**.
There will be **powerful earthquakes**, **famines** and **plagues**
    from **place** to **place**;
    and **awesome sights** and **mighty signs** will come from **the sky**.

"**Before** all this happens, **however**,
    they will **seize** and **persecute** you,
    they will **hand you over** to the **synagogues** and to **prisons**,
    and they will have you **led** before **kings** and **governors**
    because of **my name**.
It will **lead** to your giving **testimony**.
Remember, you are **not** to prepare your defense beforehand,
    for I myself shall **give** you a **wisdom** in **speaking**
    that **all** your **adversaries** will be **powerless** to **resist** or **refute**.
You will even be **handed over** by **parents**, **brothers**,
        relatives and **friends**,
    and they will put **some** of you to death.
You will be **hated** by all because of my name,
    but not a **hair** on your **head** will be **destroyed**.
By your **perseverance** you will **secure** your **lives**."

Mark and Matthew, records that Jesus actually made the threat, but places his utterance of it at a different point in his ministry and gives it a different meaning (John 2:19–21). The Gospels also report that Jesus drove vendors and moneychangers from the Temple (Matthew 21:12; Mark 11:15–16; Luke 19:45; John 2:14–16). In purely historical terms, this deed likely set in motion the chain of events culminating in Jesus' Crucifixion. The Temple was the center of Jewish national hope, Jerusalem was packed with Jewish pilgrims for Passover, the city's Roman garrison was almost certainly on highest alert, and

any disturbance at the Temple would have been swiftly and mercilessly dealt with.

In Luke, as in Matthew and Mark, the prediction of the Temple's destruction stands at the head of what is often called the "little apocalypse." But before its cataclysms and false teachers (Luke 21:7–11), before its predicted invasion of Jerusalem (Luke 21:20–24), and before the heavenly and earthly portents it says will precede the advent of the Son of Man (Luke 21:25–28), Jesus predicts a period of his followers' persecution (Luke 21:12–19).

The effort to use the "little apocalypse" with the book of Revelation as a guide to modern history occurs from time to time. Some of these efforts have become quite popular. We are wise to be skeptical of those who claim the power to read these signs in our times. Many persecutions, disasters of all sorts, false teachers without number, and repeated conflict in Jerusalem have thus far not ushered in the Son of Man. Barring any decisive information, we would do well to remain "vigilant at all times" (Luke 21:36).

OUR LORD JESUS CHRIST THE KING

Lectionary #162

READING I   2 Samuel 5:1–3

Hebron = Heh-BRONE
Stress "Here we are, your bone and your flesh."
Saul = Sawl

A reading from the second Book of Samuel

In those days, **all** the tribes of **Israel** came to **David**
    in **Hebron** and said:
    "**Here** we are, **your bone** and **your flesh**.
In days past, when **Saul** was our **king**,
    it was **you** who led the **Israelites** out and brought them back.
And the LORD said to you,
    'You shall **shepherd** my people **Israel**
    and shall be **commander** of **Israel**.'"
When all the **elders** of **Israel** came to **David** in **Hebron**,
    King David made an agreement with them there
        before the LORD,
    and they **anointed** him **king** of **Israel**.

READING I "Jesus, son of David, have pity on me!" So a blind man called Bartimaeus kept calling out, in spite of people hushing him, as Jesus approached Jericho on his journey to Jerusalem (Luke 18:35–43; also see Matthew 20:29–34 and Mark 10:46–52). Shortly afterward, Jesus, having ordered his disciples to commandeer a colt for him to ride into Jerusalem, enacts Zechariah 14:4, a text foreseeing the royal advent of a messiah of David's line. Jesus approaches Jerusalem accompanied by palm-waving crowds shouting the words of Psalm 118, a festival psalm composed in cele-

bration of the victorious return of a king of David's line from battle (Luke 18:28–38; also see Matthew 21:1–9 and Mark 11:1–10). Both Matthew and Luke specify that the male line of Jesus' family passes through David (see Matthew 1:6 and Luke 3:31).

But what has David to do with Jesus when almost a thousand years separates Jesus' entry into Jerusalem from David's royal acclamation by the elders of the tribes of Israel in this reading? The Christian concept of Christ's kingship can be seen even in the title "Christ," which comes from the Greek word for "anointed one" *(christos).*

The word messiah is a transliteration of the Hebrew word meaning the same thing. The king of Israel or Judah was God's anointed par excellence, a notion believed to have been ritually acknowledged with a smear of oil during his coronation liturgy. After the return of the exiles from Babylon, no member of David's line held power in Israel. But the religious, ethnic, and national aspirations of Israel came to be expressed in some quarters by a desire for a Davidic king. These messianic expectations were alive and strong in Israel at the time of Jesus' ministry and quickly taken up by the Church.

READING II   Colossians 1:12–20

A reading from the Letter of Saint Paul to the Colossians

Stress and pause after the words "Brothers and sisters" and look out at the assembly when you proclaim them.

Brothers and **sisters**:
Let us give **thanks** to the **Father**,
     who has made you **fit** to **share**
     in the **inheritance** of the **holy ones** in **light**.
He **delivered us** from the **power** of **darkness**
     and **transferred us** to the **kingdom** of his **beloved Son**,
     in whom we have **redemption**, the **forgiveness** of **sins**.

Pay close attention to the balance of the clauses and the rhythm of 1:15–20. Read this section slowly.

He is the **image** of the **invisible God**,
     the **firstborn** of **all creation**.
For in him were **created all** things in **heaven** and on **earth**,
     the **visible** and the **invisible**,
     whether **thrones** or **dominions** or **principalities** or **powers**;
     all things were **created** through **him** and for **him**.
He is before **all** things,
     and in him **all things** hold together.
He is the **head** of the **body**, the **church**.
He is the **beginning**, the **firstborn** from the **dead**,
     that in **all** things he himself might be **preeminent**.
For in him **all** the fullness was **pleased** to **dwell**,
     and through him to **reconcile** all **things** for him,
     making **peace** by the **blood** of his **cross**
     through him, whether those on **earth** or those in **heaven**.

READING II This reading may be an early Christian hymn (see Commentary II, July 15). No one knows for sure if it was composed specifically for singing or chanting, or if it was simply a piece of elegant prose written at the time of the letter's composition.

Most ancient people of the Mediterranean basin understood themselves to live in a world filled with spirits and invisible powers. Sickness, death, the win or loss of a lawsuit, a chariot race, or a romantic infatuation could be, and frequently were, explained by the intervention of supernatural beings

and the powers they held. The idea that one's enemy could invoke dangerous and angry spirits and force them to attack was a frightening prospect. It demanded one to seek protection, perhaps through the use of a protective magical amulet or by purchasing a curse in order to call up one's own angry spirits, demons, or ghosts to afflict an enemy before he or she had the chance to do the same. With this information in mind, this text from Colossians can be read in a slightly different light.

For this reading contains more than elegant prose about Christ's majesty and

authority. It is also about finding safety and protection in a newly ordered universe. The fact that in Jesus Christ "were created all things in heaven and on earth, the visible and the invisible, whether thrones or dominions or principalities or powers; all things were created through him and for him" was very good news indeed to people who lived in a world clogged with spirits (Colossians 1:16). Admission into the Church through Baptism placed a person into the care of Christ, who reconciled all things by the cross (Colossians 1:20).

This reading has multiple speaking parts. The rulers and soldiers speak with cruel sarcasm. The first thief, himself in great pain, speaks with hostility toward his fellow sufferer. The second thief, also in pain, somehow has the presence of mind to speak plainly and sensibly.

GOSPEL   Luke 23:35–43

A reading from the holy Gospel according to Luke

The rulers **sneered** at Jesus and said,
 "He **saved others**, let him **save** himself
  if he is the **chosen** one, the **Christ** of **God**."
Even the **soldiers** jeered at him.
As they **approached** to offer him **wine** they called out,
 "If **you** are **King** of the **Jews**, **save** yourself."
Above him there was an inscription that read,
 "**This** is the **King** of the **Jews**."

Now **one** of the criminals hanging there **reviled** Jesus, saying,
 "Are **you** not the **Christ**?
Save yourself and **us**."
The **other**, however, **rebuking** him, said in reply,
 "Have **you** no **fear** of **God**,
  for you are **subject** to the **same condemnation**?
And **indeed**, we have been **condemned justly**,
  for the **sentence** we **received corresponds** to our **crimes**,
  but **this** man has done **nothing** criminal."
Then he said,
 "**Jesus**, **remember** me when you **come** into your **kingdom**."
He replied to him,
 "**Amen**, I **say** to you,
  today you will be **with** me in **Paradise**."

Emphasize the word "today."

GOSPEL   "This is the King of the Jews." The text of the placard attached to the cross mocks Jesus and all Jews, but it also suggests that sedition was the specific crime with which he was charged (see Matthew 27:11–14; Mark 15:2–3; Luke 23:2–3; and John 18:23–38). Crucifixion was an obvious penalty for such a crime. It was public, humiliating, and encouraged obedience to the authorities through terror.

Jesus' kingship in this Gospel selection is thus portrayed ironically. Not only is the title "King of the Jews" hurled at Jesus as a cruel joke, but in Matthew, Mark, and John, he is also swathed in royal purple, crowned with thorns, and mocked by soldiers pretending to pay him homage (Matthew 27:27–31; Mark 15:16–20; John 19:2–3). It appears they abuse one more Jewish nobody whom they will shortly kill. In actuality, they have unintentionally testified to a truth neither they nor even the disciples understand. The evangelists see the profound irony. Mark, Matthew, and John especially highlight it, although Luke calls explicit attention in Jesus' words of forgiveness from the cross: "Father, forgive them, they know not what they do" (Luke 23:34). Judas, Herod, Pilate, the Sanhedrin, and the soldiers are killing a king, not in jest, but in fact.

Luke, more than the other evangelists, stresses Jesus' innocence. Pilate has declared him innocent on three separate occasions (Luke 23:4, 14, 22), the thief now offers the same judgment (Luke 23:41), and the centurion at the foot of the cross will shortly add his own voice to the chorus of exoneration (23:47). Christ's Resurrection puts this injustice right.